A Year In A Life Sentence

Chronicled by

Gregory Barnes Watson

A Year in a Life Sentence chronicles 365 days within a convicted murderer's life. The writer shares his Christian walk while dealing with the painful realities of incarceration.

Some of the names within this writing have been changed for the purpose of privacy.

Published by: Praying Hands Press

Book design by: Gregory Barnes Watson
Layout by: JoAnne Watson
Typist: Byrn Watson
Edited by: JoAnne Watson, Linda Wills and Cody Wills

Inquiries can be made to:
Gregory Barnes Watson
194 Summerside Drive
Centralia, WA 98531
gregorybarneswatson@gmail.com

Scripture taken from the HOLY BIBLE,
NEW INTERNATIONAL VERSON, Copyright
1973, 1978, 1984 International Bible Society.
Used by permission of
Zondervan Bible Publishers

Another book by
the author

A Thundering Wind
(An historical novel)

IN MEMORY OF MY SISTER,

JULIE ANN WATSON,

AT PEACE IN JESUS' ARMS

With thanks to
the many Christian brothers
who helped me along my journey;
and the dedicated
correctional staff who,
through their professional behavior,
act to keep me as safe as humanly possible.

Special Thanks To
Kathleen, Byrn, and JoAnne.
Words are Inadequate,
But my Love and Appreciation
Are limitless.

Wake up, O sleeper,
Rise from the dead, and
Christ will shine on you.

   Ephesians 5:14b

Table of Contents

How It All Began…..1

A Year in a Life Sentence...9

Conclusion...429

Epilogue..431

Follow-up..431

Afterword by Jack "*Murf the Surf*" Murphy..............................436

Biographies: Gregory Barnes Watson.......................................438

                    Jack "*Murf the Surf*" Murphy..............................440

HOW IT ALL BEGAN

On September 24, 1987, I sat trance-like in a Ventura, California courtroom listening to the black-robed superior court judge read, in a voice that intoned doom, a list of crimes that I had been found guilty, guilty, GUILTY of, and that I would be sentenced for. As an avid surfer my mind mulled over the term *body slammed*. This is when a monster wave lifts your rag-doll body up into the air and then pulverizes it against the bottom of the ocean floor. You pray for sand to cushion the impact but you get flesh-shredding coral. Your body is flattened by liquid tonnage as the oxygen that gives life is squeezed from every blood cell. It is mental white-out that never ends.

How preferable would a tsunami pounding be to: "Thirty-four years to life," that the judge pronounced, ending with the bang of his gavel.

At that instant the clock on the wall ceased ticking. A crisis had arisen; a panic with nowhere to run. A chilling sweat beaded at my hairline. Then the words of news anchors started to ring in my ears.

"The cold-hearted defendant sat without emotion as the judge sentenced him to life."

Somewhere within the crossed wires of my boggled mind, the truth jarred forth. How wrong they all are. One must be alive to have emotions. I had just experienced a death known only by others who have sat in the defendant's chair.

I would have delighted in cries, screams, to tear at my clothing, or to erupt into spontaneous combustion, but my full attention was on the picture screen clicking off scenes inside my head. They were not visions of my past but of my forfeited future. From my college degrees, a successful law career - gone. From community work, neighborly respect, a reputation - gone. From a first kiss in a restaurant parking lot, my love, my fiancée, my beautiful Angela — gone.

I was now a convicted felon of the worst kind. A murderer stamped for life as number D-67547.

I was stripped of everything, bare as if naked—alone. Worse than alone, I was by myself, or was I? I reflected back several months when the solid steel door of my county jail cell first slammed shut with a permanency that shook my bones. I was sitting, shaking, on my cold concrete bed shouting at the unresponsive walls.

"But I'm a good person!"

To myself I interrogate. How did I get mixed up in the drug trade? How could money that I did not care to spend hold so much power? How could I have endangered those that I loved while poisoning my fellow man? How could I be charged with the shooting death of a cocaine kingpin?

Throughout my self-incriminations I heard my mother's loving voice of guidance: "Greg, you have led your life to this point, let Jesus lead it from now on."

Hesitating, I whispered my reply with truthful lips, "But I'm a horrid person. Why would Christ want me?"

From a half-listened to Bible study I attended in college to impress a Christian girl who I lusted after, a scripture surfaced from my suppressed unconscious: Let him turn to the Lord, and He will have mercy on him, and to our God, for He will freely pardon. (Isaiah 55:7)

I always knew God existed. How can any rational thinking person who has taken a moment, or a lifetime, to view this glorious world and the wonders of its workings deny a Divine hand? God was there for me, but I was always too busy for Him.

I knew it was God who had saved my life when I crashed a Porsche through a telephone pole at 100+ MPH, ending crumpled and broken against a mighty oak tree. "Thanks," I said to God and then moved on.

I knew it was God who had saved my life when I lie in an isolation bed in a Chico, California hospital. Suffering from the effects of viral encephalitis and its accompanying 107 degree temperature, I nonchalantly watched as giant purple tennis shoes clomped into the room to leap onto the foot of my bed to discuss the predaceous arachnids whose bite was causing my delirium. "Thanks," I said to God and moved on.

Sitting, locked behind steel doors, I had nowhere to move on to. Desperate for help, even at 26, I felt the fear of a child who has fallen into a deep, dark well because I played too close to the edge. With nowhere else to turn, I looked up to God.

"But what can you do, Lord?" It is too late. My acts have shredded my very soul. "Can you fill my emptiness? Will you pardon my crimes? Will you direct my life?" I stopped at that thought and laughed out loud. What life? If I am convicted I will be transported to prison. I will likely be raped and then killed.

"Did I choose this path, God? Please, if your words are true, pardon me. Cleanse me. Set me free!" My cries were absorbed by the unpainted walls. All was quiet. No angels appeared; no bright lights, no heavenly voice to ease my terror. There I sat waiting. Waiting for what?

In my terror I had forgotten to breathe, but when I tried to I found that my throat was choked closed. I was panicking. I tried to scream but no sound squeezed through my frozen vocal chords. Then from deep in my quivering stomach came the eruption of bile that had been my life. A regurgitation of my sins hurled the width of the four foot cell to coat the porous wall with putrid spume. It was a portrait of what I had become. Tears streamed down my cheeks to mix with the vomit lining my caked lips. With my wrinkled jail house sleeve, I wiped my mouth to tentatively ask, "Am I clean?"

I took my first deep, fresh breath of air in a year. My tears flowed unceasing as the darkness was lifted from my soul, but the pain and sorrow I had caused to so many was revealed, plunging a knife into my heart. I was cleansed but also burdened.

After sentencing, as I exited the courtroom, and as an immature child of Christ I bitterly complained, "Where was my pardon, Lord? What happened to your mercy?"

I did not understand then, but it is seven years later and I have grown in knowledge. I recognize and accept the purifying fire that I have to go through. My fire, my tribulation, my growth in trust is called prison.

Society, led by cheer-leading politicians, may always call me scum, irredeemable, a danger to gentle folk, but I proudly call myself a follower of Christ.

The transition from a free society to the rigidity of incarceration is abrupt, shocking, and the new inmate, or *fish* as he is called, must be vigilant at all times to survive. Prison is a world unto itself. There are multitudes of rules, both written and unwritten. Some are enforced by prison staff, others by the inmates themselves. The simplest, most rewarding, yet at times frustrating, are God's rules. The Lord has allowed me not only to survive these years but to experience spiritual growth, to learn to trust His direction for my life, and to maintain hope for physical freedom from bondage equal to the spiritual freedom I now enjoy.

I will state for the record that prison is a waking nightmare. The privileges of televisions, radios, weights, and sports can numb the suffering while doing time, but only God's love and His blessings prevent the insanity that time inflicts on you from festering and destroying the mind.

It was after a visit from my cousin, Hanna who asked, "What's prison really like?" and being unable to adequately put the answer into words, I decided to chronicle the events, observations, and emotions I walk through and around during a year in my life sentence. As I sat on my bunk mulling over my decision, another reason for this undertaking bubbled forth. I have read numerous "born-again" and "rise-above adversity" Christian books that were inspiring. However, I felt most of them leapt from spiritual peak to spiritual peak, giving the new, struggling Christian a distorted, glorified picture of daily life and its many trials as a Christian. We may no longer be of this world, but we do live in it. Therefore, to struggle is constant, to slip and fall is typical, and to retreat to God's Word is a necessity for direction, growth, forgiveness, daily strength, and peace.

I have found peace in the knowledge that God's love is warmth, a flannel-comforter snuggle, and a hug in the bosom of a loving grandmother all wrapped together for eternity.

It is my desire to enlighten free people to what prison life is really like, day by endless, stagnating day. If you have bought into the revengeful joy of inflicting pain through the constant punishment of isolating one who has admittedly made tragic mistakes, you will revel in the suffering found within these pages. However, you will want to curse God because He has been and continues to be my comforter. His grace is sufficient.

I will show successes and failures of a prison system that is out of control and is eating its inhabitants as well as the futures of those who created it.

And if in any way my painful experiences cause the would-be criminal, or one who has yet to be caught, to change his ways, seek God, and thus avoid prison, every day that I have awakened to curse my incarcerated existence will have been worth it.

Please allow me to clarify myself when I say I curse my existence. It is the lifestyle and depravities surrounding me I suffer from that I curse. Christ within me is the sole joy for crawling out of my bunk to face the results of my actions; my terrible crimes against my fellow man. I have the comfort and forgiveness of God in my heart, but my body must live in constant conviction of society's punishment. In other words, my soul is soothed in a tropical oasis while my body is consumed in the scorching heat of a desolate desert.

The road from the courtroom to a prison gymnasium dormitory has been unexpected and full of blessings mixed with losses. The blessings have been of safety, new friends, and spiritual growth. The losses have been my court appeals, the relationship with my lady love and old friends, and the death of my grandmother and sister.

After sentencing I was transported from the Ventura County jail to a reception center in Chino, and then several months later to San Quentin prison, located in San Rafael on San Francisco's beautiful bay. The view may have been spectacular, but the 30-foot tall walls lined with razor wire—well, the prison's malignancy drained much of the enchantment for which the Bay is famous. However, the two and a half years spent in the 'bowels by the bay' were a molding of my character and a concentration of spiritual focus. I quickly learned the unwritten rules that would help to keep me out of trouble:

Do not borrow because if I could not pay back the debt, bad things would happen.

Do not loan because if the other person does not pay me back, I would have to do something bad to that person.

Do not steal because if a thief is caught, bad things happen.

Do not interact with homosexuals because they are usually owned by another inmate, and it could be perceived that I was trying to *cut in* on the *action,* bad things would happen.

And lastly, stay under radar, meaning, keep a low profile.

The written rules were neatly compiled in a 150 page booklet called *Title 15.* If either set of rules are violated, the punishment is swift and severe. Consequences range from time in Administrative Segregation, known as the *hole,* to time in the morgue—death. Prison is no joke, nor a game. Neither the staff nor the inmates play.

Blessedly, God guides His children. With uncertainty as to what I would find on my first Sunday in San Quentin, I entered the Garden Chapel. I was quickly spotted as a *fish* and set upon by several muscular men. Fortunately for me, their strengths were not only in their arms but in His Spirit. After the hand-clapping, rise-up-out-of-our-pews-with-praise service, I was introduced to and placed under the patient tutelage of a true God-send, Chaplain Earl Smith.

Through fiery sermons by the chaplain, guest speakers, one of them included the famed jewel thief Jack *"Murf the Surf"* Murphy, gospel concerts, Bible studies, fund-raising for victims, and Kairos, my tattered soul was nurtured. This was my cornerstone. These were my blessings. Jesus became real and my eyes were opened to His works in my daily life.

Because of the time, forever, that I was sentenced to, the distance from San Diego, where my love Angela lived and San Quentin, she chose to continue her life without me. Likewise, with friends, out-of-sight meant out-of-mind. I hold neither malice nor blame toward them for forsaking my love and friendship, only sadness by their departure and the recognition that I am responsible. I left first.

My grandmother and sister? God knew their suffering and called them home. My grandmother suffered the infirmity of old age and a stroke. My sister's sufferings came in the form of addictions. Glorifying Him, both sought Jesus as their refuge. I pray I will see them again in heaven.

In January of 1990, due to my disciplinary free behavior, my security level was reduced from IV to III. I was transferred to a new prison, Mule Creek, in Ione, California. The *Creek* is located an hour's drive east of Sacramento, our state's capital. The close proximity to law makers and the Department of Corrections headquarters places this new-style prison in the honorary, if not dubious, position of being a model for the future. This means lots of floor wax and extra water for the flowers that line the pathways around the administrative buildings. Tours of free people who are prevented from any interaction with the inmates marvel at the shine while inmates grumble at the lack of substance to assist them with personal change.

In defense of the administration, I do applaud them for their tremendous accomplishment in the reduction of violence. Unless one has a death wish to become a crispy critter and leaps onto the electrified fence, or violates every inmate canon, it is more likely he will perish from disease, loneliness, or old age, than from violence.

Of course it needs to be said that how one carries himself and what one has been convicted of has a great deal to do with how one's interaction in the inmate population will fair. Rapists, child molesters, and *snitches* still have a precarious walk. Lifers, those convicted of murder, are usually given a degree of respect.

Lifers who are Christians have a difficult and sometimes impossible task of being role models. We live with inner peace which affords an outer smile. This walk enrages some, baffles others, but gives inspiration to many. It is not I, but He who dwells within me that they see. To be led by Christ is comforting; to lead others to Christ is exhilarating.

When I refer to the *Creek* as a new-style prison, I am describing a three-in-one prison. In your mind, picture three oval recreation yards surrounding a central core of administrative buildings. The perimeter of each yard, or facility, A, B, and C consists of five housing units and a gymnasium that has been converted to a dormitory. Each facility is run as an independent prison, separating the 1200 inmates on each yard from each other. Each facility has its own basic education and vocations classrooms and custody offices called the Program Office. In the event of an incident requiring a Code 3 staff response or a lockdown, only that housing unit or facility is affected. The other buildings or facilities remain Code 4, normal program.

This new style of prison effectively manages and contains violence but is an inefficient utilization of scarce resources. Needing three of everything: medical-dental clinics, chapels, libraries, etc., requires a miniaturization of their physicality and reduced time allotment by the doctor, minister, or librarian who has to split his time between the three facilities.

Chaplain Smith at San Quentin had the luxury of a 500+ seat Garden Chapel that filled to capacity for both services on Sunday. He was also available five days a week to minister to inmates' needs.

Here at the Creek, Chaplain Drake must divide his time among the three facilities and share the two-car garage-size chapel on each yard with those of the Muslim, Jewish, Catholic, American Indian, and Seventh Day Adventist faiths. And, so as not to offend the sensitivities of any faith group, no group may display any form of religious icon.

It may be true that it is not the number of coals in the fire that determines its intensity, but when the goal of not-to-offend supersedes the passion to praise, growth is inhibited. This lack of fire has been the cause for me and a friend to form a Bible fellowship that meets weekly for study, praise, and prayer on the recreation yard. Over the years our group has been as humble as two, and as rambunctious as twelve, depending on the ebb and flow of inmate transfers in and out of this facility; facility B.

After my arrival at the Creek, and for nearly four years, I was housed with another inmate in a 5'x 9' two-man cell. Quite roomy compared to San Quentin's narrower abodes. Being a skilled typist with a basic understanding of the English language, I have been assigned as a clerk for the facility lieutenant and then for the facility program administrator.

In October of 1993, because of my disciplinary-free behavior, my security level was reduced from a III to a II. As a reward, I was given the 'privilege' of being moved from the two-man cell to a double bunk in the converted gymnasium to reside with 159 other 'privileged' inmates.

This was another shock to my mind. This was where my Christian tenets would strenuously be put to the test. This is where I decided, prodded by my cousin's question and my desire to enlighten and help struggling Christians, that beginning with this year's classification review, I would chronicle my walk, both the successes and failures, honestly and faithfully.

This is my year in a life sentence. May God have mercy on me.

Thursday, October 28, 1993

```
┌─────────────────────────────────────────────────────────────────┐
│ STATE OF CALIFORNIA            DEPARTMENT OF CORRECTIONS           │
│ INMATE PASS                         CDC 129 (7/88)                 │
├──────────────────────────┬──────────────┬────────────────────────┤
│ INMATE'S NAME            │ CDC #        │ HOUSING #               │
│   WATSON                 │ D-67547      │ BG-152                  │
│ ISSUED BY                │ DATE:        │ PASS FROM:              │
├──────────────────────────┼──────────────┼────────────────────────┤
│ PASS TO:                 │ DATE:        │ TIME:                   │
│   Program Office         │              │    0900                 │
│ REASON:                  │              │                         │
│   UCC                    │   PRIORITY                             │
│ ARRIVAL TIME:            │ RECORDED BY:                           │
├──────────────────────────┼──────────────┬────────────────────────┤
│ DEPART TO:               │ TIME:        │ RECORDED BY:            │
└──────────────────────────┴──────────────┴────────────────────────┘
```

HAPPY NEW YEAR?

9:00 a.m.

Continue Present Program (CPP), and I begin my seventh year striving to live as the angels, but in hell.

Today I was summoned to appear before the Unit Classification Committee (UCC) for my annual review. This event took place in a bedroom size conference room within the office complex of the Program Offices wherein I toil. Working within bathroom size offices of this mini complex are two facility sergeants, a lieutenant, a correctional counselor I and II, the office technician (a politically correct way to give a fancy title to, but still underpay the secretary who shoulders the majority of paperwork not assigned to the inmate clerks), and leading us all is the program administrator.

Presiding over my annual review was my supervisor, who is the Program Administrator, Alfred T. James, Correctional Counselor II, Steve Lloyd, and my previous counselor, a CCI, Bob Myers. My current counselor was unavailable because he, Karl Burton, was wheeled out of his office last Friday after suffering a mild heart attack. I have yet to meet Mr. Burton, but it is a fact that he is not well liked among the inmate population. I am told it has to do with his gruff personality and lack of efficient work habits, but I prayed for him anyway. He is someone's husband and father.

My classification review lasted a total of three minutes.

"Mr. Watson, you've again remained disciplinary free this past year and have maintained an above average work record," expounded my stand-in counselor as he reviewed my prison file. If staff only knew how difficult it is to kowtow without question to every rule changed at whim without rhyme or reason by staff, or how much crap I have to take from fellow inmates to remain disciplinary free, they would celebrate and congratulate me with fireworks and a cake. I suppose, simply because I am doing what is right, that intrinsically that should be enough, but I don't feel it is. This is my humility problem. I know I have to work on this issue and will continue to pray about it.

"Your custody points are being reduced to 19. Congratulations, you are now a level II. Do you want to transfer or remain here? If you choose to stay here you'll be re-housed in the gym."

I want to go home. I want to go surfing. I want to be held by a beautiful woman who has eyes only for me. I am surrounded by too many snitches, molesters, and psychopaths content in their lifestyles of abnormal behavior that becomes their perceived norm. Can you not see they are driving me crazy? Do you understand my nightmare that I cannot wake up from? Do you care?

I looked across the wood veneer table at the suited men patiently waiting for my reply. I sighed, resigned to my self-inflicted fate and said, "I'll stay here."

A new year has dawned. Three hundred and sixty–five days of relative certainty that I will remain here at the Creek, remembering that nothing is ever 100% certain in prison. I took a deep breath, steeling myself, and believing that I can make it, keeping in the forefront of my mind that Jesus will carry me.

2:30 p.m.

There was only one set of footprints on the recreational track as I pushed a cart with my few belongings from my cell to the gymnasium. As I looked in the door I paused, wondering if Daniel felt as nervous when he entered the lions' den.

Psalms 107:6-11. *Then they cried out to the Lord in their trouble, and He delivered them from their distress. He led them by a straight way to a city where they could settle. Let them give thanks to the Lord for His unfailing love and His wonderful deeds for man, for He satisfies the thirsty and fills the hungry with good things. Some sat in darkness and the deepest gloom, prisoners suffering in iron chains, for they had rebelled against the words of God and despised the counsel of the Most High.*

☩ ☩ ☩

Friday, October 29, 1993
4:00 p.m.

Whirling whine of tattoo gun motors, homosexual phlegm cough-ups, and repetitive "Mother – fu-----" to assist in completing complex sentences are the sounds that inundate me in my new quarters as I lie prone on my bunk, forced to remain in place during the afternoon count.

The gymnasium is a cavernous cube with double bunks lined closely together as dominoes. So close that I can reach out and touch my neighbors and they me. I shiver at this thought while inhaling air that smells like a wet dog. Wait, I apologize to the wet dogs of the world and would gladly embrace them instead of this fecund, decaying marsh vapor.

The competing discussions piercing my ears remind me of those in junior high school locker rooms, but these are not boys lying about what *base* they made it to with what girl, but lost men gleefully playing one-upmanship in discussing their crimes. God, what happened to the minds of these men? "Garbage in—Garbage out."

I refuse to be a tape recorder soaking in this offensive ambiance. It is a Chinese torture chamber of dark noise. I flee inward to the promised peace of the Spirit's temple. I picture in my mind Christ's supplication to our Father on my behalf. A small smile forms at the corner of my lips. Careful, Greg. Do not be proud in God's love. My goal is contentment under any circumstance. Peace. I only need to ask.

5:30 p.m.

Literary workshop: the Laubach Way to reading. Something positive. This was my third class, which is held in one of the five classrooms in the educational hallway next to the Program Offices. This course is where inmates are taught how to teach illiterate inmates to read and write. For every man we teach to read we help him escape into the past, present, and future worlds of great and not-so-great authors.

I have taken this course for several reasons. The first is purely self-interest in that I dream of all these men reading quietly, which could be the tearless death of the cartoons that blare from the televisions, but I believe our sequestered society could bear that loss. The second reason, I suppose that it too is self-interest, because with the ability to read and comprehend, and with gentle persuasion, many of these men could be led to the Lord. As I have said before, being a small part of helping one to know Jesus is a joy unmatched. Hopefully, prayerfully, this class of thirty can change the lives of multitudes.

7:45 p.m.

I went back to work. Though I am not assigned to work in the evenings (third watch) I had been asked, which is a polite way by my supervisor of ordering me, to train a new clerk. His name is Alex Payne.

Payne is the spitting image of the goateed snowman who narrates on a *Rudolph the Red-nosed Reindeer* television special. Now add to the image the years required to equal seventy-five, a foul smelling pipe that Payne constantly packs for, in his words, a better smoke, and there he sits.

Payne is intelligent, but he has had no experience with disciplinary terminology which is required to type staff reports. That is the essence of the job, so we were both frustrated.

"Yard recall! Yard recall!" reverberated across the facility from amplified speakers mounted atop the buildings. Emergency count. Someone was observed walking along the road near the prison wearing blue jeans. Blue jeans and blue chambray shirts are what make up the official inmate uniform. And, because many in the free world also wear these, emergency counts are a regular occurrence.

The 114D (Administrative Segregation lock-up order) report that I was helping Payne to type concerned an assault on staff by an inmate. When I process these reports, I always wonder what straw pushed the mental button that caused the inmate to snap.

8:15 p.m.
(Emergency Count)

The red count light on the wall above the officers' raised station flashes its warning to remain on my bunk. The torture of noise begins a fresh. "Garbage in—Garbage out". I turn inward. Jesus is there for me as always.

Philippians 4:12-13. *I know what it is to be in need, and I know what it is to have plenty. I have learned the secret of being content in any and every situation, whether well fed or hungry, whether living in plenty or in want. I can do everything through Him who gives me strength.*

✝ ✝ ✝

Saturday, October 30, 1993
7:00 p.m.

My feet burn from raw blisters. My skin tingles from a mild sunburn. My muscles are exhausted from a thousand leaps, dives, and arm jarring snaps. The cause of all this discomfort? My blessed fault. I played four and a half hours of volleyball with Christian brothers, and any other challengers, only having to sit out two games. I cannot wait to get back to the beach and answer the question: "Say, man, where did you learn to play so well?" "California Penal," I will reply without hesitancy. I will never deny the truth, the source of my fiery purification.

In my mind's eye I see all the players that were on the court at various times today. Some were *trucks* (terrible players) and some were very skilled, but each brought a smile to my wind-blown and cracked lips. The scene was unlike any prison yard or experience I had ever seen. Hispanics, blacks, Asians, and whites all playing together, having fun, not caring the least about skin color or what neighborhood the other was from.

Another smile, this one a bit perverse, stretches from ear to ear. It is for the district attorney who prosecuted me beyond the fullest extent of the law. I have cheated her out of several hours of misery. Through energetic play, I was able to temporarily forget I was in prison. Enjoying the company of laughter-filled human beings can lift the heaviest burdens to allow one to float over the tallest fence. Thank you, Lord. I look forward to tomorrow.

Ecclesiastes 2:25-26. *For without Him, who can eat or find enjoyment? To the man who pleases Him, God gives wisdom, knowledge and happiness.*

✝ ✝ ✝

Sunday, October 31, 1993
9:30 a.m.

Another beautiful day filled with hours of volleyball. Of all the possible sport pastimes available here, horseshoes, basketball, softball, volleyball, and soccer, I prefer volleyball. It is meant to be non-contact, it takes a measure of skill to play well, and with several experienced players the volleys are invigorating.

Today I was the first one on the court, as the gym dwellers were released to the recreation yard before the other housing units. I was given a few moments with the broom as I swept the rain puddles from the court.

"Honk...honk...honk," echoed above in the drifting clouds. I looked up and saw a southbound migrating flock of Canada geese. They were so graceful in their arrowhead flight. Historically, the land I stood on belonged to the Miwok tribe of Indians. I wondered what those band of early natives thought as they watched the passing flocks a hundred years ago. The sky was likely filled with tens of thousands of geese instead of these twenty passing overhead. At that moment my heart ached for the tremendous loss, both for the Miwoks and the geese as only a few of each are left.

"Clang...clang...clang," shattered my thoughts as the steel doors of the five remaining housing units opened. Men streamed from the doors with an urgency to reach their desired diversions. There are twelve hundred men on this yard. There are over 130,000 in the California penal system with more and more on the way. There are less and less Miwoks and less and less geese. Is this progress?

10:00 p.m.
ALL HALLOWS EVE

Halloween used to be my favorite night. I would cavort in costume, celebrating in gyrations of dance and hypnotic drum beats. Since my incarceration I have learned of Halloween's source, that being the Druids, their worship of nature, and how this night was a celebration of the dead, not the living God. I neither worshiped nature, nor did I commemorate the spirits who no longer walk the earth, but I need to rethink my party attitude regarding this night. I have to be very careful because Satan's treat is always a trick. I fell hard for the red devil once. I do not ever intend to allow that to happen again.

Romans 1:22-23. *Although they claimed to be wise, they became fools and exchanged the glory of the immortal God for images made to look like mortal men and birds and animals and reptiles.*

✞ ✞ ✞

Monday, November 1, 1993
7:30 p.m.

The moon hangs low in the eastern sky as the man that occupies it is not smiling. I, too, have sadness for my upper bunk mate, Brain. He senses trouble on the home front, and though he only has several years left to serve on his sentence, to him it is forever. His hard-timing has begun. I wish I could ease his pain because I know it all too well.

It has been five years since Angela said her good-byes, departing from my life, but her memory still quickens my heart and rolls my stomach with an ache that will not ease.

Angela - 1986

Angela was my exotic, brown-skinned lady with root beer eyes for whom I pray God has blessed with a better mate than I was. I will never forget her full-lipped smile, infectious laugh, and loving touch with exquisitely delicate fingers. My poor choices proved that I was not worthy to gaze upon her beauty and grace, or to have enjoyed her intelligence and wit, though I pray that my growth spiritually and in character will someday, in His divine time, allow me to be blessed with another.

I always pray for Angela's happiness. Is that not what I am supposed to do if I claim to have loved her?

I see it time and again, the hope for words of forever, and for better or worse, ending with the judge's gavel. Maybe if couples turned to each other for support, and to Christ for guidance, hearts would beat more peacefully and the gavel of divorce less often. It is just a thought—a lonely one.

Just like the man in the moon.

9:40 p.m.

I paused in the reading of my escape magazine, the *Conde´ Nast Traveler*, and glanced to my right toward the tattooed man who usually entertains me with an unending repertoire of mother-fu---- as he communicates with his *homies*. What has caused me to turn his way was the quiet. He was writing a letter to someone and by the expression on his face, the words he wrote were from his heart. Was the letter to a wife, a girlfriend, his son, a daughter, mother, or father? I do not know. I do know; however, that whoever the recipient will be, the words they will read are not from the B.S. storyteller, impresser of homeboys, but from a man who wishes he was somewhere with his family.

I thanked God that I am part of His family and that He is always with me.

Romans 8:14-15. *Because those who are held by the spirit of God are sons of God. For you did not receive a spirit that makes you a slave again to fear, but you received the Spirit of sonship. And by Him we cry, "Abba, Father."*

✟ ✟ ✟

Tuesday, November 2, 1993
4:00 pm.

Mail! Yes, I do exist. I am handed two letters; one from my mother and the other from my friend, Curt, who I met in San Quentin and is now housed in Soledad prison. The tone of both letters is they are doing well. This is always a relief to hear, because when tragedy strikes, being incarcerated, I am helpless to assist. As I read my mother's letter I do become anxious as she related the selling of her car. This is good for her, bad for me. It means she and her husband, Walt, are one step closer to moving to Texas—so far away from me.

The move will be very good for them financially, but it will deny me my bi-weekly visits that I cherish so much. Living in Pollock Pines and teaching in a local high school, my mother is only 45 minutes from the Creek.

These years of incarceration have brought a wonderful twist in the relationships with my parents. We are not only mother and son, father and son, but friends who share more than one way conversations. I do admit that I now eagerly follow their guidance as God has lifted a veil to allow me to see their success in life. I appreciate their love which is given without judgment to my offenses, and I truly enjoy their company, seeing them as three dimensional people struggling with life's ups and downs, not simply parents with restrictive rules. The change in me is another positive outcome of a terrible situation which I and I alone created.

Now; however, I must depend more on God for support, as my mother will be living in Texas and my father is 600 miles away in San Diego. It is a very hard thing to give up fleshly hugs for spiritual ones. I am very nervous. I need to pray.

Matthew 10:37. *Anyone who loves his father or mother more than me is not worthy of me; anyone who loves his son or daughter more than me is not worthy of me.*

✝ ✝ ✝

Wednesday, November 3, 1993
4:00 p.m.

Mail again? This week is shaping up to be quite positive, postal speaking. This letter is from my step-sister, Beth, and her husband, Roger. I find it interesting that the only people I receive mail from are Christians. Is it they can better see the Spirit working within me and wish to support the change? Are they following Biblical instruction to visit the prisoners? Are Christians, by their walk, forgiving?

This is something to ponder.

Beth stated that she thinks about and prays for me daily. I know that her prayers along with my family and friends have helped to keep me safe, healthy, and as positive as I am. Beth also mentioned how my positive attitude is an inspiration to her. That, quite frankly, is the best compliment I could ever ask for.

Actually, I see this as a circle. Their loving prayers to God on my behalf, God's hand of protection over me, and my faith in Him that allows me to be positive and continue to be productive.

We have to work together to lift each other up. So far so good.

Hebrews 10:24. *And let us consider how we may spur one another on toward love and good deeds.*

✝ ✝ ✝

Thursday, November 4, 1993
10:00 a.m.

One responsibility of my job assignment as a clerk in the Program Office is to supervise inmates taking the typing test. Inmates who want to be considered for clerical positions have to pass the test by successfully typing 15 words per minute. Many claim to be proficient; few are.

Today, Teri with an 'i' came in to be tested - a handsome black-effeminate, with a Michael Jackson copy-cat voice and stunningly silky waist-length, ebony hair that any woman would envy. What a darling?! He/she/it claims to be the niece/nephew of Jeronimo Pratt, the famous Black Panther, who the police set up to take the rap for a murder. As I was privileged to know Jeronimo while I was in San Quentin, it was interesting to listen to Teri speak of their relationship. Was he/she/it really related to Jeronimo? I can't be sure, but Teri told a great story.

I have to admit that I find the social interaction of prison homosexuals and transgenders to be a fascinating soap opera. The majority of them are very insecure and always in need of attention. Their lives are solely on a sexual, seductive-minded level, so when I have to interact with one, as today, and I treat them like a normal person, not trying to sex-play them as they are used to, they are unsure as to how to act.

The Lord said homosexuality is detestable (Lev. 18:22) but He also said thou shall not judge yet ye be judged. I neither understand nor approve of their lifestyle but can still address them as humans. There is an old saying: You hate the sin but love the sinner.

Oh, Teri failed the typing test and pitched a bitch...drama, drama, drama.

3:30 p.m.

I can't believe it. I almost lost it. Six years of staying clean, being cool, taking all the crap as it comes, then the straw, and snap. The young kid, 18 or 19, who sleeps on the top bunk next to me, has his leg in a full cast due to torn ligaments. Upon entering the gym, staff asked me if I would give up my lower bunk and allow Jason to have it. A simple request? NO WAY.

On my walk back to my bunk I grumbled to myself. "They take me out of a cell and move me into the gym with a bunch of *diverse* individuals. I can no longer watch my television because my bunk is in the center of the gym with no access to an electrical outlet, nor can I type on my typewriter, and now they want my lower bunk, too? NO WAY! The taking has to stop somewhere."

Jason hobbled over on his crutches. I told short-timing Jason (he has three months left to serve on his two-year sentence) that he does not have enough time left to warrant a lower bunk. Jason got all smart-ass and said, "That's too bad for you. Maybe you should have thought about doing life before you did the crime. I will just have staff take your bunk from you."

That disrespectful little bastard. I wanted to smash his face and I told him so using a surprising number expletives. Then, as if materializing out of the ether, my big and burly Christian friend, *Bull,* stepped up and in between Jason and I, giving me a bear hug, and reminding me that my potential freedom was at stake. The parole board would not look kindly on me if I beat up a cripple.

Jason took advantage of my being restrained and quickly hobbled away. Man, I felt terrible. Too much stress in here. Thank God for friends.

3:50 p.m.

Time is a good cooler of tempers. I located Jason near the water fountain, apologized, as I did not mean what I had said, and offered him my bunk. He, too, apologized for his comments, realizing that he had crossed the line.

7:30 p.m.

Five inmates are moving out of the gym, being transferred to level one, which is outside the electrified fence. These transfers opened up a lower bunk for Jason. As a further apology I helped him move his property and settle in.

Yes, I still have my lower bunk. Do I feel bad? Yes. I should have given Jason my bunk without being asked. He was in need and I was being selfish. The timing was bad, but that is no excuse for my inconsiderate behavior. I failed the stress and generosity tests. Forgive me Lord.

Romans 12:18. *If it is possible, as far as it depends on you, live at peace with everyone.*

✝ ✝ ✝

Friday, November 5, 1993
9:00 a.m.

My closest Christian friend, Aaron, transpacted (took his property to Receiving and Release) today. Receiving and Release is situated between A, B, and C facilities and it is a building where staff search and pack property of inmates who are transferring to other prisons or are paroling. R & R is also where our care packages from home are searched and distributed.

Fourteen months ago I was Aaron's best man at his wedding, which was held in the visiting room, and he was the shoulder I cried on when my sister, Julie, passed away earlier this year.

Aaron and I met as co-workers, fellow clerks in the Program Office. We have learned a lot from each other, growing spiritually as we discussed His word. I will miss him dearly when he leaves. I know that this transfer to James' Town Fire Camp will take him closer to his wife, Roni, who lives in Oakdale, 40 miles away. This will be a blessing for them. I am also confident that the Lord wants Aaron to spread His wonderful light on others. I have been blessed by Aaron's companionship, his jokes, and his understanding as a Spirit-filled man. Looking at Aaron now, one would never know that he was once a member of the San Diego Crips street gang. God's transformation of Aaron is miraculous.

God knew that I needed someone special to continue my growth and someone who would not be embarrassed when I needed to let my grief pour out. Now it seems God has other plans for Aaron, and though his departure will feel like a loss, his friendship will remain in my heart.

Ephesians 4:32. *Be kind and compassionate to one another.*

✝ ✝ ✝

Saturday, November 6, 1993
8:00 a.m

HAPPY BIRTHDAY TO ME!
I was born today, 33 years ago…not much else to say.

1:00 p.m.

I elected to give myself a present by telephoning a special lady friend who just happens to be my childhood sweetheart. A lot of miles and years have passed since our last kiss at 18, but one's first love never seems to fizzle out completely. For me, my first love is an ember forever warming a corner of my heart.

Mickie was my teenage bombshell. A sweater-stretching Pamela Anderson who possessed a tomboy attitude that challenged even me when it came to athletic adventures. Case in point: The Tandem Jump of Fright.

Prom Night
- 1979 -

San Quentin
- 1989 –

She and I were 15 and 16 years old, respectively. I had been teaching Mickie how to ride motocross at the *Secret Track,* which was known to all as four dirt acres situated in the middle of Chatsworth's industrial complex in the San Fernando Valley. She was a fast learner and wanted me to ride behind her while she *putted* around the track on my Yamaha 125YZ. I consented, momentarily forgetting Mickie's natural inclination for thrills. The ride started out quite enjoyable as the bumpy dirt track jiggled Mickie's two endowments onto my hands as I happily embraced her. It was then, as we rounded a turn leading toward a monster jump and she revved the throttle to full, that my heart skipped a beat.

I tried to reassure myself that she would veer around the jump, but as the engine's RPM's continued to increase, whining to a shriek (or was that me?), Mickie steered straight, her path never wavering.

My mind echoed with shouts: *She can't make this jump. We'll crash.*

Mickie's body leaned forward, pulling my terror into accepting her determination. The motorcycle's wheels raced up and over the jump's steep lip, the shocks extended fully from the absence of terra firma as we shot skyward. A chaos of sounds mixed as we flew through the air; the high-pitched whine of the engine, my screams, and Mickie's laughter, and then whump. We landed hard, but Mickie held firm to the handle bars and steered to a patch of tall grass where she skidded the motorcycle to a controlled stop. Falling playfully off the tamed mechanical contraption and into each other's arms, we laughed ourselves to tears. I knew I was with someone very special who would always exceed my wildest expectations.

Mickie's voice raised several octaves when she recognized my voice on the telephone line. My heart never ceases to jump when I hear her sparkling words of encouragement and care for me. The 15 minute time limit for telephone conversations always flies by too quickly, but we utilized it as best we could in a spirit-lifting, seems like old times chat about our daily activities, and about God's grace.

It is good...no, it is wonderful, a cherished thing to have a connection through treasured memories that lasts over time. True friendships can survive personal mistakes. How does that saying go? We are friends in spite of our faults.

As the minutes ran out, and before the automatic disconnect, we said our good-byes with an electronic, reach out and touch someone hug, which included a promise by me to call again soon. I definitely will. I deserve a gift or two.

3:00 p.m.

My co-workers and friends, Smitty and Aaron, delivered three candy bars and a birthday card to me. The candy was sweet to the taste buds, but their words of friendship and respect go beyond description.

I have known them both for nearly three years and have found them to be men who do not dispense words lightly. Smitty is serving life with dignity, and Aaron is a strong catalyst for Christ. I have been blessed by their wit at work and revelry while we try to exist in this suffocating cube we call a house.

7:30 p.m.

Parents. They are a wonderful creation of God. I am so blessed to have their support and love. When speaking with my father on the telephone, he told me that one of my self-addressed, stamped postcards was returned by an agency that is interested in reading two of my screenplays. Because I will be too old to work if I am ever released, I am working toward becoming a screenwriter or a writer in any form. My goal is to earn an income for retirement and not be a burden on society as I have been. I hate to use the girlie word giddy, but that is how excited I am about this request, though admittedly I have a long way to go before an actual sale of a script.

It has been said that artists should never be fed too much and that creativity comes from adversity. If this is true then I will win the Oscar for best screenplay because suffering is what my existence is all about—except for God's intervention.

Back to my father. Without his support in routing mail and forwarding copies of my scripts I would be dead in the water, or in this locale, floating face down in the Creek. Just a pun. It is okay to laugh.

With so many inmates on their own, with no support from anyone outside, it is not surprising that recidivism is as high as it is. Not to exaggerate, but being in prison, inmates become armless, legless, and their voices are silenced. An inmate may have a great idea, but without the assistance of a free person, nothing can be accomplished. It is bad enough that inmates cost taxpayers approximately $28,000 a year, but it is worse when an inmate is released unprepared mentally, vocationally, and financially.

Thank you, Lord, for my parents.

HAPPY BIRTHDAY TO ME. It was a good day.

John 3:5-6. *Jesus answered, "I tell you the Truth, no one can enter the Kingdom of God unless he is born of the water and the Spirit. Flesh gives birth to flesh, but the Spirit gives birth to the spirit."*

✝ ✝ ✝

Sunday, November 7, 1993
5:30 p.m.

I chose not to go to the chow hall tonight for dinner. Instead I had a *spread* (dinner) with Aaron on his last night before he transfers. Our entrée consisted of Top Ramen noodles mixed with smoked oysters, sliced salami, spices and hot sauce. The *wine* was a '93 fountain tap, chilled then allowed to air. Very fresh though a tad bland, but what did I expect from water?

It is very hard to say good-bye to someone who has been so important in one's life, even if only for a few years. I now understand all the tears that girls shed at the end of high school and college graduation ceremonies. I do not know how many years, if ever, it will be until I see or talk to Aaron again. I am sadder than I expected. We hug in a masculine, just-scored-a-touchdown way. His embrace is spiritually comforting. Who said men are not emotional. We vowed to keep each other lifted up in prayer.

Aaron, unlike his Biblical predecessor, is a good man who follows God's instructions. From violent gang member to God's family member, I am confident that God will keep Aaron safe as he travels and adjusts to his new physical prison.

God does change men if they are willing, and Aaron and I certainly are.

Numbers 20:23-26. *At Mount Hor, near the border of Edom, the Lord said to Moses and Aaron, "Aaron will be gathered to his people. He will not enter the land I gave the Israelites, because both of you rebelled against my command at the waters of Meribah. Get Aaron and his son Eleazar and take them up Mount Hor. Remove Aaron's garments and put them on his son Eleazar, for Aaron will be gathered to his people: he will die there."*

✞ ✞ ✞

Monday, November 8, 1993
5:30 a.m.

Aaron woke me per my request at 4:30 a.m. to say a final good-bye. I then awoke again at 5:30 a.m. for breakfast to find a Christmas candy cane hanging from my bunk with the following note attached:

Greg,

You've become a very special friend and person in my life. It was extremely difficult to tell you "Bye".

But you and yours will always be in my prayers. And though I'm not with you in the flesh, I'm with you in spirit, as we each are born from the same Spirit.

Don't let discouragement get the best of you, but KEEP SEEKING THE FACE OF GOD as I truly believe that time is short and God has a great work for you.

Start where you are at and He will open doors according to His purpose and your faith.

Don't feel alone and don't listen to the lies of Satan. Claim the promises of God as they are rightfully yours.

I love you, as my Christian brother, my friend, and just a good guy with some screwy ideas and a great big heart.

"Dare to walk on water."

Aaron

I sat on my bunk as tears moistened my checks.

Malachi 3:16-17. *Then those who feared the Lord talked to each other, and the Lord listened and heard. A scroll of remembrance was written in His presence concerning those who feared the Lord and honored His name. "They will be mine," says the Lord Almighty, "in the day when I make up my treasured possession. I will spare them, just as in compassion a man spared his son who serves him."*

✠   ✠   ✠

Tuesday, November 9, 1993
9:00 p.m.

I returned to work, though I was not scheduled to be there. I went in for the peace and quiet. Upon my return a letter was waiting for me. It was from Marie Bell, who is now Marie Khwak. She is a pen-pal who I originally started writing to through an international pen-pal club that I joined. In the letter, Marie announced her marriage to a Korean businessman and that she is expecting her first child. That was terrific news, especially as I had not heard from her in about five months and I had started to worry about her absence.

Marie is my longest running, though at times sporadic, pen-pal, having written for two and one-half years.

Marie experienced a difficult childhood, being physically abused at a young age, and then being thrust into a life that dipped into the darker side of the entertainment business. Living on her own by the age of 14 on the streets of Paris, she became an *exotic* dancer. She belonged to, and was owned by a troupe that traveled throughout Europe and the Orient to dance and to please men, and surprisingly, many women.

While in Korea, and now age 22, an old woman for her trade, she was kicked to the streets. There she met a Christian businessman who helped her escape the only lifestyle she knew. Marie is not proud of her past but accepts it and is moving on. She is thankful for the peace and forgiveness God has given her and the love from a husband who does not judge her for her past.

Marie's letter was brief, but she still thinks of me and always sends her best. I will write her back immediately to catch her up on the latest in my life and to celebrate her transformation, her marriage, and her coming child. Marie is a ray of sunshine, and I thank God for her ongoing friendship and salvation, both physically and spiritually.

1 Corinthians 7:1-2. *Now for the matters you wrote about: It is good for a man not to marry. But since there is so much immorality, each man should have his own wife and each woman her own husband.*

✝ ✝ ✝

Wednesday, November, 10, 1993
12:30 p.m.

Hope is a scary thing. My volleyball partner, Ed, who is the best player I have ever met, and who was on the AVP professional tour until a poor decision brought him, thankfully only temporarily to this abode, informed me that after speaking to his attorney about my case, his attorney believes that I should receive a reversal in the federal courts. Also, at the federal level, an attorney would be appointed to assist me.

I had appealed my conviction through the state court system and actually won an issue, but as they say, "I won a battle but lost the war." My issue was simple: The right to confront my accuser. The bodyguard of the drug dealer I killed lied when he testified at the preliminary hearing. He then fled the country to Argentina, a country without an extradition treaty with the

United States. During the trial, an officer of the court read the bodyguard's statements to the jury ultimately condemning me. Without the bodyguard being present, my attorney was unable to cross examine him to prove to the jury that he was lying about the reasons for the shooting.

God, I know I am not worthy, but I do try to follow in your Son's footsteps.

Ed also said that if the issues are substantial, meaning likely to prevail, the court may grant me an appeal bond that would allow me out of prison until the retrial, if any. So many *ifs*. So many hurdles to climb over. I have no money. Who will still be around to testify for or against me? Will my ex-business partner lie to save his own skin, or will the Lord help him to see the light? I only want this chapter of my life to end.

This I suppose is where faith and prayers come in. Oh, for the love of hope.

7:15 p.m.

I telephoned Mickie. I had to share my new hope, and because both my parents are out of state on vacation, she was the first one I thought of to be a part of my happiness since she has willingly shouldered my sadness. Mickie was ecstatic. We made plans for a surf trip. A little premature I agree, but we are counting on God's promise of: "Ask it in my name and it will be given."

Mickie was suffering from a cold and feeling rather blue. She was pleased that I chose to call her, and my hopeful news and cheerful voice lifted her spirits. Mickie then asked if she could attend the new trial and I replied, "Of course." I will need all the support I can get.

Hope is not scary. It is absolutely terrifying because it allows me to imagine all the wonderful and exciting things, the possibility for a normal life.

9:45 p.m.

CRASH! A television is smashed to the cement floor. Alarm buzzers sound as the amplified speaker system blares: "Code 3! Code 3!" A big black, normally calm inmate named Connor is wrestled to the ground as batons and then handcuffs are applied. Several other inmates step toward the kneeling officers, the inmates' eyes glaze over with dangerous thoughts. This could get out of hand quickly.

Additional officers rush into the gym, responding to the alarm to help secure the area. With no gun coverage in a level II setting, this place can ignite into a conflagration with the strike of the smallest match.

Connor's problem? He was not getting quick enough service from the officers at their station. Gee, life is tough. It will now get tougher for Connor as he goes to the hole. Attitude and patience is everything.

James 5:11. *As you know, we consider blessed those who have persevered. You have heard of Job's perseverance and seen what the Lord finally brought about. The Lord is full of compassion and mercy.*

✞ ✞ ✞

Thursday, November 11, 1993
VETERAN'S DAY
3:30 p.m.

Out of respect for our country's warriors, who in my opinion, are not lauded enough, I have been given the day off from work to enjoy what many sacrificed their lives for—our right to leisure time as we choose—or in my case, allowed. Among the many sporting events, a two-on-two volleyball tournament was scheduled. Last year on Veteran's Day the recreation yard was cancelled due to a stabbing on the yard that resulted in a subsequent lockdown. I was worried about today's tournament as heavy rain fell throughout the night. My concern was that it would not let up. It is true that winter is upon us, but this is California. We are supposed to be tan all year. Well, aren't we? Ha ha.

Thankfully, the sun shone through diminishing clouds and the temperature was in the 60s. Just right. As usual, a glutton for verbal punishment, I was in charge of refereeing the game when I was not playing. Good heartedness abounded and I was not too abused, as I am recognized as a referee who calls fouls fairly and with the understanding that all players are not at the same skill level. It is a balancing act.

By 2:45 p.m. the teams were whittled down to two, mine and Ron's. Ron is a member of the informal Bible study. He is a Vietnam veteran who humbly wears his colostomy bag as his badge of courage. Because of Ron's small stature, 5'5", his military specialty was as a tunnel rat. He would crawl down into the dark, narrow tunnels dug by the North Vietnamese to search them out. It was during one of these forays deep underground that Ron was shot by the enemy who were silently hiding in a side tunnel. With only a hand gun, Ron engaged the battle, taking several more metal slugs to the gut. Through fortitude, Ron won the battle, but to this day he fights a psychological war that the horrors of combat manifested.

My team had beaten Ron's once, but they worked their way back up through the losers' bracket to challenge us again. The battle for yard domination had begun, but due to better tactics and height advantage, my team beat Ron's two out of three games. As a reward, my team receives winner's certificates. These certificates are mementos of success, something to hang on one's wall, or in the case of those in the *cube*, on our locker doors.

As I left the volleyball court I shook Ron's hand. Even in defeat he was all smiles. I recognized the real winner and said with sincerity, "Thank you."

Reality's ugly head reared itself. Back in the gym, after yard recall, all the inmates, including me, were ordered to strip naked for a body examination: evidence of scratches to flesh, scraped knuckles, developing bruises. The staff was searching for signs of a combatant. Obviously they have one. He was easy to spot with red stuff leaking from his nose and mouth.

No luck. The sought-after party was not found within these four walls. Staff set off to the other housing units to continue their search.

Ester 8:11, 16. *The king's edict granted the Jews in every city the right to assemble and protect themselves; to destroy, kill and annihilate any armed force of any nationality, or province that might attack them and their women and children; and to plunder the property of their enemy. For the Jews it was a time of happiness and joy, gladness and honor.*

✟ ✟ ✟

Friday, November 12, 1993
8:00 a.m.

A new rule: Inmates are now required to wear state-issued blue jeans, blue shirts, and boots to the visiting room. We are no longer allowed to wear personal Levi's blue jeans or personal tennis shoes.

Why? The captain will say it is for security reasons. We all know it is for our degradation in front of our families.

"Make inmates wear torn and improperly fitting clothing. Break their spirits, their will, their pride, and we can easily control the sheep." That is the mantra spoken freely by staff.

It is sad that (some) staff believe they have to destroy us as opposed to lifting us up and inspiring us for the good of mankind.

3:00 p.m.

The new rule: Temporarily suspended pending review. It seems the cost to outfit all the inmates would prohibit its implementation.

1 Thessalonians 1:3. *We continually remember before our God and Father your work produced by faith, your labor prompted by love, and your endurance inspired by hope in our Lord Jesus Christ.*

✠ ✠ ✠

Saturday, November 13, 1993
3:00 p.m.

While at work, I trained Brian in the position (Aaron's old one) of the lieutenant's clerk. Brian is having a hard time. His difficulty is not due to any lack of typing or spelling skills, but due to his finding out that his wife is seeing another man. Betrayal is a pain that twists the stomach and crushes the mind. Lord knows I am trying to give him sound, experienced advice as I remember my own unanswered cries of, "Why?"

When my Angela spoke the crushing words over the telephone, informing me that she was leaving, that she was in a relationship with another, my heart, mind, and world imploded. I understand her right to a normal, fulfilling life, but logic did not quiet my sobs, nor unknot my stomach from the thought of another man receiving the attention I cherished from her.

I also know that as Brian is in the middle of it, it is hard, if not impossible, for a normally rational mind to override emotions of the wounded heart.

During our afternoon Bible study today, we lifted Brian up in prayer. I prayed the Lord will ease Brian's pain. I know He can if Brian will allow Him to do so. God is the only way.

I am confident that Brian will be a fine clerk once he can concentrate, once his heart is healed. The unanswerable question is: How long?

Four years later, my heart is still is broken.

Proverbs 16: 24. *Pleasant words are a honeycomb, sweet to the soul and healing to the bones.*

✞ ✞ ✞

Sunday, November 14, 1993
3:00 p.m.

I spoke with my mother on the telephone. She and her husband, Walt, have returned from Texas. I thank God for His travel mercies. From the conversation it sounded like the big move is on as everything went like clockwork while they were looking for investment properties. They made offers on several and two were accepted by the property owners. I was happy to hear they will not be moving until June of 1994, after my mother finishes this year of teaching. In my heart I feel like this is God's will for them, so I will focus on that and not my loss of visits.

9:30 p.m.

It appears the Spirit is shining through me and that my trust is worth risking. Standing by our bunks, speaking softly, Brian confided in me that he is an ex-police officer who was convicted of having consensual sex with a minor (statutory rape). He is appalled by the way inmates are degraded and abused in so many subtle and not so subtle ways. As a police officer he believed that after arrest and conviction, and once a person was incarcerated, they had the opportunity along with appropriate programs to assist them in changing for the better.

"Wow! Reality, it is an eye opener," Brian whispered.

I feel honored that he believes he can trust me with his secret. Being an ex-police officer in prison must be a scary thing. I knew I did the right thing by bringing him under my wing. I shouldn't be surprised that others find me trustworthy, since I am trusting in the Spirit to guide me in acting appropriately.

Proverbs 11:13. *A gossip betrays a confidence, but a trustworthy man keeps a secret.*

✝ ✝ ✝

Monday, November 15, 1993
4:00 p.m.

Mail! I received a letter from my father. It contained the addresses of two cousins who want me to send them visiting application forms. Why now? It has been six years with no letters from them - nothing. I know God would want me to set the example and be gracious, but I do not know if I want to. Why am I always forgiving others for their inconsiderate behavior? I suppose I should pray about this resistance, this prideful behavior because I feel abandoned.

Included in the letter were photographs of a Halloween party held at my father's home. It looked like a lot of fun and no one was costumed as a ghoul. My father parked my 1931 Model 'A' Ford pickup, which is affectionately named "Rackety Boom", orange and black in color, in the driveway with a skeleton at the wheel drinking from a Jack Daniel's bottle. It looked scary and sent a pertinent message.

I do miss parties, the celebrations of life with laughter and the camaraderie, but it is not a Halloween party that I look forward to and ache for. What I want is a welcome home party…someday.

Proverbs 23:20-21. *Do not join those who drink too much wine or gorge themselves on meat, for drunkards and gluttons become poor, and drowsiness clothes them in rags.*

✝ ✝ ✝

Tuesday, November 16, 1993
10:00 a.m.

The review of the proposed visiting rule requiring the wearing of state-issued clothing only has been completed. We inmates have official permission to wear our own jeans and tennis shoes to the visiting room. Apparently the D.O.M. (Directors Operational Manual) section the captain was attempting to enforce has not been approved by the muckety-mucks at departmental headquarters in Sacramento. Rules on…rules off…back and forth. It gets confusing and frustrating for both the inmates and line staff who are trying to figure out today's policy. I have no doubt that one day the rule will be implemented at a cost of tens of millions of dollars to the taxpayer. Yes, this is a security measure, and though in jest or verbal retaliation, inmates often refer to the odd or offensive guard as having the mentality of a box of rocks. I am confident that no officer would allow a man to freely walk out of the visiting room simply because the rivets on his jeans were stamped with Levi's.

4:15 p.m.

Mail! I received a letter from the Chairman of UCLA's Script-writing Department, wherein he critiqued my script *Joshua's Home.* There was sweet with the bitter. Of course I was dreaming of a reply that stated Spielberg had been notified and we would soon "Do lunch." Well, I am fully awake now as he said I need to work on my dialogue. The chairman did like the overall story-line and remarked that I had a good grasp for crisis. Heck, my life is a crisis, but I was pleased and thankful for the encouragement. I will go back to the drawing board with the hope to improve where needed.

At times like this I truly wish for a word processor. Having only a typewriter means rewrites are a major undertaking. They are also a waste of scarce resources because to change one sentence, which pushes lines onto the following page, I may have to retype three, four, or even five pages. This is where perseverance comes into play. Fight through the obstacles.

7:00 p.m.

No yard tonight. The staff is receiving Hepatitis B shots...against us? The administration believes there will be an outbreak and wants to protect its employees. Common sense would be to give the shots to the inmates to prevent the outbreak in the first place.

These are the moments I especially have to ask for God's hand of protection. I do not want to get sick because the medical care in here is zippo. There is lots and lots of nice shiny equipment, some well preserved in their shipping crates, but for the remedies the medical advice is to drink a lot of water and walk around the track.

I admit that I am not in possession of the statistics and I have no access to other inmate's medical files, but I have a gut feeling that many of the *naturally caused* deaths in here could have been prevented. If I were only smarter, or more experienced in civil law, I would sue the Department of Corrections to uncover the truth and demand better preventive health care.

Suing for money is sometimes appropriate, but if you are dead money does not do you any good.

Psalm 91:5-6. *You will not fear the terror of night, or the arrow that flies by day, nor the pestilence that stalks in the darkness, or the plague that destroys at midday.*

✟ ✟ ✟

Wednesday, November 17, 1993
8:00 a.m. – 4:00 p.m.

There was a planned power outage for the administrative offices today so I was told not to report to work. Instead, I chose eight straight hours of volleyball. I enjoyed many exciting games as my eye-hand coordination kept up a steady thwack of ball spikes that could not be blocked. The team I was on only lost one out of the twelve games played. Yes, it was a spirited, spike-filled; bask in the warm sun day.

Even though today was warm, and the rays of the sun shone brightly, I could perceive a change. Early mornings and evenings possess a hint of a chill, reminding me that the calendar is moving deeper into the winter season. This being the case, I am extra grateful to God for today's balmy temperature.

I was also pleased to watch as men of all colors played together, enjoying the competition, and each other's company. I wish all men of diversity and division could see this and learn from it. We are all the same inside. We love, we laugh, we hurt, and we cry. We are all God's children. Some have lost their way while others have been found.

7:45 p.m.

Mr. Moore's sweet words ring wonderful in my ears. I replaced the telephone receiver after talking to Mickie's father. I have always been frightened by this steel-barrel of a man whose lifetime occupation as a big rig trucker forged a commanding, no-nonsense character who accepted no guff. Yet, even after all the terrible things that have been said about me, some true, he still sees in me the decent young man who was to be called, "Son-in-law." His words of encouragement and emotional support are extra special. I often wonder how my life would have been different if I had married Mickie back in high school when *she* asked me.

It warms my heart that Mickie and I still have a special friendship and that I am still accepted by her family. A little understanding, acceptance, encouragement, and dignity is all anyone ever needs to keep one's head up in a world that is full of uncertainty…and of course, God, to bring it purpose.

1 Peter 4:8. *Above all, love each other deeply, because love covers over a multitude of sins.*

✞ ✞ ✞

Thursday, November 18, 1993
7:30 p.m.

He is dazed and appalled, mumbling confusedly, "Privileged?" My old cellie, Doc Mahar, was moved into the gym a few minutes ago. He is walking around, being overwhelmed by the constant commotion, and the unrelenting chaos of the activities of the other gym inmates. The nefarious activities include gambling, fighting, shooting heroin, smoking marijuana, and stealing illicit sex. Doc asked me when one gets used to this? I smiled, shook my head and said, "Hopefully never." Remember, residing in the gym is a reward for good behavior.

Mutiny, Mr. Christian. Mutiny!

8:00 p.m.

Brian returned from a visit with one of his policeman buddies, an ex-co-worker. Due to his peace officer status, his buddy carried his service revolver onto the prison grounds and immediately notified staff per procedures. He was promptly given the third degree, double-talked, harassed, and basically abused by the prison staff. He could not understand what he had done wrong. He is still a police officer. He holds up the law and catches bad guys.

This is the problem. *He* catches the bad guys and walks the *toughest beat in the state*—the streets. Many officers who work in prison are jealous, and would prefer to be in his street shoes, but for some reason they were unable to pass the educational or psychological requirements. It is a simple case of badge envy.

And yes, he was doing something wrong. He was supporting his friend who fell to temptations and the seduction of a 17-year-old girl who looked and claimed to be 22. It is true. I read her court testimony transcripts.

There was no violence, but Brian violated the law and justice must be meted out. News flash! The statutory rape laws are different in other states. It is a strange world. Guilt or innocence is determined by geography.

Proverbs 14:30. *A heart at peace gives life to the body, but envy rots the bones.*

✟ ✟ ✟

Friday, November 19, 1993
2:30 p.m.

I was too, too busy today at work. Classification paperwork of orientation inmates to be organized and recorded on the proper forms, logging and processing of the never-ending disciplinary reports, overseeing typing tests for wannabe clerks, and staff from education and vocations wanted me to make photocopies for them because their copy machine was broken. Did I mention that every twenty minutes or so the coffee needed to be made? The work of a clerk is never done.

I took many a deep breath throughout the day as I waded through my tasks. With each breath came a private smile. I was busy, productive, and doing a darn good job. Sure, my compensation is only 26 cents an hour, but I really work for the Lord and not for *the man* as most of the staff never expresses appreciation for my efforts. Only God does, always. And, as He was the one that blessed me with a good job, comparatively, as I could be picking up litter on the yard in the rain, I will keep smiling.

Wow. What a great, busy day.

5:00 – 7:30 p.m.

It was a good visit with my mother and Walt. They explained their purchases of two mobile home parks in Texas. It appears the Lord has dispensed blessings without reserve. I am happy for them and trust that God would not have blessed them with such good fortune if this move was not in His will. I know I can trust Him.

While I was seated in the visiting room I noticed Brian with his wife. They sat together at a corner table. I was concerned for Brian as I know his fears and desperate pain. I prayed silently that God would fill them with forgiving hearts.

8:00 p.m.

Back in the crazy circus of the gym, Brian told me that his wife is no longer *in* love with him but still loves him. Ouch! There is the knife to the heart. Brian did take my advice of giving her the freedom she believes she needs. This way she will have the room to come back and he can give his heart some peace, no longer having to worry about who will answer the phone or if she will show up for a visit. Now they can start again, as friends, hopefully to grow back into love again.

Love is a decision, not an emotion. I can only believe that God chose to love me because emotionally I have been quite a problem for Him, or at least my old self was. I am trying hard to do right for you, Lord.

9:30 p.m.

Super cop Bartels strikes again. Bartels spent an hour and a half searching *Silent's* 3x4 foot locker. Really? Was it necessary to unroll the toilet paper? That was going a bit overboard especially since *Silent* does all he can to stay out of trouble, following to the 'T' every rule.

Officer Bartels desires to be liked by staff and respected by the inmates, but he possesses no social skills. It is apparent that Bartels was the kid in school who was always picked on, beat up, and likely never asked to play team sports. I feel sorry for him.

Silent is assigned to a bunk three down from mine. He is a 40-year-old Hispanic who sits on his bunk all day and draws. He is quiet, friendly, slightly portly with short hair, and is missing a front tooth. How sad a sight the extensive search was and for what purpose? Even the accompanying officer was embarrassed, rolling his eyes and shrugging his shoulders helplessly. But, I must remember the prime directives: Break their spirits; Destroy their pride. Then, you will have an emotionally crippled inmate to be prized.

Sorry. What you create in the inmate population is hatred toward all authority. I lie back on my bunk and turned on my Walkman radio to listen to soothing music to calm this seething beast.

Colossians 3:17. *And whatever you do, whether in word or deed, do it all in the name of the Lord Jesus, giving thanks to God the Father through Him.*

✝ ✝ ✝

Saturday, November 20, 1993
7:00 p.m.

Brrr… I have shivered all evening. I bundled myself in sweat pants, a sweat shirt, and an extra thick beanie, all sent with love in a care package from home, but they are inadequate against the winter's biting cold that has snuck in on us. Occasionally I looked toward the ceiling at the wholly inadequate heater attached with wire straps and wondered if it would ever be turned on. A work order has been submitted, back in October, but hey, the maintenance people are busy making sure the administration building has adequate heat…we are just inmates. We do not need any stinkin' heat.

Alarms! Code 3. Building 8. A man is down. I learned he was jumped on and brutally beaten by several other inmates. He will spend several days in the infirmary recovering. Did he steal? No. Did he forget to pay a gambling debt? No. What he did was move his lips and tongue before engaging his brain.

As the Lord warns: The smallest member of the body, the tongue, can steer one to doom. So many times I have wanted to yell, "Shut the f—k up!" at those inconsiderate jerks who constantly yell across the gym, who slam the dominoes on the metal tables, and who blast their radios. But, my tongue would lead my fists and thus all of me to ruin. The ultimate goal is freedom and I will endure all to obtain it.

James 3:5-6. *Likewise the tongue is a small part of the body, but it makes great boasts. Consider what great forest is set on fire by a small spark. The tongue also is a fire, a world of evil among the parts of the body. It corrupts the whole person, sets the whole course of his life on fire, and it itself set on fire by hell.*

✞ ✞ ✞

Sunday, November 21, 1993
10:30 a.m.

The night's chill may have remained, but I shook it off and was rewarded with wild rallies of volleyball on a court slick with black ice. Opponents battled each other and gravity, but the ball was not allowed to touch the ground.

Alarms! Code 3. We all dropped to the pavement as staff ran across the yard toward housing unit 10. The volleyball rolled onto the grass, breaking the frosty blades.

Two black men with muscles rippling with violence were furiously fighting each other. Fighting over what? Another man? For the *privilege* and *pleasure* of sexual gratification they will bruise and bleed. But *it* has such a cute walk, and the voice, oh so sweet and feminine. "Detestable," cried the Lord. A man shall not lie down with another man as he does with a woman.

I am lonely, my heart cries out for affection, and my flesh aches for a gentle touch, but I can wait. I can wait a lifetime if need be. No, never with a man. Never! Never! Never!

How strong of a man could they be if they are so weak as to seek sexual pleasures from another man?

Romans 1:27-28. *In the same way the men also abandoned natural relations with women and were inflamed with lust for one another. Men committed indecent acts with other men, and received in themselves the due penalty for their perversion. Furthermore, since they did not think it worthwhile to retain the knowledge of God, He gave them over to a depraved mind to do what ought to be done.*

✝ ✝ ✝

Monday, November 22, 1993
9:00 p.m.

Perfection of one's work to reach the heights of despisement. Sergeant B's last night. The crowd cheers...HURRAY!!!

Staff and inmates alike are thrilled with her transfer to another prison. It is sad when an individual such as Sergeant B, with unfettered power, treats others, both officers and inmates with such disdain, always seeking ways to humiliate simply because she can. The old saying of: "You can catch more flies with honey than vinegar," is true. Staff does not have to be buddy-buddy with each other or with inmates, but they can ask instead of order, and more likely than not, they will receive the compliance they wish just as fast. And, as a supervisor, he or she will not have to watch his or her back for the political or metal knife.

I should mention that Sergeant B is a self-professed lesbian. I often wondered if her treatment of others, men in particular, was a reflection of how she feels about herself. This is only speculation on my part, but how could a person love herself and treat others so hatefully?

Staff did not have the usual going away party for Sergeant B as they have in the past for other departing staff. The sentiment was, "Good-bye and good riddance."

Daniel 4:27. *Therefore, O King, be pleased to accept my advice; Renounce your sins by doing what is right, and your wickedness by being kind to the oppressed. It may be that then your prosperity will continue.*

✟ ✟ ✟

Tuesday, November 23, 1993
11:00 a.m.

One teaches one. I took a break from typing reports at work, deciding to watch the inmate activities on the recreation yard through the conference room window. It was a *Winnie-the-Pooh* blustery day outside, but Max was on the volleyball court teaching a new player how to bump pass the ball.

Thirty-two year old Max; timid Max; skinny and frail Max. A scarecrow of a man who would regularly be assaulted and have his canteen and personal property taken from him until we took him into our volleyball circle to encourage, and to show the abusers on the yard that Max has friends. There is a quiet strength in numbers.

A little kindness, some praise, and Max has blossomed. He stands straighter, more confident, less a victim in waiting. Most of the men who play volleyball are Christians and attempt to let the Spirit shine in their daily walk. It is encouraging to see new faces wanting to play, hopefully drawn to Christ's light shining through us. Later, if the timing is right, I will ask Max if he would like to join our fellowship group.

One teaches one.

Romans 14:19. *Let us therefore make every effort to do what leads to peace and mutual edification.*

✟ ✟ ✟

Wednesday, November 24, 1993
8:00 p.m.

I went into work to get away from the chaos in the gym and to hopefully write a few lines of my screenplay in progress. As I was in the creative zone, the images in my head flowed smoothly onto the paper. A very rare event as writing is very difficult for me.

I was so engrossed in concentration that I had not noticed Officer Clark standing in front of my desk. She coughed to get my attention. When I looked up, there was that big smile of hers. She asked, "Have you learned to spell yet or are you just drawing pictures?" Always a joker.

I have only known Officer Clark for several months but it has been a pleasure because even though she can be the joker she is always professional, and neither she nor the inmates cross the invisible line of over familiarity. She exhibits a confidence in her position which I believe gives her the privilege to share her toothy grin below the rich earthy eyes of a country-girl face. Somehow Officer Clark has that special ability, by simply saying, "Hello," to take control of any situation, turning a negative to positive, metaphorically turning our gray skies bright blue. Too much? Let me just say Officer Clark is a breath of fresh air.

Attitude, it is so important regardless of which side of the bars one is on. I would like to ask Officer Clark if she is a Christian, but that would cross the invisible line. I will simply be grateful for the light she brings to our normally dark world.

Matthew 5:16. *In the same way, let your light shine before men, that they may see your good deeds and praise your Father in heaven.*

✝ ✝ ✝

Thursday, November 25, 1993
THANKSGIVING DAY
3:00 p.m.

We won! Doc Mahar, Ed, and I won the three-on-three volleyball tournament. Forgive my lack of humility for a moment, but our success was not too difficult as we three are the most experienced players on this yard. What I did find interesting today was how well the Hispanic team played. They placed second. Because the tournaments are played by the American college rules and the Hispanic players are not familiar with them, this gave my team the advantage. I have been considering asking the other players if they would be willing to have a tournament where we play by the rules the Hispanics are familiar with…namely none.

6:00 p.m.

The holiday meal was properly prepared tonight. And, surprisingly it had a flavor that my taste buds recognized. We were served real turkey not processed, mashed potatoes, a dollop of canned cranberry sauce, green beans, salad, a slice of pumpkin pie and a cold soda. I have no doubt that many inmates found something to complain about; overcooked turkey, pie slice too small, or limp salad, but I felt very blessed that the state went out of its way to spend the few extra dollars to provide felons with a special Thanksgiving meal. I am embarrassed at times by my fellow inmates lack of gratitude and their sense of entitlement. There are a lot of law abiding citizens on the street that are not eating as well as we did tonight.

On the flip-side, if only penologists, law makers, and victims of crime could understand that if broken men were lifted up every day, treated with dignity, they would have a model to follow. I accept that prison is meant to be deterrence, punishment of offenses against society, but what is really being taught is that if you possess the power, the gun, that might is right.

One or two good meals a year does not make for a healthy body and mind.

9:00 p.m.

I could not outrun it. I thought I could make it through the day, but depression caught me. I ache to be with my parents this evening as Thanksgiving is traditionally a day where families drop whatever it is they are doing to find time to spend with each other. I ruined that. What makes my absence from their dinner table worse is the thought that my mother and father may somehow think they are responsible for my poor choices. They are not, but parents think that way and I do not know how to relieve them of this unfair burden.

My only thoughts are to continue to show them, to prove to them, that I do know right from wrong, and that I did listen each time they directed me down the correct path. I want to scream, "Look at me! I have changed!" But these walls do not allow my words and deeds to penetrate.

Thankfully, through visits, letters, and telephone calls, my family and friends can hear and see the changes in me through Christ's workings. This is my hope: for them to find peace, and me to receive freedom.

Depression sucks.

I am going to crawl under the covers and end my day.

Psalm 100. *Shout for joy to the Lord, all the earth. Worship the Lord with gladness; come before him with joyful songs. Know that the Lord is God. It is he who made us, and we are his; we are his people, the sheep of his pasture. Enter his gates with thanksgiving and his courts with praise; give thanks to him and praise his name. For the Lord is good and his love endures forever; his faithfulness continues through all generations.*

✝ ✝ ✝

Friday, November 26, 1993
5:30 p.m.

Aaauughh!!! Where is my script??? Someone removed the pad of paper that contained six months of work from the locked locker at work.

God, I am going to throw up. Please, please, please, someone tell me who did this?

I have some hope as an 8 ½" x 14" pad of lined paper was put in place of my 8 ½" x 11" pad, which indicated, hopefully, that whoever did remove the tablet did not know my draft was on it. I prayed earnestly that my pad finds its way back into my hands. I do not want to attempt to reconstruct all those scenes and all that dialogue.

God, I am going to throw up.

Philippians 4:6. *Do not be anxious about anything, but in everything, by prayer and petition, with thanksgiving, present your requests to God.*

✝ ✝ ✝

Saturday, November 27, 1993
2:30 p.m.

Emotionally I could not play volleyball today. I was still so unnerved by the disappearance of my script. So much work...vanished.

3:00 p.m.

During our weekly Bible fellowship, Ron shared his walking-on-clouds week. Ron's 18-year-old daughter sent him a photograph of herself in a letter. Ron has not seen or heard from her in four years. Maybe she was ashamed that her father was in prison. Maybe she was angry because he left the family to fend for itself. Who knows, but whatever the reason, she is now opening the lines of communication with him.

It scares me to death to get married and to have children. I suppose I do not have much to worry on that account as I do not have a girlfriend. There is Mickie, and as a bonus she too has become a Christian, but I believe she is hedging her bet by not making any commitments unless I regain my freedom. That makes me believe her love is conditional, but then again, what kind of husband could I be from behind bars? Not a very good one.

But...hells bells, everyone else in here seems to be able to find girlfriends and wives. Why not me?

I am happy for Ron, but thankful that I do not have the responsibility of a family at this time.

3:30 p.m.

Doc Mahar, who speaks fluent Spanish, spoke with the Hispanic porter who cleans the Program Office. The subject of discussion was the *missing* pad of paper with my script on it. The porter *thinks* he knows who may have it.

Psalm 62:5. *Find rest, O my soul, in God alone: my hope comes from him.*

✟ ✟ ✟

Sunday, November 28, 1993
8:30 a.m.

All night I heard rain as it pounded down, splattering with heavy drops on the roof. I was relieved. I was not in the mood to spend the day refereeing for the Hispanic volleyball tournament, especially since it would be oxymoronic to referee games with no rules. It is true that I pushed for this as it would be a fair thing to allow those with different ideas about how to play a sporting activity to have their way once in a while. The tournament will be rescheduled for the next weekend and by then I will be in a brighter, more energetic mood.

I skipped breakfast and stayed in bed as my dreams are usually more pleasant than my reality. That I suppose is why they are called dreams.

10:00 a.m.

Ah… A hot shower, a shave, and I am ready to write. I am surprised by the unusual quiet that surrounded me. I decided to stir the creative juices at my bunk instead of going to the Program Office to write. I want to always give acknowledgment where due. In the evenings or weekends when I am not assigned to work, and only a skeleton crew of staff are in the office, I am allowed to go there to sit quietly at an unused desk, to think, to read, and to write. I appreciate this privilege, this kindness by staff.

2:45 p.m.

Ouch. My butt hurts. To quickly clarify why my posterior aches, I sat on my hard footlocker, using it as a stool, for almost five hours. For further clarification of my unfortunate ailment, I sadly suffer from the not too uncommon Caucasian disease called, "No-ass-at-all," thus no padding. However, the reward for the pain in the rump is 20 pages of writing completed. Not too shabby of an output for working in the giant cubical.

3:15 p.m.

During the 3:00 p.m. gym unlock I walked over to work to see if…Yes! The script that was lost had been returned to the locked locker. Prayers and the appropriate approach worked wonders. I bumped into the suspected culprit as he was emptying the trash cans and thanked him and then let him know that if he needed writing paper in the future to ask and I would make sure he received some.

All is well that ends well…at least in regards to my script.

Romans 8:28. *And we know that in all things God works for the good of those who love Him; who have been called according to His purpose.*

✞ ✞ ✞

Monday, November 29, 1993
8:45 p.m.

Brian sat down on my bunk next to me. He looked like someone had killed his dog…he only wished. He finished speaking to his wife's boyfriend on the telephone. The boyfriend is living in Brian's house. That had to be a big knife stab to the heart.

"Hey, buddy, twist it harder, why don't you?"

There seems to be no honoring of the marriage vows these days. Actually, it would be hypocritical to completely blame Brian's wife, Tami, as Brian was convicted and incarcerated for infidelity with a minor. Maybe this is Tami's way of getting back at Brian for the pain he caused her? Still, I can sympathize with the hurt he is experiencing.

I can sympathize because before my lady, my dear Angela, told me she was leaving, she stated that she was seeing another man. His name was Greg. He drove a black Ferrari. He, too, was a surfer like me. Regardless of how painful that was to hear, I will never blame Angela because if I had not committed my crimes, causing our physical separation, it is likely that we would still be together, as husband and wife. I am to blame.

If all parties, Brian, Tami, and I had obeyed God's commandments; none of us would be going through this pain. I believe I have learned and grown and hopefully they will too.

Whoever first coined the phrase, "Hindsight is 20/20," spoke the truth. I can look back and see my blind, stumbling, stupidity for running in the dark. Now my eyes are open with Jesus' light guiding the path. His commandments are the road signs clearly directing my steps. I admit that I do not know my life's destination, but praise-worthy, God has eliminated many of the ditches I would have fallen into.

God sees the future, and I will follow Him as I walk toward it.

Psalm 121:1-2. *I will lift up mine eyes unto the hills. From where does my help come from? My help comes from the Lord, the Maker of heaven and earth.*

✝ ✝ ✝

Tuesday, November 30, 1993
5:45 p.m.

Fate? Karma? Or God's irony? I was sitting in the chow hall with Anthony, who is a Jehovah's Witness, and he was telling me how the Great Frisbee Caper transpired. He had committed an armed robbery and was fleeing the scene on foot. An off-duty policeman spotted Anthony running and took chase.

Anthony climbed onto the roof of a dry cleaning store and was being pursued by the plain-clothes officer. The officer shouted for Anthony to "Freeze" and pulled out his concealed pistol. Though Anthony is not a large man, he is a tough, bull-dog scrapper. Anthony was able to disarm the officer so as not to be shot, but the officer refused to let loose of Anthony and the two of them continued to struggle, throwing blows with fists and elbows.

Anthony's literal downfall came when he and the officer stepped onto a skylight and broke through, crashing to the floor of the dry cleaners. Both the officer and Anthony were injured in the fall, but because the officer landed on Anthony, Anthony's wind was knocked out of him, allowing the officer to handcuff and arrest him. A good bust, right?

Now here is the Great Frisbee Caper as Anthony explained it. Because Anthony had removed all identifying clothing, and had tossed away his weapon, he claimed in his statement to the police that he was climbing onto the roof of the dry cleaners to retrieve his Frisbee. While doing this, a deranged man with a gun attacked him. At no time did the officer identify himself as a policeman.

It came down to one man's word against another, and as Anthony was able to produce a friend to corroborate his statements, the district attorney had no choice but to drop the case. Thus, the Great Frisbee Caper. Quick thinking ingenuity. Amazing, but not admirable.

I was momentarily puzzled. If Anthony was not prosecuted for the armed robbery, why was he now in prison? Normally, I never ask another inmate what he is in prison for but this situation begged the question, so I asked. Anthony chuckled when he answered. It seemed that the very next day, the friend who had corroborated Anthony's statements loaned Anthony a car, which unknown to Anthony, happened to be stolen. When the police pulled Anthony over for what he thought was a traffic infraction, the police discovered a stolen handgun and marijuana hidden under the back seat.

Continuing his laughter, Anthony concluded by saying, "I would have received less time for the armed robbery."

Fate? Karma? Or God's irony?

Thankfully, during this extended sentence, Anthony has left that lifestyle in the past, and embraced God for the future.

What a character.

Psalm 119:9-10. *How can a young man keep his way pure? By living according to your word. I seek you with all my heart: do not let me stray from your commands.*

✧ ✧ ✧

Wednesday, December 1, 1993
9:00 p.m.

They are precious links to the outside world; our telephone calls. Surprise, surprise, surprise. We have a new addition to our party line. I say *party* with disdain because all inmate telephone calls are monitored and recorded. I certainly understand the need for security, and I even applaud it, but there does not seem to be any guidelines for staff to follow when it comes to monitoring our calls. All calls must be collect and the service fee is expensive. I have observed staff repeatedly turn off a telephone simply to watch the inmate become upset.

It's entertainment.

The new addition is a tape recording that blares over the line every few minutes, announcing: "You are speaking to an inmate in a California correctional institution. BEEP."

Gee, thanks. My mother, my father, my friends did not know I was in prison. Yeah, right. Would it be unrealistic for me to believe that the receiving party who accepts my collect call would know who I am and where I am calling from? Especially when a recorded message states: "This is a collect call from an inmate in a California correctional institution."

This is one more way to throw the fact that I am in prison in my face and in the faces of my family and friends. And, let us consider the simple annoyance of interrupting our conversation. The new addition is rude and unnecessary.

Oooops. I forgot. I am scum, but remember, scum always rises to the top.

Praise God.

Psalm 91:14. *Because he loves me, says the Lord, "I will rescue him; I will protect him, for he acknowledges my name."*

✝ ✝ ✝

Thursday, December 2, 1993
6:30 a.m.

Fog Count. Yahoo! No one was allowed out of the housing units, which meant I could not go to work. Therefore, I chose to sleep in, but since I closed my eyes, I missed watching the staff as they ran all over the recreation yard counting the fog droplets. No. Actually, they count us, but I look for humor wherever I can find it, even if it is in my own head. The purpose of the fog count is staff believes that if they cannot see across the recreation yard we may slip away in the fog…did they forget about the electrified fence?

It is sleepy time. Zzzzzz…

12:30 p.m.

Fog count cleared, meaning all felons were present, and the fog cleared at about 10:30 a.m., two hours ago. What was the delay in releasing us back to normal program? It is a mystery. Regardless of the reason, I went off to work as I was still in the middle of my end-of-the-month reports. With the shortened day, I would be pressed to finish by the deadline of 3:00 p.m.

Thank God I am blessed with speedy typing fingers and brain power…run hamster run.

2:00 p.m.

Warden's Message. I sat at my desk working steadily through the reports while a lieutenant of 20 years sat at her desk reading the prison's newsletter. She giggled and then laughed out loud. I paused, curious, and always wanting to share in any revelry, I entered the lieutenant's office to inquire.

"It is the Warden's Message," she replied. "What a joke. Warden (Ms.) Latham is always praising her troops, but she has neither walked among us since her probation period ended, nor does she have a clue as to what is really going on in the trenches."

It is quite telling of leadership's failings when the majority of underlings believe she is out of touch. I say, "Majority," because I have heard the same statement from many other staff.

There is such a concentration of power at the very top that no one near the bottom has the ability to stand up and point out the stupid rules and regulations that the lower staff readily admit to each other, and surprisingly, to the inmates that make no sense. This top heavy power without regard to the input or experience from below is why the system stays the same—broken.

Hey, the emperor has no clothes.

Ephesians 6:13-15. Therefore, put on the full armor of God, so that when the day of evil comes, you may be able to stand your ground, and after you have done everything, to stand. Stand firm then, with the belt of truth buckled around your waist, with the breastplate of righteousness in place, and with your feet fitted with the readiness that comes from the gospel of peace.

✟ ✟ ✟

Friday, December 3, 1993
3:00 p.m.

Legal mail? What could it be? Oh, cool. It was the reply from the Australian Consulate General. My passport has been approved; I leave next week. Yeah, I wish. No, seriously, it was the answers to my requests for addresses to an anthropological museum in Australia and to music stores that carry native aboriginal music.

Why have I been seeking out Aboriginal music? To help me get into the mood, or actually the spirit, of *Dreamtime*. *Dreamtime* is the name of another screenplay I have been working on. It is also the name of the creation story of native Australians. I have been using aspects of their beliefs in the adventure drama. Cool music that didgeridoo. Fascinating story—their creation, that is. My only dilemma now is how to get the cassette tapes sent in because the prison has only a few approved vendors that inmates may purchase from, and obviously none of the ones in Australia are on the list.

4:00 p.m.

I spent an hour strolling around the recreational track while waiting for the gym unlock. The housing units, including the gym, only allow inmates to enter or exit at specified times, which are every two hours. No exceptions.

One lap around the track is one-third of a mile. During my walk I was entertained by several of the more unique inmates and their rituals. One in particular is Carl Kimble. Carl stands in the middle of the yard, religiously playing a flute to placate the death song spirits. Between stanzas, Carl does a brief hop-dance all the while facing the setting sun.

This tune and dance would be cute except for the compulsory reasons behind them. They are Carl's reluctant substitute for killing. Carl believes that if the dark spirits are not appeased, they will unleash an earthquake that will destroy California, and cause the deaths of many millions. Therefore, the half-dozen people Carl killed in sacrifice to the spirits is a paltry trade-off for the millions he saved...it is Carl's logic backed up by the fact that California has not fallen into the ocean.

I turned my attention away from Carl to gaze up at the passing clouds—something less disturbing. There were a mixture of cumulus with white fluffy edges; cumulus nimbus, dark gray and black, bumping up against the Sierras; and wisps of cirrus feathered high, high above. I sighed deeply recognizing an envious fact.

Clouds are so free, so peaceful, even with their potential for storms, and thus inspiring. They are God's ships riding across a sea of air. They go where the Lord directs, willingly, they simply rise up. A lesson was there, but instead of ciphering it out, I chose to simply enjoy their passing.

1 Kings 3:14. *And if you walk in my ways and obey my statutes and commandments as David your father did, I will give you a long life.*

✠ ✠ ✠

Saturday, December 4, 1993
2:30 p.m.

Anthony, the Jehovah's Witness, approached me in a very distressed state. He wanted me to know he was a true Christian and all those other bastards could go fu-- themselves.

Apparently, during the dinner we had together the other night, when someone had said he did not act like a Christian, I jokingly commented: "He's not. He's a Jehovah's Witness."

Someone must have put a bug in his ear, or all of a sudden he felt I had insulted him. Using a soft, non-confrontational voice, I gently explained that each *religion* believes that they are the one and only true religion and I would never condemn him because his religious practices are different from mine. As well, he should not be offended when someone's beliefs are different than his.

My words were as leaves tossed to the wind. Anthony was in no mental state to listen to reason. He had set his demeanor to agitation, causing his bald head and flaring ears to flush bright pink.

Religion and love of it, or in defense of it, has caused more deaths throughout recorded time than all the wars put together. Then again, most wars are somehow about whose god is the correct god. Does not the Bible and most religions have the tenet of love they neighbor? Curious, I think so.

I apologized one more time to Anthony and then slowly backed away.

Revelation 17:6. *I saw that the woman was drunk with the blood of saints, the blood of those who bore testimony to Jesus.*

✠ ✠ ✠

Sunday, December 5, 1993
3:00 p.m.

Exhausted, drained, spent, tuckered out. Yes, I like that last adjective. I was tuckered out from a vigorous day of smacking and chasing the volleyball around the court. Today was the Latin League Tournament to recognize the Hispanics' style of play.

I did have difficulty at first convincing the regular players to play by the Latin rules—none, but after we got started, and the men realized today would be a free-for-all, it worked out well. Not surprisingly the Latin team won and will receive certificates as awards. I am pleased for them. I can mark this day, this tournament, as a success.

Recognizing the way others do things, accepting differences without negative judgment, and realizing that my way is not the only way goes a long way to building trust and friendships.

8:00 p.m.

Fights. Shots fired. Boots in the face, fists to the belly, and scratching like junk yard dogs. The holiday blues are setting in. The inmates have begun to act out, to rock and roll: six shots fired on Facility C when a staff member was assaulted; three separate fights on Facility B, and a man dropped dead in a shower on Facility A of a massive stroke. Today has not been a happy or healthy day for some of the residents of the Creek.

I am willing to die just about anywhere when the time comes, but please, Lord, do not let it be in prison.

Psalm 49:15. *But God will redeem my life from the grave; He will surely take me to Himself.*

✝ ✝ ✝

Monday, December 6, 1993
4:00 p.m.

Mail. It's a letter from Bonnie and her husband, Rod. She is a faithful pen-pal. I receive a letter from them every three or four months. Each letter is filled with the simplest, but precious topics of everyday life. In the brief time we have been corresponding, they have made me feel important and worthy to share their life with.

I was introduced to Bonnie and Rod through Someone Cares. It is a Christian pen pal organization that matches inmates across the country with Christians who are willing to reach out, or I should say, reach in to lift a man or woman up, and to be examples of God's love for all man, even wayward ones.

Bonnie and Rod are a light that I am so blessed to be illuminated by.

8:45 p.m.

Telephone talk with Mickie. Up talk. Down talk. I wish I could be closer or out to help cheer her up. As a single mother, Mickie is having a rough time financially. This fact brings her down emotionally. She then feels defeated and only cares to spend time raising her son and daughter. Focusing her energy on her children is in itself admirable, but I heard the flatness in her voice. The spark was absent from the vibrant girl I called my princess in younger days. Life is tough on both sides of the wall, but Mickie's woes are multiplied by an ex-husband who cares only for his needs. Without the Lord in his life directing him, he believes the money he earns is for himself, and that somehow children can raise themselves.

Selfishness. It is a sin, isn't it?

Mickie and I ended our conversation with a few laughs and an "I love you." That made me feel good, but I am hoping she, too, was feeling a little better. Mickie is not perfect, but she is a godly woman, and like most people, she deserves a measure of happiness. Unfortunately, no where can I find in Scripture that God guarantees joy in this world—only in His kingdom and in the knowledge that He loves us.

After our conversation I prayed my supportive words were able to supply more than a bit of what she needed to fill her cup. I also prayed that her faith does not waiver but only strengthens during this time of hardship.

I know for me, it is sometimes too easy to cry out, "Why?" to the Lord, but then I remember Job who did everything right and still was tested. I failed miserably and deserve every test I am given, every chastisement, so that I will learn and be steadfast on the straight and narrow path.

Psalm 34:17-18. *The righteous cry out, and the Lord hears them; He delivers them from all their troubles. The Lord is close to the brokenhearted and saves those who are crushed in spirit.*

☩ ☩ ☩

Tuesday, December 7, 1993
10:00 a.m.

Everyone hide! Something terrible has happened to the office technician Donna.

Apparently, some staff member believed she has been too pleasant to us scumbag inmates. She was instructed to get tough with us. So this morning she came in snapping at me and the two other inmate clerks, questioning every move we made.

"What are you typing?"

"What documents is Smitty photocopying?"

"Brian, why did it take you fifteen minutes to deliver the memorandums to the housing units?"

How sad. *They* believe they can never ease up. Never loosen the screws, not even for a moment, because maybe for a second, the fleeting idea might cross our minds: I am not an animal. I am human. I can strive to rise above my past.

I hope this crush-them phase will pass quickly. Donna was a bright light to our day. She was a glowing example of how to treat others...exactly how each of us would like to be treated—with dignity, respect, and high expectations.

4:15 p.m.

I am depressed. I am feeling the weight of loneliness again. The cause, no mail. The mail officer zoomed past my bunk without a sideways glance in my direction. I do not expect mail every day, and as I did receive a letter yesterday I should feel blessed.

My heart goes out to the men who never receive mail. I cannot bear it when the mail officer walks by more than four or five days in a row, so the feelings of abandonment must be unbearable at times for these other men. All I need, all any of us need, is for someone to take a moment to write on a small card a few words of care. I hear all the time, written in my parents' letters, that friends or relatives that I have not heard from, say, "Tell Greg I'm thinking of him." Well, thoughts are very nice, but I am not a mind reader.

Okay, okay. I am having a small pity party, but that is how I am feeling at the moment.

Hebrews 13:3. *Remember those in prison as if you were their fellow prisoners, and those who are mistreated as if you yourselves were suffering.*

✝ ✝ ✝

Wednesday, December 8, 1993
1:00 p.m.

Crack! The ball is out of the park. Well, not exactly. In this case, the bat was a 2"x4" made out of oak and the ball was a man's skull.

The Mill and Cabinet vocational shop is a very dangerous place to disrespect someone. Never threaten a small in stature man as he will never come at you face on, but from behind with a metal shank (knife) or homemade bat. Respect all men—always safety first.

7:15 p.m.

I waited 45 minutes in the cold rain to pick up my quarterly care
package. That is a new record in brevity. I usually have to wait several hours
to be escorted to R&R by a plaza officer.

Included within my package were a new pair of tennis shoes, a Casio
G-Shock watch (surfer watch), and Asian candies. The candies, which I came
to relish when I lived in Hawaii as a young teenager, always cause the package
officer to view them and me with an odd, "What the hell are these," stare. Le-
he-mui, shredded cuttlefish, marinated mango strips, and hot and spicy
tamarind wrapped in multi-colored packages with Japanese and Chinese
characters are always a mental stretch for the Nestlé Crunch consumer.

I smiled during the close inspection of my candies while salivating like
Pavlov's dog at their tongue-tasty memory. It is the little things that become
more and more important when one has less and less.

Also, I find it interesting how God is becoming a closer friend as those
I once knew on the streets fall away into the chaos of their own lives.

Ephesians 2:3. *All of us also lived among them at one time, gratifying the
cravings of our sinful nature and following its desires and thoughts. Like the
rest, we were by nature objects of wrath.*

✟   ✟   ✟

Thursday, December 9, 1993
12:30 p.m.

Marty (Mr. Someone Else's Severed Penis In His Pocket Freeway
Killer's Assistant), who has somehow adopted me as mentor and friend, saw
me standing in front of the Program Office, taking my lunch break. Marty was
returning from his appearance before the parole board today, and even though,
many years ago, the judge told Marty that he would recommend that Marty
never be released, the parole board commissioners stated during the hearing
that they might consider him for parole next year.

Who is kidding who? In this era of un-forgiveness and "Let them rot
in prison" sentiment, no one is receiving parole dates. Forgive me. I used the
no one term. That is an absolute and not exactly true. Out of the four to five
thousand parole hearings held each year, the commissioners and the governor
are allowing .02%. So there is hope.

At least the commissioners spoke in a kind tone to Marty while they fed him shovels of sh--.

When I picture myself going before the parole board, it scares me to death. I am afraid as I am neither an actor nor a game player. My fear is that I will not be able to express my true feeling of remorse, for the pain I have caused so many, to these commissioners who are total strangers, ex-police officers and victims of crime. I will have to give my fear over to God. I will need to surrender completely and have the faith of a mustard seed that Christ's light will shine through me.

The question then will be: Are the commissioners' eyes and hearts open to receive Christ's light?

4:15 p.m.

Mail. A letter from Mickie. Be still my beating heart. She writes that her children's school work is getting harder and she needs an intelligent male role model around to help. Then she asked, "When are you coming home?" A wonderful compliment, but if I am so smart, why was I acting so stupidly? Can I say, "Short Cut?" How about, "Dead end?"

Mark 13:9. *"You must be on your guard. You will be handed over to the local councils and flogged in the synagogues. On account of Me you will stand before governors and kings as witnesses to them."*

✞ ✞ ✞

Friday, December 10, 1993
6:00 p.m.

Holiday stress boiled over. Facility A: a rare riot between the white and black inmates. Facility C: a riot between the Northern and Southern affiliate Mexicans, and Facility B: three separate cell fights, and two, fall-down drunken inmates from the consumption of homemade alcohol (*pruno*).

There is no cheer in this holiday air.

8:00 p.m.

I finished reading a memorandum posted in front of the officers' station regarding holiday carolers coming into the prison to serenade us later this week. Gee, why don't they pump the aroma of grandma's Christmas dinner in through the air vents to torture us more?

I know the carolers' hearts are filled with good intentions, but they are misguided. Inmates neither want to be reminded that it is the Christmas season nor of all the things we are missing: the warm hugs of family and friends, the tasty holiday foods made with love, and the gifts wrapped with glittering paper.

Do not throw the poor animals a plastic Christmas bone. Spend your energies in preventing others from coming to prison in the first place. That would be the greatest gift to all.

1 Peter 5:6-7. *Humble yourselves, therefore, under God's mighty hand, that He may lift you up in due time. Cast all you anxiety on Him because He cares for you.*

✟ ✟ ✟

Saturday, December 11, 1993
8:00 a.m.

Let it rain. Pitter-patter was the tune played atop the gym's tin roof. It was a lullaby tune. How nice. I turned over in my bunk, snuggling deep into the warmth of my covers and sought out sleep. I closed my eyes, and like a child playing peek-a-boo, nothing of this prison existed. Off to dreamland. I was whisked away to allow happier times of skateboarding in the Los Angeles summer sun.

If only I could sleep through the madness, but then, how would I learn anything?

3:00 p.m.

Still raining. No Bible fellowship today. Bummer. I can, however read The Word on my own. Isaiah will be *it* on this lazy day of precipitation.

Isaiah 26:3. *You will keep in perfect peace him whose mind is steadfast, because he trusts in you.*

✟ ✟ ✟

Sunday, December 12, 1993
7:00 p.m.

A difficult but not unusual situation arose at work. Placed before me was a thick pile of reports written by officers that would not pass the grammatical scrutiny of the lieutenant or program administrator. The difficult part is explaining the request for changes in the reports, and doing so in a way that does not sound uppity or cause the officers to lose face in front of a no-good, low-life inmate such as I am viewed.

The alternative was to type the reports as they were, then to retype them after being rejected, and then called on the carpet as to why I did not catch the errors. No thank you.

I gave the 'request for changes' plea to the sergeant first. BULLS EYE! I was given carte blanche to correct the reports.

A smidgen of humility and a cautious angle of tact worked perfectly. I am thankful that the Lord has been able to teach me this lesson. I know my place, my lowly standing in this world, but I still need to put forth my best effort.

Daniel 12:3. *Those who are wise will shine like the brightness of the heavens, and those who lead many to righteousness, like the stars for ever and ever.*

✝ ✝ ✝

Monday, December 13, 1993
1:30 p.m.

What a female dog! I speak of the non-custody wench who delivers office supplies to the Program Office and housing units. Is there something in her job description that requires her to demean inmates? Is rudeness part of the orientation course? How do I describe the snotty-bitchy tone of voice when her words are mere instructions to do this or carry that box?

2:00 p.m.

When the sh-- rolls downhill, guess who catches it?   Not only did I get sh-- from the supply delivery wench but from Donna as well. As I have said, Donna used to be a shining light, but in addition to the instruction from above to get tough on us, Donna is stressed because the program administrator dumped a month's worth of paperwork on her desk and wants it completed yesterday.

I apologize in advance for the following chauvinistic statement but my observations have merit. Excluding the delivery wench because she has always been a female dog, many of the female staff, both custody and non-custody, have been on the proverbial rag lately.

I have been unable to figure out the cause, but these emotional swings are not good at all. Inmates, including myself, need stability to function well in this unnatural setting.

Is it too much to ask that professional staff be the same today, tomorrow, and every day? And come to think about it, they are all free to quit if they do not like their jobs. What could possibly trouble a free person?

"Give us structure or give us..." Oh never mind. Some in society would gladly give us the latter of the incomplete sentence.

4:00 p.m.

Mail. I received a Christmas card and letter from Weila, a pen-pal who lives in the Philippines. Weila works as a seamstress fixing flaws in tee shirts in a textile factory. She earns the equivalent of $15 a day. She constantly writes how fortunate she is to have her position even if she has to work six days a week, fourteen hours each day. Weila works in Manila and is hopeful that this Christmas she will be able to travel home to one of the other islands. She has not been home in three years due to the cost of transportation being expensive, and she sends the majority of her income home so that her three brothers can pay for school.

Knowing that a postage stamp to mail me a letter costs 80 cents, I offered to send her international postage but she declined, stating that it would not be proper.

How very humbling.

Weila's card said, "Have a nice smile." I certainly will try.

8:00 p.m.

With each inmate's name that is called off by the escort officer, I sink deeper into depression. These inmates are being taken from the gym to Level I, and within a few months they will be going home. The majority of these men have only served a few years, and simply put, they are jerks, the trouble makers. They have not learned a thing, and when they are released, it is obvious to all who observe them, that they will again apply whatever dastardly deeds they were doing that brought them to prison in the first place.

Prison sucks, and yes, the rules seem unfair. Life seems unfair, but who said it ever was, or was supposed to be?

Help, God, I need a nice smile.

Isaiah 50:9. *It is the Sovereign Lord who helps me. Who is he that will condemn me? They will all wear out like a garment: the moths will eat them up.*

✝ ✝ ✝

Tuesday, December 14, 1993
9:30 a.m.

I offered to help Donna put away the supplies.

"I've already done it and you can tell Smitty that he's not getting any of the bond typing paper," was her accusatory retort.

Jeez. Donna basically insinuated that I give away state supplies for personal use. F.Y.I., Smitty buys his own bond paper, thank you very much. I hate having to take crap from these better-than-thou S.O.B.'s. Who the hell do they think they are?

I turned and left the room. Think, think, think, of the ultimate goal—FREEDOM, and what would be pleasing to God. I also reminded myself that *they* have not been convicted of a felony so they are better than I am.

3:00 p.m.

As I walk around the track after work, I conversed with Mr. Miami (Joey). Joey is very flamboyant but says he is not gay. Fine. It is his closet to live in. Regardless, he asked about writing novels. I offered him a few pointers about organizing his work and character development, not that I am any kind of expert. Mainly, if he wants to write a novel then he has to sit down and dedicate himself to writing.

Joey mentions his cellie, Charles Watson. Yes, that Charles "Tex" Watson, the *ex*–follower of wacked-out Charles Manson, Helter Skelter, and all that crazy stuff. Joey told me that Charles is working with a Christian production company on a movie. Hmm...I made a mental note to talk to Charles about this. He may have some helpful suggestions for my screenwriting. Networking is important whether a person is inside or outside of prison. It is about who you know, and the more Christians a person knows the better off he or she will be.

5:30 p.m.

While I waited for chow release to be called, *Bull* stopped by my bunk and we chatted. He is a great inducer of smiles. *Bull* told me of his latest grand dream for his future. He wants to purchase an ocean liner cruise ship to live and work on. That is a very lofty goal. I asked him if he would be satisfied just to be able to live and work on one. *Bull* thought about it for a minute and then replied, "So long as I have a window." We both laughed.

Psalm 49:15. *Wait for the Lord: be strong and take heart and wait for the Lord.*

✝ ✝ ✝

Wednesday, December 15, 1993
12:15 p.m.

Mmm-mmm, chocolate-covered cherries. I stepped out of the Program Office for a post lunch break breather from the hectic morning of paper pushing and supervisor ducking. Shocked by the unusual lack of a line at the canteen window, I bought a box of six of these delicious treats. I decided as I popped each into my mouth that they would be the reward; a chocolate-covered, cherry-sweet delight for surviving this day of administrative turmoil. I savored each messy, dripping bite.

Please don't think this tasty treat is a regular offering. At Christmas time, the canteen manager orders something out of the ordinary to remind our taste buds of what they were created for. My tongue is exceedingly grateful, and I asked of God that this kindness not go unblessed.

2:30 p.m.

Utilizing the 'stay under radar' rule I avoided nine out of ten abusive remarks that were hurled by supervisory staff this afternoon. Contrary to the sweet taste that filled me, today program staff were infected with irritation, frustration, and a spirit of negativity, but for reasons unspoken by them, they did not indicate why. Basically, nothing went right for them.

I'm stuck with this prison life, but I choose to focus on God's light and a confectioner's creation—sweetness. Staff chose their careers, and today the darkness of prison overwhelmed them—bitterness. I'm praying that they will shed this when the steel gate slams behind them. It's only a job. It's not their life.

9:00 p.m.

My name was announced over the gym's loud speaker. I was ordered to report to work. There were a dozen reports that needed typing. The on-duty clerk, Mr. Payne, would be unable to finish them by 10:00 p.m. when he had to lock-up for count. The 3rd watch lieutenant was pleased to see me, and it was a pleasant change to be wanted for something positive that I can do, even if it is only my typing skills.

For this skill, my digital dexterity, I have my mother to thank. Prior to my senior year of high school, when I was traveling overseas with my father in England, Iran, and Bahrain, and without consulting me first, my mother registered me for classes, including a typing class.

When I returned home and reviewed my class schedule I was annoyed because I believed my life would consist of being the boss. And, bosses employ secretaries to do the typing. I did not need to learn how to type. Yep, there's that chauvinistic pig side showing through. Then, when I walked into the classroom filled with girls, I being the only teenage boy, I silently thanked my mother—and learned a skill that has become invaluable.

As I look up from my lowly position as inmate clerk, I would be honored to rise to the level of secretary.

Colossians 4:1. *Masters, provide your slaves with what is right and fair, because you know you also have a Master in Heaven.*

✞ ✞ ✞

Thursday, December 16, 1993
7:00 p.m.

Whoa! What an earful. Brian, the 30-year-old man who I recommended and then trained in the position of a clerk in the Program Office has turned out to be a rat. Hell, what did I expect? Once a cop, always a cop.

It seems someone stole Brian's Walkman radio and he went to staff about it. That is a no-no. If Brian had not left the radio unattended on his bunk it would not have been stolen. Where does Brian think he is? Staff is searching everyone's locker, tossing their property here and there without regard for damage or disorder. They will never find the radio, as stolen items are quickly taken to the yard and sold. The unfortunate result is that Brian is labeled as a snitch.

My instinct is to not want to be associated with a rat as it could affect my health and life span. Guilt by association, you know. However, the Spirit is strong, and instead of ostracism, I pray Brain will understand and accept my advice to keep his mouth shut and deal with situations like this on his own. Never involve staff in personal problems. Even if staff do take an interest it usually only makes matters worse.

Matthew 6:14. *For if you forgive men when they sin against you, your heavenly Father will also forgive you.*

✞ ✞ ✞

Friday, December 17, 1993
3:00 p.m.

We have been locked down all day due to the fog that hangs heavy, thick, and low. Bored, bored, bored, so I took a walk around the gym to see if there was anything I could find to do or anyone I wanted to talk with. As I passed the gym's door which contains a narrow view port made of bullet proof glass, I saw a vision floating through the fog. It was scabby-gay Scott.

Pimple picking, feces licking, gross-me-out Scott was being escorted in handcuffs by two officers across the yard toward a housing unit. Scott must have done something wrong, or more likely he was *touched-up* (assaulted) in level I, and now he is back on our facility after leaving only a short time ago.

Scott has a serious problem other than his hygiene and eating habits: it is with the truth. Scott is unable to speak it. Unfortunately for tellers of lies, they are quickly ferreted out and the consequences are severe. I was unable to tell from the distance and the obscuring fog if Scott carried any marks of battering.

When Scott and his escort disappeared into the mist, I thought of the unsuspecting man in a cell whose door will shortly open to reveal Scott as his new cellie. That will be one unhappy man. I said a silent prayer for both.

The diversion took up 30 seconds of time. Bored, bored, bored.

Matthew 10:8. *"Heal the sick, raise the dead, and cleanse those who have leprosy, drive out demons. Freely you have received, freely give."*

✟   ✟   ✟

Saturday, December, 18, 1993
4:00 p.m.

The blanket of fog continues to cover the yard. There is no outside inmate movement. Several inmates and I had an interesting discussion around my bunk. The subject: who should go home and is there any justice?

Child molesters and rapists, the sickos of the yard receive no counseling or help of any kind and they walk out of prison in only a few years.

Then there is Ellie Nestler, the woman who killed a man, shot him execution–style, in open court because he was *accused* of molesting her son. Will she be punished? What about the victims? What about the dead man who never had the opportunity to defend himself at trial and the child of Ellie Nestler, who now lives with this killing. What about them?

What about inmates who are trying to do good time, change their ways, and wanting to become productive citizens? The consensus around my bunk was that we want to believe that free people, the normal Joe and Jane on the street, do care if we succeed or fail, but so much of the time the impression we receive through the media is just the opposite.

Frustrated by not being able to see any light at the end of this penological tunnel, we concluded there was too much politics in the prison system. All of it driven by emotional, knee-jerk laws paid for by special interest groups. There are answers wrapped in common sense, but who would listen if it came from inmates.

Only God can save us now but maybe not in this lifetime.

2 Peter 3:9. *The Lord is not slow in keeping His promise, as some understand slowness. He is patient with you, not wanting anyone to perish, but everyone to come to repentance.*

✟   ✟   ✟

Sunday, December 19, 1993
5:00 p.m.

I dropped a letter into the mail box addressed to one of the museums in Australia with the hope they will respond with the names of books on *Dreamtime,* cassettes of Aboriginal music, and their prices. I must keep moving forward on my dreams.

9:00 p.m.

Santa! Santa! Santa is everywhere but is he Satan in disguise? Commercialism...where did the Christ child go? Replaced by elves and reindeer, Christmas trees and ornaments. Paganism all the way. Are we celebrating the winter solstice, the *sun,* or the *Son?* I believe Christ was born in the summer, not the winter, but God should not care if we fudge the date. Heck, we have named a pagan day after His Son. How proud of us He must be.

Wake up people. Thou shall not follow after pagan ways.

Today, the 1990's, we worship the antics of the Bundys. What happened to the moral teachings of the Cleavers? Who should we thank for this progress? I do know who we can thank for the jolly old man in the red suit: that would be ourselves.

Santa or Satan?

The reason for this outburst? The movie *It's a Wonderful Life* concluded on television. It reminded me of what we should be celebrating. It is family. It is love. It is God and all He has given us. The most important is of course His Son, Jesus.

Because decorations are taboo in prison, but even if they were allowed, putting a dress on a pig does not make it date-worthy. This Spartan environment allows me the opportunity, without distractions, to focus on the Spirit for the true meaning of Christmas, regardless of the date.

Peace and praising Jesus' Name...HALLELUJAH!

1 Corinthians 10:21. *You cannot drink the cup of the Lord and the cup of demons too; you cannot have a part in both the Lord's Table and the table of demons.*

✝ ✝ ✝

Monday, December 20, 1993
9:30 a.m.

I am sooooo special. NOT. My supervisor, Mr. James, had me
escorted into work even though there is pea soup fog outside and no inmate
movement allowed. It seems the paperwork to keep the wheels turning was
spilling off my desk, bogging things down. Hmm? Staff did not want me to
work Friday when I could have easily processed all the incoming work, but I
was supposed to go happily in and wade through it at their pleasure. I know I
am not that humble yet, but I am praying for an increased measure. I will
admit it was a nice change to get out of the cacophonous concrete cube for a
few hours. The only sound that assaulted my ears was that of the keys on the
typewriter. A pleasant tap-tap-tap.

4:00 p.m.

Mail. It was a Christmas card from my trial attorney. How thoughtful.
It is strange that I feel bad because I ruined his perfect record. He had never
lost a murder trial until I showed up on his door step. I am surrounded by
many inmates who complain they were inadequately represented. I have no
complaints. I occasionally ask those inmates if they are guilty and they reply,
"That's not the point."
     Everyone in this country has the right to a vigorous defense, but if you
are guilty, regardless of the adequacy of that defense, I do not believe a person
has the moral right to complain.

10:00 p.m.

Age: full gray beard. Maturity: thinking before acting. Prudence:
choosing the right battles. Two bunks over, an acquaintance named Odom,
who has been around the prison mills, both federal and state, who has ridden
with the A.B. (Arian Brothers gang), who kicked many asses and took no
names, guards included, is now aging into his late fifties and has realized he
cannot win the war, though he still relishes the memories of venting venom on
staff.
     Listening to Odom's stories, I agree with him that it is very frustrating,
that being our inability to fight city hall and gain any sort of victory. What
Odom preaches from hard learned lessons is as follows: "Do whatever *they*
want in order to reach freedom. Be cordial. State your requests in a respectful

manner and in most cases staff will assist you. Manipulation is for losers, especially when it is not needed. Keep your eyes on your goal. Keep your dreams alive. Staff is not the enemy. It only seems that way at times."

I know that God has blessed me with the look and observe trait. My name, Gregory, means "the watcher." Watch and learn and stay out of harm's way.

Old dogs can be taught new tricks.

Colossians 3:16. *Let the word of Christ dwell in you richly as you teach and admonish one another with all wisdom, and as you sing psalms, hymns and spiritual songs with gratitude in your hearts to God.*

✠ ✠ ✠

Tuesday, December 21, 1993
11:00 a.m.

Leonard, a skinny Santa Claus Christian in a suspicious suit came up to me as I was walking across the yard to use the outdoor restroom. He was in a state of panic because his life had been threatened again. Maybe Leonard should think about his actions. He hangs out with child molesters and runs to staff daily with complaints about perceived injustices.

"Do your own time, Leonard," I advised him.

Inmates are labeled by their actions and associations. Forgive my hypocritical-sounding statements complaining about staff not standing up when they see a wrong, and then chastising a fellow inmate, especially a fellow Christian, for doing so. First: staff is part of the system and inmates are ruled by it. Staff is viewed as righteous, who can do no wrong, and whose statements matter. Inmates are viewed as scum, who always lie, and whose statements are viewed as whining, and it's-not-fair cry-babying. Second: I do applaud Leonard's attempts at righting a wrong, but do not come running to me when staff becomes annoyed by the constant pestering or inmates retaliate for being told on.

I cannot save Leonard's butt. I spend all my time taking care of my own.

However, if a person stands up for a cause, then he should stand up all the way, or leave it alone. Make a decision either way and do not whine about the consequences of the decision.

Proverb 3:25-26. *Have no fear of sudden disaster or the ruin that overtakes the wicked, for the Lord will be your confidence and will keep your foot from being snared.*

✝ ✝ ✝

Wednesday, December 22, 1993
10:00 a.m.

The inmate clerk from housing unit 7 came into the Program Office to pick up clerical supplies for his building. He had to wait for Donna to return because she had gone on an errand to Facility A. So he, *Big Daddy D,* told me his life story. *Big Daddy D,* appeared to be in his late 50's, with a military style crew cut and expanding paunch, but in his youth he led a life, disc jockeying while establishing radio stations across the country during radio's and rock-n-roll's infancy. He said he even worked with the legendary Wolf Man Jack before Wolf Man became a household name. AAAOOOOWWWUUUUU!!!

What never ceases to amaze me is the variety of men who lived productive lives and are now incarcerated for crazy crimes. *Big Daddy D* is serving four life sentences running wild (consecutive) plus five years. He kidnapped four people over a money dispute.

Wow. My 34 years to life sentence seems piddly in comparison. I, at least, have hope of parole. *Big Daddy D* has none. Still, he has a great attitude and seems, on the surface, to accept responsibility, and his fate, which more than likely is his demise in prison. Amazing? No, not really, *Big Daddy D* is a Christian trusting in something larger than us all.

3:00 p.m.

I entered the gym after work to find that staff had roped off the television alcove with bright yellow caution tape as if a murder had occurred there. The television in the alcove was turned off as were the two bolted to opposite walls in the main bunk area. The crime? It was a shocker. It was unbelievable. It was outrageous. During the day, some inmate, one without a job, and likely bored, plugged up the door lock to the circuit breaker room so staff would be unable to turn on the light in the television alcove. This light causes a harsh glare on the television screen.

Staff response: they turned off all televisions. To me, and many other inmates, especially those who work all day, we cannot find the logic in punishing those who were not responsible. This mass punishment breeds animosity toward staff, and by the way, is against Title 15 rules.

Hey. Who is running this place? Think. Please think. What are you trying to teach us?

Hebrews 12:1-3. Therefore, since we are surrounded by such a great cloud of witnesses, let us throw off everything that hinders and the sin that so easily entangles, and let us run with perseverance the race marked out for us. Let us fix our eyes on Jesus, the author and perfecter of our faith, who for the joy set before Him endured the cross, scorning its shame, and sat down at the right hand of the throne of God. Consider Him who endured such opposition for sinful man, so that you will not grow weary and lose heart.

✝ ✝ ✝

Thursday, December 23, 1993
9:00 a.m.

Cool. I talked to a professional athlete. Well, ex-pro anyway. The newest addition and co-clerk to the Program Office is Frank. He used to play football for the San Francisco 49ers. Frank played and lived the all American dream of a football star, and then after his sports career, dabbled in real estate until he used a crossbow on a target that one cannot get a license for. So sad. All his talent; all his intelligence; stuck behind bars.

What a waste.

With so many smart people in positions of power, it seems mystifying that they cannot figure out what to do with us misfits, the misguided, and those who are seeking to change. Is there not something more productive than stagnating in prison?

I could have the answer, but I do not have the power to implement it.

6:30 p.m.

I tried to make several telephone calls but no one was home.

In the gym the 160 inmates have to share four telephones. There is a timer on each telephone that is set for 15 minutes and then automatically disconnects the call. This mechanism was designed to limit each inmate's usage, so as to allow others access to friends and family. Unfortunately, staff cannot be bothered to monitor how many times an inmate redials.

This discourtesy by some causes fights when many inmates are waiting to use the telephone. To avoid confrontations I look for times when fewer are waiting, such as during sporting events on television.

I have noticed that with each passing year, my list of people to call has become shorter. Friends who swore to be with me to the end have drifted away. I guess their definition of the end was interpreted differently by me.

I dialed again but the telephone at the other end kept ringing. Being unable to reach out and touch someone, I felt myself slipping into darkness. Depression for me has come to be like easing into a warm tub of chocolate pudding. I no longer fight it. I have even learned to embrace it. Depression will not kill me so I have attempted to make a friend of it. It is only an emotion and it will eventually pass.

I lie on my bunk and placed my headphones over my ears, and deliberately finding a radio station with sad music, I allowed myself to cry inside. When the tears slip past my eyelids, regardless of the time, day or night, I crawl under the covers, cover my head, and refuse to be there. No one on earth can make me say I am in prison.

In my cocoon of sheet and blanket I turned inward to find the light shining through the thick gel of depression. There. There is the Spirit of God; always attentive, always loving, always waiting on me to call. I have found it okay to be depressed, because it means I have feelings. And as long as I still feel I know I am alive.

Isaiah 43:2. *When you pass through waters, I will be with you; and when you pass through the rivers, they will not sweep over you. When you walk through the fire, you will not be burned; the flames will not set you ablaze.*

✝ ✝ ✝

Friday, December 24, 1993
9:00 p.m.

"Twas the night before Christmas and all through the gym, ruthless convicts scurried within. Stabbings? Fights? Tattooing or drugs? No, just handshakes, well wishes and hearty, muscle-bound hugs. The gifts were tiny, a piece of candy or shots of mud (spoonfuls of coffee), but the emphasis my dear reader, though unspoken, was love."

10:00 p.m.

For my closest friends, Doc Mahar, *Bull,* and Smitty, I made stockings from wool socks. Each sock contained a Top Ramen soup, bouillon cube, pieces of toffee, ginger spice, and dried seaweed to top it off. These were items out of my care package from home. I included in each sock a short note of thanks for their friendship and a scripture blessing from God. The stockings looked silly but the men appreciated my gesture.

It was a good night.

Philippians 2:1-2. *If you have encouragement from being united with Christ, if any comfort from His love, if any fellowship with the Spirit, if any tenderness and compassion, then make my joy complete by being like-minded, having the same love, being one in the Spirit and purpose.*

✟ ✟ ✟

Saturday, December 25, 1993
CHRISTMAS
All Day

I slept in as the fog was thick as two week old refried beans. When I finally awoke, I noticed an act of kindness by staff that I will credit to Christ's Spirit. The televisions were back on. We were able to watch two entertaining movies: *Scent of a Woman*—witty dialogue, and *Sidekick*—hilarious story about a boy who idealized the martial arts star, Chuck Norris.

Besides the 4th of July and Thanksgiving, Christmas is the only holiday where we are fed a sparingly better meal. Tonight we received instead of cool-aid, a soda, and again for dessert it was pumpkin pie. I would have to say that it was an Oliver Twist delight: "Please, Sir. May I have another?"

The best part of the evening occurred after dinner in the form of appetizing creations that Doc Mahar and *Bull* pieced together. With culinary ingenuity they created from their care packages, rolled rice in seaweed; peanuts, sugar, banana slices, brown sugar, and sunflower seed balls; vichyssoise (potato soup); and crackers topped with walnuts, dried tomato slices and honey.

My stomach had not been so full in years. Should I hazard to say, though not wanting to raise the ire of the rack-and-stock-punishment public, that at that moment, life was good?

It is true that today is not Christ's birthday, but thankfully His Spirit moves across the earth without regard to the calendar, blessing all that allow Him into their lives.

Psalm 103:5. *Who satisfies your desires with good things so that your youth is renewed like the eagle's?*

✟ ✟ ✟

Sunday, December 26, 1993
10:00 a.m.

Seeing an unattended telephone, I grabbed it and tried to call Mickie but she was not home. Her aunt informed me that Mickie was off to places unknown and is not expected to return until after the first of the year. Her ex-husband has taken the children for the holidays.

My heart goes out to Mickie for the pain I know she is feeling. The children are her life, and as I was told by her aunt, Mickie handled the departure of her children with maturity, a stiff upper lip and all, but in her soul she was torn apart.

Where did Mickie go? No one knows. I wish she would come to see me as I care so much for her and would do my best to cheer her up. It has been four and a half years since I last saw her. A month before my transfer from San Quentin, Mickie came for a visit. I imagine walking into San Quentin's imposing castle-like structure must have been frightening, but in she came wearing a beautiful smile. The hugs we shared that day were heart-warming and strength giving.

I prayed continuously for Mickie today.

10:30 a.m.

Good ol' MCI. The telephone company that is always willing to kick back a portion of the call to the Department of Corrections for the privilege of allowing me to call home. My mother answered, and after the "Merry Christmases" she told me the loan for the sale of her home had been approved. She and Walt are one step closer to moving to Texas.

I felt a panic churning in my stomach.

Lord?

Proverb 3:5-6. *Trust in the Lord with all your heart and lean not on your own understanding; in all your ways acknowledge Him, and he will make your paths straight.*

✿ ✿ ✿

Monday, December 27, 1993
3:00 p.m.

Holding Back the Tears by Simply Red. It is not only a beautiful song but a state of mind. Damn, I am too sentimental. Doc Mahar transpacted his property today. He is transferring to California Men's Colony at San Luis Obispo.

I was very fortunate to have him as a cell mate before being moved to the gym. Besides his stimulating, not always about prison, conversations, a rarity in here, he is a miracle healer. As an ex-chiropractor, he assisted in the rapid healing of my ankle when last year on the volleyball court I rolled my ankle, badly twisting it.

I wished him well and hope to see him again someday. He began as a stranger, a convicted felon, who became a friend, and is now moving on.

I am still here. Sigh.

Jeremiah 30:17a. *But I will restore you to health and heal your wounds, declares the Lord.*

✿ ✿ ✿

Tuesday, December 28, 1993
9:00 a.m.

The sun was shining brightly, our work supervisors were in a good mood, and the new clerk, Dario, from Colombia that I spent most of the day training was quick, accurate, and pleasant.

Dario is 65, from a wealthy family, and if I were a betting man, I would say he is very well connected in the cartel, drug cartel, that is. How do I know? I have no positive proof, but his demeanor and the respect he commands lean in that direction. The co-clerks and I have jokingly and respectfully anointed him *Don* Dario. He smiled at that moniker.

So the reader does not become confused by all the co-workers I refer to, I will enlighten. The prison runs on three watches. First watch is from 10:00 p.m. to 6:00 a.m. Except for early morning kitchen workers, all inmates are locked up during first watch. Second watch is from 6:00 a.m. to 2:00 p.m. During this time approximately half the inmates are either in education, vocations, or a work assignment such as clerk, yard crew, building porter, or maintenance. Third watch is from 2:00 p.m. to 10:00 p.m. The majority of inmates are off work and school and attempt to find ways to entertain themselves. In the Program Office, there are a total of five clerks; three for second watch, one for the correctional counselor II, one for the lieutenant, and one (me) for the program administrator. For third watch there is one clerk for that watch's lieutenant, and there is a relief clerk to cover the regular days off (RDOs) of the two lieutenant's clerks

4:00 p.m.

Back in the concrete cube, Smitty brought me his latest issue of Writer's Digest magazine. Smitty is writing a crime novel so we share resources and bounce plot ideas off one another.

In this issue of the Writer's Digest there was an ad for screenwriting fellowships with the possibility of $25,000 for five lucky winners. Could I be good enough to be one of them? I do not want to confuse ego with skill level but I have to reach high. I will send for the information.

Who knows? If I won I could pay off my court-ordered restitution and have a little left over to buy new tennis shoes.

10:00 p.m.

I said good-bye to Doc Mahar. I want to give him a big hug but my macho holds me back. I can sense the same thing from him. Being tough guys sucks at times. In the morning Doc will be gone and his bunk filled with another dazed soul wondering how he got to be so privileged.

I will pray for travel mercies for Doc.

Isaiah 26:3-4. *You will keep in perfect peace him who is steadfast, because he trusts in you. Trust in the Lord forever, the Lord is the rock eternal.*

✝ ✝ ✝

Wednesday, December 29, 1993
6:10 a.m.

I was rudely awakened this morning, but hey, who cares how my day was started. To combat the glare of the ceiling lights that are on in the gym all night, those of us who sleep on the bottom bunks hang curtains from the edges of the upper bunks. The curtains are made from towels or sheets and they help keep out the light in the hope for better sleep. The men on the top bunks tie bandannas round their heads to cover their eyes.

Staff on first watch does not object to the curtains so long as they can see that we are breathing and that the bunk is not occupied by a dummy...let me clarify...that the bunk is not occupied by a mannequin. Many of the bunks, including mine, are occasionally warmed by a dummy. This request by first watch staff to be able to observe a live person is reasonable and accommodated.

However, second watch, beginning at 6:00 a.m., and depending on who is assigned to the gym post, work by a different set of rules. Unfortunately, we had an officer this morning that walked around and yanked the towels and sheets down, and then threw them in our slumbering faces. It was a very unpleasant way to start the day.

Why is it that staff so easily treats us in a manner that they would never put up with themselves? Prison is truly a humbling experience which entails a huge degree of self-restraint in order to accept this kind of abuse. I hate it to my core, but I realize that most of the staff are unhappy and unempowered people in their everyday lives. Most importantly, I remember that my small sufferings are nothing compared to that which Christ suffered for me. I also acknowledge that Christ was innocent and I am not.

Removing the towel from my face I glanced down the aisle to confirm that Doc Mahar's bunk was empty: it was.

2:00 p.m.

Leonard came to me today seeking advice on where to transfer. His annual classification committee is scheduled for tomorrow. Leonard's counselor, for reasons not expressed, is putting him up for transfer. At least the counselor is allowing Leonard to choose where.

"What about San Quentin?" Leonard asked. I replied that I believed he would be fine at the 'Q' if he made two changes in his behavior. Do not snitch and do not hang with the molesters.

Leonard then confided in me that he was here for child molestation. My advice was the same. There is the old saying of: "It is better to be thought of as an a-- than to open one's mouth and remove all doubt." Or in this case, one's actions.

If Leonard does transfer to San Quentin, he will be enriched by the uplifting programs in the Garden Chapel. He will also be safe if he restricts his ministering to those who either follow His light into the chapel, or those who Leonard invites, but while on the yard he must learn to associate with everyone and no one. That way a person cannot be labeled anything but a Christian.

Deuteronomy 31:6. *Be strong and courageous. Do not be afraid or terrified because of them, for the Lord your God goes with you. He will never leave you nor forsake you.*

✞ ✞ ✞

Thursday, December 30, 1993
3:00 p.m.

Energize me! Visits from family and friends always perk me up and allow me to realize that all the hassles in here are just like hassles out there. Though I am verbally mistreated at times, if I were on the street I would also encounter people who are rude and discourteous. I have to remember to thank God for what is more important, that being my safety, my health, and my mental well-being.

Thank you, God.

My father and his wife, JoAnne, came for a visit. I am only able to visit with them three or four times each year because they live near San Diego, nearly 600 miles away.

We always have positive and productive conversations. It is a shame that I did not take advantage of their wisdom years ago. If I had, I would not be in prison now. But that is neither here nor there...water under the bridge. Dad told me he mailed a 'shooting' script of *Major League II* to me. It is the movie sequel to *Major League I* and now in production. This will be a great opportunity to review an actual paid for screenplay.

Thank you, God, again.

Isaiah 48:18, 22. *If only you had paid attention to my commands, your peace would have been like a river, your righteousness like the waves of the sea. "There is no peace," says the Lord, "for the wicked."*

✟ ✟ ✟

Friday, December 31, 1993
1:30 p.m.

I screwed up. I left work an hour early today. My tasks were completed and my supervisors had left for their New Year's Eve celebrations. So who would know? Well, the relief lieutenant knew. As I walked out the Program Office door, he asked me who keeps my time card. Obviously the lieutenant is going to inform Donna of my premature departure.

I could use the excuse that I work ten to fifteen hours extra each month without pay but that will not fly.

The rule: It is forbidden to leave one's work assignment without permission (even if one is not being paid). I will have to deal with it later.

No New Year's Eve celebrations for me. Stupid. Stupid. Stupid.

Peter 2:13-14. *Submit yourselves for the Lord's sake to every authority instituted among men; whether to the king, as the supreme authority, or to governors, who are sent by him to punish those who do wrong and to commend those who do right.*

✟ ✟ ✟

Saturday, January 1, 1994
A NEW CALENDAR YEAR
12:01 a.m.

I was unceremoniously awakened by shouts of, "HAPPY NEW YEAR!" I wish I possessed that kind of exuberant enthusiasm. For me, today is just another day. As I slipped back into slumber, I thanked God for keeping me alive to see it. There will be untold possibilities in the future where I will count on the mysteries and miracles of the Lord to reveal them.

9:00 a.m.

The lights were on then they flickered like a disco strobe, and then pop, they were out.

"Get on your damn bunks," shouted three officers from the raised platform. Courage, with a hint of nervousness rang in their words. Darkness gave rise to dangerous opportunities. I kept my ears open and my spider senses turned up to wary as several inmates scurried past my bunk on hands and knees. To where? I did not know. For what purpose, I did not ask?

9:45 a.m.

Lights, Camera, Action. The cause of the blackout was never disclosed, but as I was released to the recreation yard, my thoughts were on the games to be played.

3:00 p.m.

Whew! What an exhaustive day! All the skilled players came out and we volleyed game after game. The air was chilly, causing each bump pass or block of the volleyball to sting the skin, but the sun shone, and there was no wind to wiggle the ball in flight. Today began a new calendar year with what felt like the Son shining on me.

Each day seems like the preceding, a long unending series of body counts, lock downs, bland food, degradation and potential for violence, but when I look closely, when I open my eyes, I am inspired to have each new day as a blank slate where I can fill it with God's hope for betterment. I have this hope, since faithfully through His Son's blood; God has forgiven my failure, tossing away my sins forever.

Praise God.

11:00 p.m.

Shut eye did not come easy. I know it was long past my usual 10:00 p.m. slumber when I finally dozed off to a restless sleep. The troubling cause? My victims, known and unknown, swirling in my head. They are always present…my heavy burden that God has helped me to shoulder, but on the days that for me are better, when my joy in an activity overrides my sadness from being away from my family, it is my victims' suffering that rightfully resets my elation to reality.

I am able to laugh.

The person I murdered cannot.

I am able to receive encouragement from my family.

The person I murdered cannot.

I am able to hope for a second chance to be a good citizen.

The person I murdered cannot.

Even though I acted as if I were a god, deciding who would live and who would die, I am able to ask God for forgiveness.

The person I murdered cannot.

My friends and family can be uplifted by my love and prayers.

The friends, family, and the person I murdered were robbed by me of each other, and there is no restitution for that crime.

As a male I am genetically wired to fix what is broken. What I have done cannot be fixed. I have destroyed so many hopes, dreams, and lives that I can barely breathe, let alone slumber. Then as I take a breath, the Spirit reminds me of the reason I have to keep going. I have to try, even if trying is futile, because I prevented another from ever trying again.

Acts 26:18. *"To open their eyes and turn them from darkness to light, and from the power of Satan to God, so that they receive forgiveness of sins and place among those who are sanctified by faith in me."*

✞ ✞ ✞

Sunday, January 2, 1994
10:00 a.m.

Morning came too quickly and I found myself stuck in bed. I could not move. I thought I was paralyzed. Actually it was better that I did not move. The muscles in my neck, shoulders, arms, and legs—so sore—OUCH. I overdid it yesterday. Playing any sport against quality opponents always makes me ratchet up my game to the level of "Give all I have and then double that effort."

Lying under the covers, I accepted the lesser of two painful propositions. I could lie in bed immobile and suffer several days of muscular freeze-up, or I could order my protesting body to get up and go back outside to smack the volleyball around until the painful rigor in my limbs eased to a manageable ache. The lesser would be the latter. There is always a price for too much of a good thing. Thankfully I could pay this one.

Praise Christ. He paid the rest.

Though I am still worried what Donna, the office technician, will say come Monday about my early departure from work on Friday, my thoughts are mostly on my victims. As I carried their burden to the recreation yard, I prayed that God will help them to have peace in their lives, in spite of me.

Ephesians 5:8-9. *For you were once darkness, but now you are light in the Lord. Live as children of light (for the fruit of the light consists in all goodness, righteousness and truth).*

✝ ✝ ✝

Monday, January 3, 1994
7:30 a.m.

I decided that the best defense was an honest offense, so I went in early to work and told Donna exactly what time I left work on Friday. She replied, "No problem." Whew. Honesty is the best policy, but you can bet the farm I will not be *bending* any rules again.

I must toe the line. Unfortunately, the line in prison often moves without warning.

10:00 a.m.

My throat, cough-cough, announced its distress, turning scratchy. Being sick is no fun regardless of where one lives, but in prison, illness is terrifying because it reminds me of how alone I am.

I reminded myself to drink a lot of water and walk around the track. Not funny, but those are the doctor's orders.

6:00 p.m.

I was sitting in the chow hall with three inmates who have been in and out of prison more times than they can remember. They each have successfully completed parole, discharging their prison number, but due to drugs, lifestyle, or *friends,* they keep coming back.

They were discussing the proposed Three Strikes & You're Out law that is likely to pass, especially after the killing of little Polly Klaas. Each of my dinner companions have been *down* five or more times and were saying that they will have to kill their next victim(s) because they cannot leave witnesses. They said they have no other choice.

"Petty theft or murder, the sentence is the same—25 years to life," the man to my left said.

Choice? What did they mean they have no other choice? They can seek help to discover why they continue to re-offend. What are the triggers that begin their downward spiral? Stop that trigger and remain crime free. That is the only choice.

6:30 p.m.

I pulled the covers over my pounding head. My body ached. My stomach flipped and flopped. Nobody cared. A football game began on the television. The color commentators called the play by play and the inmates' cheers and jeers were deafening.

Rest was futile.

Prison is punishment.

Luke 6:19. *And the people all tried to touch Him, because power was coming from Him and healing them all.*

✠ ✠ ✠

Tuesday, January 4, 1994
2:30 p.m.

Work was difficult today. I had a hard time concentrating due to my dizzy-foggy head. I was glad that the workload was light because my typing fingers would not cooperate and kept hitting the wrong keys.

Running across the yard to vomit did not help either.

7:30 p.m.

Officer Bartels returned from his week off due to his own illness. He walked among the bunks trying to strike up conversations of a probing nature. Nosy, which is his job, but viewed by fellow staff and inmates as being anal retentive and insecure, which is strange and sad for a person with his innate power as a correctional officer. Behind his idiosyncrasies I sensed a decent man searching for a way to fit in. I treat Officer Bartels with respect and courtesy, but due to my being a resident and him wearing a badge, I am unable to be as friendly as I would like to be. It is a safety thing—someone is always watching.

I cannot be viewed by other inmates as being cop-friendly, and besides, there is that Title 15 regulation against over familiarity. To be specific, it is Section 3400.

At times I overhear Bartels' co-workers comment that he is an irritant super cop because he enforces the rules beyond the letter of the law, causing unnecessary paperwork. Again, I believe Bartels wants to be accepted, as we all do, but he chose a tough place to want to feel a part of a group.

All I can really do is put forth Christ's example as when He asked a hated tax collector to follow Him. Jesus saw the good in Matthew. I can see the good in Officer Bartels and act appropriately. That is a difficult line to walk, but I know God will give me the proper balance.

8:30 a.m.

I went to bed early as I still felt achy, weak, and nauseous. Thankfully, the soreness in my throat has lessened so swallowing is easier.

It appears I will live.

Hebrews 10:23-24. *Let us hold unswerving to the hope we profess, for He who promised is faithful. And let us consider how we may spur one another on toward love and good deeds.*

✝ ✝ ✝

Wednesday, January, 5, 1994
5:30 p.m.

The annual State of the State message was given by Governor Pete Wilson. The speech was depressing. The Governor wants to build six more prisons. He wants voters to pass Three Strikes & You're Out life sentences for serious or violent offenders, and One Strike & You're Out for child molesters and rapists.

Like many in our society, I have difficulty separating the sin from the sinner when it comes to those who commit crimes against children and women. However, I have learned from watching inmates who have been convicted of these crimes that a larger percentage has their convictions overturned than other criminal offenders. This occurs because the victims in these cases are not the best witnesses. I am not saying that women or children are less able to describe their assailants. What I am saying is there are documented cases of women misidentifying their assailants and later DNA proves innocence. Children can be manipulated by a parent who wants custody or by a well-meaning but overzealous social worker.

My thought would be for Two Strikes & You're Out life sentence because the odds of a miss-identification or frame up twice would be incredibly rare, if not unheard of.

Throughout the Governor's tough talk on crime and increased punishment, there was no mention of programs or preventive measures for children so they do not get into trouble as they grow through adolescence and into adulthood. I was a registered Republican, but I have been disgusted of late by the G.O.P.'s use of scare tactics. Tonight's speech was more of the same. Governor Wilson is trying to incite the populace into acts they otherwise may not do if they thought them through or if they had all the facts.

I agree that repeat offenders need more *down* time to get their lives straightened out. Three Strikes and One Strike laws are not the answer, especially since repeat offenders can be tried under the current Habitual Criminal Act and sentenced for life. These Strike laws the way they are written cast a wide net and will likely ensnare many unintended minor offense criminals.

Richard Allen Davis, the man who kidnapped and murdered Polly Klaas, was an eight time loser. He was eligible for the Habitual Criminal life sentence on any one of his three prior offenses before killing Polly. Why did those three district attorneys choose not to impose it? The answer to this question would be impossible for me to speculate on, but I believe it is a valid question. In addition, were any in-prison programs afforded Mr. Davis during his eight prior incarcerations? Ultimately, Mr. Davis is responsible for his actions, but there were many opportunities for those in positions of power to intercede.

The Bible (God) says we are supposed to follow those that are placed in authority over us, but I suspect that command is only to be adhered to when our leaders follow God's commandments.

Could Governor Wilson's trek down a destructive penological path, even if he believed it to be correct, be a sin? Maybe it is our sin to follow a prison-building fanatic to our state's financial ruin. Another politician, a wise woman once said, "Building prisons to solve crime is like building cemeteries to cure AIDS."

An insightful statement. Think about it.

The State of the State. Dismal.

1 Corinthians 4:8-9. *We are hard pressed on every side; but not crushed; perplexed, but not in despair; persecuted, but not abandoned; struck down, but not destroyed.*

✝ ✝ ✝

Thursday, January 6, 1994
7:30 p.m.

I had a wonderful visit with my mother. Weekday visits for me are after the 4:00 p.m. count which takes on average 30 minutes to clear. This allows me about three hours, which includes two heart-warming, strength-giving hugs. My mother would give a thousand more but the rules allow only one upon greeting and one upon departure. Sigh.

As I was processed out of the visiting room, stripped naked, and made to bend over, spread my butt checks and cough, the usual procedure, the strip-out officer commented that I am another Watson. I was unsure as how to take this comment, and then the officer asked if I knew "Tex". I said, "Yes, I know Charles, and I have been privileged to become friends with such a Spirit-filled and peace-filled man."

"Oh, that Bible crap. I've seen the games before. Inmates pick up the Bible on the way in and drop it off at the gate on their way out," he snorted.

I immediately realized that this was a disillusioned and unforgiving man who did not believe the life-changing ways of the Holy Spirit. The most wonderful gift we can give ourselves is to forgive others and live in peace. It has been a strange turn, one that I would have believed improbable, that I find the company of convicted murderers, those who have accepted Jesus and no longer judge, more uplifting than some of the gate keepers who are supposed to be my role models, but are constantly negative, judging the man instead of the act.

Maybe I and others convicted of crimes have more to be thankful for, and are humbled before the Lord, as He has forgiven us, and opened our eyes to our potential.

Praise God.

Isaiah 55:7. *Let the wicked forsake his way and the evil man his thoughts. Let him turn to the Lord, and He will have mercy on him, and to our God, for He will freely pardon.*

✟ ✟ ✟

Friday, January 7, 1994
9:00 p.m.

Flashing red light. Alarms! Code 3. The gym doors swing open as staff responded to the gym to peel apart the brawlers. For the winner an extra 30 days here at the Creek. For the loser a broken nose. Gambling is not for everyone. It should not be for anyone if you cannot pay your debt.

Two tattooed white inmates with shaved heads and bushy beards were playing poker. One lost more than the value of the canteen in his locker. He could not pay, so the other took it out in flesh. I do not see the profit in it. Does anyone?

Oh, it helps to pass the time. It was entertainment.

Galatians 6:7b-8. *A man reaps what he sows. The one who sows to please his sinful nature, from that nature will reap destruction; the one who sows to please the Spirit, from the Spirit will reap eternal life.*

✟ ✟ ✟

Saturday, January 8, 1994
All Day

Ignoring the calls from friends and my competitive urge to play volleyball, I chose another activity today. The sun was shining with considerable warmth for a winter's day. There was not a single cloud to mar the pure blue sky. Perfect for a leisurely walk around the track and to shake off the last sniffles of my illness.

With each step I inhaled the fresh country air and felt the touch of rays against my face. They were the spice that lifted my spirit to soar with the seagulls. God made this day for me. Unhurried. Unmolested. At peace. I know I did not deserve it but I do appreciate it.

It is important that I never again forget to praise God for His bountiful blessings. In my life and in this setting, the blessings are simple, but at the same time, extraordinary: vibrant green grass, rolling hills dotted with proud oak trees, and a brilliant unending sky. All these usually go unnoticed and unacknowledged in this hectic place, but I only have to stop and look around at what God gives every day, and not focus on what my acts allowed man to take away.

Psalm 92:1-5. *It is good to praise the Lord and make music to your name, O Most High, to proclaim your love in the morning and your faithfulness at night, to the music of the ten-stringed lyre and the melody of the harp. For you make me glad by your deeds, O Lord; I sing for joy at the works of your hands. How great are your works, O Lord, how profound your thoughts!*

✞ ✞ ✞

Sunday, January 9, 1994
8:30 p.m.

Inmate Davidson, the cripple, the telephone hog, the reneger of debts owed, the man who argues over the tiniest thing, and is a total pain in the a--, finally hobbled his way across the line.

Today, while using the telephone, he crutched himself into the hole for threatening to kill his girlfriend. Not too smart since all telephones are monitored and recorded.

Four officers and a sergeant entered the gym and made a bee-line to Davidson. He would not be too difficult to subdue, weighing a buck-forty soaking wet. However, he cannot be handcuffed, unless staff want to carry him because without his crutches, he cannot walk. And, because staff never know in advance how an inmate will react when informed he is going to administrative segregation, they usually come with overwhelming force.

Davidson acted indignant, swore up a storm, and stated, "You're taking my words out of context," but allowed the officers to escort him out of the gym without a physical fuss.

I have always said; "The world is round and if you screw people over, the screwing will come back to get you sooner or later. And if it is later, boy, you better watch out."

Proverb 14:16-17. *A wise man fears the Lord and shuns evil but a fool is hotheaded and reckless. A quick-tempered man does foolish things and a crafty man is hated.*

✠ ✠ ✠

Monday, January 10, 1994
8:00 a.m.

The lieutenant called me into his office and asked me to find him a new clerk as the one he has, *Don* Dario, is not working out. I was surprised to hear this because Dario is a fast typist, but apparently his age is working against him. He misses the little things and has to be constantly reminded to log the incoming and outgoing reports.

I talked at length with the lieutenant and he agreed to give me a few more days to work with Dario. Hopefully I can oversee his work and catch any mistakes or oversights before the lieutenant does. Dario is enjoyable to work with as he has many interesting stories of his adventures as a young boy in the jungles of Colombia. A regular Mowgli of the *Jungle Book*. I would hate to see him get fired because of diminishing faculties caused by advanced age.

It is better that a friend cracks a gentle whip than a dissatisfied supervisor with the cat o' nine tails.

Proverbs 20:29. *The glory of young men is their strength, gray hair the splendor of the old.*

✠ ✠ ✠

Tuesday, January 11, 1994
9:00 p.m.

Sheet exchange. Once a week we line up in the gym, like cattle in a chute, waiting to receive what are supposed to be clean sheets. In the morning, prior to departing for work, the line forms in the moldy, tile-peeling toilet and shower area to turn them in at the laundry window, and then again at night we process through to pick them up.

The sheets, thousands of them, are collected throughout the prison, and stuffed into washing machines by inmates who do not give a damn. You would think pride in a job well done would be incentive enough, or the fact that the workers are in the very same line obtaining their sheets, but no. If no one is proud of you or praises you for quality work, how can the inmate be proud of himself? It is a crap shoot as to how clean the torn and stained sheets will be.

"Name and bed number?" the officer demanded as I stepped to the window. "How many did you turn in?" he asked as he checked his list. Not waiting for my answer, he stated, "Give 'em two," to his inmate assistant.

Glen, who is an elderly man with misfitted dentures assigned as a porter (cleaner) in the gym, slid me three. I did not ask and I did not need, but that is what friends are for. A little extra without seeking anything in return. The extra sheet also increases the odds that as I unfold them, at least two will be suitable to make a bed with.

I smiled at Glen as he smirked in return.

John 15:12-14. *My command is this: Love each other as I have loved you. Greater love has no one than this that he lay down his life for his friends. You are friends if you do what I command.*

✝ ✝ ✝

Wednesday, January 12, 1994
6:00 p.m.

The two chow halls on Facility B each hold 200 inmates. We are allowed between ten and fifteen minutes to eat the meal. When we *dine* we are seated at tables that accommodate four, and we sit with whoever may be standing next to us in the chow line. This is called controlled seating.

Tonight I was required to sit with three 20-something-or-others who are three of my rambunctious neighbors. I was not pleased because even when eating their talking volume level is set at SHOUT. I have come to hate noise because it is almost constant. There has to be something in the Geneva Convention that prohibits torture by noise. Drat, that only applies to prisoners of war. Would political prisoners count? No, I'm not one of them either.

I am seriously considering becoming a hermit when I (if I) get out of prison, but on a tropical island with excellent waves for surfing. Oh, sorry, I have digressed from my dinner companions.

One of these youngsters respectfully asked if I was lifer. Then he asked if I thought there was ever a time when committing a crime was justified or excusable. He was not pleased with my answer.

I said, "No." Then I took the opportunity to tell them how I thought that prison time was so important. The furrowed brows and twisted lips plainly expressed confusion on their part. I explained that this time gives us the opportunity to get our minds and lives straightened out. If we do not use it productively we will be right back. I wished I had said, "This time is a real blessing from the Lord." Dang, missed a chance, but hopefully the message got through.

Stop the games. I, we, you will only lose in the end.

8:00 p.m.

A shaved headed inmate with *White Power* tattooed on his forearms approached me as I sat on my bunk. He asked if I wanted to trade bunks? A bunk next to the wall? A bunk with an electrical outlet for my typewriter and television? Yahoo. But wait. What was the catch? He said the wall fan is too cold for him. Sounded reasonable and since I have sweats I believe I would be able to cope with it. POWER ON!

The difficult part will be getting staff to agree to put in the paperwork for the bed change.

Romans 5:12. *Therefore, just as sin entered the world through one man, and death through sin, and in this way death came to all men, because all sinned.*

✝ ✝ ✝

Thursday, January 13, 1994
6:30 a.m.

I asked Officer Jones, our gym officer, if she would facilitate my move to the wall bunk.

"Not today. Those are considered convenience moves and will only be submitted on weekends," was her reply.

Damn. I do not want to wait two days. Mr. *White Power* could change his mind. I am so close to acquiring a little comfort but it is still out of reach.

My thoughts flashed back to a tee shirt I owned as a teenager. The design on the front depicted two buzzards sitting on a limb of a dead tree. One buzzard says to the other, "Patience my ass; I'm going to kill something." As a 15-year-old, the caption was funny. It is not so funny anymore. I will exercise patience, and exercise my legs as I head off to work.

9:15 a.m.

Damian Williams, the black youngster who pummeled the white truck driver, Reginald Denny, with a brick during the Los Angeles riots, sat on a bench in the Program Office waiting to be classified. He sat like a king holding court as his *admirers* congratulated him. Damian was so cool. He was surprisingly a little man; not large at all, except maybe on the fat side. Now I understand why he and his associates had to gang up on Mr. Denny to subdue him. I had the urge to walk up to him and bitch slap him, the ultimate in disrespect, to see how tough Damian thought he was when it would be one on one.

The Spirit had other plans, and tapped me on my shoulder, reminding me to let the anger pass. Damian has to deal with his own actions and will face God when the time comes.

Forgive me, O Lord, for my evil thoughts for I do not want to be judged.

Romans 12:17, 19. *Do not repay anyone evil for evil. Be careful to do what is right in the eyes of everyone. Do not take revenge, my friends, but leave room for God's wrath, for it is written: "It is mine to avenge; I will repay," says the Lord.*

✝ ✝ ✝

Friday, January 14, 1994
7:00 p.m.

The tension was thicker than axle grease as the races and gang affiliations within the races grouped for protection and power. One black man punched another in the face. One was a Crip and the other was a Blood. Personal reasons or politics, I am not told. Staff was neither aware of the assault, nor did they notice the grouping as friends, associates, and gang members chose sides.

An anonymous note was dropped on Tad's bunk. Tad is a fresh faced 39-year-old who looks 16. Unfortunately, Tad has a thing for 12-year-old boys. The note read: Lock it up or else. Of course Tad went straight to staff to tell. A few minutes later a wannabe tough-guy youngster was cuffed-up and escorted out of the gym and to the hole. Anyone who leaves a note is usually too scared to do anything. This looked to me like a P.C. (request for protective custody) move, meaning the tough-guy youngster probably had problems of his own and needed to be removed from this facility.

The groupings of blacks, whites, and Hispanics shuffled here and shuffled there. Who would make the first stupid move? By the way, have I mentioned there is no gun coverage in the gym?

Staff was now alerted by the lack of noise, the shuffling of groups, the shifting of eyes, and the whispers as the coalitions built strength. I would call it a dance of the dunces, but not out loud and not to their faces. For the participants, this is about pride and honor. So sad! So misguided!

Brian's *new* radio is missing. He loaned it to Jason who has a gambling problem. The problem is Jason owes a lot of money that he has no way of paying. Jason told Brian that someone stole the radio. That is a possibility but more likely Jason gave the radio as a partial payment to whoever he owes. Who loses? Brian. Will Brian ever learn?

Never borrow! Never loan! Never gamble! Do not steal! Do not mess with homosexuals and stay under radar (for those who do not want problems or drama). I do not know if Brian will ever grab hold of these concepts. He has a good teacher in me, but he does not take my instructions to heart. These are not school yard games.

Ten officers have entered the gym in a show of force. "Yard release," is announced over the gym speakers. As the grouping inmates dispersed to the yard, each is searched for weapons, just in case any had intentions of escalating the initial offense.

The tension in the gym, the threat of violence has passed...for now.

The majority of bad things in prison, and in life, are brought on by one's own actions. If one minds his own business in here, usually he will be left to survive.

Exodus 23:22. *If you listen carefully to what He says and do all that I say, I will be an enemy to your enemies and will oppose those who oppose you.*

✞ ✞ ✞

Saturday, January 15, 1994
4:30 p.m.

I high-stepped it to the wall bunk, finally. Patience does pay off. Even though I will be on the top bunk, I can set my television on the locker next to my bed and plug it in. Public Television, here I come. It has been close to three agonizing months since I have be able to watch *Nature, National Geographic, Nova,* and the other cerebral stimulating programs. I am not able to handle watching hours and hours of people-problem talk shows or substandard animation that passes for cartoons these days. One's mind becomes what we fill it with.

The man residing in the bed below mine is an old school, muscle-bound bigot who misses the days of sheet wearing and cross burning. No, it was not his southern accent that gave him away. It was the full back tattoo of the scene that he proudly showed me. I complimented Nevel on the artist's attention to detail, specifically how lifelike the flames were as they consumed the cross. However, I reserved my personal thoughts on the theme.

I inhaled deeply, as I recognized that with the privilege of electricity had come a challenge of gentle persuasion toward a light other than the fire of hate, but I would wait until Nevel and I were better acquainted.

Thank you, Lord, for this opportunity…this challenge would be a whopper.

John 13:14-15. *"Now that I, your Lord and Teacher, has washed your feet, you also should wash one another's feet. I have set you as an example that you should do as I have done for you."*

✞ ✞ ✞

Sunday, January 16, 1994
10:00 a.m.

No showers? What did staff mean? Could they not smell that malodorous air? One hundred and sixty sickly sweet and sweaty men with no way of cleaning their bodies. What would become of my olfactory? Oh, it was killed off a long time ago.

Okay, I exaggerated. Out of the 160 gym inmates, about half went to the yard this morning at 8:00 a.m. to exercise. Only half of them have returned to find they cannot wash the sweat off.

The prison's water treatment plant clogged. That will happen now and again as it processes the effluent (waste) of 3,200 inmates, but was designed, as was the prison, for 1,700.

Overcrowding? I think yes.

9:00 p.m.

The treatment plant has been unclogged. I would not have wanted that job, and could you imagine the size of that plunger? Ha ha. The 12 showers in the gym have been turned back on, but will be off again for the night at ten. That is the rule. No showers after ten o'clock. No exceptions. Many will not shower today, including me. I am not into sharing. Can someone open a window? Sorry, no windows in the gym.

"Breathe deep the gathering gloom. Watch eyes tear from the human fumes." I must be losing my mind…not yet. I am just a little crazy.

Romans 8:18-21. *I consider that our present sufferings are not worth comparing with the glory that will be revealed in us. The creation waits in eager expectation for the sons of God to be revealed. For the creation was subjected to frustration, not by its own choice, but by the will of the one who subjected it, in hope that the creation itself will be liberated from its bondage to decay and brought into the glorious freedom of the children of God.*

✚ ✚ ✚

Monday, January 17, 1994
4:21 a.m.

A major earthquake rocks Los Angeles. The early television news reports are horrible. I thank God my family was not in the area. My prayers go out for those who lost family, friends, and property. Last year, 1993, was a rough year for Californians with summer wildfires and winter mud slides, and now with this quake, it appears that 1994 will truly test our citizens' strength.

I am morbidly curious as to what Kimble will be saying to his cellie after learning of the destruction. Something bizarre like: "I told 'em my songs and dances were only so effective. There has to be human sacrifice to the death spirits or they will shake California into the ocean."

Kimble aside, God said He will protect His Children and their homes. It would be interesting to take a survey to find out who was injured, killed, or lost property, and to find out what their spiritual beliefs were, if any.

The telephone lines will be extremely busy with loved ones trying to connect, so I will wait a while until I attempt to get through to Mickie in Simi Valley. I am very concerned for her parents who live in the quake's epicenter of Northridge in the San Fernando Valley.

I will trust in God and not worry, however I will remain concerned. Yeah, yeah, I know they are sort of the same thing.

Luke 10:19. *I have given you authority to trample on snakes and scorpions and to overcome all the power of the enemy: nothing will harm you.*

☩ ☩ ☩

Tuesday, January 18, 1994
6:00 p.m.

Tonight I sat in the chow hall eating dinner with Howard. Howard was convicted of eating human hearts for the pleasure of Satan. We were discussing the wonder of wives, which I do not have, and the thrill of children, which again, I do not have. Howard said he had changed his ways due to the fact that he has a grown daughter and wants to set a good example. He said he used to be very wicked and a sick person.

"Yeah, I have heard the rumors," I interjected. Howard sadly nodded his head in affirmation.

Despite Howard's past appetites, I accept him for who he has become after 27 years of incarceration. And, as Howard is the one who has had to come to grips with the terrible things he did and the people he hurt, I do not have the right of judgment. I believe if more people would act in this manner there would be less vindictiveness and more success stories in the world.

Besides families, we discussed the CDC-602 appeal system (Interdepartmental Grievances). Howard had a meeting today with a Sacramento representative concerning the appeal he filed and was told: "Only inmates have to follow the laws and regulations set forth in the Title 15. It is only considered as guidelines for staff and the department."

That bit of news was scary to hear, and shows how powerful the Department of Corrections has become. When a high ranking official of the department can openly and blatantly disregard the laws set forth by the legislature to protect the basic human rights of incarcerated men, it is not surprising that so many abuses occur.

The tax paying public has been bamboozled when it comes to what incarceration accomplishes for the majority of its captives. Politicians say one thing, prompted by huge campaign contributions for the prison guards' coffers, and like sheep, the public accepts these false statements as truth. Or maybe the people who foot the bill cannot be bothered, but I do not believe that. The public does care, but they do not know the truth about *rehabilitation* in prison. It does not exist unless it is self-motivated and God centered.

Should someone with a past like Howard's, or even mine, ever be given another chance to be part of a free society? This is a question for others to answer.

How would Jesus answer this question?

We all need the true Shepherd to guide us.

Luke 17:3. *So watch yourselves. "If your brother sins, rebuke him, and if he repents, forgive him."*

✟ ✟ ✟

Wednesday, January 19, 1994
10:00 a.m.

Each morning, my first task at work is to review the Daily Inmate Movement Sheet and record the new arrivals, placing the names on the appropriate counselor list for classification purposes. This morning I noticed that Geronimo Pratt, ex-Black Panther, has arrived from San Quentin, but he has been placed on Facility C. I would have enjoyed it if he were on this facility because I always enjoyed our interactions while in San Quentin. His peaceful and friendly demeanor was certainly contrary to the Black Panther's militant history. I do not know whether or not Geronimo killed the man he is convicted of murdering or if it was an FBI setup to cripple the Panther movement as Geronimo's lawyer, Johnny Cochran, claims. In any case, the hype the media feeds the public about this so-called infamous and brutal murdering convict is way out of proportion to the reality of the man.

What happened to truth in journalism?

3:00 p.m.

I felt good, a little hope-filled high, as I left the law library. Facility B's library seats ten inmates. However, it is tasked with the responsibility of serving the needs of 1,160 inmates. While sitting in the cramped room, I wondered if the law library, its measly square footage tucked back in the far corner of the education area, was a reluctant afterthought by prison designers.

Regardless of the library's small size, I was able to find the book that had the Sacramento address for the Federal Public Defender's office. My plan is to write them this evening to inquire as to what forms I will need to fill out a request for their appointment to my case.

One step at a time.

10:00 p.m.

I tossed and turned on my bunk trying to lure the Sand Man. Instead, I caught a weeping depression. Its source was last night's discussion about wives and lovers. My heart and stomach still ache over losing Angela. It has been six years since she said good-bye, but it feels like only hours since her painful words rang in my head.

"I'm sorry, Greg," she said, "but I can't live apart like this. I love you too much. Good-bye."

I may have treated her like a goddess in the beginning of our relationship, but I recognize, with my arrest, the awful charges, the trial, conviction, and separation, I put her through hell in the end. A relationship can only be judged over the long term. My actions, which were in the very least selfish, destroyed any possibility for a long term anything. I failed Angela in all aspects.

Angela deserved happiness and instead I gave her pain. I pray that she has been blessed with the true love and joy worthy of all she has to offer. I only have one prayer, and if it is God's will, I would like to see Angela again, even if it is only from an admiring distance.

Psalm 34:17. *The righteous cry out, and the Lord hears them; He delivers them from all their troubles.*

✞ ✞ ✞

Thursday, January 20, 1994
9:00 a.m.

The lieutenant stepped up to my desk and just stood there. I stopped typing to look up at him. The lieutenant's gaze turned from me to *Don* Dario, who was seated at the next desk and typing, and then the lieutenant turned back to me. He stated, "Much better," and then turned on his heels and entered his office.

I understood. *Don* Dario will keep his job. I enjoy success stories, especially when I am able to have a small part in them.

3:00 p.m.

It has been three days since southern California's earthquake and I am still unable to get through to Mickie on the telephone. The more film footage I watch of the destruction to homes and apartment buildings and the long, long lines of people waiting for essentials, raises my concern to the level of worry for Mickie and her family's safety.

Some things are difficult to give to God to handle, but because I am totally helpless to assist in any way I must give my worry and their care to Him. He must protect those that I pray for as it will bring glory to Him and validation of Scripture. I can and do seek comfort in His promises and I do believe in His words as He has always done what He proclaimed.

I may be helpless, but I am not hopeless.

Hebrews 11:1. *Now, faith is being sure of what we hope for and certain of what we do not see.*

✟ ✟ ✟

Friday, January 21, 1994
7:30 p.m.

She answered! I finally got through to Mickie. She and the house where she lives in Simi Valley are fine, but unfortunately her parents' home suffered extensive damage. The quake damaged the living room and cracked the home's foundation. Mickie said their home looks like a bomb exploded, but the only thing that matters is her parents were not injured. They are now living in a cousin's camper in their front yard.

I next telephoned my father. He is in the construction business. I asked him if he would contact Mickie's parents to recommend a contractor that does residential, and who would not gouge them with an exorbitant estimate. Well, what do you know? Come to find out my step-brother Tom does small contracting, and my father will ask him to stop by the Moore's for a look-see. I wished I could do more but prayers and family relations will have to do.

THE FRUSTRATION OF IT ALL....but I can count on God to help put the right people in the right places when the need arises.

1 Corinthians 1:3-4. *Praise be to the God and Father of the Lord Jesus Christ, the Father of compassion and the God of all comfort, who comforts us in all our troubles, so that we can comfort those in any trouble with the comfort we ourselves have received from God.*

✝ ✝ ✝

Saturday, January 22, 1994
9:30 a.m.

Where is the rain? Ha! The local television weather forecaster is cute, with bouncy brunette hair and a sing-song voice, but she is wrong again. What a great job she has. Retainment even in the face of continuous errors. I looked at that brilliant sun and knew the dew clinging precariously to the volleyball net would quickly evaporate. I closed my eyes to the concrete and barbed wire, choosing to focus on the sun splashed California winter day. Sunscreen and volleyball. I was truly blessed.

8:00 p.m.

Mail? This late at night and on Saturday? We have not received mail deliveries on Saturdays since 1988. Budget cut backs, you know. I assumed the mail room staff was so far behind that they had to work overtime to catch up. However, confidential sources tell me that if they actually worked during their regular work hours, instead of B.S.ing and drinking coffee that was purchased for the inmates' consumption, maybe they would get the mail delivered on time.

Hey, I am not the one saying this. It is other staff members who would probably like to have what is perceived as a cushy job. I wonder if this is a case of a fence and green grass.

Contrary to the perception of sluggishness, I have to commend the mail room workers because my outgoing mail quickly reaches its destination and only two or three of my many, many letters have failed to arrive. So, bravo on that account.

Dig it. Five letters for me. Uh-oh, some are dated as far back as January 3rd. Oh well, better late than never. The letters were from Mom, Dad, Charlie, Weila and Madeline in the Philippines. Total love. All these friends and family took the time out of their own struggles to write and express their concern for me.

Charlie, a Christian friend from San Quentin days, shouts, "I'M FREE!" Well, sort of, as he is still on parole. Charlie is three years my junior, five inches taller at 6'5" with hair redder than pomegranate juice. Charlie was convicted of involuntary manslaughter for driving his ski boat while intoxicated. One of his passengers fell overboard, and when Charlie turned the boat to pick her up, he hit her and she died.

Charlie was celled next to me and helped me through my deepest *hard-timing* (depression) when Angela said her good-bye.

Madeline, five years my junior, answered my ad in an international Christian pen-pal newsletter. She, like Weila, lives in Manila, but she works as a cashier, earning $12 a day. She, too, sends the bulk of her income home to a small village where she is from so that her brothers can continue their education. In Madeline's introduction letter, she asked, "Will you allow me to pray for you?" She and I have been friends ever since that day two years ago.

My day began filled with a bright sun and healthy exercise, and culminated with words of inspiration and encouragement. I will remember this ear-to-ear smile because it hurts my cheeks so wonderfully.

God is to be praised. I needed a day like today.

John 15:9-10. *"As the Father has loved me, so have I loved you. Now remain in my love. If you obey my commands, you will remain in my love, just as I have obeyed my Father's commands and remain in His love."*

✞ ✞ ✞

Sunday, January 23, 1994
5:00 p.m.

I telephoned my mother tonight as it is her birthday. I had sent her a birthday card with words written from my heart. Still, written, and even spoken words are so inadequate when it comes to expressing love and appreciation. Where would I be without her support, prayers, guidance, and love? I would be "tore-up" as a convict would say. Additionally, I agree wholeheartedly with a cute little saying I once heard. It goes: "God invented mothers so He could rest." I realize God does not need to rest, but He sure did right when He created mothers, at least when He created mine.

Happy Birthday, Mom. Thank you, God.

7:00 p.m.

Brian is getting a divorce. He was supposed to go on his family (conjugal) visit today. He was going to utilize this private time to talk things through with his wife. She did not show up. After four or five tries, Brian finally reached her at home. The brief telephone conversation elicited her decision to divorce.

Without a positive or productive avenue for release, I know Brian's emotions are running wild. He can only sit and stew in the wreckage of what was once a happy home. At least the shoe was dropped, a decision has been made, and he can start concentrating on himself and stop *hard-timing*—fat chance of that.

Relationships in prison are almost impossible. It takes a very special lady, a lady willing to sacrifice, willing to accept half a life at best. Unfortunately, there are too few of these rare ladies, and if I were asked, there should be none. We men should stay home, stay focused on God and family.

I know. No one asked.

9:30 p.m.

Brian returned from a regular visit with two policemen friends. He tried to explain the mental horror that goes on in prison and pleaded with them to never write *creative* police reports to bust (frame) a criminal.

"Prisons do more harm than good," Brian reiterated, "because prisons and the hypocrisy that is systematic in their culture causes the inmates to lose any respect for authority they may have had, especially when police or prison staff lie."

I could not agree more.

Brian was walking in the shoes of many who came before him and was becoming a great advocate. Not for warm and fuzzy coddling but for understanding and change. The question is: Will anyone listen to Brian now that he is tainted with a felony?

Matthew 19:8-9. *Jesus replied, "Moses permitted you to divorce your wives because your hearts were hard. But it was not this way from the beginning. I tell you that anyone who divorces his wife, except for marital unfaithfulness, and marries another woman commits adultery."*

✝ ✝ ✝

Monday, January 24, 1994
3:00 p.m.

I watched four inmates, two white and two Hispanics argue over who was going to use one of the five, four-seat tables, in the gym. It began with who was waiting first and then quickly deteriorated into derogatory remarks about who was born where and that three of the other tables were already occupied by a certain race.

The three officers at their station kept a wary eye on them.

Tolerance: A fair and objective attitude toward those whose opinions, practices, race, religion, or nationality differ from one's own; freedom from bigotry.

Tolerance is a wise policy for prison survival. Unfortunately, inmates demand respect but what they need is tolerance. I am surrounded by closed-minded individuals who are missing out on the good things that come with diversity. Yes, some people are very annoying, but this annoyance has very little to do with skin color, place of birth, or their religious beliefs. It has to do with immaturity and lack of social graces. It is easily assumed that many in prison were never taught manners, or if they were, they believe that being courteous is weakness.

God requires us to love our neighbors and enemies. If we practiced this commandment with social graces, and then if two sides rise up in conflict, it is likely that both sides will find accommodation and unexpected rewards.

Tolerance and love; two interesting concepts need to be brought into the practical applications in our daily lives.

One of the argumentative white inmates called one of the Hispanics a "stupid wetback." In return he got his nose broken.

Alarm! Code 3.

John 13:31, 34-35. *Jesus said, "...A new command I give you: Love one another. As I have loved you, so you must love one another. By this all men will know that you are my disciples, if you love one another."*

✟ ✟ ✟

Tuesday, January 25, 1994
3:15 p.m.

I lie on my bunk, plain worn out. Why? It was from the mental stress and strain of work and having to duck and dodge the varied personalities of both staff and inmates. During my many months here, I assumed the position of unofficial coordinator in the office. I insure that each clerk is able to complete their tasks, anticipating the needs of the supervisors, all the while avoiding the slings and arrows of those who are in a mood. It is mostly a thankless job, but as I have stated before, I work for God, and the alternative, chaos, would only end in my being dismissed from the position.

My solution to my exhaustion was to kick off my boots and curl under my blanket for a well-deserved nap. Ah.... Zzz...

7:30 p.m.

Huh? I slept through dinner? I probably saved my life. Ha ha.

President Clinton was on television giving the State of the Union speech. There are so many problems facing our society today: crime, teen pregnancies, drug abuse, corruption, and so on. How can it all be dealt with?

If we would all turn toward God and His wonderful love and guidance, we would have a change. However, this message has been preached for 2000 years, but too many are hard-headed or blind. I was both. It is not difficult to be good, and I have found the rewards are far more enriching than silver and gold.

In this country, do we not "pledge allegiance under God?"

Romans 8:35-37. *Who shall separate us from the love of Christ? Shall trouble or hardship or persecution or famine or nakedness or danger or sword? It is written: "For your sake we face death all day long; we are considered as sheep to be slaughtered." No, in all these things we are more than conquerors through Him who loved us.*

✟ ✟ ✟

Wednesday, January 26, 1994
7:00 a.m.

Gone in the name of "Investigation." Two friends, *Tree Top* and *Big Mac*, have been taken to the hole. Why? Suspicious circumstances. They were helping two staff members with a project for revamping the quarterly (care) packages. Their plan would increase security by preventing the introduction of contraband: i.e. drugs and weapons, and would make millions of dollars for the Department of Corrections. Unfortunately, somehow this plan stepped on several high-ranking administrators' toes, and so they must go. The proposed plan will die from neglect.

What about the low-level staff the inmates were helping? They are still here but were reassigned to work the prison's perimeter from 10:00 p.m. to 6:00 a.m. It is only the discard-able inmate who gets the royal shaft down the hole. If you wear blue, you are replaceable in a blink of an eye, no matter the quality of work you may do, if you have offended someone.

I believe it is only by the grace of God that I am still surviving in my position as the program administrator's clerk. If I near an invisible land mine or walk too close to an unknown precipice, the Spirit taps me on my shoulder so I can back quickly away. To have such a protector provides me with great piece of mind as long as I listen to Him.

I will miss *Tree Top* and *Big Mac*.

John 16:13-14. *"But when He, the Spirit of truth, comes, He will guide you into all truth. He will not speak on His own; He will speak only what He hears, and He will tell you what is to come. He will bring glory to me by taking from what is mine and making it known to you."*

✟ ✟ ✟

Thursday, January 27, 1994
1:00 p.m.

I never thought I would hear such an intense discussion between the sergeant and lieutenant over the merits of eyebrow waxing, cheek bone highlighting, and supplemental incomes with Mary Kay cosmetics.

During their conversation I sat typing at my desk, grinning at this sneak peek into their other side. I had my suspicion that under their rough and tough exteriors wait persons counting the minutes until the end of the work day when they can shed the faux masculinity, their starched uniforms, and don the niceties and daintiness of sexy, sensual women.

Of course I am speaking about the sergeant and lieutenant who are both females.

What a contrast; the talk of primping techniques compared to their tyrannical attitudes they believe is required by their career choices. It was quite pleasant to eavesdrop on their female talk even if it was only for a few minutes.

I so miss the wonders, the specialness of ladies.

I never forget that God saved His best work for last, that being the creation of a woman.

Proverb 31:25-26, 30. *She is clothed with strength and dignity; she can laugh at the days to come. She speaks with wisdom, and faithful instruction is on her tongue. Charm is deceptive, and beauty is fleeting; but a woman who fears the Lord is to be praised.*

✝ ✝ ✝

Friday, January 28, 1994
1:00 p.m.

Carrie, your stuck pig is squealing. And the cup runneth over, not with wine, but with the life blood from the chest cavity of a Mexican gang member whose torso has a sharpened broom handle through it. This violent intrusion does not bode well for a healthy life. I pray he does not die. Death at age 22 would be a waste.

"Yard recall! All inmates return to your assigned housing unit," blared from the speakers.

This incident occurred in the minimum dorms (level I) outside the fence line, not in our facility. Remember, minimum is where the guys that are going home within two years are housed.

A re-evaluation of who should occupy the Level I beds might be in order.

6:00 p.m.

I dined with the "They're no good" crew. I was seated with three black men ages approximately 45, 35, and 20. They were negatively commenting about the black lieutenant who supervised feeding tonight.

"He's no good," remarked the eldest.

"An Al Jolson wannabe," the second sneered.

"Just an Uncle Tom," the youngest spit out.

Being the odd man out and a little nervy tonight I put in my two cents.

"Maybe he is what you say, but he makes $60,000 a year, and we are the ones in prison. He must be doing something right."

My dinner companions did not want to hear that. From their point of view it was a greater accomplishment being in prison for going against the establishment—committing crime, than achieving success, especially by a brother who has excelled within the establishment. To me, their talk sounded like envy, a failure to accept personal responsibility, and striking out at those who have risen above adversity.

We cannot blame others for our place in life. Accept what is and move forward to attain one's own greatness. I will succeed because I believe in myself, my family and friends believe in me, and I trust in God who believes in me, too.

Isaiah 1:19-20. *"If you are willing and obedient you will eat the best from the land; but if you resist and rebel, you will be devoured by the sword."* For the *mouth of the Lord has spoken.*

✟ ✟ ✟

Saturday, January 29, 1994
9:00 a.m.

"Return to normal program," was announced. The lockdown is over. The inmate who was skewered did not die. Thank God.

10:30 a.m.

A big honcho meeting was held in the warden's office. The subject, broom handles. How to control them: Should they be taken away? Lots of talk but I doubt if anything will change. The floors have to be swept somehow.

I suppose if soft, bendable broom handles were used...nah...that would not work, though it would be funny to watch.

6:00 p.m.

Tonight, my table companions were not so unique, sadly so. They were physically huge, tough as case-hardened nails, and sexually, they would take it as they could get it. I have found it bewildering, as well as disturbing, that a large segment of the toughest, tattoo-covered men in prison will kill you if you call them a fag or a queer, but behind the closed door of a cell will sodomize and are sodomized to their sexual delight.

Disgusting as it is, if it only affected them, that would be their downfall, but most of these men are married, or on the hunt for a wife, and will eventually be exposing them to many potentially dangerous diseases, including AIDS. Throughout dinner I was forced to listen to the conquests of these men while in prison and the fine-looking *girlfriends* they had had.

I have often wondered if imprisoned men were treated like the troops of the French Foreign Legion of old, meaning, willing ladies were made available, would there be these high numbers of inmate on inmate sex?

Nope, I could not finish my dinner as graphic descriptions in the one-upmanship were shared by each. Where were my Christian brothers with their uplifting conversations when I needed them?

Romans 8:6-8. *The mind of sinful man is death, but the mind controlled by the Spirit is life and peace; the sinful mind is hostile to God. It does not submit to God's law, nor can it do so. Those controlled by the sinful nature cannot please God.*

✝ ✝ ✝

Sunday, January 30, 1994
9:00 a.m.

I made sure that I had stretched my limbs and loosened my muscles, because it was going to be a beautiful volleyball day. It will be sixty degrees, sunny, brisk and bright. I so enjoy this sport, but not the bickering that often comes with sporting activities. Whether it is volleyball, softball, basketball, or horseshoes, they are only games and should be fun. The arguments in volleyball over close calls; did the ball hit the line, or did the player touch the net, are a waste of time and create such negative energy. And, as many of the players on the court are Christians, it is important how we are viewed by non-Christians because others tend to judge Christ by His followers. I only want to give them positive perspectives, not negative, or hypocritical.

Besides, wining a volleyball game does not let the victor go home any sooner.

3:00 p.m.

I almost forgot, today is Super Bowl Sunday. It is the day when many who hate, unite in support of "Their Team" irrespective of race or religion. It is the sport that matters, especially when large quantities of Top Ramen soups have been wagered on the outcome.

Me? I always root for the underdog because I can relate to their uphill battle.

6:00 p.m.

Sadly, the pup could not overcome. The favorite, the All American team, the Dallas Cowboys won…at least I believe they did. My focus was on their cheerleaders; magnificent specimens with dazzling smiles.

1 Peter 2-21. *To this you were called, because Christ suffered for you, leaving you an example that you should follow in His steps.*

✞ ✞ ✞

Monday, January 31, 1994
4:00 p.m.

News Flash! California criminal frenzy continues with the Three Strike's & You're Out band wagon careening out of control while everyone tries to leap aboard. Today in the legislature, no less than five separate bills were introduced concerning three felonies; wherein the criminal loser will receive a life sentence.

Selfishly, I believe it is terrific, because inmates like myself who can prove they have changed their ways will have to be paroled because the prisons will be so overcrowded, and the state so broke that the parole board's boss, the governor, will have to do the right thing and release suitable inmates.

On the downside, everyday life in prison will get very tough, dangerous, and uncomfortable. The prison guards' association's propaganda slogan of "Walking the Toughest Beat in the State" will become a reality.

That scares me.

4:15 p.m.

Mail. Foreign mail? From the Philippines? No. From South Korea? No. It was from Australia. The museum in Sydney responded with names of Dreamtime books, Aboriginal cassette tapes, and their costs. Excellent.

6:20 p.m.

I telephoned my father to share the information I received in the mail. He was pleased and eager to mail off an international money order to help me in my creative pursuit.

My father ROCKS!

9:00 p.m.

I sat on my bunk and casually watched four inmates in succession being tattooed on a bunk near mine. What a deadly game of tattoo, tattoo, who has the killer flu? Hepatitis C and AIDS carrying inmates were giving all the others the death sentence since the same unsterilized needle was used on each of them.

The Bible clearly states: Thou shall not mark (tattoo) the body. God made us in His beautiful image. Why would we want to graffiti it up? Do we think we are more creative than God?

Leviticus 19:28. *Do not cut your bodies for the dead or put tattoo marks on yourselves. I am the Lord.*

✝ ✝ ✝

Tuesday, February 1, 1994
7:30 a.m.

First of the month and I was busy, busy, busy with reports: staff ethnic-gender report, disciplinary report, In-Service Training logs, and never forget the most important one, the inmate payroll. Except for inmates who are assigned to Prison Industry Authority (P.I.A.) jobs or joint venture with outside private companies, my position receives the highest pay on the facility at 32 cents an hour. It may not be much with the pay cap of $48, any extra hours are free, but if I am frugal, my pay will keep me in soups, stamps, and candy bars.

I am fortunate that I do not smoke or drink coffee. Those who do, find themselves going without or in constant debt to inmates who run black market stores. If an inmate borrows from a *store*, the charge is three items for every two borrowed. If an inmate gets stuck in this cycle, it is tough to get out. And, if the inmate cannot pay his debt, well, it can then become a dangerous situation.

The frenzy of monthly reports was good for my mind and soul. Keeping focused on the tasks kept me from dwelling on the unpleasant environment that surrounds me, and for my soul, well, I believe that my job done well pleases God. Another benefit of busy, busy, busy was that the hours passed quickly. Then again, my reward was to return to the concrete cube. Maybe I should not have been so efficient.

3:30 p.m.

Legal mail call. I received a large envelope from the Federal Public Defender's Office. They sent me the necessary forms to request the appointment of attorney by the courts after my federal appeal is filed and accepted. This was exciting. It could be the turning point in my legal battle. I prayed with all my heart that it would be in the Lord's will.

5:00 p.m.

The menu posted at the officer's station read Pot Pie for dinner. I am not a picky eater, but yuck. For me, tonight would be Top Ramen soup and a Snickers candy bar.

Hebrews 11:6. *And without faith it is impossible to please God, because anyone who comes to Him must believe that He exists and that He rewards those who earnestly seek him.*

✝ ✝ ✝

Wednesday, February 2, 1994
3:00 p.m.

My work day was over. I began the long trudge down the track to the concrete cube. I thought to myself, at least I do not have to fight freeway traffic jams.

Alarm buzzers sounded above building 8, shattering my false sense of peace. The officer manning the yard gun tower (O.B.B.: Observation Booth B facility) shouted over the P.A. system, "Get down! Get down!" as he racked a round in his mini-14 rifle. Officers ran from every building, from the Program Office, and the plaza area, their side-handle batons swinging as their arms pumped forward and back. Like a piercing wedge the green wall of uniforms funneled at full speed in through building 8's sally-port door.

From the volleyball court I could hear six to eight Hispanic inmates laugh and jeer at several less fit officers as these staff huffed and puffed. That was not a smart thing to do.

Wave off. It was a false alarm.

The attention focused on the volleyball court. Staff surrounded the offending inmates and ordered them to strip naked for searches and the appropriate level of humiliation. Did I mention it was 50 degrees today?

After the strip out, each Hispanic was allowed to put their boxers back on, and then they were handcuffed and escorted back to their cells where they would remain locked up for the remainder of the day. Maybe these inmates and those that watched the spectacle would learn something, or maybe they would become angry and vengeful for being humiliated in front of their peers and gawking staff, female officers included.

What I learned is that staff (being human) do not like being laughed at or embarrassed. To prove this fact, that people should not be made fun of or embarrassed, they did the same thing to the offending inmates. Does that make sense? What happened to communication?

9:00 p.m.

It is another early night in the sack. I am feeling defeated again. Not quite a chocolate pudding depression night, but simply mentally worn out, and wanting to be in the arms of a loved one.

Diagnosis; tired and lonely.

Someone once coined the phrase: "The world *was* my oyster." The shining pearls in my life were a lady who loved me and a law career that had no limits. I was an idiot. Selfish, selfish, selfish to throw it all away on a financial short cut that ended up being a dead end.

I constantly rub my eyes as I look around at my constricted world because I cannot believe that I am in prison. It is too surreal.

I want to sleep forever. Please wake me when the bell tolls.

Isaiah 51:11. *The ransomed of the Lord will return. They will enter Zion with singing; everlasting joy will crown their heads. Gladness and joy will overtake them, and sorrow and sighing will flee away.*

✞ ✞ ✞

Thursday, February 3, 1994
8:00 a.m.

On my way to work I was asked by a passing inmate, "Hey, how ya doing?" I replied "Great. I'm having a wonderful day." I lied through my teeth. But if I said it enough I would hopefully start to believe it.

Feeling blue, thinking positive.

I am confused and depressed over my appeal and possible retrial. Boy, that is worrying about chickens before they hatch. My confusion is how do I stay within God's grace and will while fighting the devil? My depression is because the reality is that rarely do the good guys come out on top in the courts or within the Department of Corrections. Many times it appears that only the sneaky and conniving get ahead.

Do not get me wrong. I am guilty of my convicted offense, but what I want is acknowledgment by the courts, so that it is as *they* say, "On the record," that I was not attending a tea party when I played god and took a life.

I will have to pray for guidance and peace of mind.

8:00 p.m.

I was watching the movie *Top Gun* on television. What an exciting story. It got my adrenaline pumping with each aerial dogfight. It inspired me to set sky high goals, but the love story depressed me. The first time I saw the film was with Angela during happier times—I was still FREE. My life held so much potential; it was filled with so much love and overwhelming happiness that comes with youth. Pitifully, all I do now is cling with bloody fingernails to sweet memories that once were, and to hopes that may never be.

Top Gun did inspire me to write the ultimate love story. If not between me and a lady, how about between me and God?

John 14:27. *"Peace I leave with you; my peace I give you. I do not give you as the world gives. Do not let your hearts be troubled and do not be afraid."*

✝ ✝ ✝

Friday, February 4, 1994
12:00 Noon

"Only inmates with less than two years are assigned to live in the gym," the prison's Public Information Officer and tour guide told the visitors.

"But what about lifers?" I interjected as I walked past the huddled visitors after returning to the cube for my forgotten lunch.

"These are non-violent inmates," the guide continued.

I would agree that many in the gym are now non-violent, compliant, and chomping at the penal bit to prove their worthiness to rejoin society.

I wished I only had two years left to serve.

Did I care if the staff person who gave the tour was displeased by my comments? Did I care if he had to answer uncomfortable questions posed by the confused visitors? Not one iota. So many lies are told to the public to cover the financial manipulations under the guise of "Safety & Security Needs."

Gym beds needed to be filled, and because prison officials know that the majority of lifers are model inmates trying to prove they are suitable to be released, staff subject them to the worst living conditions. Lifers are shuffled between buildings and are transferred to different prisons to suit administrators' needs, not society's desire for a system that encourages rehabilitation and then rewards changed men with release.

It should be reform and release, not finagle for financing.

Mark 16:15-17. *He said to them, "Go into all the world and preach the good news to all creation. Whoever believes and is baptized will be saved, but whoever does not believe will be condemned. And these signs will accompany those who believe: In my name they will drive out demons; they will speak in new tongues."*

✝ ✝ ✝

Saturday, February 5, 1994
12:30 p.m.

Bright sun. Azure blue sky. Lovely. If I could only remove the barbed wire, electrified fences, guns, guards, concrete buildings, and the sorrowful faces of inmates wearing prison blues, the vibrant green grass and recreating men participating in volleyball, softball, horseshoes, and weight lifting would remind me of a park atmosphere. The adjective, festive comes to mind, until: "Yard recall." Damn, another stupid count. How many people on the street own blue jeans?

1:00 p.m.

Count. Count. Count.
What? No showers? It will be a smelly time in the cube. The pilot light for the locomotive size water heater has gone out again. "What about cold showers?" I asked, thinking I would rather shiver for a minute than stink for hours. "Sit on your bunk. The count hasn't cleared," the officer responded.

2:30 p.m.

"Count's clear, but the showers are still closed," the officer announced.

9:30 p.m.

"Back to your bunks, Count Time," grunts the officer over the speakers.

10:10 p.m.

"One more time, back on your bunks, Count's not clear," is announced by a first watch officer. Did staff in Control need to borrow my calculator? This is really irksome. So what is new?
Sniff-sniff. Pee-yew!

Psalm 143:10. *Teach me to do your will, for you are my God; may your good Spirit lead me on level ground.*

✝ ✝ ✝

Sunday, February 6, 1994
9:30 a.m.

Ah... The shower was deep muscle warm, edging near hot. A rare treat. Now I needed to change my sheets as I had to sleep in them all sweaty and icky. Yuck. Sorry, sheet exchange is only on Tuesdays. Crusty sheets for two more nights. Sigh.

11:00 p.m.

Black clouds hovered overhead all day, providing an excuse to veg out. I watched movie after movie, relaxed, teared up, was inspired, and entertained. A good day to re-energize the body, mind, and spirit.
That fuzzy pink bunny and his little drum have nothing on me.

11:15 p.m.

Time for this lad to hit the hay. I stood to stretch, and as I looked out across the gym with my boob-tubed eyes, the many fully-covered bodies sleeping on their bunks resembled an overflowing makeshift morgue. The guards, as resident ghouls, walked about to check the corpses for signs of life. The staff does this, not out of care, but per regulations, and I suspect some self-interest. Do you know how much paperwork is required to be completed if one of us dies? Hours and hours. Staff do not want to hang around here filling out forms. As much as I want, they also want to return home to loved ones. Hey, on that topic, we are not much different.
I praised God for my health and sanity.

John 3:16. *For God so loved the world, that He gave His one and only Son, that whosoever believeth in Him should not perish, but have eternal life.*

✝ ✝ ✝

Monday, February 7, 1994
10:00 a.m.

There was very little work to do this morning. An anomaly. I stood by the office door and watched all the oysters at play. These men possessed rough exteriors with slimy, seemingly unappetizing fleshy interiors. But given the proper care and nurtured guidance, I believe there can be found a beautiful pearl in each of them.

Politicians, police, and victims of crime would strenuously disagree with me, and no, my glasses are not rose-colored. I have seen change happen again and again to men whom I thought were not redeemable. As a result of positive encouragement from outside by caring people who would not give up and inspiration from inside by the Holy Spirit, this combination can transform anyone.

2:30 p.m.

"Peeling the cap." A very graphic phrase for a severe head injury. When a metal mop ringer and a human skull do battle, the head loses.

A moment of silence and a whispered prayer for the injured man.

I acknowledge there are some inmates who need to be cultured longer than others to bring forth their preciousness.

Hosea 2:19. *I will betroth you to me forever; I will betroth you in righteousness and justice, in love and compassion.*

✟ ✟ ✟

Tuesday, February 8, 1994
7:30 a.m.

The *brownies* have arrived. Not the cute little girls with cookies but new cadets from the CDC academy, who, every couple of weeks come through the institution. Inmates unceremoniously call them brownies because of the color of their temporary uniform.

Okay, you caught me in a half truth. Some inmates call them brownies. Others call them by the much less flattering term that is the product of one's bowels…same color.

Each cadet is paired with an officer for a few hours to observe the goings on of a prison, their soon-to-be work environment.

One staff member, Officer McCormick, who is a professional in all respects, usually takes the cadets into the Program Office classification room for a pep talk. If the door is left open, I am able to overhear this pep talk/instruction, which is fair as it relates to inmates. McCormick's talk goes along these lines: "Don't bring an attitude, and remember, you are not the judge. They have already been sentenced. Attempt to treat each as an individual and use common sense for your safety. Inmates react to staff, not the other way around."

It is too bad too many cadets forget these wise words after they graduate and don the green uniform of an officer. I have always wanted to ask these officers-in-training: "What in the heck made you choose prison guard as a career?" I suspect the majority would reply, "The money." It is true that a career in corrections pays very well, not to mention the benefits and retirement, and to apply, a person only needs a G.E.D. (General Education Diploma).

The cadets dispersed with their escorts. When they passed me at the Program Office door I could see fear and apprehension in many of their eyes. They were, for the first time, face-to-face with a convicted criminal, a man in blue. I purposely smiled. I would not be a stereotype regardless of their academy indoctrination.

The voice in my head echoed Quasimodo, screaming, "I am not an animal!"

1 Timothy 6:10. *For the love of money is the root of all kinds of evil. Some people, eager for money, have wandered from the faith and pierced themselves with many griefs.*

✞ ✞ ✞

Wednesday, February 9, 1994
8:30 p.m.

While in the middle of watching a *Nature* program on PBS about a family of close-knit African elephants, I was unexpectedly called into work. I did not mind as this on-call status was my nominal repayment to the third watch lieutenant for him allowing me to come into work of my own accord to use an unoccupied desk for my creative writing.

There are five tables in the gym, but they are reserved for playing cards, dominoes, and chess, and as there are no quiet places in the gym, it makes it all but impossible to be productive unless one's goal is to be a champion dominoes slammer. Also included in the constant commotion are announcements over the loudspeakers that nearly cause my eardrums to bleed from the volume and inmates interrupting me, curious and wanting to know what I am doing.

I rapidly typed several disciplinary reports for staff that had to be completed due to time limitations, and then was swiftly on my way back to the gym, to arrive in time to watch a new addition, the birth of a baby pachyderm to the family of elephants.

Sometime in the Night

I dreamed of a combination pizza restaurant, spy hideout, and swim center. Boy was that a stretch of subconscious imagination. The best part of the dream was the location, the island of Oahu in Hawaii. I was showing a girl, the first girl I ever kissed, around my multi-use facility. Naturally, because it was my dream, she was impressed. So was I, actually. Then my bladder gave me a wakeup call. Bummer.

As I plodded my way to the urinals and back, I pondered the significance of the dream, and then decided it was too deep, so instead of taxing my half-asleep brain, I just enjoyed the feeling of momentary escape.

Her name? Kathy. I will never forget my first kiss. Heaven.

Acts 2:17-19. *"In the last days, God says, I will pour out my Spirit on all People. Your sons and daughters will prophesy, your young men will see visions, your old men will dream dreams. Even on my servants, both men and women, I will pour out my Spirit in those days, and they will prophesy. I will show them wonders in the heaven above and the signs on earth below, blood and fire and billows of smoke."*

✝ ✝ ✝

Thursday, February 10, 1994
9:30 a.m.

Surprised? Not really. Old Leonard, a charismatic child molester, was escorted in handcuffs to the hole for unlawful influence. Did he do it? I do not know, but rumor has it he was pressuring other child molesters to move near his cell so he could have more control over them. Leonard's ploy: if they did not move, Leonard would tell inmates on the yard who the child molesters were, or in prison vernacular: "Pull their covers." An interesting strategy, but as I said, I do not know if it is true. Leonard, if it is true, may be a busybody and a manipulator for drama's sake, but for the rest, only he knows.

Unfortunately for Leonard, all staff need is a whiff of wrong doing, and the suspect will be whisked away. Due process? Maybe later, but in the interim, a bare cell in administrative segregation will be Leonard's new residence.

What is hard to believe is that those who are convicted of any type of crime would believe that they can keep their offense a secret. There are no secrets on a prison yard, not from staff and especially not from other inmates…someone is always watching, listening and snooping.

7:00 p.m.

Damn that reality check. I spoke with a wise, older inmate named Sal. He has battled in the State and Federal courts for years on his own case and on behalf of other inmates. This is his take on the judicial system: "If you are arrested, there is a 95% likelihood of conviction. On state appeal, the likelihood that the conviction will be overturned is about one percent. If the appeal is filed in the federal courts; the likelihood of success is one-half of that one percent."

In other words, it is like climbing up a greased razor blade.

Sal went on to say, "It is not that all convictions are perfect, in fact, most arrests and trials are filled with errors. Unfortunately the appeals courts set the bar of burden of proof so high for the convicted person that even if you are legally in the right, it is nearly impossible to bring forth the adequate evidence." He then concluded by saying. "The judicial system is not evil, it is not unfair because it treats all inmates the same, it is just what it is. The best way to defeat it, or to win, is to stay out of it."

These are very wise words, but too late for me. God, give me strength.

Next week I have scheduled time with a prison legal beagle who has agreed to review my paperwork so that I would have another opinion. I will still go forward regardless of his thoughts. I have to. I have to try as it is my life that is at stake. I am so tired of living this life of degradation.

2 Timothy 1:7. *For God did not give us a spirit of timidity, but a spirit of power, of love and of self-discipline.*

✝ ✝ ✝

Friday, February 11, 1994
4:00 p.m.

Mail. A Valentine's Day card from across the ocean. My heart soars. My eyes see sparkling joy in the face on the enclosed photograph. My ears conjure whispered words laced with honey. My nose imagines the delicate fragrance of a lady's perfume mixing with tropical flowers. Ah... remembrances of loves past evoked by the simple act of opening a paper card.

I had not received a Valentine's Day card for a number of years, three to be precise. Even though the sender of this one is only a pen-pal in the Philippines, and not a lover, Madeline's words warmed my hungry heart. It does not take a lot to keep me positive, but at times those little bits of encouragement seem far apart in coming.

Hmm... if newborns are fed, kept warm, and their bedding changed, but they are not held, they will die. How long would it take for a grown man to succumb to the same fate?

1 John 1:3. *We proclaim to you what we have seen and heard, so that you also may have fellowship with us. And our fellowship is with the Father and with His Son, Jesus Christ.*

✟ ✟ ✟

Saturday, February 12, 1994
8:00 a.m.

An inmate talent show pre-empted the volleyball games today as the *talent* utilized the concrete court to perform on. Knowing that my usual outdoor activity would not be allowed, I decided to spend the day studying in the law library. While waiting in line with the 23 other inmates desperate for one of the ten seats, I listened to music, songs, and poetry. Two or three of the inmate groups registered on the good side of the mediocre scale. I again concluded that there was a lot of talent going to waste behind bars. However, because the Arts are difficult fields to break into, and a home is easier, that was where these inmates focused their efforts. What a shame.

8:00 p.m.

The Winter Olympics in Lillehammer, Norway, opened tonight. Watching the broadcast of the Opening Ceremonies I marveled at the pageantry, the excitement of the parading athletes, and the world unity in the name of competitive sports. I believe God was happy at this moment as He looked down on His many children, together, and in peace. Why can we not do this year round?

9:30 p.m.

All the inmates in the gym, including me, were buck-naked, standing in front of our bunks so that flashlight-wielding staff could inspect our bodies for signs of a physical altercation. Four droplets of blood were discovered on a towel in the shower area so it was assumed that an assault occurred, which more than not would be the case. I am tired of men staring at my naked body.

10:00 p.m.

Old man Pepe came shuffling past on his cane, saying, "I had a nose bleed this morning but *they* wouldn't listen to me." Oh, was that bit of indifference supposed to be a news flash?

"Hey, Pepe," I sniped, "You're only about 130. You probably beat some smart--- down and stuffed him into your locker. Am I right?"

Pepe smiled at the compliment and shuffled on.

Romans 15:5-7. *May the God who gives endurance and encouragement give you a spirit of unity among yourselves as you follow Christ Jesus, so that with one heart and mouth you may glorify the God and Father of our Lord Jesus Christ. Accept one another, then just as Christ accepted you, in order to bring praise to God.*

✞ ✞ ✞

Sunday, February 13, 1994
12:00 Noon

Bump…pass…spike…point!

"Watson, report to the Program Office," boomed from the loudspeakers.

What; in the middle of a volleyball game, and on my day off? An inmate was going to the hole and the sergeant wanted me to type the paperwork. It was an inmate who believed he was not receiving enough mail, money, care packages or visits from home. He started making threats to his loved one in the visiting room. Not a smart thing to do and very ungrateful.

It was a great compliment to be trusted enough by staff to type semi-sensitive material. Gossiping leads down the road to destruction, and besides, this was someone else's business. I stay clear of their problems.

12:45 p.m.

I left a few dirty smudges on the lock-up reports from my fingers, but the reports were typed accurately, and I was back on the volleyball court in 45 minutes. I was immediately asked by the other players what the call was all about?

"Someone was a bad boy," I replied.

"Who was it?" they probed.

"His name? Oh, I forgot. Let's play ball," I said, and the games continued without missing a beat.

James 1:26. *If anyone considers himself religious and yet does not keep a tight rein on his tongue, he deceives himself and his religion is worthless.*

✞ ✞ ✞

Monday, February 14, 1994
VALENTINE'S DAY
8:00 a.m. – 3:00 p.m.

I worked my tail off organizing the Men's Advisory Committee's archives. The M.A.C. is an inmate-elected body tasked with representing inmates concerns and communicating such to the prison administrators. Though elected by the inmates, the body serves at the will of staff. I have observed time and again an executive body member who was too effective, or did not know his humble place, be fired, sent to the hole, or transferred out of the prison.

The three boxes of archival paperwork consisted of memorandums, proposals, and by-laws that date from 1987, when the prison first opened, to the present. Can we say, "No method to their filing madness?" It did make sense as it was madness to be on the M.A.C. because they rarely accomplished anything except what the administration wanted them to accomplish. They are a bunch of inmates who believe they are running something, but mostly it is their mouths.

I do not mean to be too harsh on these inmates because there are some who stand for election with good intentions, and I applaud them. However, they are naive, and quickly learn their limitations. Prison is a top down authoritarian system and anyone who believes otherwise has deluded himself.

4:00 p.m.

No mail. No "Be My Valentine." Sigh. Love is a fleeting thing.

I admit to being a hypocrite when it comes to relationships involving women and inmates. I want a special lady—a love, but I question a woman who would want a relationship with an inmate unless each knew the other before incarceration. On the other hand, why was she unable to find someone who had not committed a felony? On the other hand, there are many good men and women in prison who would love, and honestly adore and care for a person who chose to take a lover's leap. As I am the odd-man-out, I have a third hand—God. When His time is right for me, whether I am in prison or out, God will bless me with a wonderful partner, and then I will be thankful and not question her motives.

I have asked in Jesus' name...so it will be...if it glorifies God.

John 14:21. *"Whoever has my commands and obeys them, he is the one who loves me. He who loves me will be loved by my Father, and I too will love him and show myself to him."*

✞ ✞ ✞

Tuesday, February 15, 1994
5:30 a.m.

As I waited, lying on my bunk in a half-sleep stupor for breakfast to be announced, the first watch officer approached and informed me that he wrote me a CDC-115 disciplinary report.

"What?!" I said, fully awake.

"In two of your outgoing letters there were photocopies, presumable made without permission," replied the officer as justification.

There was no arguing with an officer who has made his determination, so I kept my mouth shut, but thought: Well, buddy, you presumed wrong. I made and paid for those photocopies.

What a way to start the day.

My only recourse was to go over the officer's head.

7:30 a.m.

At work, I waited until the lieutenant was not busy to talk to him about the 'write-up.' I explained Donna's kindness in allowing me to make copies and run a monthly tab with a pre-signed trust withdrawal form held in her office. The lieutenant said he would look into it. That was all I could hope for.

Without the blessing of being able to make copies I would never accomplish my creative writing goals. What a hassle. Every day there was something new to test me, to see if anger or the Spirit would win the moment. Today it was a guard trying to save the world one photocopy at a time. Save yourself, pal, and leave me the hell alone.

I took a deep breath and looked skyward while the two polar entities battled within me for supremacy.

10:00 a.m.

The lieutenant verified that I had been paying for the photocopies. Then, with me in attendance, wrote in large block letters across the write-up: WITHDRAWN.

Thank God that was over. This round goes to the Spirit.

6:00 p.m.

I had a lengthy discussion with the legal beagle who was willing to guide me through the federal appeal system. This promise of assistance has my hopes rising slightly as at least I would get the procedure right. He and I have a date for next week, same bat time, same bat station, to review the legal issues raised in my state court appeals. I will be waiting, with high hopes, in my bat cave.

8:00 p.m.

I chatted with Mickie on the telephone. She had mixed reports to relay concerning her new job as manager-in-training at Thrifty's. Mickie was learning quickly, but the hours were long, and the store was purposely short-staffed to save money. We agreed that the job may be tiresome, but to bring home a paycheck after years on the welfare doles raised her self-respect and at the end of a long day, gave her a feeling of accomplishment for a job well done.

After we hung up, a tsunami of loneliness crashed down on me. I missed Angela. I missed Mickie. I missed my parents. I missed everyone.

Isaiah 41:10. *"So do not fear, for I am with you; do not be dismayed, for I am your God. I will strengthen you and help you; I will uphold you with my righteous right hand."*

✝ ✝ ✝

Wednesday, February 16, 1994
All Day

No water. This time a water main outside the prison has broken. No water to drink. No water to shower with or flush the toilets. An institution filled with 3,880 inmates, plus several hundred staff with no ability to cast away their bodily functions after relieving themselves. The urinals sloshed with dark yellow liquid and the commodes overflowed with brown...they were not a pretty sight, and the smell, well, use your imagination while picturing the odoriferous haze as it thickened, wafting through the buildings. Gag!

10:00 p.m.

I went to bed to talk to God. I was having difficulty dealing with reality. I had always been blessed in that if I screwed up I managed to avoid the harshest crack of the prosecutorial whip. Meaning, if I misbehaved in school, at home, or received a vehicular citation, I was called on the carpet and punished, but the penalty was short; an apology, a night in, a fine, was my punishment. However, I admit those steps across the line pale in comparison to why I am in prison. Futilely, I keep waiting for someone to say, "April fools," or "Time's up," but after six and a half years, it still has not happened.

I need help, and it does not seem to be available. No one is coming to rescue me.

The scream not heard in space still reverberates between my ears.

I am not sure what a panic attack is but if it is an immeasurable fear that I have fallen into oblivion, I would at least be able to name the beast that holds me in its claws.

Psalm 145:14-16. *The Lord upholds all those who fall and lifts up all who are bowed down. The eyes of all look to you, and you give them their food at the proper time. You open your hand and satisfy the desires of every living thing.*

✞ ✞ ✞

Thursday, February 17, 1994
5:00 p.m.

Plan A: Something was amiss.

I looked at my watch for the tenth time and it confirmed that my visitor was an hour late. My worry meter bent further into the red because my mother is always on time and dependable. If she said she would be here at a specific time, she would be…unless. I had to beg staff to allow me to use the telephone to call home because the telephones are turned off between 4 p.m. and 5:30 p.m. I needed to find out what was going on so I humbly pleaded my case.

"Sure. Go ahead," was the third watch officer's reply.

I hoped mom was okay. There had been a savage storm last night with 80 mph winds that whipped rain and snow, causing power outages. Because my mother lived in the mountains she could have had any number of problems.

Busy signal…busy signal…busy signal…Damn.

"Hello," Thank God. All was well…sort of. My mother was feeling under the weather and did not want to risk driving the slick, icy, and winding roads. She will visit next week. Mom said she was sorry and wished she could have come. Even though I could have used the energizing hugs tonight, her health and safety are more important.

I will survive, and I wanted her to do the same.

Plan B: Veg out.

I turned on the Olympics and watched ice skating. This is not my favorite winter sport, but those twirling girls are sure pretty, just too young for me.

Colossians 3:15. *Let the peace of Christ rule in your heart, since as members of one body you were called to peace. And be thankful.*

☩ ☩ ☩

Friday, February 18, 1994
3:00 p.m.

Disrespect was in the gym air and consequences quickly followed.

A smart-alecky Hispanic threw remnants of his Top Ramen soup on the floor after a black inmate (a gym porter) finished sweeping and mopping. The black inmate asked the Hispanic inmate if he was going to pick up his mess. The Hispanic told the black, "Go fu-- yourself." The battle was on and the Hispanic got his clock cleaned.

The real danger is not the one-on-one fight, unless you are one of them, but when the combatants are of different races. Then I have to watch to see if the 'friends' of one of the fighters jumps in against the other, changing what was a personal dispute to one of race against race. A battle between two could quickly become a melee of twenty or two-hundred. Or, the fight could be a diversion. It's a tactic to get staff to look one way while the real assault or stabbing occurs in another place to another person.

7:00 p.m.

Two Hispanics fought over a magazine, bouncing like pin balls against the steel bunks that lined the aisle. Sounds rather stupid and petty to fight over a magazine, but if it was taken, without consent, you have to 'get busy' (fight) to stand up for what is yours, or you will lose everything.

Without respect, a person cannot survive in prison. Sadly, this is the way it is; however, I prefer to give courtesy as its costs me nothing and I found it returns much.

Proverb 15:1-2. *A gentle answer turns away wrath, but a harsh word stirs up anger. The tongue of the wise commands knowledge, but the mouth of the fool gushes folly.*

☩ ☩ ☩

Saturday, February 19, 1994
ALL DAY
Presidents' weekend

Heavy rain pelted the roof, cleansing the world outside, but kept the horde inside to share the same stale air, air that is thick with germs. It is no wonder that I am sick again. Is it a winter cold, or the flu? To properly name the aches, the runny nose, sneezes, and hot and cold sweats will not ease my discomfort.

I seem to be unable to get fully well, back to 100% in this gym full of disease carriers. One sneeze and everyone is re-infected. I cannot get used to living like a pig in an overcrowded pen. I turned over in my bunk, shaded my eyes from the bright, ever-glowing lights, and tried to sleep. Maybe when I wake up everything and everyone will be gone.

Would it be too much to ask for the Lord to come back today? If not, couldn't some pissed off politician push *the* button?

Whoosh!

Sweet nothing.

1 John 3:2-3. *Dear Friends, now we are children of God, and what we will be has not yet been made known. But we know that when He appears, we shall be like Him, for we shall see Him as He is. Everyone who has this hope in Him purifies himself, just as He is pure.*

✝ ✝ ✝

Sunday, February 20, 1994
2:00 p.m.

The All Star brick thrower, Damian Williams, snuck into the gym. Tension rises as he and several other young blacks make snide remarks to passing whites. Mr. Williams better be careful. In the gym whites outnumber his posse. They hate him and are looking for any excuse to pay him back for his ill treatment of Reginald Denny.

Things could get ugly fast. I stay put on my bunk watching and waiting.

4:00 p.m.

Mr. Williams exited the gym at yard recall. He was certainly playing with fire. It would be rare for someone at this institution to 'take him out' (kill him). The majority of the "kill 'em now because I don't care" inmates here have matured or are tired and want desperately to go home, but 'touch him up' they could still do.

Staff may have appeared indifferent to Mr. William's incursions into the gym and his inciting remarks, but they are not deaf, dumb, or blind. Staff will likely bide their time, observe, document, and then transfer Mr. Williams to a less hospitable prison—yes, there are many prisons worse than the Creek. Or, Mr. Williams could slide by long enough to go home from here, act up again in his neighborhood and end up with a bullet rattling around in his brain. However, even though my flesh has issues with Mr. Williams, my spirit prays that he will learn the lesson society is trying to teach him and become a valued member of his community.

God has worked greater miracles.

Colossians 2:10, 15. And you have been given fullness in Christ, who is in the head over every power and authority. And having disarmed the powers and authorities, He made a public spectacle of them, triumphing over them by the cross.

✝ ✝ ✝

Monday, February 21, 1994
8:00 p.m.

After a long, sickly day at work, using what seemed to be a full roll of toilet paper to blow and blow and blow my runny nose, I was rewarded by talking with my father on the telephone. Even though I was feeling poorly, and we were separated by hundreds of miles, he was able to cheer me up and make me feel special. I know that is what fathers were created for, but it means so much more when I am in this terrible place. It matters not that at age 33, when I am supposed to be an adult, that my father's warmth lifts my mental outlook as if I were a seven-year-old with a skinned knee.

I wanted what all sons crave; to be the pride of a father's eye, to give my father bragging rights over my accomplishments. My father raised me to be a good son. Instead, I chose an alternate route, ignoring the bright and flashing 'Road Out' sign.

Above all things, I pray that my parents will still be alive when I am finally set free. God knows how important this is to me and my parents. For me, to be able to show them that their belief in me over all these years was not misguided. For them, to know their son once again has a future where each day is met with a smile, not a sigh, would be an answered prayer. Hopefully, this is God's will, too.

9:00 p.m.

Finally, ten days after putting in a medical request slip I received a pass (ducat) to go to the clinic for my sore throat, aches and pains, and general malaise. Usually, trips to the clinic would be a waste of an inmate's time, but I can always pray for that exception to the rule.

Exodus 20:12. *"Honor you father and your mother, so that you may live long in the land the Lord your God is giving you."*

✝ ✝ ✝

Tuesday, February 22, 1994
10:45 a.m.

T.L.C. I was in shock by the tender loving care. The MTA that I saw in the clinic was pleasant, attentive to my descriptions of my symptoms, and actually prescribed medication for my throat that was a wee bit stronger than aspirin. In addition, I was in and out of the clinic in 30 minutes, not the usual two hours of sitting in the sick tank staring at walls decorated with gang names.

Amazing. Another confirmation that there is a God - kindness toward the detestable.

9:00 p.m.

I curled under my covers as I was tired, dizzy, wishing for a massage, and wanting to escape into dreamland. As I closed my eyes trying to shut my ears to the rap music blaring from a nearby radio, I thought for a moment and thanked God for the kindness of the MTA who treated me today. I acknowledged the rarity of her kindness while I was in physical discomfort. I believe more than ever that most of the inmates' illnesses are real, not made up for attention or for drugs, and caused by a virus or bacteria, but also because of the excessive mental and physical stress. Our bodies are worn down. A depleted body is unable to combat the onslaught of germs that surround us in prison that a free person's body, with less stress, would easily ward off.

Prison administrators try to save a few dollars by sardine packing inmates into smaller and smaller spaces, but end up spending more, though not enough, on the consequences in the form of medical treatments. I understand a no-luxury system, but to maintain a system period, a few dollars spent on peace-of-mind amenities or preventive health care would save the taxpayer untold millions of dollars and help to sustain this growing monster.

Psalm 107:20-21. *He sent forth his word and healed them; He rescued them from the grave. Let them give thanks to the Lord for His unfailing love and His wonderful deeds for men.*

✝ ✝ ✝

Wednesday, February 23, 1994
1:30 a.m.

I was awakened by the same 1st watch officer who previously tried to write me up. It seemed I had forgotten to place a stamp on a piece of outgoing mail and he wanted to bring this to my attention so that my letter would not be delayed. I appreciated this unnecessary act of kindness and graciously thanked him as I placed a stamp on it.

Yes, I can let bygones be gone.

5:10 a.m.

A dream of unquenchable fire and I with an inadequate fire hose. No longer are my dreams a sanctuary from the tormenting beast that is the Department of Corrections. I was trapped in a room without doors, fighting a blaze with every ounce of subconscious imagination. I rallied my make-believe fire engine company, which resembled law books, to have courage even as they were consumed. Then, from within the raging fire came my worst childhood fear.

Wasps.

Not small swat-able ones, but car-size, mechanical, killer wasps that multiplied exponentially. Seething with an evil buzz that changed into the laughter of the district attorney who prosecuted me, they advanced to overwhelm me, stinging me until I awakened drenched in sweat.

I hate my life.

It is the beginning of another day and I am already emotionally defeated. I know God is always around to help, but I am too beaten down to look.

Chocolate pudding washed over me.

4:00 p.m.

Mail. It was a letter from the Screenwriting Academy Foundation with script submission instructions that I had requested. If I finish *DREAMTIME* by the cutoff date of May 1st. I will send it. If not, I'll ask my father to mail *Pacific Moon.*

Isaiah 59:1. *Surely the arm of the Lord is not too short to save, nor His ear to dull to hear.*

✝ ✝ ✝

Thursday, February 24, 1994
3:00 p.m.

My fingertips hurt from too much typing. My ears hurt from too many people asking stupid questions, and because I was still ill, it seemed as if everyone was pushing my impatient button causing my normally pleasant demeanor to bend close to the breaking point. I always try to help others, but many do not know when to stop pursuing my kindness.

To celebrate surviving my work day, I climbed up onto my squeaky bunk and allowed my plastic pillow to woo me into a needed nap. Ah…

4:00 p.m.

"Watson, what's your number?" the mail officer asked as he startled me out of a thankfully, dreamless sleep.

"Huh? Mail? Oh, D-67547." I stammered.

It was a letter from Mickie's parents. They included photographs of their post-earthquake home in Northridge. Wow. Words are wholly inadequate to describe the damage a fallen brick chimney can do to a home. The roof had an unintended skylight; living room furniture pulverized; knick-knacks and items of a family's life strewn about and covered with dust and pink ceiling insulation.

Again, I thanked God that no one was injured. In their letter they thanked me for putting them in touch with a good contractor through my father.

I sat back and thought with a small smile on my face; it may have been a small thing but I was able to help. It felt good to contribute as it had been so very long since I made a difference...a positive one anyway.

Hebrews 6:10. *God is not unjust; He will not forget your work and the love you have shown Him as you have helped His people and continue to help them.*

✞ ✞ ✞

Friday, February 25, 1994
4:15 p.m.

I missed the gym's unlock because I had to finish typing a report at work, so I had to remain outside until 4:00 p.m. To pass the time I walked around the track with Coleman. He has been *down* for 13 years on a seven years to life sentence. Coleman would have been paroled six years ago if the parole board had been following the law that mandates the parole commissioners to "shall parole" the inmate, instead of the whims of the political powers, or the emotions of those who demand revenge for wrongdoings. It is a scary thing for an inmate seeking parole when two of the three *impartial* parole commissioners who sit in judgment were specifically appointed by the governor because they, or a family member, have been a victim of crime. And, the third commissioner is usually ex-law enforcement. Talk about a stacked deck. With this kind of impartiality, it is not surprising that Coleman, a model prisoner with many opportunities waiting for him on the street, is still incarcerated.

The real tragedy is that society, the taxpayers, becomes victims again by having to support through their tax dollars Coleman's cost of continued incarceration, including increased medical expenses as he ages.

On a semi up-note, during our stroll, Coleman shared information to research in the library concerning what could be the illegal administration of my sentence. It's another possible angle to look into.

Every stone must be turned.

Romans 16:20. *The God of peace will soon crush Satan under your feet. The grace of our Lord Jesus be with you*
.

✟ ✟ ✟

Saturday, February 26, 1994
7:30 a.m.

Shots fired! Over a fist fight? Watch out. The officer in the gun tower has an itchy trigger finger. I would never want to be in a position to be shot because those spinning 9mm bullets are designed for maximum tissue damage. I was glad I was at work and not on the yard. It can be a dangerous place, and the danger can come from many directions. Fortunately for the two Hispanic combatants, the officer only fired a warning shot into the ground.

Following the rules does have its advantages—safety.

8:00 p.m.

Scabby-gay Scott was moved into the gym today. Knowing I work in the Program Office, Scott came by my bunk inquiring into the personal traits of Lieutenant Davenport. Scott wanted a psychological edge because he has to appear before the lieutenant for the disciplinary hearing from a write-up he received while in level I.

I blew my top, giving, what a military person would call, "a proper dressing down." This was the second time Scott had tried to obtain information from me. If I knew anything and passed it along, I would lose my job and go to the hole. Scott was a manipulator, attempting by batting his eye lashes to appear naive, but all told, a very dangerous, loose-lipped man. He tried to compliment me, but I told him to take his deceptive act down the road. I refused to be woven into his destructive web.

I was once the naive one who dangled from the puppeteer's strings; that puppeteer's name was Financial Temptation. My eyes have been opened by the Lord so that I can see the true face behind the smiling mask.

Matthew 4:10. *Jesus said to him.   "Away from him, Satan! For it is written: Worship the Lord your God, and serve Him only."*

✞ ✞ ✞

Sunday, February 27, 1994
10:00 a.m.

The sun was shining brightly and the volleyball court was dry. It was volleyball time. Besides the camaraderie, the vigorous exercise frees me from any inner demons that I may have picked up during the week from other staff or inmates. Whether spiritual demons or common ones such as frustration, anger, or hate, smacking the volleyball as hard as I can while giving a war cry that would make any Native American proud, sends those demons flying. And, if I have hit the ball just right, besides the emotional cleansing, I score a point.

Exercise and exercising, is a win-win scenario for me.

3:00 p.m.

Pooped and tuckered out. Five hours of volleyball with good friends, Christian friends, and very few arguments. Christ's Spirit filled us. I also believe I may have even bronzed my pale winter skin. And to top it all off, my stomach was filled by two humongous and delicious homemade burritos courtesy of *Bull.* I was ready for a nap. I felt content, relaxed, and at peace. It was a moral imperative that I remember this feeling...remember this feeling...remember this feeling...zzzz...

11:00 p.m.

The Olympics in Norway are over. If it were not for the stupidity and cruelty of the pipe-wielding attack on Nancy Kerrigan in the attempt to take her out of the ice skating competition, the events would have been a serene success. I saw another person trying a short cut that led to oblivion. Short cuts are never worth it, Tonya Harding.

Watching the athletes striving to attain greatness was inspiring, but I do not want to live vicariously through others. I must succeed in my own right beyond the boundaries of these walls. God instills greatness in all of us and I need to tap into His blessings. The decision to strive for greatness will be difficult and fraught with rejection after rejection, but I have to try.

Psalm 37:4-6. *Delight yourself in the Lord and He will give you the desire of your heart, commit your way to the Lord; trust in Him and He will do this: He will make your righteousness shine like the dawn, the justice of your causes like the noonday sun.*

✟ ✟ ✟

Monday, February 28, 1994
6:00 p.m.

I was dining with the rough and tumble crew tonight. The long beards, head to toe tattoos, and missing teeth were evidence of fights won and lost. Unexpectedly, this conversation was of concern for one of the men's aging father who drinks too much, and how abuses of any vice eventually catch up to a man.

To look at these men, my first impression would be there was not a caring bone in their bodies, but I have been fortunate to see many different sides to many of society's outcasts, the strange and bizarre men who are imprisoned here. At moments such as that, I envy God's ability to see past the outer skin to a man's heart and true nature. I wished all of us were blessed with more of that ability, or at least possessing the patience to allow the first impression, which could be wrong, to pass.

4:00 p.m.

Mail. From Australia. It was the cassette tape and a book from the museum in Sydney that my father ordered for me. Receiving them in the regular mail was both a mistake and a blessing because these types of items are supposed to be sent to R&R, not the mail room. After examining this package the R&R officer would state, "Not from an approved vendor. Denied."

I prayed this kindness by the mail room staff would not go unrewarded.

9:00 p.m.

I spent the last two hours sitting on a yard bench listening to Australian Aboriginal music on my cassette player, watching the stars blink in the night sky, and fighting the futility blues. I understood why suicide looked like an easy way out of this mess called prison. Men walked in circles around a track going nowhere; Kimble danced on the pitcher's mound attempting to placate the death song spirits in his head; and a football game, where the players moved up and down the field with no apparent winner. It all seemed so futile.

Then, Charles Watson walked up, sat down, and asked, "How ya doing?" I told him the truth. "Not so good." With the momentary high of receiving something great in the mail comes the emotional crash. As I explained what I was going through, I felt utterly foolish to complain to a man who has done three times the amount of time in prison than I had, and who seemed to have all of society against him—a real pariah.

Looking at Charles and all he was up against put my feelings of despair in perspective. God sent the right man at the right time. If Charles could smile under the weight of his burden, then surely I could, too.

Psalm 30:5. *For His anger lasts only a moment, but His favor lasts a lifetime; weeping may remain for a night, but rejoicing comes in the morning.*

✝ ✝ ✝

Tuesday, March 1, 1994
3:00 p.m.

A potentially huge setback in my ability to move about within my limited space. My custody level is Medium A which means I am allowed to be out of the gym from 6:00 a.m. to 9:00 p.m. Custody levels range from Maximum A, which is the strictest down to Minimum B, the least restrictive. These are determined by how long an inmate was sentenced to, how much time he has already completed, and if he had ever escaped from jail or prison. My level, Medium A is two steps above Minimum, and the lowest a lifer can achieve.

Achieving this level allows me the luxury of movement, except for count time, between 6:00 a.m. and 9:00 p.m. In response to an inmate who escaped from a prison in southern California, our warden is proposing that all lifers be placed on Close B custody. This is a stricter level, which on the upside, would require that I be moved out of the gym and placed back in a cell where I would have a small measure of peace and quiet. The downside, I would only be allowed out of the housing unit from 6:00 a.m. to 4:00 p.m. and have to return, at noon every day to be counted. I would be restricted from evening library, showers, and telephone usage and my exercise time would be severely curtailed.

Have I done anything to warrant this new proposed restriction? No. I am a "model prisoner." Unfortunately, once a person is convicted of a crime, they join the collective of being subject to knee-jerk reactions. I am sick and tired of being lumped as a group and not treated as an individual. What is prison supposed to teach us? That if we follow the rules we will have the opportunity to be productive and prosper, or if one has made a mistake, that the rest of our life is doomed to suffer arbitrary and capricious setbacks?

I know God will help me to rise above this additional and unwarranted punishment if it occurs. I fear that many inmates who do not have the Lord in their lives will wrap another layer of hatred around their hearts, later to be unfurled on a society that claims innocence because it chose to shut its eyes when a salvageable misfit was turned into a monster.

10:00 p.m.

Ancient prophesies. A *NOVA* special. Prognostications of the end of time. Armageddon, cataclysmic world reformations scheduled for the late 1990's and early 21st century. These revelations are scary but looked to with anticipation. Heck, if the world did come to an end as some predict, I will only have to spend six more years in prison. I will then be with God and all my questions answered, such as: was free will such a good thing?

Though I believe in Jesus' teachings, there are many times each day that I do not feel worthy to be in God's presence. Thankfully, Jesus took care of that with the shedding of His blood. I have only my faith to hang on to and that is enough.

Romans 1:17. *For in the gospel righteousness from God is revealed, a righteousness that is by faith from first to last, just as it is written: "The righteous will live by faith."*

✝ ✝ ✝

Wednesday, March 2, 1994
9:00 a.m.

Killing the rumor. Relief washed over me. I spoke with the program administrator and he explained that the new Close B custody proposal would be for inmates serving sentences of life without the possibility of parole. Also, that lifers now living in the gym would be moved out 'relatively soon' and placed back into cells. And, during *acute fog* (pea soup) conditions, no lifers would be allowed outside.

This, if it came to pass, I could handle. So life as I currently know it would go on, and for now, it seemed as if wisdom had prevailed.

Shocking. Prison and wisdom are words rarely uttered together.

8:00 p.m.

I spoke with my father on the telephone. He mailed more of my legal transcripts to me, was tracking down other court papers that we had misplaced, sent another one of my screenplays to an inquirer, and was re-doing my introduction letter to agents.

Thank you God for good ol' dad. Thank you. Thank you. Thank you.

Acts 16:23, 25. *After they had been severely flogged, they were thrown into prison, and the jailer was commanded to guard them carefully. About midnight Paul and Silas were praying and singing hymns to God, and the other prisoners were listening to them.*

✝ ✝ ✝

Thursday, March 3, 1994
8:00 p.m.

In the four years that I have resided at the Creek, I have noticed that many of the inmates who have been incarcerated longer than myself and who are older, come to me for counsel, or include me in their circle to disseminate truthful information. I feel honored that these men trust my judgment. I believe this is a positive reflection of my character. It is a strange thing to learn about trust, honor, and honesty in a prison setting. However, if one thought about it for a moment, these are the only possessions that staff, rules, regulations, or laws enacted by politicians, cannot take from us. Consequently, if trust were ever broken, if I were to lie, it is unlikely that I would ever be given a second chance.

Thank you for the lessons in character, Lord.

Psalm 9:9-10. *The Lord is a refuge for the oppressed, a stronghold in times of trouble. Those who know of your name will trust in you, for you, Lord, have never forsaken those who seek you.*

✟ ✟ ✟

Friday, March 4, 1994
6:30 a.m.

Nevel informed me that he will be transferring next week. This means he will be vacating the lower bunk and I will move down to the bottom bunk. Time to celebrate. Sort of. The next inmate on the seniority list to move to the wall bunk, which will be above me when I move down, is Robert. He and I do not get along. Actually, we are not on speaking terms as he has lied to me several times.

I asked the sergeant if Brian could move over me. Robert could move into Brian's vacated bunk which is also a wall bunk. The sergeant said, "No problem, just check it with Officer Jones." That could be a problem. Officer Jones is a black female whose words are all sugar and spice but her actions are very racist. To be specific, white inmates have nothing coming.

Per the sergeant, I politely asked Officer Jones and she said, "No." I was not too upset because that is exactly what I had expected from her. Even so, it is very difficult to respect someone who denies a reasonable, pre-approved request, simply because she can. I accepted this as a test. I smiled, turned and walked away. I wanted today to be a good day and was determined not to let her ruin it for me so early in the morning.

Regarding Nevel and my gentle attempt to open his eyes to the wonder of racial diversity...baby steps. Since moving above him I have steered conversations to achievements of blacks in America, inventions or discoveries that have enriched the world, and items that Nevel could personally relate to.

When Nevel's daughter was young, she needed a blood transfusion during a surgery. The process of blood plasma storage (blood banks) was perfected by a black doctor named Charles R. Drew. Nevel has a sweet tooth second to none. It was a black man, Norbert Rillieux, who revolutionized the sugar-refining industry with his invention of a vacuum pan evaporator. Nevel told me his best memories are as a young boy on his grandparents' farm in Georgia. It was a black man, George Washington Carver, who transformed the agricultural economy of the South through his research of the peanut, land rejuvenation, and education of the Southern farmer.

Nevel admitted, "I guess they're not all bad."

It is a hopeful start.

Hebrews 10:35-36. *So do not throw away your confidence; it will be richly rewarded. You need to persevere so that when you have done the will of God, you will receive what He has promised.*

✧ ✧ ✧

Saturday, March 5, 1994
2:00 p.m.

The truth is simple. Stress kills. However, the cure is simple. Exercise. After four hours of vigorous volleyball I was ready to celebrate with a victory siesta. My team did not win all the games, but because I kicked stress' a--, mentally I am a champion.

5:30 p.m.

"I smell tobacco smoke. The televisions will be turned off," announced Officer Bartels. The inmates' response was quick: shouts mixed with obscenities, pounding and kicking on lockers, unrest and anger. Twelve additional staff were summoned. The uproar continued. Would there be violence? The sergeant arrived to discuss the situation with the inmates, reiterating the no smoking rule in the gym. The sergeant did listen to several of the more composed inmates, and, as no one was actually seen or caught smoking, the televisions would be turned back on at 9:00 p.m.
One strutting and stupid inmate bumped against an officer as the officer turned to walk away. The inmate was quickly handcuffed and taken to the hole. The tension decreased as both sides made their point—détente.

10:00 p.m.

Officers Bartels and Wynon end their shift and exit the gym to the cheers, jeers, and raucous applause of the inmates. Bartels re-enters, bows, and then exits again.
I decided that both inmates and staff are immature at times.

Jude 24-25. *To him who is able to keep you from falling and to present you before His glorious presence without fault and with great joy to the only God our Savior be glory, majesty, power and authority, through Jesus Christ our Lord, before all ages, now and forevermore! Amen.*

✟ ✟ ✟

Sunday, March 6, 1994
6:00 p.m.

Dinner was delayed an hour due to the control officer/gunman in building 10 leaving his post and locking himself out of the secure area. The facility has to be locked down, securing all inmates either in their cells or in the gym, while staff used ladders to climb onto the roof of building 10 and break through the roof/control hatch to gain access into the control booth. It was entertaining watching the proceedings through the narrow slit of a window in the gym's door. However, I am sure that particular officer who was responsible was not enjoying it, but it does show that everyone, even officers, are human and makes mistakes.

Everyone, regardless of his profession or position in life makes mistakes that affect others. I believe, as Jesus teaches, that we should all be forgiven and offered an opportunity to prove ourselves worthy.

Hopefully that officer's reprimand would not be too severe.

1 Peter 1:24-25. *For, "All men are like grass, and all their glory is like the flowers of the field, the grass withers and the flowers fall, but the word of the Lord stands forever."*

✟ ✟ ✟

Monday, March 7, 1994
10:00 a.m.

With fanfare, bells, and whistles, Governor Pete Wilson signed the Three Strikes & You're Out bill into law. Times they will be changing. Unfortunately, in all reality, your basic criminal who is on the street rarely stays current with politics or watches the nightly news. Those in the know would be the inmates now in prison. Some of their responses to this signing were not encouraging.

"They will have to kill me before I do life."

"I will have to kill the witnesses."

"The first cop that pulls me over will get a bullet in his head."

As I listened I prayed these were statements of bravado. However, I am fearful for our society, as these are men who have not changed their ways, and are going home soon.

It seems more appropriate that a man's sentence should be determined by the man and not the crime. Though I have been disappointed by the mistreatment of some inmates by some staff, there are many who are helpful, encouraging, and insightful. These men and women who work with inmates on a daily basis know by observation who will be the repeat offenders. It makes sense to me that these staff; the housing officers, work supervisors, chaplains and counselors, should determine when a particular inmate ought to be released. Politics should not play a role in a man's incarceration. Neither should blame be placed on any person if a good candidate for release relapses. No one is perfect. If line staff had a greater say in who goes free, I would wager there would be a reduction in recidivism.

Will the Three Strikes & You're Out law work? Will the courts be clogged to a standstill? Will the taxpayer sink under the weight of prison costs? Only time will tell. It always does.

8:15 p.m.

One shot and he was dead. Two inmates, one named Mark Adams, were involved in a fist fight. Staff ordered them to stop but they continued. A warning shot was fired. They continued fighting. A second shot rang out and Mark Adams lie dead.

It is true that Mark Adams was a convicted murderer who had embarrassed the Department of Corrections by a past escape, but should his punishment be death? An insightful person once said, "The death of one diminishes us all."

What potential was snuffed out? We will never know.

I am deeply saddened for Mark's family, for the officer who has to live with the knowledge that he, too, is a killer, and for the other inmate involved in the fight, for he will be charged with Mark's murder. This is the law. Justice is demanded. There should only be sadness.

I wondered how the family of Mark's victim will feel after learning of Mark's demise. An eye for an eye?

I cannot praise the Lord enough for my safety.

Revelation 21:4. *He will wipe every tear from their eyes. There will be no more deaths or mourning or crying or pain, for the old order of things has passed away.*

✞ ✞ ✞

Tuesday, March 8, 1994
8:00 p.m.

In general, today was a good day. My spirits were balanced. I am healthy, regaining my strength, and I was able to speak with my father on the telephone. It has been several weeks since my mental outlook edged to the positive side. For people who have not spent time in prison, they need to understand that even the air is heavy. With each deep breath of sorrow for my victims, my family, and my friends, my lungs are filled with a great weight that burdens my heart. To live any length of time under these mental and physical conditions, to survive is a constant battle.

I need to savor this feeling of contentment as it is rare. If I only had more faith, I believe this inner peace would last longer.

"As small as a mustard seed," Jesus said.

I am able to hold on to the good feelings, clinging to my faith for a while, for several hours, and maybe even a day, but then it will eventually slip away and down I tumble into the waiting vat of pudding. However, for the moment I taste and enjoy this sweet happiness of success. My success is staying alive and continuing to fight this emotional battle.

I also acknowledge that with every battle there will be moments of rest that I attribute to Jesus' love for me, His manning the rampart in my place. I am smiling, thanking Him for always standing strong to beat back that which afflicts me, allowing me to regain my strength and have a good day.

Ephesians 4:14-15. *Then we will no longer be infants, tossed back and forth by the waves, and blown there by every wind of teaching and the cunning and craftiness of men in their deceitful scheming.*

✞ ✞ ✞

Wednesday, March 9, 1994
5:00 a.m.

Nevel, my bunkie, transferred this morning. Believe it or not I will miss him. There will be a void in the gym as he was a character of unusual traits. Despicable in his racial outlook, yet honorable in his word and deed. Grotesque in vocabulary, yet always willing to help a friend. I do not know how much my attempt to be an example as a Christian made an influence in his attitude toward others, but hopefully God planted a seed through my non-racist attitude. I wished Nevel the very best.

11:20 a.m.

I returned to the gym. Having been re-assigned to the lower bunk, I needed to move my bedding and property. Ah... Now I can get comfortable...relatively speaking. Suddenly it dawned on me that I am assigned to the bunk I first wanted when I scanned the possible sleeping sites in the gym. This bunk is at the end of the row, next to an emergency exit door. This meant I only had bunks to one side, a little more room. This bunk, against the back wall also butted up to an intake vent that provides me with more fresh air—a precious commodity.

Applying patience and daily prayer paid off. It took four months for the Lord to provide my request. This seems to be another lesson of proof that God wants me to be happy even in the little things. I only had to allow Him time to work. One could say it's a miracle as there are 159 other bunks that I could have been assigned to.

God is amazing.

Isaiah 30:21-22. *Whether you turn to the right or to the left, saying, "This is the way; walk in it." Then you will defile your idols overlaid with silver and you images covered with gold; you will throw them away like a menstrual cloth and say to them, "Away with you!"*

✝ ✝ ✝

Thursday, March, 10, 1994
8:00 p.m.

The visiting room was exceptionally crowded tonight, but after an hour sitting in chairs against the wall, my mother and I were seated at a table. Next visit I will have to tip the escorting officer more Top Ramen soups. Ha ha. As always, the vending machine food was delicious (compared to chow hall food) and the conversation was light and cheerful. My mother was fully recovered from her illness and looked great. I receive a rush of euphoria during and after each visit. Talking with my mother, or anyone for that matter, who has a real life in the world is like watching color television for the first time. Even though I have seen the real world, after almost seven years of incarceration, I begin to doubt my past experiences. Talking with, being seated next to a free person, and watching her expressions, her animation as she talked of what she had been doing, is like seeing it, hearing it, fresh for the first time.

When my mother moves to Texas there will be far less color brought to my black and white memories of the world.

9:30 p.m.

Back in the gym after the visit, I had a warm smile for everyone I passed. Heck, I know most of them. It is a strange comfort to be able to walk among these *supposed-to-be, once-were,* and *could-be-if-provoked,* dangerous men, and to know they are pleased to see me and happy for me that I had a good visit. Knowing this, I only wanted God's light, love, and glory to be seen coming from me.

9:45 p.m.

There was an emergency cell extraction in building 7. A cell extraction is an 'event' of military precision and over-whelming force. Officers, five to ten, including sergeants and a lieutenant to supervise, 'suit-up' in gladiator apparel: helmets, face shields, pads, gloves, and a plexi-glass shield, some of which are electrified. Staff then orders the non-compliant inmate to exit his cell. If he refuses, staff rushes in to pinion the ill-mannered inmate to the floor or bunk so as to subdue and remove him. In this instance, the offending inmate, Kyle Hazewood, had slipped too far from our reality, believing that the shower water contained acid and therefore he had refused to shower, proclaiming that no one could make him.

Never challenge staff.

The officers had to fight to subdue, and then hog tie Kyle to a stretcher to remove him from his cell. Was he taken to the hole or to the infirmary for psychiatric evaluation?

Thank you, Ronald Reagan for closing many of the psychiatric institutions in California. Kyle never should have been placed in a prison regardless of his crime. He should be a patient in a mental health hospital. Care, concern, and medication are what Kyle needed, not clubs, plastic shields, and shackles.

10:45 p.m.

I fell into a contented sleep while watching a PBS special presentation of The Moody Blues. The group was giving a concert at Red Rock stadium. Their hypnotic music was being accompanied by the Colorado symphony and transmitted in stereo. I was at peace. God had been very, very good to me today.

I wish everyone a good night.

Psalm 42:8. *By day the Lord directs His love, at night His song is with me, a prayer to the God of my life.*

✞ ✞ ✞

Friday, March 11, 1994
1:00 p.m.

The warden walked through our facility today. She claims to be pro-program to help inmates rehabilitate, but I have not seen any evidence to support this fact. Although, in the warden's defense, I am not incarcerated in the Department of Rehabilitations. The warden did; however, give us Christmas trees for the holidays. Pretty stupid idea if you ask me. How about expanded library hours or return of the college courses? Those were two positive programs in need of improvement. I wanted to ask the warden some questions, but would never have been able to get through her security entourage.

8:30 p.m.

The inmates who did the tattooing in the gym were caught. Their lockers were *tossed* (searched) and their property, whether legal or illegal to possess was confiscated for punitive purposes. These inmates were so blatant about their activities, and with all the snitches looking for someone to tell on, it was amazing they were able to continue for as long as they did.

9:15 p.m.

The tattooists are back in business. Apparently it is difficult to stop creative expressionism.

Romans 6:12-13. *Therefore do not let sin reign in your mortal body so that you obey its evil desires. Do not offer the parts of your body to sin, as instruments of wickedness, but rather offer yourselves to God, as those who have been brought from death to life; and offer the parts of your body to Him as instruments of righteousness.*

✞ ✞ ✞

Saturday, March 12, 1994
2:00 p.m.

A new upper bunkie is moving in, making his bed and stowing his personal items in his locker, and it's not Robert. Robert declined his turn at a wall bunk. This was probably a wise decision as our close proximity would be uncomfortable for both of us. My new bunkie goes by the name of *Wolf.* He, like me, is a lifer, but unlike me he is only 5'9" tall and covered head to toe, including his face, with tattoos. As opposed to looking like a flesh-artist's canvas, *Wolf* appeared to be the victim of a drive-by tagger. I was only guessing of course, but I would say *Wolf* received his nickname because of his long shaggy mane and frilly beard, because it certainly is not derived from his personality.

I have known *Wolf* for about six months and he has always been a quiet person, courteous, minds his own business and reads Louis L'Amour westerns. Hey, a man who reads about cowboys who save damsels in distress has to have some good qualities.

8:30 p.m.

After a sun filled day of vigorous volleyball and an uplifting Bible fellowship, I was relaxing on my bunk being caressed by the warm tingles of a new tan. To take me away from my surroundings I listened to Phil Collins sing a ballad on my radio while I read my *Islands* magazine. I gently eased into remembrances of surfing perfect left to right overhead waves at San Miguel beach in Mexico. I closed my eyes to concentrate, to summon up the color of life, and I was pleased to find I could, after all these years, smell the ocean's salty air. And, yes, Angela was there, right beside me on my spare surfboard. Her root beer brown eyes were wide with excitement as we paddled to catch the approaching swell.

Concentrate, concentrate, ah... there, I could remember Angela's gentle kiss on my wet salty lips as we returned from the sea to relax on the warm sandy beach. I was her Salty Dog,

I hoped I would not start to cry.

Hebrew 13:5. *Keep your lives free from the love of money and be content with what you have, because God has said, "Never will I leave you; never will I forsake you."*

✞ ✞ ✞

Sunday, March 13, 1994
9:00 a.m.

Vanity, thy name is sunscreen. It is 80 degrees of bright sunshine outside and this face needs all the help it can get. I was the kind of guy who relied more on my personality than *GQ* looks to attract the ladies. I certainly am not ugly by any definition, but Brad Pitt doesn't have to worry about me stealing his girl. And as I look forward to the day when a lovely-intelligent lady caresses my face, I don't want it be covered with vinyl record grooves. Wow! That's dating myself. So a dab of sunscreen will do me and keep me safe from the ravages of the sun's rays.

2:00 p.m.

Interesting volleyball with unique cheerleaders. The games were vigorous two-on-two, skilled, exciting, sweaty, and provided a forum for escapism as my mind kept flashing to Redondo Beach in Southern California with the many ultra-attractive, bikini-clad ladies shouting encouragement with each accomplished spike of the ball.

Unlike Redondo, here we had four of the sadly confused men wearing improvised makeup, cheek-tight shorts, and twisted up tee-shirts to expose their shaved bellies. Their high-pitched cheers were confusingly uplifting due to my female memories, but to look at them brought my daydream back to an ugly surrealism. I did not know whether I should laugh or cry so I spiked the ball instead...Point!

Psalm 107:8-9. *Let them give thanks to the Lord for His unfailing love and His wonderful deeds for men, for He satisfies the thirsty and fills the hungry with good things.*

✞ ✞ ✞

Monday, March 14, 1994
8:30 p.m.

My day went smoothly with my mental meter staying in the positive until I was called back to work to type a report regarding another who did not have a good day. A young, plump, homosexual was hit in the head with a 'sap' (a sock containing several D size batteries) as he entered his cell. He was knocked unconscious, and for an hour, until the next unlock when he was discovered by staff, he was repeatedly sodomized and forced to orally copulate seven men who lined up to take turns, all because the homosexual would not give *it* up of his own accord.

"He should thank us. He's never had so much attention," was the joke among the assailants.

I suppose one could say, "What's the big deal? He's a fag. He participates in sodomy all the time." Women also participate in intercourse, but they only become traumatized when participation is forced and violent. I do not condone the lifestyles of homosexuals, but neither can I accept the rape of anyone, male or female, nor should anyone.

Statistics validate the fact that there are more rapes per capita in prisons each day than in a whole month in free society. Why are these screams not heard? Are they absorbed by the thick concrete walls or discounted by society's belief that criminals deserve what they get?

I thank God for my safety.

Colossians 3:2, 5. *Set your mind on things above, not on earthly things. Put to death, therefore, whatever belongs to your earthly nature; sexual immorality, impurity, lust, evil desires and greed, which is idolatry, because of these, the wrath of God is coming.*

✝ ✝ ✝

Tuesday, March 15, 1994
11:00 a.m.

An impatient crush of blue-clothed men waited in bunched lines for their monthly supply of goodies. Dozens of inmates were standing in front of the canteen to purchase food and sundry items.

Each inmate eyed the other, daring the other to cut in line to find out the consequences of such foolishness and disrespect. Then, as if witness to a snowman in hell, the jostling crowd of men turned in unison as two muscular black inmates carried a white inmate in their arms chair-style off the recreation field. The white had been injured playing football. The men in the canteen line stopped talking as they stared with mouths agape as the injured was carried toward the medical clinic.

Brotherhood was forced on the blue-clothed men with shocking reality. Kindness among the races. The three men disappeared into the clinic and with them so did the moment. Hatred and suspicion was welcomed back like an old friend or a comfortable pair of shoes. Though for a moment, the Spirit reigned among us and it was glorious.

1 John 4:10-12. *This is love: not that we loved God, but that He loved us and sent His Son as an atoning sacrifice for our sins. Dear friends, since God so loved us, we also ought to love one another. No one has ever seen God; but if we love one another, God lives in us and His love is made complete in us.*

✝ ✝ ✝

Wednesday, March 16, 1994
4:00 p.m.

The mail has been a parched stream bed. Dry. No cool words to soothe my heart's thirst. Hey out there, I am still alive! Somebody write me...please.

Craig, a defunct rock and roller, who sleeps three bunks down the row from me, offered me several addresses of women who had advertised in a sex catalog, seeking *friendship*. I declined. Yes. I am lonely, but that is not the kind of friendship that I am looking for. I trust in God to provide me with a special lady; one of grace, Christian values, brains and beauty. My request for a special relationship will probably take God time to fill, requiring a lot of patience on my part. I reflected that I have plenty of the former (time), and I am working on the latter (patience).

6:00 p.m.

The inmates in the chow line were jockeying for position so they did not have to sit at the same table with Scabby-gay Scott. Sore-picking, feces-eating Scott; he is a disgusting sight. I am grateful to my parents for teaching me manners, and I thank God for protecting me from Satan's curses of grotesque fetishes.

I do pray for Scott as being afflicted as he is causes him to be an outcast among outcasts and that has to be miserable.

9:00 p.m.

I finished watching an episode of *Beverly Hills 90210*. Okay, I admit it, I like the show. This particular episode was where the teenaged character named Brenda goes to jail for burglary. Well, in the end, as always in television land, everything worked out. It was the pat happy ending.

"One day in jail and all I wanted was to go home," was Brenda's end of episode revelation through tear-filled eyes.

Reality is a bitch because I can't write myself out of this mess I created. My reality is here every single dreaded day.

"All I want is to go home, too," I sighed. One of my greatest fears is that by the time I am released there will no longer be a home to go to.

Revelation 3:20-21. *"Here I am! I stand at the door and knock. If anyone hears my voice and opens the door, I will come in and eat with him, and he with me. To him who overcomes, I will give the right to sit with me on my throne, just as I overcame and sat down with my Father on His throne."*

✢   ✢   ✢

Thursday, March 17, 1994
8:00 a.m.

The weight pile, approximately the size of two basketball courts set side by side, the surface of which is gravel, where the benches, dips, and pull-up bars are cemented into the ground, and the weights are made of pig iron, is scheduled to re-open today after nine months of closure. There are new rules and procedures posted in each housing unit that have to be followed if an inmate wants to use the *pile,* including taking a safety test.

Forgive me if I am pessimistic at the pile remaining open for very long. Someone will get into a fight over whose bench or weight is whose, which then causes staff to close it. The frustrating thing is that the combatants usually are not working out but only hanging around and reserving an area or waiting for their friends who may or may not show up. My hopeful side would like to see the pile remain open because lifting weights, like rigorous volleyball, reduces stress, which in turn lowers overall violence. I will keep my fingers crossed.

12:00 Noon

During a break in my work I went to the canteen to pick up food and sundry items as I have been doing off and on or the last four years. When I returned to the office, the relief lieutenant called the three of us clerks into her office to chastise me, and to warn others against going to the canteen during our work hours. I was a bit; let me find the right word… miffed. Yes, I was miffed, especially since we had had prior approval by Donna. Besides, we clerks work hard and do a good job. This had allowed us in the past to have a few measly perks, one of which was not having to stand for hours in the canteen line, but to go during work hours. It only takes a few minutes to pick up our groceries because we give our order forms to the canteen supervisor and she has it ready at break time.

It's difficult to constantly adapt to the changing whims of each supervisor who happens to pass through on random duty, but we clerks smiled politely and nodded like bobble heads in understanding as we left her office, knowing that this restriction would pass with the end of the lieutenant's shift.

3:45 p.m.

Yo, Adrian! I was pumped up. I finished my first weightlifting workout in many months. I conceded that I approved of the new set up and the new rules. What I did not like was the removal of the hand held dumbbells because I could better isolate muscle groups with them as opposed to the long bars. Staff view dumbbells as potential weapons and history has proven their belief to be fact. Safety and security first. I hope my muscles will not be too sore tomorrow.

4:00 p.m.

Mail. The drought is over. I received letters from my mother, Madeline, and American Express. It seems that American Express has chosen me to apply for their preferred card because, in their wise eyes, I am special and have a financially secure future. I appreciate a good joke. In all fairness, American Express got it half right. My future will be secure, secure behind concrete and steel.

The letters from my mother and Madeline were uplifting and put a smile on my face as they shared their daily triumphs and defeats while attempting to act as Christ would want them to. My mother is of course prejudiced in my favor in her unwavering words of support, and even though Madeline has only known me through our correspondence, she has welcomed me into her life with Christian fellowship. Her generosity of spirit is overwhelming and her scriptural insight is inspiring.

The longer I am surrounded by negative poor-me people, the more I cherish positive I-can overcome attitudes. My outlook on life is greatly influenced by the type of people I associate with. As I look back and evaluate the people I associated with prior to prison, I can clearly see how our poor choices were encouraged by our flawed characters.

Associations matter. I need to always ask, "Would Jesus approve of this person in my life?"

Colossians 3:22-24. *Slaves, obey your earthly masters in everything; and do it, not only when their eye is on you and to win favor, but with sincerity of heart and reverence for the Lord. Whatever you do, work at it with all your heart, as working for the Lord, not for me, since you know that you will receive an inheritance from the Lord as a reward. It is the Lord Christ you are serving.*

✝ ✝ ✝

Friday, March 18, 1994
2:00 p.m.

Mr. Lloyd, the head man in charge of all the counselors is changing positions. He will no longer work on this facility but on Facility C. Working with him has been a great experience these past four years. His kindness and sharp wit has made my work assignment more than tolerable because he treated me and the other inmate clerks as humans. I will sorely miss him.

Staff threw Mr. Lloyd a going away party, even though he will still be working within this prison. That is respect and appreciation for a quality individual. And, because Mr. Lloyd is a good sport, staff called "Teri" with an 'i' off the yard to serenade him. Though Teri tried to steal Michael Jackson's voice, he was teeth-gratingly tone deaf. Teri sang *Jesus Loves Me,* and though the words were touching, the pitch was unbearable. I did not know how staff was able to keep a straight face. Mr. Lloyd vowed to get even with everyone involved. The party was a success.

Neither I nor the other clerks who worked with Mr. Lloyd were invited.

4:00 p.m.

Mail. Quite some time ago I ordered three books on script writing and a copy of the screenplay *Dances with Wolves* from the Screenwriters Guild. Finally they arrived. I am hoping that I can glean some guidance and wisdom to improve my writing skills.

Psalm 32:8. *I will instruct you and teach you in the way you should go; I will counsel you and watch over you.*

✝ ✝ ✝

Saturday, March 19, 1994
3:00 p.m.

After a morning of enjoyable volleyball games, I treated the seven men in our Saturday fellowship group to a 'spread.' It consisted of burrito fixings that I purchased from the canteen: flour tortillas, instant refried beans, canned meat, jalapeño peppers, and chips. I wanted to celebrate friendship and have a good-bye party for *Bull.*

Bull received confirmation from his counselor yesterday that he will be transferring to CMC (San Luis Obispo) within the next couple of weeks.

Bull can be stubborn and thick-headed at times, but he is so in a loving, child-like way, never purposefully trying to offend. *Bull* has a hopeful innocence and a thirst for knowledge that will be missed by his many friends. I will especially miss our afternoon and evening discussions around my bunk on whatever topic drew his attention that day. *Bull* and I exchanged addresses so hopefully our friendship will continue after his departure.

The burritos were delicious.

Ephesians 2:19-20. *Consequently, you are no longer foreigners and aliens, but fellow citizens with God's people and members of God's household, built on the foundation of the apostles and prophets, with Christ Jesus himself as the chief cornerstone.*

✟ ✟ ✟

Sunday, March 20, 1994
8:00 a.m.

The commodes in the gym are in a row of eight, bolted to the floor, 12 inches apart. They were purposely placed in the open with no doors or partitions for privacy. This forbids modesty. After breakfast, there is a line waiting to be seated, cheek to cheek.

This morning a white inmate cut in front of a black inmate. Harsh words followed and shoving began but the two were separated by associates who did not, or could not be delayed in their turn at a commode by a code…bowels wait on no man and no man may move from his position on the floor during a code.

It sounds silly to fight over a toilet, but the real issue was respect, saving of face, and lastly, relieving of interior pressures, all of which are essential to prison survival.

9:00 a.m.

A memorandum was posted in the gym (and all housing units) stating that hair curlers and *du rags* (head coverings) will no longer be allowed to be worn on the recreation yard. This new prohibition is obviously directed toward the black population because they are the only inmates who wear them.

Needless to say, the blacks were upset and began shouting: "Racists!" and "This is discrimination!" I am loath to say it, but for many African American inmates, who in their life felt disenfranchised, those were their rallying calls, and because it is rarely true, I am tired of hearing it.

Staff's intention is directed at gang members identifying themselves by their headgear, and staff is attempting to prevent intimidation.

Unfortunately, many inmates refuse to see past their own little wants and desires. There is a bigger picture here, and besides, the blacks can still wear their curlers and *du rags* in the housing units.

Psalm 37:8. *Refrain from anger and turn from wrath; so do not fret—it leads only to evil.*

☩ ☩ ☩

Monday, March 21, 1994
1:00 p.m.

A scheduled power outage for 1:00 p.m. allowed my co-worker Frank, and I to leave work early—no power, no typing. We decided to take advantage of the weight pile because without power to the buildings, there would be no unlocks. We were stuck outside on a clear, blue sky spring day.

The benches, dip and pull up bars are color coded, with each race having their own exercise area. This posed a dilemma and an opportunity. It was a dilemma because I am white and Frank is black. Where would we work out? It was an opportunity because we were examples of what should be, not what was expected of inmates simply because they are in prison.

Frank and I chose a bench and began pumping iron to the disapproving stares of many. No one said a thing. Maybe the displeased observers remained silent because both Frank and I are quite muscular, though strength in prison rarely deters an attack. Hopefully it was because they saw in us an inner strength, two people doing what they wanted to regardless of peer pressure.

I felt blessed that God had given me the inner strength to do what was right, not what was the 'thing' to do because others were doing it. Our workout was strenuous and the conversation between sets was enjoyable. Hopefully, Frank and I will have this opportunity again in the future.

True strength comes from within and from breaking rules that should not exist.

1 John 2:6. *Whoever claims to live in Him must walk as Jesus did.*

☩ ☩ ☩

Tuesday, March 22, 1994
9:45 a.m.

I processed an Incident Report on a victim of a sap attack. Kevin took seven stitches to the head. He is a short-timer, with only two and a half months until parole, and from all reports, both staff and inmates, Kevin was minding his own business.

So why was he attacked? It was a case of a *51-50* going berserk and lashing out at the first person he came in contact with. That unlucky person was Kevin.

A 51-50 is a mentally disturbed person, and by his accounts, Kevin did not 'look' right as he sat across the breakfast table from him. So after chow the 51-50 returned to his cell, prepared his sap. Then as the cell doors re-opened for yard, the 51-50 raced down the tier to greet Kevin as he exited his cell, SAP.

It was frightening how much blood gushes from a head wound.

Violent incidents such as this, random in their nature, vividly show me the hand of protection that God has placed over me. I praise Him constantly, but it really is never enough. For me, to feel confident in my safety is a blessing that brings me peace of mind beyond compare. Not too many people can say that.

Not enough people know Christ.

2 Thessalonians 3:3. *But the Lord is faithful, and He will strengthen and protect you from the evil one.*

☩ ☩ ☩

Wednesday, March 23, 1994
11:00 a.m.

I walked into Donna's office to do something. What, I cannot remember. We started talking but her words were lost to me because the top buttons on her blouse had come undone. The position she was seated in allowed for an unobstructed view of her ample right breast. I was startled by the sight and hoped I maintained my composure.

I quickly found a reason to leave her office.

That one brief glimpse brought back wonderful memories of a woman's supple form, which for years I have been trying to suppress. Needless to say, I have not been successful as I achingly miss the wondrous curves, the hills and valleys that make women so alluring to gaze upon.

It seems to me that because a man's gruff, testosterone-filled flesh is in such stark contrast to a woman's soft, soothing touch, filled with and exuding love, that a simple caress by a woman is a Shaman's salve for any ailment of the skin or soul. Daily, my nerves are scraped raw to rival a metal peeler on a stubborn potato. An embrace or fingernail tipped tickle from a lady has become my desire for nightly dreams until the Lord finds and delivers a real flesh and blood one. Until then I will employ that patience thing to get by.

Isaiah 40:31. *But those who hope in the Lord will renew their strength. They will soar on wings like eagles; they will run and not grow weary, they will walk and not be faint.*

✝ ✝ ✝

Thursday, March 24, 1994
8:00 p.m.

Our telephone calls to the outside world are again used to harass. Every two minutes or so a recording now comes on to announce that the caller is in a correctional institution. No duh! At the beginning of the call, when the called party picks up the telephone to accept the collect call, they are informed that the caller is in prison. Some people may at times be forgetful, but I doubt that within two minutes, my father, mother or friends began to believe that I am in the Bahamas and calling to inform them on the status of the pina coladas.

Prison officials call it security, the public's right to know. I call the first announcement understandable; the second, third, fourth, and fifth, undo harassment. Conspiratorially speaking, if prison officials discourage family ties, many inmates will not have a support base in the future. This could increase the likelihood of the parolee's return to prison, thus confirming the theory of: once a criminal, always a criminal.

I will endure, with God's grace, any and all 'security' measures prison administrators place on me. I pray that God also blesses my family and friends with the strength to overcome this added negative pressure.

Isaiah 54:13. *All your sons will be taught by the Lord, and great will be your children's peace.*

✞ ✞ ✞

Friday, March 25, 1994
2:00 p.m.

Rumors, regardless of whether they originate in prison or the free world, are wild fires. They burn hot and travel fast.

Someone started a rumor that I had either been sent to the hole or transferred. Several inmates came into the Program Office wanting to apply for my job. My friends on the yard had been in a panic trying to find out the true scoop. Fortunately, this rumor, though interesting, was not damaging to my reputation. My appearance in the doorway of the Program Office for all to see killed the rumor's falsehood.

Other rumors, allegations of drug possession or interludes with homosexuals, can be devastating. A rumor of drugs, or possession of other contraband, will cause staff to *roll-up* (place in the hole) an inmate until the investigation is completed. A rumor of homosexuality will forever mark an inmate's character.

Even if there is a suspicion of something, people should keep their mouths closed. Voicing a rumor without proof usually inflicts damage to another's character, spirit, or body, and more times than not the rumor turns out to be false.

The tongue is a powerful tool and weapon.

Proverbs 12:18. *Reckless words pierce like a sword, but the tongue of the wise brings healing.*

✞ ✞ ✞

Saturday, March 26, 1994
3:00 p.m.

I learned during afternoon fellowship that yesterday, Ron, the Vietnam veteran, received a surprise visit. Surprise visits are terrible because they usually bring bad news. This one was no different.

Ron's elderly parents came to inform him that his son had been arrested and was in county jail for causing the death of a live-in girlfriend's toddler. The facts surrounding the child's death were sketchy, but Ron said the child was acting up, and his son slapped or hit the child, causing him to fall backward hitting his head against the bricks of the fireplace hearth.

The child lapsed into a coma and then died several hours later. What a terrible turn of events for all concerned. One death, but so many victims. Ron is shattered and feels a sense of responsibility due to his being incarcerated and not being home to properly give guidance to his teenage son.

A father's guilt, so many times unwarranted, is still a tough emotion to live with.

Many prayers are needed for all concerned.

Matthew 5:4. *Blessed are those who mourn, for they will be comforted.*

✞ ✞ ✞

Sunday, March 27, 1994
ALL DAY

Code 3 alarms, again and again and again, as if they were going out of style and every staff member wanted to push their alarm button one more time. I sat on the ground more than I stood today. Several of the alarms were false, accidental bumps against a desk or chair, half a dozen were fist fights, and the one in the gym was due to what I believe was nerves and gender. Nerves, because the petite female officer who stood five feet in boots, was frightened of the giant; the six-foot four inch male inmate that she was having an argument with. And gender, because the inmate was not obeying her commands quickly enough. As a woman placed in power over men, she could not tolerate his challenging behavior, even though it never rose to the level of threatening.

If it had been a male guard verses a male inmate, they would have continued their disagreement so long as it remained verbal even if profanities were involved, until the argument was resolved. Again, there was no posturing as a prelude to violence by the inmate, but due to the female officer's basic and natural fear and her personal inability to effectively communicate with a testosterone-filled man, a complete disruption of the program (daily activity) occurred.

God has His reasons for specifying that women are not to be placed over men. Women can and should walk side by side with men when they follow God's commandments. In many instances the presence of women in a prison setting has a calming affect but at other times they can be a danger to all concerned.

If I am ever forced into a physical altercation, I want a huge, muscle-bound, male guard responding to break us up, not a petite female who stands by, pushing her alarm button, and waiting for other guards to arrive. By then I could be dead.

God is wise beyond our comprehension so why do we constantly go against His teachings? This is a hard question to answer. I know it is difficult because I am guilty of this offense.

1 Corinthians 11:3. *Now I want you to realize that the head of every man is Christ, and the head of every woman is man, the head of Christ is God.*

✟ ✟ ✟

Monday, March 28, 1994
5:00 a.m.

Bull, I will miss you. Another friend walked out the door but hopefully not out of my life. *Bull* was escorted by an officer to Receiving and Release for his journey to California Men's Colony at San Luis Obispo. Many inmates who have come from there say it is great, for a prison anyway. Inmates judge the quality of a prison based on its food, and whether there are vocational, educational, and handicraft programs. By the high recidivism rate it would appear that inmates do not care, but many do want to better themselves. They only require the opportunity.

With luck, *Bull* will meet up with Doc Mahar as that is where Doc went. As they both only have a little more than a year left on their sentences it is likely they will be housed in the same facility. I do not know what program will be available to *Bull* at CMC, but as *Bull* is not a sit around type of guy, I am confident he will find productive activities to his liking. Hopefully, CMC has a Mill & Cabinet shop. That is where *Bull* excels and it is the career path he wants to pursue after his release.

Bull has been a good Christian brother and he helped me through a tough moment when my buttons were pushed out of joint. My prayers for safety and spiritual enrichment go with him as he, too, continues to struggle daily in his walk down God's straight and narrow path.

I already know I will be depressed today as it always seems that I am being left behind. I need to remember to turn my sadness around and be happy for the experience of knowing a special man such as *Bull*.

Deuteronomy 13:4. *It is the Lord your God you must follow, and Him you must revere. Keep His commands and obey Him; serve Him and hold fast to Him.*

✝ ✝ ✝

Tuesday, March 29, 1994
11:00 a.m.

My appointment with the Sacramento Appeals Coordinator was for 9:30 a.m. but because time is not money, except for the taxpayers; he was taking his sweet time. I appealed, by way of the CDC-602 interdepartmental grievance process, the institution's closure of the state-mandated handicraft program, and the forced mailing home of my hobby supplies. I wanted the Department of Corrections to reimburse me for what I was allowed to purchase for this program. Five hundred dollars was my conservative estimate, but the Department is fighting it, and to date has spent about $600 saying, "No." Forgive me, I misspoke. The Department has spent, in man hours defending their unlawful act, $600 of taxpayers' money.

The representative was very cordial when he finally called me into his temporary office. He also agreed with everything I said. However, if the past repeats itself, as it usually does regarding inmate 602's, the coordinator will return to his plush Sacramento office and then deny my appeal.

I can peacefully accept not being able to be productive in the handicraft program, but I am irritated by the prison's flagrant violation of state law.

What I will never understand is why would a program be discontinued which costs the taxpayer very little, which the individual inmate pays to participate in, which generates revenue for the state when inmates sell an item, and occupies an inmate's time in a productive activity?

I am not smart enough to figure this out.

9:00 p.m.

Ferris Bueller (in the movie *Ferris Bueller's Day Off)* told me to, "Go home already." I wish I could. What a free spirit. You had to admire Ferris, his attitude toward life, and he did have a fine looking girlfriend. Sniffle. I hate living vicariously through characters in the make-believe world of television, but Ferris quite rightly reminded me to take a moment and smell the flowers.

Even prison flowers smell sweet.

Romans 13:1. *Everyone must submit himself to the governing authorities for there is no authority except that which God has established. The authorities that exist have been established by God.*

✟ ✟ ✟

Wednesday, March 30, 1994
4:00 p.m.

Mail. Awesome! A new pen-pal. I received a letter from Arlene who lives in the Philippines. She says she is 19 and a Mormon. This potential relationship will be interesting. I have strong beliefs as a Protestant and I am sure she, as a Mormon, does too. I want to make a friend, not alienate her by trying to push my belief on her. I enjoy learning about different people, their cultures, and beliefs, and of course receiving letters. Mail ROCKS!

With sensitivity to beliefs, I will cultivate our friendship and then if the opportunity arises, I will gently give her insight into why I believe what I do and the glory it has allowed me to see. I shall respond immediately, taking this evening to write back because it is a minimum of 15 days for a letter to travel to a specific address in the Philippines. I have discovered that their mail distribution system is not as efficient as ours in the United States.

For the price of a stamp and a few words of friendship I will hopefully have another long term window to the colorful world outside.

Thank you, Lord.

Ephesians 5:1-2. *Be imitators of God, therefore, as dearly loved children and live a life of love, just as Christ loved us and gave Himself up for us as a fragrant offering and sacrifice to God.*

✝ ✝ ✝

Thursday, March 31, 1994
4:30 p.m.

News Flash! Pete Wilson, our Governor, is pushing hard for a One Strike & You're Out law for sex offenders. Wow. That would surely stop rapists and child molesters from re-offending but what about mutual consent statutory rape? Or a molestation charge spawned by a heated divorce case because of a desire for custody over children? Do not think it will not or has not happened. Therefore, a life sentence for these types of crimes is going overboard. It is crazy out there in the political world and I am overjoyed that the end may be near...if the PBS prognosticators are right.

6:00 p.m.

Rob, the blond-haired, perpetually tired-eyed, assistant number two to the freeway killer, stopped by my bunk to ask for a shot of mud (coffee). As I am a tea drinker I could not help him with his request. Even so, Rob was in a good mood because he is being put up for transfer to a prison closer to his family. Rob has been incarcerated for many years, and looking into his eyes, it was easy to tell he would give anything to erase his past. Rob is quiet, unassuming, and in need of a friend. I thank God for the strength to overlook Rob's past mistakes and accept him for the potential which God blessed him with.

We all need kind words, no matter what monstrous deeds we may have committed. Someone must make the first peace offering. Christ did it for me. I can do it for others.

10:30 p.m.

I slipped into depression on a greased rail. I did nothing productive this evening. I watched 4½ hours of stupid, mind-numbing sitcoms on television while eating a whole box of saltine crackers that I smeared with peanut butter. They were not so much a culinary delight but a chewable salve for despair. The *I'll Never Make It Home Alive* blues snuck up on me and has me pinned as a poorly trained wrestler to a mat.

I hold dearly to hope. I pray faithfully. I have a possible appeal issue, but the stark and overwhelming reality is I have 13 years until my first parole board hearing. It is unheard of to receive parole at the first hearing, even though the law mandates it. How will I make it? Who in my family will be left alive? I look around at all the men and bunks...what a waste... what a life. What a pitiful sight I must be, covered in cracker crumbs with sticky, peanut butter fingers.

Laugh, Ms. District Attorney, laugh. Today's emotional battle goes to you. Wave high that victory flag.

I need to crawl under the covers and pray. This yoke is heavy Lord. Please help me before...

Colossians 3:13. *Bear with each other and forgive whatever grievance you may have against one another. Forgive as the Lord forgave you.*

☦ ☦ ☦

Friday, April 1, 1994
APRIL FOOLS DAY
5:30 a.m.

April Fools and the joke is on me. I am still in prison. Sigh.

3:00 p.m.

Whoa! My blood was pumping hot. I was nearly goaded into a fight. I was sitting at my desk at work, typing, when the third watch inmate porter walked in and helped himself to a large stack of colored paper which is a saleable commodity on the yard. I quietly asked him not to do that because I am responsible for the supplies, at least while I am on duty. He got all crazy, talking loud, asking me if I was a cop, puffing up his chest, and challenging me to step outside.

Yeah, it was easy to be a tough guy with the lieutenant, program administrator, and secretary a few feet away in their offices and ready to push their alarm buttons if we *got off* (began fighting). I wanted to smash him good, to teach him a lesson for such disrespect, but that would neither have pleased God, nor would violence have accomplished anything. I backed down and ate crow. It did not taste very good, but I was confident that God was pleased.

The porter helped himself to several hundred pieces of colored paper as he smiled at what he thought was a victory.

Proverbs 14:29. *A patient man has great understanding, but a quick-tempered man displays folly.*

✝ ✝ ✝

Saturday, April 2, 1994
12:30 p.m.

While the volleyball was being spiked back and forth across the net, Ed, one of the better players went to Receiving and Release to pick up what I believed would be his care package full of tasty goodies. When he returned he had a thick book—for me?

The book was a writer's handbook and appeared to be expensive. I was so touched, stunned really. I could not find the words to express my total surprise and appreciation for such an unexpected gift. I gave Ed a big bear hug as I stammered, "Thank you." I know I will utilize the book's information for many years to come.

Thank you, Lord, for friends.

Proverbs 17:17. *A friend loves at all times, and a brother is born for adversity.*

✝ ✝ ✝

Sunday, April 3, 1994
EASTER SUNDAY
All Day

The significance of today surpasses Christmas by leaps and bounds. Christ's birth is special, but it is His death and then resurrection that should cause all of humanity to shout praises toward heaven.

Jesus paid the ultimate price for me, for us all. He was executed in my place to cover my sins. This act will allow me, with all my faults, to live in His Father's kingdom for all eternity. The majority of the time I feel so unworthy, especially when I reflect on the crimes I committed and the hurt I caused. However, knowing Jesus loves me to the extent of sacrificing Himself in such a horrific way, forces me to realize that I am worthy only through Him.

With this feeling of worth comes a desire to please and to be thankful even under these circumstances. I constantly pray that I can do or say at least one thing each day that will please God. It seems like a simple goal, but following through on this desire is far from easy; however, I will keep trying.

Romans 8: 1-2. *Therefore, there is now no condemnation for those who are in Christ Jesus, because through Christ Jesus the law of the Spirit of life set me free from the law of sin and death.*

✝ ✝ ✝

Monday, April 4, 1994
7:00 a.m.

Donna came to work today suffering from hysterical laryngitis. This was surprising as she is usually a happy-go-lucky person, except when she is commanded to crack the whip. It would be interesting to know what or who was the source of her hysteria.

A pregnant counselor, whose eyes sparkle with pleasure at making sure inmates know their place, left on bereavement leave. Someone close to her died. Who and how I did not know.

Neither of these women, Donna or the counselor, are Christians. I know this by their negative comments when the subject comes up. So to have their tragedies occur over the Easter weekend brings my mind to puzzling. Is it a coincidence? I think not. God is our salvation and our chastiser. I hate prison, but I am thankful that God loved me enough to rebuke me into line and has allowed me to find salvation. I hope Donna and the counselor can see His love through their pain.

6:00 p.m.

News Flash! The judicial review board of the California legislature gave unanimous thumbs up to a bill that would take away prisoners' rights. Yes, believe it or not, we do have a few. I am concerned about what will happen with the massive influx of lifers that are expected to be coming to prison under the Three Strikes & You're Out Law, combined with the proposed removal of all baby-sitting items such as televisions, radios, typewriters, correspondence courses and the like. The old timers say the days of thunder are returning, meaning, if a caged man has no outlet, no productive way to spend his time, he will turn his agitation against those he perceives as his tormentor—prison staff. That is never a good idea, and in reality, each of us is our own tormentor.

Time, circumstances, and conditions of confinement are constantly changing for the worse. The future, if there will be any for inmates, is grave. My hope in man, in his wise leadership, is all but gone. However, my faith in God grows stronger each day.

Is it equivalent to a mustard seed? Probably not but I am trying.

Psalm 91:4. *He will cover you with His feathers, and under His wings you will find refuge; His faithfulness will be your shield and rampart.*

✞ ✞ ✞

Tuesday, April 5, 1994
3:50 p.m.

Ten minutes before the 4:00 p.m. yard recall, my muscles were comfortably tight. I felt strong, and my allergy irritation was just tickling my nose as I strolled around the track after an invigorating solo work out on the weight pile. Nearing the empty basketball court I saw Charles Watson seated on a bench and decided to join him. After a few pleasantries regarding the excellent weather, temperature in the high 70s, our conversation turned to the Inmates' Bill of Rights revocation bill pending in the legislature. Charles was concerned with the possible loss of conjugal visits as he has participated in the positive program for many years. Together with his wife, Charles has brought several beautiful children into this world. I have met and observed them while in the visiting room and have admired their gentle Christian nature.

Some non-Christians and Christians lacking compassion or forgiveness, object to a man, who was involved in a terrible crime, having any pleasure. I find this attitude both sad and very shortsighted. Sad, because without compassion and forgiveness, where would we be in God's eyes: and shortsighted because the majority of inmates serving a life sentence will eventually be returning to the streets. What frame of mind they return in will depend on how the non-Christian inmate felt he was treated, and for the Christian inmate, how his faith was nurtured.

Charles and I agreed that our only power to affect the decisions of others was through God. All we could do was pray and hope for the best.

Psalm 128:1-4. *Blessed are all who fear the Lord, who walk in His ways. You will eat the fruit of your labor; blessings and prosperity will be yours. Your wife will be like a fruitful vine within your house; your sons will be like olive shoots around your table. Thus is the man blessed who fears the Lord.*

✟ ✟ ✟

Wednesday, April 6, 1994
10:30 a.m.

Achoo! I am dying here. My allergies to spring pollen erupted with a vengeance this morning, and my body is rebelling with sneezes, itchy eyes, an itchy mouth, and a running nose. The only medication the doctor has given me in the past has been little yellow pills, but their only effect is to make me antsy and shake. I will put in a request for sick call and hope there is something new in the pharmacy that will reduce my suffering. Achoo! Achoo! Achoo!

Speaking of sick call requests, I have been waiting two months for an appointment with the optometrist to have my eyes examined for a new prescription. It has been four years since my last exam and my vision has steadily worsened. Even when wearing my glasses, I find myself leaning closer to the typewriter to be able to see clearly.

Even with the many frustrations, and a long, long wait for medical/dental/optical services, at least they are available. And though we are required to pay a *Brubaker* five dollar bill for a diagnosis and prescription of aspirin and a walk around the track, if I were coughing up blood or a metal object sticking out of my body, staff would transport me to a real hospital for treatment. It is difficult to accurately document the ailments, the cancers and heart disease, where medical staff failed to diagnose because of indifference, lack of funds or a belief that the inmate is faking and that the long, long wait results in unnecessary complications and a suffering death. But hey, they're criminals and deserve what they get or don't get. Right? Wrong. Surprise. They are human beings and should be treated s such even if only to teach the lesson that every life is precious.

Prayerfully, those ailments will never happen to me, and I thank God for my current good health and general well-being.

6:00 p.m.

News Flash! Wiser heads have prevailed? The Legislature voted against cancelling conjugal visits for the time being. I know it was not politically correct for the representatives of victim advocates to vote in favor of inmates, but these visits are important for the maintenance of the family unit. Some people see these visits as an unnecessary privilege for the inmate. I would encourage those who think this way to flip it around and view these visits as a need of the family members who have not broken the law. In addition, only programming inmates who remain disciplinary free are eligible. Conjugal visits are a carrot that promotes non-violence and that should be everyone's goal.

Galatians 5:22-23. *But the fruit of the Spirit is love, joy, peace, patience, kindness, goodness, faithfulness, gentleness, and self –control.*

✞ ✞ ✞

Thursday, April 7, 1994
10:30 a.m.

I was ordered to report to Receiving and Release to have my photograph retaken. It has been more than four years since the last photograph and staff wanted it updated. Have I changed that much? While in R&R, I was able to look at the first photograph taken of me when I arrived at San Quentin in 1987, the one taken here at Mule Creek in 1990, and the one taken today. I am happy to report there has not been much of a change. Well, maybe a little less hair on top, but no bags, no sags, no creases, or overt signs of a beaten man. I must hide it well. Ha ha. I give full credit to God for keeping the Spirit strong inside me, to maintain a healthy body with a twinkle in my eyes.

If the rapture does come soon and I disappear, staff will have my most recent smile to remember me by. Yes, I smiled in each of my mug shots, asking, "Mr. DeMille, is it time for my close-up?" I believe it is important to keep a sense of humor, or at least try to, even under these unhappy circumstances.

8:00 p.m.

Hugs and smiles of love; I am so blessed to have such a close relationship with my mother. Our visit tonight was emotionally uplifting and I find it comforting that parenting never stops. The relationship should mature and change with the times, but a child, regardless of age is always in need of love, guidance and moral support.

At times during the visit, I wondered if my mother could see the dread in my eyes when she spoke of moving to Texas. I could see it in her and hear the uncertainty in her voice. Big changes. It will be a new town, a new school to teach in, and a whole new state with a lot of unknowns. It is only natural that she would be apprehensive. Even so, I believe God will provide for my mother's needs, but I will miss her hugs and smiles of love.

I will always be my parents' child.

1 Corinthians 15:51-53. *Listen, I tell you a mystery: We will not all sleep, but we will all be changed—in a flash, in a twinkling of any eye, at the last trumpet: For the trumpet will sound, the dead will be raised imperishable, and we will be changed. For the perishable must clothe itself with imperishable, and the mortal with immortality.*

✟   ✟   ✟

Friday, April 8, 1994
4:15 p.m.

New rule: telephone sign-up time.

In an attempt to stop the few inmates from monopolizing the four telephones in each housing unit, a sign-up schedule has been implemented. After mail is distributed at 4:00 p.m., the housing officer will walk to each cell or bunk while we are restricted to them during count time. This will be our only opportunity to sign-up to use the telephone. That is the rule. No ifs, ands, or buts.

When the officer came around, my new Bunkie, *Wolf,* was asleep. Being observant, the officer knew *Wolf* tries to call home on Fridays, but did not want to wake him. Instead, the officer asked me what time *Wolf* would like to call and then signed him up.

I bet you thought: what's the big deal? Well, let me tell you. The little, very simple act of consideration is so rare, so uncommon, so unknown in a place like this that it was grossly noticeable and supremely appreciated. When *Wolf* awoke and I told him the officer signed him up, *Wolf* was stunned.

The little things do count and for his kindness I prayed that the officer would receive many blessings.

5:00 p.m.

News Flash! Kurt Cobain, lead singer and rock superstar of the music group Nirvana thought his life was so terrible that he had to take a shotgun and remove the top half of his head. That bastard! How dare he? All that success, fame, fortune, and he was not happy. Did he know God? Obviously not. My life sucks, but I would never commit suicide. That would be disrespectful to my parents, friends, and especially God, all of who love and care for me.

Another person died today. Mrs. Winn, the oldest woman in America. She was 118 years of age and the daughter of slaves. The news anchor reported an interesting note about Mrs. Winn. Apparently, her doctor told her that her heart was in poor shape and that she should not work as hard as she does or it would kill her. The doctor made this diagnosis in 1924. When asked about the doctor's warning, Mrs. Winn was known to reply, "Hard work and God keeps me going."

Mrs. Winn is an inspiration.

Kurt Cobain is a disappointment.

Luke 1:78-79. *Because of the tender mercy of our God, by which the rising sun will come to us from heaven to shine on those living in darkness and in the shadow of death, to guide our feet into the path of peace.*

✞ ✞ ✞

Saturday, April 9, 1994
8:00 a.m.

Volleyball today? Nope. It is into the law library for me. Study. Study. Study. I need to be able to file the best federal appeal that I am capable of so that the judge will understand my issue(s) and grant me relief; a new trial where I can confront my accuser, or if he has remained in Argentina, that his prior false statements are ruled inadmissible.

12:00 Noon

Exiting the library I learned that all the blacks and Hispanics on our facility have been placed on lockdown. There was a Code 3 in building 10. Fist fights which turned into a melee between a half dozen blacks and Hispanics over the use of the telephones. I can only assume someone, or several someone's decided not to follow the sign-up list. It's that respect/courtesy thing again.

Prison administrators clamp down hard on any race issue to prevent it from escalating. Unfortunately, their actions entangle many inmates who were not involved in the altercation. Their mindset is that it is better to punish everyone of that race, attempting to make a point, to hopefully prevent a re-occurrence of the event. In all the years that prisons have existed, group punishment has not worked...but administrators keep trying.

12:30 p.m.

It had been my hope to attempt to occupy a table in the gym to continue working on my legal draft, but with the blacks and Hispanics restricted from the yard, no such luck. I will have to hunch over my bunk and try to concentrate. Yeah, good luck with that, I say.

8:00 p.m.

After chow I commandeered an unused desk in the Program Office. I was able to write out three more pages to my legal brief. This was surprising because each time Sergeant Myers walked by with another officer's report on the melee to be typed; I knew he eyed me, wanting to recruit me for the task. I am grateful for Sergeant Myers' restraint.

Psalm 4:8. *I will lie down and sleep in peace, for you alone, O Lord, make me dwell in safety.*

✞ ✞ ✞

Sunday, April 10, 1994
10:00 a.m.

I stood alone on the empty volleyball court. With two-thirds of the inmate population locked down and the white players choosing other things to do, there would be no volleyball today. Instead, I enjoyed the yard which was unusually empty of inmates and pleasantly quiet. There was a blue sky overhead and two acres of green grass surrounding me. I felt as though I was standing in the middle of a meadow as a light, warm breeze drifted by. I cherished the rare moment. Uh oh. Achoo!

2:00 p.m.

The downside of this lockdown is that Frank will be unable to make our workout appointment. As I said, many inmates, solely because of the color of their skin are entangled in the lockdown, despite their non-involvement. It's a better safe than sorry sort of thing. I will miss his company. The upside is I will have more weights to choose from than I can use.

3:00 p.m.

I saw a guy walking around the track who was visiting with a pretty, young lady the same evening as I was visiting my mother. I had spoken with him in the past...I think his name was Dale. He claimed to be a pure bred hillbilly dwarf. Does that mean he is the product of mountain siblings? I do not know. Catching up to him, I asked who the lady was. He said it was his 16-year-old niece and she is engaged to be married.

Wow. In my opinion, 16 is too young to be married. I wondered if I should ask who she was marrying. Before I could, Dale turned the conversation to what he was in prison for, and he proceeded to explain how it was impossible for him to have committed rape because he was high on PCP (animal tranquilizer) at the time. Dale went on to describe how he was going to shoot both of his accusers as soon as he gets out, which was in nine months. There was no doubt in my mind that he was speaking the truth, not merely venting or posturing. His eyes were glowing with evil.

Very scary.

I understand anger caused by lying witnesses, but there has to be a point in every adult's life when you have to move forward, and not fester over transgressions committed against you. If God can forgive us, it is up to us to forgive others. Right? Can I get an amen? Amen!

Mark 11:25. *And when you stand praying, if you hold anything against anyone, forgive him, so that your Father in heaven may forgive you your sins.*

✞ ✞ ✞

Monday, April 11, 1994
11:00 a.m.

"Freed at last. Freed at last." The blacks and Hispanics have been freed from their lockdown. The scare of a prison-wide race riot is over and a life of noise and disorderly chaos can resume.

4:00 p.m.

Where is the mail? The first watch staff Sunday night did not *feel* like processing the outgoing mail so it and the gym's mail bag remained in the gym. If the mail room has no bag to place the incoming mail into, none will be delivered.

6:00 p.m.

I want to seal the edges on an 8½" x 11" envelope with tape due to the fact that the ones I am required to purchase from the canteen are cheap and flimsy and fall apart in the mail. I asked Officer Wynon for 14 inches of Scotch tape. She gave me three inches. "Take it or leave it. We're not in the business of supplying tape," she snapped. I shook my head in dismay and walked away.

8:00 p.m.

The yard sergeant came into the gym to 'kick-it' with the officers seated on the raised platform. I watched as Officer Wynon left the gym for reasons unknown. I decided to try for tape again. I explained the reason for my request, informing the sergeant that I had asked Wynon and she had given me three inches. The sergeant shook his head, dismayed, handed me the tape dispenser off the officers' desk and said, "Knock yourself out."

God blessed me with restraint in the face of purposeful antagonism and led me to a source of relief. God is great.

1 Peter 5:8-9. *Be self-controlled and alert. Your enemy, the devil, prowls around like a roaring lion looking for someone to devour. Resist him, standing firm in the faith, because you know that your brothers throughout the world are undergoing the same kind of sufferings.*

✞ ✞ ✞

Tuesday, April 12, 1994
9:10 a.m.

I received a ducat (pass) to report to the clinic at 8:00 a.m. At 9:10 a.m. I was ushered into the doctor's closet-size office. Sniffling and with bloodshot eyes, I explained my allergy symptoms. The doctor reviewed my medical file to verify my yearly condition and then prescribed the little yellow pills.

I sighed; another summer of being antsy and shaking.

9:30 a.m.

Domestic troubles.   At the announcement of yard release, and the opening of the cell doors in building 9, an inmate began throwing his cellie's property and mattress out of the cell, over the railing, and off the second tier. It was apparent, from the profanities tossed with the clothes and food items that the one did not want the other to reside within their domicile any longer. Of course staff could not tolerate this type of disruptive behavior, so both inmates were placed on CTQ (confined to quarters) status—separate cells of course.

It's true there are a number of incidents that mirror this one each month. What I am astonished by is their relative infrequency. Married couples would find living together in a room the size of a bathroom very difficult, and they are in love and want to be together. Inmates in general are dysfunctional. They do not love each other, and they certainly do not want to be housed together.

Patience and tolerance are the watchwords, qualities that have to be cultivated to survive peacefully in here…and out in the free world.

How about a self-help course on conflict resolution for non-couple, couples?

It is just a thought.

1 Peter 1:22. *Now that you have purified yourselves by obeying the truth so that you have sincere love for your brothers, love one another deeply, from the heart.*

✟ ✟ ✟

Wednesday, April 13, 1994
4:00 p.m.

I ran back to the gym for count time. Normally I would have been off work an hour ago but the classification (UCC) of new inmates ran late. As I am responsible for typing the status changes of all the inmates on Facility B, and then distributing them to the housing units, I had to stay until the counselors reviewed each file and spoke with the inmate. I peered into the classification room at 3:45 p.m. The committee members had two more inmates to classify, but count time neared, and it waited on no man. I will have to finish today's work this evening. I am not thrilled by that prospect because I reserve my evening for legal studies, Bible studies, and creative writing, with a PBS program thrown in for the occasional educational entertainment.

However, in weighing all aspects of my job, I admit I have it better than many inmates. I am not breaking a sweat on the yard crew or in the sauna-like kitchen washing pots and pans. Therefore, I will not grumble, but be thankful, even though I missed my workout from 3:00 p.m. to 4:00 p.m., and have to return to work after the evening chow.

4:05 p.m.

Mail. It was a letter from Bonnie and Rod. The pages were filled with encouragement for both my legal and creative endeavors. Bonnie shared her passionate pastime of keyboard playing and asked if I am musically inclined.

Bonnie's encouragement was perfect timing because, if I can acquire more tape to seal the envelope, I will be mailing *DREAMTIME* to the screenwriting Academy Foundation tonight. Yes, I finished it. Big Smile. It is a long shot, believing I can win, but I have to try. Success is built on a ladder of failures.

Musically inclined? I enjoy listening.

10:00 p.m.

A busy day is done. Inmate status changes complete. *DREAMTIME* is in the mail box. Praise God. I did more than survive today.

1 Timothy 6:6-8. *But godliness with contentment is great gain. For we brought nothing into this world and we can take nothing out of it, but if we have food and clothing, we will be content with that.*

✝ ✝ ✝

Thursday, April 14, 1994
ALL DAY

Sweatin' the telephone. My friend Rick, 28-years-old and a failed car thief, was on and off the telephone all day with family and friends. His wife, Linda, was having a baby, their second, and he was trying to obtain updates. What a wonderful time. A new life entering the world, and a child with unlimited possibilities.

I am both happy and sad for Rick. Happy, because Rick is excited about having another child, yet sad because he cannot be with his wife when she gives birth. Then I asked myself, who should I feel sad for? I decided that it will be his wife. I will wager that she, too, is overjoyed by the birth, but angry beyond words with Rick for his selfish acts that brought him to prison and left her to go through this most special of occasions without him. There are no cards, no flowers, and no candy to make up for Rick not being by her side.

I often wish I had a wife to ease my loneliness, but I would not wish this lifestyle on my worst enemy. I pray that all will go well for Rick, Linda, and their new child, which Rick discovered in one of his many calls, that Linda has named Melissa.

3:30 p.m.

Yard recall? It was a little early, was it not? Not near to 4:00 p.m. As I walked from the weight pile I could see staff lined up in front of the doors to each of the housing units. They were checking the hands of the inmates as they entered the buildings. Apparently a victim has been found but the assailant is still on the loose. I approached Officer Davis, holding out my hands which were free of swelling, cuts, or bruises, but he waved me past without inspecting them.

Having known me for three years, it's my hope that Officer Davis waved me by because he knows my godly character, and that I would use words and not my fists to resolve a conflict.

7:00 p.m.

A lockdown has been instituted for the whites and Hispanics. The victim of the earlier assault, who is white, was punched once in the mouth, but could not or would not identify his attacker. He only described him as white or light-skinned Hispanic. Humph. Punishment in the form of a lockdown for many, to serve the needs of a few.

There is a bright side to this lockdown and that is I could sleep in tomorrow, but I cannot. The law calls and I will heed it. If I get up early enough I may be able to commandeer a table for a couple of hours, or until I can no longer stand the glares of those who want to play cards.

Isaiah 48:18. *If only you had paid attention to my commands, your peace would have been like a river, your righteousness like the waves of the sea.*

✞ ✞ ✞

Friday, April 15, 1994
10:00 a.m.

For 2½ hours I held a table, writing, writing, writing, and then I retreated to my bunk, but only after fending off three less than polite requests to use the table.

2:30 p.m.

I decided to call Mickie. I have to admit the availability of telephone access is one benefit to living in the gym. If I were in a cell, there would be no opportunity during a lockdown.

Lockdowns are of varying degrees, meaning what staff allows us to do during a lockdown depends on who is locked down and why. Sometimes we are allowed to shower and use the telephones, other times, we are not.

Lovely Mickie, my childhood sweetheart, is now a close and dear friend. She answered on the second ring. We spoke for the allotted 15 minutes, but the conversation was weird. She said I sounded spiritually distant. She asked how my keeping in the Word was going. I said fine. I lied, being embarrassed. Except for Saturday fellowship and constant prayer I have not read much in the Bible lately. I had known this was not good, but the question is: How did Mickie know?

After hanging up the telephone I glanced toward my bunk and noticed the sign painted over it that read: NO FUMAR (No Smoking). The words were appropriate because I have not been on fire for God's word lately even though my heart is for Him always. I count my blessings daily, and I am very thankful, but my embers are burning low. I need to better balance my legal and creative writing with studying the Bible. In my embarrassment, it's comforting to know God is always ready and willing to re-ignite my burner.

Besides cracking open The Good Book tonight, I will sit down and write Mickie a thank you letter for sharing her woman's intuition. That is what friends are for.

2 Timothy 2:15. *Do your best to present yourself to God as one approved workman who does not need to be ashamed and who correctly handles the word of truth.*

✞ ✞ ✞

Saturday, April 16, 1994
7:00 a.m.

The lockdown continues.

With last night's promise in my pocket, I resumed Proverbs. I have found in the past that is where to turn if one wants to know what to do and what not to do. Each verse is so simple, but filled with a whole lot of wisdom; plain English that will guide me to a successful and eternal life.

My world today would have been so different if I had heeded those words earlier. I know it's not too late for my eternal life, but I wonder how much of my mortal life will be ruined by my terrible choices. How long will I be punished? Will society ever forgive me? I doubt it, but then, many in society have not read Proverbs recently, or ever.

10:30 a.m.

The majority of the whites and Hispanics in the gym are awake now. For them the lockdown meant late nights, sleep-ins, and more time to do whatever. To walk around the gym and observe the menagerie of inmates involved in different activities is intriguing. Some are involved in self-improvement activities: reading, writing, studying, while others have personalized and monogrammed handmade cushioned covers that slip over the metal seats at the card and domino tables. Between the two groups it is easy to predict who will be coming back to prison after release. Unfortunately, it is the inmates from the latter group that go home every day. The former group is made up of lifers.

How did this system evolve so that the changed group remains in prison?

Hebrews 3:12-13. *See to it, brothers, that none of you has a sinful, unbelieving heart that turns away from the living God. But encourage one another daily, as long as it is called today, so that none of you may be hardened by sin's deceitfulness.*

✟ ✟ ✟

Sunday, April 17, 1994
12:00 Noon

It is as if the blacks are being punished along with the whites and Hispanics who are still locked down. Yard unlocks are usually at 8:00 a.m. but both yesterday and today the morning unlock was not until 9:30 a.m. For the most part, the majority of staff enjoys lockdowns as the workload is reduced to near zero. There are no unlocks, no answering of questions, no supervision of inmates because none are out of their cells or building, and a lockdown based on violence looks good in support of their association's motto: "We Walk the Toughest Beat in the State."

What a load of cr--. It's far safer in here for staff than out on the streets because on the streets the criminals can and do shoot back.

I cannot say for sure why the unlock for the blacks was late. Maybe staff training? Not likely as the officers were seated at their station. It is a mystery that I cannot solve, but hopefully, tomorrow after the administrators return from their fun-filled weekend, they will evaluate the situation, and return us to normal program.

There is rumor floating around that says we will be locked down next weekend for tuberculosis (TB) testing. Testing for infectious diseases certainly is a legitimate reason for a lockdown so that no one is missed. I can deal with that inconvenience, except for the needles. I hate needles.

Psalm 55:22. *Cast your cares on the Lord and He will sustain you; He will never let the righteous fall.*

✟ ✟ ✟

Monday, April 18, 1994
10:30 a.m.

"And the crowd goes wild." We are off lockdown. I had guessed 11:00 a.m. and I was close.

At work I overheard the program administrator tell the lieutenant that the fight and subsequent lockdown was simply bad timing. By Friday evening both the victim and assailant had been identified, but because policy does not allow inmates to be released from a lockdown on a weekend, we (inmates) were stuck.

The thinking behind this, and it's logical, is the administration does not want hundreds of inmates with pent-up energy or frustration being let loose on the yard. The administrators want us to have a full day of work behind us before we freely mingle on the recreation yard.

Oh well, I made good progress on my legal writing and stoked my Biblical fire – downtime well spent.

4:00 p.m.

Mail; another tribulation to test me. I received a notice in the mail that Receiving and Release staff returned the creative writing books I ordered because staff did not know the package contained books. They thought it was a Special Purchase item such as a radio, television, or typewriter. Staff wrote, "Has to come from an approved vendor." *Excuse me*: Books no longer have to come from approved vendors. Did they not read the memorandum? Now I have to challenge, by way of a 602 appeal, their actions and policy that return packages without first opening them to discover the contents. If staff, in the inmate's presence, were to open the box, it would eliminate the presumption of "Unauthorized Package." What a hassle, but it is typical of this beast.

I only want a couple of books to enhance my writing skills. Why must everything be so difficult? Oops, sorry. I momentarily forgot. Prison is for punishment.

Hebrews 12:1. *Therefore, since we are surrounded by such a great cloud of witnesses, let us throw off everything that hinders and the sin that so easily entangles, and let us run with perseverance the race marked out for us.*

✞ ✞ ✞

Tuesday, April 19, 1994
4:30 a.m.

Snakes were not only in the Garden of Eden but they are around us in everyday life. In our modern, citified world, usually we only need to worry about the two legged kind that speaks with forked tongue. Except on this day, an inmate sleeping on his bunk in building 6 was bitten by a slithering rattler that decided to come in out of the cool night air. The inmate will survive but he had to be transported to an outside hospital for treatment.

We all need to be vigilant and pray daily for protection. God did promise protection to His children and I take it on faith that His words in the Bible are truthful. So far so good.

Oh, the snake? It was beaten to death by an officer with a side-handle baton.

6:00 p.m.

Dinner with speculating intellectuals. Now and then I am seated at chow with a few reasonably intelligent men who walk the line. Tonight I had the pleasure of dining with three and the topic of conversation was: What is really housed within Dreamland?

Dreamland is the super-secret air base in Nevada where futuristic aircraft are tested. The speculation was: Were alien space ships hidden there, specifically, the one that crashed in Roswell, New Mexico, and if so why was our government not telling us the truth about their existence? Did our leaders believe we would not be able to handle the knowledge of beings more powerful and more intelligent than ourselves? Would this knowledge somehow invalidate religion and God? My contribution was, "Hell no." Was there some prohibition on God that would prevent Him from creating other beings on other worlds?

Some may argue that there is no mention of extraterrestrials in the Bible so 'they' do not exist. Really? That argument assumes God had told us all His secrets. Heck, we cannot understand most of what is written in the Bible, and that is why we study, study, study. Can you imagine Jesus trying to explain microbiology or quantum physics to the disciples? Why add to the mysteries that already stupefy us?

Speculation and theorizing was fun. The two hot dogs and chunky potato salad we were served were enjoyable, too.

Revelation 12:11. *They overcome him by the blood of the Lamb and by the word of their testimony; they did not love their lives so much as to shrink from death.*

✝ ✝ ✝

Wednesday, April 20, 1994
8:00 a.m.

Seated at my desk at work, I paused between typing reports. Suddenly it dawned on me that mentally I was fine and physically I was well. A simple appraisal of well-being, but believe me, it was a rare conclusion in this world of stress, worry, and fear. I leaned back to stretch and to relish the moment while I thanked God.

3:30 p.m.

Exercising. I worked out alone with the weights because my routine was shorter than most others, only an hour, and because Frank's work schedule had been changed. Today I was grateful to have friends in the vicinity because while I was on the bench press, after my 5th set of 10 reps, I suffered sudden and total muscle fatigue. I was stuck under the weight, which totaled 230 pounds, and was unable to get the bar off my chest. I looked around, not yet allowing myself to panic, and then groaned, "Smitty." Seeing my predicament, Smitty quickly came to my rescue, helping me to lift the bar back onto the rack. I am sure I will be kidded about this later but his help is worth it. I will gladly accept friendly ribbing in place of broken ribs.

By the way, Smitty is black. Can you believe it? A black man helping a white man in prison. Quick, alert the media.

6:00 p.m.

Dinner with the intellectuals tonight? Fat chance of that. I was sorely disappointed with the conversation tonight as it centered on wishes for the genocide of another race. "What good are wetbacks (Mexicans) anyway?" was their sentiment. Having been in love with a Mexican American, and admittedly, I probably always will be, I kept my opinion to myself.

Prison brings out the best and worst in people. I want to be the best, a light. . .His light.

Psalm 119:105-106. *Your word is a lamp to my feet and a light for my path. I have taken an oath and confirmed it, that I will follow your righteous laws.*

✞ ✞ ✞

Thursday, April 21, 1994
10:30 a.m.

The 40 or so lifers in the gym were all in a flutter because one of them had been moved out this morning. He was re-housed in a cell and placed on Close B status (higher custody, less freedom). These lifers were like a clutch of hens gossiping over every action or event and how it affects them.

The real skinny on the inmate is that he was not a lifer, but instead is serving a 180 year sentence, and only had a few years in.

New policy: Any inmate with more than 20 years left to serve before parole or parole eligibility will be housed in a cell.

Once this new policy was disseminated, the cackling settled down and the hens took roost on their bunks or resumed their preferred activities.

9:00 p.m.

The man who sleeps in the bunk next to me has a nickname of *Swede.* Yep. He's from Sweden. His nickname is not very creative but it is easier to pronounce that his real name. *Swede* is serving a second degree murder sentence of 15 years to life for killing his drug supplier with a hammer. His legal fight is with the California political system. *Swede* wants to be allowed to return to Sweden to complete his sentence.

Sweden and the United States have a treaty that allows for the transferring of inmates back to their native country. The Swedish government wants *Swede* back; officials of the Department of Corrections want to send him back, and the California courts have ruled that he should be sent back per the treaty. The problem is coming from a politically appointed person who is preventing *Swede's* transfer. This person is the Chairman of the Board of Prison Terms and he is appointed by the governor.

Why should politics rule the day while common sense, judicial review, and financial loss by the taxpayers take a back seat?

Swede showed me a document submitted by the Chairman which summarized his argument. It read: If Mr. *Swede* were transferred for incarceration in his native county of Sweden after only serving 17 years of his life sentence, it is probable that the Swedish government would release him. This probability is based on information provided by the Swedish Consulate that stated, "Rehabilitation of the offender is the foremost goal of our government. Once this has been achieved, full reintegration into society is the objective."

This stated goal is contrary to the California penal code which requires the offender to be punished. If a California offender chooses to rehabilitate himself, it is the responsibility of the commissioners of the Board of Prison Terms, who are appointed by the governor, to determine whether the offender is to be released from prison, not the Swedish government.

This writer (Chairman) acknowledges Sweden's less than one percent recidivism rate for *Swede's* category of offenders, but speaking for the victims of these crimes, I am appalled by the high percentage of releases, 85%, after an offender has served less than 12 years. This in comparison to a near zero release of California offenders convicted of the same offense. It is apparent that Sweden's and California's correctional systems are diametrically opposed. If *Swede* were to be returned to Sweden, California's goal would be negated and justice denied.

Poor *Swede.* His head is constantly bandaged from beating it against the political wall.

10:00 p.m.

ABC news. Federal Bureau of Investigations statistics reveal that crime has decreased over the last 30 years.

"That's a lie!" screamed the politician who was interviewed for comment regarding the story.

But it's true. Statistics are manipulated every day, but looked at as a whole and in the proper non-political context, overall crime decreased by 2% over the last quarter century. The problem is we as a television culture are constantly bombarded by gruesome scenes of violence from around the country and around the world. It is information overload and Nielsen ratings grabbling. What can we do?   We can get the facts and ask tough questions of our politicians.

The truth is comforting.   The truth will someday send *Swede* home. The truth should give free people peace of mind.

John 8:12. *"Then you will know the truth, and the truth will set you free."*

✝ ✝ ✝

Friday, April 22, 1994
10:15 a.m.

"The roof. The roof. The roof is on fire," were the appropriate song lyrics as black, broiling smoke billowed from the chow hall's tray scullery. The prison's inmate fire company, held on tight, as the fire truck barreled through the open gate between buildings 9 and 10. The truck's diesel engine roared and its siren wailed as it took the curving track toward the chow hall. Inmates, who were scattered across the yard, staring at the conflagration, moved closer to that which fascinates every young boy – a shiny fire truck.

Then, above the sirens, the firemen's shouts, and crackling flames, that distinctive sound of a rifle round being chambered by the officer in the gun tower, echoed across the yard, followed by, "Move away from the vehicle. Now!" To staff, any vehicle is considered an escape apparatus that could be used by an inmate to make his break. Then, another warning, "Don't breathe the smoke. It's poisonous." Someone had relayed the fact that what was burning were the plastic cups, bowls, and trays.

Above, news helicopters flew, filming for tonight's broadcast. In addition to the media hounds, a California Department of Forestry helicopter circled the prison. Suspended on a long cable from the CDF helicopter's belly was a missile-shaped air sensor to check for toxic air contaminants. Watching the plaza gate, I saw blue and gray suited administrators, more than I had ever seen; fill the yard shouting orders that contradicted those who had arrived a moment earlier.

"Where will we eat?" murmured through the inmates.

"Forget the food. What about the gym and our property? It's right next to the kitchen," was my stated worry.

11:30 a.m.

With the assistance of local fire engine companies that arrived in 10 minute intervals, the fire was extinguished. The tray scullery was destroyed but the gym was saved. Inmates who are housed in buildings 6 through 10 were ordered back to their cells.

2:15 p.m.

Four hours later we gym dwellers were still waiting on the recreation yard but were told to move to the volleyball court. Thank God for this beautiful day with the temperate weather; not too hot, not too cold.

5:00 p.m.

Change of location. As a group herded like cattle, we were moved from the volleyball court to the basketball court. Due to my skinny, no padding type of butt, it was sore from sitting on the hard concrete for five hours.

A smile crossed my face as I remembered when I was a little tot and my mother would nudge me off her lap, lovingly saying my rear bones hurt her thighs. Ah… memories.

Though the fire had been out for many hours, we were not allowed to return to the gym until a HAZMAT (Hazardous Materials) guy from Sacramento arrived to inspect the gym for toxins.

Really? That sounded as if they almost cared about our well-being.

5:30 p.m.

Dinner was sack lunches served picnic style on the basketball court. Again, I thanked God for this summer-warm evening and no bugs to spoil the meal. Surprisingly, all the inmates were exhibiting maturity and cooperation with each order given. This positive attitude was met with calm flexibility by most staff members. Example: When an inmate raised his hand in need of the restroom, he was allowed to walk a narrow route to and from the yard toilets.

6:30 p.m.

HAZMAT guy reported that the inmates may return to the gym, but all clothes, linens, and mattresses must be replaced. Wow. That's going to be a major cluster----.

The summer-like sun has taken its toll on me. I am drained and my face and receding hairline are the color of ripe tomatoes and are hot to the touch.

The one day I forget my hat, but who would have predicted a fire?

8:00 p.m.

New mattresses? Thick and soft mattresses arrived with new clothing on trucks from other prisons. It turned out that it's a good thing that California has more prisons than most countries because it did not take too long for these supplies to be gathered and trucked in.

New blankets, sheets, towels, and clothes, too. It's almost like Christmas. It was almost worth it, all this waiting, the exhaustion, sore butt and sun burn, to have, for once, new clothes and linens. Staff should be commended for their ability to solve this major problem efficiently. It was not a cluster----.

What an adventure. I will sleep soundly tonight.

Isaiah 65:24. *Before they call, I will answer; while they are still speaking, I will hear.*

✣ ✣ ✣

Saturday, April 23, 1994
7:00 a.m.

Lockdown. Flee. Run away if you can. The ladies with the needles have arrived in the gym. It's TB testing time. As I have said, I hate needles. I am sure this negative sentiment is a throw-back to my childhood and the vivid memories of pain each time I was stuck for some vaccination or another.

Nowhere to run so I got in line. Staff checked each inmate's identification card against their roster so as not to miss anyone. Too fast. The line was moving too fast. I summoned my inner strength. I shuffled forward, hesitantly closer. Why did the MTAs' smile when they jabbed each inmate? Shivers ran up my spine.

"Hold out your left arm," she coaxed in a sweet voice. My God, that needle was huge. I took deep breaths as I submitted my limb to the torture. Look away, Greg. For the love of God, look away.

"Next," echoed a voice from a distant planet. What? Did she stick me? I did not feel a thing. Wow. My fear overrode the pain factor. The MTA smiled at me as I stepped away from the table.

She must have been an angel.

7:30 a.m.

The ladies with the needles have departed. No one fainted. Monday they will return to check our arms for any reaction. I pray mine will be negative.

8:00 a.m.

The gym inmates were split into groups and fed in the dayrooms of buildings 6 and 7. The feeding was exceptionally slow as staff adjusted to the lack of a chow hall. Come Monday it will be unlikely that any inmate will be on time for work due to the delay in feeding.

3:00 – 4:00 p.m.

With the TB shots completed in all the housing units, the inmates were released to the recreation yard for an hour. There was enough time for a brief, but uplifting Bible fellowship. Five men attended...we only needed two for the Spirit to attend.

Hebrews 13:6. *So we say with confidence, "The Lord is my helper; I will not be afraid. What can man do to me?"*

✞ ✞ ✞

Sunday, April 24, 1994
7:00 a.m.

While waiting for chow, I overheard staff say the cause of the fire was a faulty heating coil that did not turn off, catching the trays on fire. No inmates will be punished.

8:00 a.m.

Breakfast feeding was late again. Today I decided to take my own man-sized plastic fork and spoon to eat with because the ones given on the paper plates were meant for infants. Hmm... I pondered a thought. Is this place really a giant child care center? It certainly is an extended time out.

8:30 a.m.

Rain? Will these April showers bring May flowers, or will they be yard weeds? No volleyball today. Instead I remained prone on my comfy new mattress, read my *Islands* magazine, and dreamed of adventures sailing the winds within my mind.

11:30 a.m.

Darkness? Have I been struck blind? No. It's a power outage. What's next? We had fire. How about floods? Oh well, no light, no reading. Apparently it's nap time.

2:00 p.m.

"Power up, Mr. Sulu," must have been Captain Kirk's order as the dilithium crystals are back on line. We have light again.

11:00 p.m.

Scabby-gay Scott was caught with his fingers up his rear while in the toilet area. I hope he was not looking for a late night snack. Yuck. Oh my, I lent him a magazine. He can keep it. It is the few inmates with the bizarre behaviors that taint the rest of us.

1 Peter 2:11. *Dear friends, I urge you, as aliens and strangers in the world, to abstain from sinful desires, which are against your soul.*

✚ ✚ ✚

Monday, April 25, 1994
7:00 a.m.

I passed the test. The MTA ran her finger across my forearm where I was injected, and then she stated, to my great relief, "It's negative."

9:00 a.m.

The slow feeding in the buildings put me to work two hours late. Actually, that was not too bad considering the food had to be transported in carts to each of the buildings. I wonder how long we will be eating in the housing units. I had peeked in through the slender window in the chow hall door at the damage and it looked to be a total loss.

4:00 p.m.

Mail. I received a letter from Greg Reed. He is a Christian brother residing behind the walls of Solano Prison. Greg writes inspiring letters that always cheer me up when I am feeling blue. Even though, as with Mule Creek, Solano has eliminated many of the programs that help keep inmates productive; programs such as handicraft, college, music, and the majority of the weight pile equipment, Greg continues to find ways to keep himself productive, putting forth a positive, can do attitude. When Greg and I were in San Quentin, he always exhibited a real entrepreneurial spirit. I know that if Greg finds a project he enjoys, despite the cut backs and limitations, he will sink his whole self into it to succeed.

Unfortunately, Greg is also a lifer, but if ever released, knowing his Christian walk, the lessons he has learned, and his drive to succeed, he will be a positive asset to the community. For both our sakes, I hope these prison trials will pass within a relatively short time, but if not, Greg and I are dedicated letter writers, and we will continue to lift each other up throughout this journey of tribulations.

That is what friends are for.

8:00 p.m.

There are times when being the program administrator's clerk is a real pain. Many know-it-all inmates ask me to take their ideas to my boss concerning ways for improving the running of the facility. Well, first of all, I am not a messenger, and second, my boss does not want or need to be bothered. He has a chain of command and inmates are not part of it. To quell this problem I have been instructing the would-be idea men to write their ideas down, and then I would give them to my boss. This requirement-solution has cut way down on the suggestions because the vast majority of inmates do not want to take the time to write their *great* ideas down.

8:30 p.m.

A telephone conversation with my father and his wife, JoAnne. They arrived safely home from their trip to the Chesapeake Bay Area in Maryland. My father's hobby is duck decoy carving and painting so he and JoAnne travel to different shows throughout the state and country to participate in competitions and view other carvers' work as well as paintings of wildlife, especially wildfowl.

I am so grateful to God for His travel mercies. My family's safety is number one on my prayer list.

Romans 12:10-11, 13. *Be devoted to one another in brotherly love. Honor one another above yourselves. Never be lacking in zeal, but keep your spiritual fervor, serving the Lord. Share with God's people who are in need. Practice hospitality.*

✞ ✞ ✞

Tues, April 26, 1994
4:00 p.m.

Mail. I received the response from Sacramento headquarters regarding the 602 appeal I filed about the closure of the handicraft program. I skipped the summary and read the DECISION; Appeal denied. To paraphrase: "Though handicraft is a mandated program, it is a privilege not a right. Therefore, a warden may modify or discontinue the program at his/her discretion. … Additionally, any items purchased by the inmate to participate in the program were done so at the inmate's risk." Sigh.

9:00 p.m.

It was a slow day in prison. No fights, no fires, no juicy gossip. Not a single, sit on your butt, alarm. Someone obviously was not doing his job.

Sometimes, actually most of the time, when I walked around this gym, or on the recreation yard, I feel as if I am in a bad B movie, but have not been given the script. I do not feel as though I fit in. It is the "In the world but not of the world" sort of thing. I am content to be by myself, read my Bible, work on my creative writing projects, listen to music on my radio, or watch the Public Broadcasting Station.

Musing aside, and needing a drink, I walked the length of the gym from my bunk to the toilet area where the drinking fountain is bolted to the floor (somebody must have seen *One Flew Over the Cuckoo's Nest*). I marveled at all the illicit activities in progress: smoking while peeking around the bunks, tattooing with a converted cassette player and AC/DC adapter, and gambling in plain view of staff. Not very productive and not very wholesome…hold it. There sat Mr. Giles. He was holding an informal Bible study at his bunk with three other inmates. Four convicts, three incarcerated for murder, seated quietly, and holding hands with heads bowed in prayer.

I felt warmth and I believe I saw a glow about them. It was the presence of the Holy Spirit. I continued on and smiled as I sipped cool water from the fountain and thought: I did fit in somewhere and that place was with Jesus.

Romans 12:1-2. *Therefore, I urge you, brothers, in view of God's mercy, to offer your bodies as living sacrifices holy and pleasing to God—this is your spiritual act of worship. Do not conform any longer to the pattern of this world, but be transformed by the renewing of your mind. Then you will be able to test and approve what God's will is—His good, pleasing and perfect will.*

✟ ✟ ✟

Wednesday, April 27, 1994
3:00 p.m.

As quitting time approached, I finished typing 90 status changes, placing these inmates on CTQ (Confined to Quarters). Can we say "Overkill?" The inmates assigned to three vocational shops were locked down because one inmate lost, hid, or had a tool, a protractor, taken from him.

For accountability of tools, the shops utilize a 'chit' system. Each inmate who checks out a tool must submit his chit. At the end of the work day, all tools must be accounted for before the inmates in the shop are released from the secure vocational area.

Obviously staff knows who the protractor was checked out to, so I say, put that man in the hole, strip search the other inmates that work in that vocational shop and be done with it. Again, I asked myself the $10,000,000 question: Why punish so many for that act of one who they have in custody? Silence. No answer.

What have we learned today, Dorothy? That it is A-Okay to discipline those who had nothing to do with the misconduct? I witness everyday how this course of action breeds animosity in inmates toward staff. Punishing people for a wrong they did not commit is not right, but despising the punisher is wrong, too. The evil cycle has to be broken. I doubt that staff will ever change. This form of *correction* is too ingrained in the system, so it has to be the inmate who rises above and turns the other check seven times seven times seven. There is great peace in forgiveness, and in this peace we can bear any mistreatment.

Fortunately, I am a clerk in an area that usually requires that I be the screw-up before I am locked down, unless it is facility wide. With a little luck, the protractor will be found before Friday evening, so these 90 men will not have to remain CTQ'd over the weekend.

Psalm 32:1-2. *Blessed is he whose transgressions are forgiven, whose sins are covered. Blessed is the man whose sin the Lord does not count against him and whose spirit has no deceit.*

✞ ✞ ✞

Thursday, April 28, 1994
7:00 a.m.

Many mornings I go directly to work, going without the breakfast entrée because I am tired of eating the same thing over and over and over each week: hard French Toast or crusty pancakes with cold syrup; rubbery fried eggs; soupy oatmeal; gray hash; impossible to peel hard-boiled eggs, or concrete biscuits soaked in lumpy gravy.

Today, for some reason, the staff in the gym would not let me go to work until everyone on the entire facility had been fed. Because we are still eating in the buildings, by the time feeding is completed, I will not get to work until nine, or maybe even ten o'clock. This really sucks.

Wait. Bible study opportunity. I have been reading Songs. Love and loving under God's eyes and blessings, as described by scripture, is out of this world. I can hardly wait until I am blessed with a beautiful and intelligent lady to share God's kind of love with. It has only been four years without that special kind of love, but it feels like a thousand, and I am wilting.

9:00 a.m.

Why not? Since I am still waiting to be released to go to work I decided to try and telephone my cousin Penny. I have not spoken with her in four and a half years, and have only received one letter from her in the six and a half years that I have been incarcerated. To say I am disappointed is an understatement because Penny only lives an hour and a half away in the Tahoe region. I often wonder what reasons my cousins, aunts, and uncles could have for their decision not to keep open the lines of communication. I have not betrayed them in any way that I am aware of. Maybe it is because they are not Christians and are wrapped up in their lives and consumed daily by the world.

Penny accepted my collect call and was excited to hear from me. I have to admit that our conversation was like picking up from yesterday—from my day of freedom. Penny was curious to know if I would like to receive postcards. Would it make me sad to see the sights but not be able to experience them? "Heck no," I replied. Just include me in your thoughts; remember me positively when you do fun things, and afterward, share them with me. A postcard with "Thinking of you," or "We love you," written on it would bring me great happiness to know that I have not been forgotten. I do not need or ask for a lot.

I thoroughly enjoyed talking to Penny and she hopes to visit me this September with her new baby and husband, Brad. I certainly will look forward to that. Her visit would be a great opportunity for me to show God's work within me, and my attempt at happiness even in a place such as this.

John 12:49-50. *"For I did not speak of my own accord, but the Father who sent me commanded me to say and how to say it. I know that His command leads to eternal life. So whatever I say is just what the Father has told me to say."*

✝ ✝ ✝

Friday, April 29, 1994
9:00 p.m.

Care of another's property? What ever happened to conscientiousness? I know, I know, we are not supposed to worship idols, and I do not, but why is it that my possessions get broken by other people's carelessness, and why does it bother me so much?

Two years ago, while still housed in a cell, my father purchased a television for me. It was assumed that I would need a quality one to last me many years, so he bought an expensive one. The first week I had it my cellie accidentally bumped into it while he was watching it, breaking the plastic that holds the headphone jack in. Sure, he was sorry. Big deal. He could not fix it and it remains broken to this day.

Tonight I had planned to only watch my friends play volleyball while enjoying music on my Sony Walkman. No. That would not do. They wanted me to play, and truth be told, it is difficult for me to pass up on a spirited game. For safe keeping I asked Tommy, one of the more temperamental players, if I could wrap his jacket around my radio. "Sure," he said, and the games began.

At the conclusion of the last spike and point, which I failed to block, and after I had to run to retrieve the ball, I watched from a distance, with horror, as Tommy began to pick up his jacket. Panicked, I shouted, "Tommy, don't pick up your jacket." Everyone but Tommy heard me. Crash! My Walkman hit the concrete. Broken pieces of plastic flew everywhere. Six and a half years I have kept my radio safe from thieves, from damage, and it only took one forgetful person to break it. Sure, Tommy was sorry. Big deal. He could not fix it. It is broken and I am pissed.

Ephesians 4:26-27. *"In your anger do not sin": do not let the sun go down while you are still angry, and do not give the devil a foothold.*

✝ ✝ ✝

Saturday, April 20, 1994
7:00 a.m.

Alarm! Code 3. The inmates in building 8 are fed up with the puny food portions served on the children's size paper plates. The *incident* was more food fight than a fist fight as two inmates threw their plates and food back at the inmates serving on the makeshift line—lockdown.

9:30 a.m.

It was decided that only building 8 inmates would be locked down. Building 8 is Tommy's building. It is too bad for him, but better for me and the other volleyball players. Tommy is a scream in your face, argumentative, tantrum throwing, kick the volleyball over the fence when he does not get his way, 5'7", 135 pound 40-year-old. I will not miss him today. I am still annoyed by Tommy's carelessness. I know it is not very Christian of me to hold a grudge, but I have so little, and cherish each item as a blessing, and that is why I feel this way. I am not perfect, and at times it is a great burden trying to be Christ-like, but I know God and I will work through this test, this example of my own shortcoming. This is the important thing.

1:30 p.m.

Fast-paced games to exhaustion. The volleyball was spiked to point more times than I could count, and not once was it kicked in frustration. Time to rest...

2:00 p.m.

...in God's word. Fellowship on the recreation yard with friends, sharing our understanding of Scripture, limited though it may be, while the afternoon breeze cooled me. Ah...heaven.

10:15 p.m.

Being a Saturday evening, I can make as much noise as I want because the inmates in the gym are awake. No work tomorrow. The clack, clack, clack of my typewriter as I put finishing touches on my federal appeal bothered no one. Sigh. It's done. Will it make a difference? Only God knows.

Proverbs 16:32. *Better a patient man than a warrior, a man who controls his temper than one who takes a city.*

✟   ✟   ✟

Sunday, May 1, 1994
11:00 a.m.

I carried my future, my appeal, within an envelope, properly addressed to the federal court, to the officers' station. Officer Lewis inspected (searched) the envelope for contraband, double-checked the address to insure it was for 'legal' purposes, and then sealed and signed the flap. Into the mail box it went. Do I dare hope? Hope is too scary. As I walked back to my bunk I reminded myself to have faith in God. What will be, He would see me through.

7:00 p.m.

Scabby-gay Scott, the bodily excretions eater, argued with the officers, his work supervisors, because he did not believe he had to work during his assigned work hours. Scott is assigned as a porter (cleaner) in the gym (whose brilliant idea was that?). Scott thought it should be okay if he went to the yard or library instead of sweeping or mopping. The officers disagreed, handcuffed Scott, and then escorted him out of the gym to a standing ovation from the rest of the inmates.

What a lonely existence it must be when not one person likes you. Scott is the most disgusting person I have ever come in contact with, but I do have great empathy for him. No, I am not Christ-like enough to be his buddy, but I will not be his enemy either. Cordiality is the first step. Understanding is the second step. Acceptance and then hopefully change.

Luke 17:12-16. *As He was going into a village, ten men who had leprosy met Him. They stood at a distance and called out in a loud voice, "Jesus, Master, have pity on us." When He saw them, He said, "Go show yourselves to the priests." And as they went, they were cleansed. One of them, when he saw he was healed, came back, praising God in loud voice. He threw himself at Jesus' feet and thanked Him—and he was a Samaritan.*

✝ ✝ ✝

Monday, May 2, 1994
9:00 p.m.

A man's inability to express emotions is a real stumbling block to communications of the heart, but hopefully, the quality of time spent together allowed for the feelings to show through, and spoke volumes of affection.

Tonight I spent two hours sitting on the lawn talking with Ed Thompson. Ed is a masterful volleyball player, a person of intelligence, and a Christian with a positive attitude. I can always pick him out of the walking masses even with my dwindling eyesight. Ed has a bull-buster's gait. His bowed and worn-out knees give him a comin' along stride, but beware of the smiling cripple because his tattered cover hides an athlete to be reckoned with.

Ed has been here at the Creek for ten months and is going home in five days. I will miss his charisma immensely. I have a lot of associates here, but Ed is one of the few people who I would want to and do call a friend. I pray he will be able to stay on the straight path when he returns to the streets and that he will be able to stay in contact with me. I would so enjoy, to one day play beach volleyball with Ed in real sand, with real waves crashing in the background, and with cheerful squeals of lovely ladies punctuating each powerful spike of the ball.

Thanks for the great times, Ed-me-bucko; you made my life a little easier. My prayers for blessings go with you.

1 Corinthians 13:13. *And now these three remain: faith, hope and love. But the greatest of these is love.*

✝ ✝ ✝

Tuesday, May 3, 1994
10:00 a.m.

In a rare moment of not having a pressing report to type, I asked Donna if I could slip into the library through the back door. She replied, "Fifteen minutes."

Standing at the library's counter, I searched the Yellow Pages for the address of the Sears Service Center closest to the Creek. On a whim, I decided to write them to find out if I can purchase replacement pieces for my broken radio. Though it is an older model they may still be able to order parts for me. If so, I am going to give the bill to Tommy. Then I will find out if he takes responsibility for his actions by reimbursing me. Will he or won't he? Only the Spirit knows for sure.

9:15 p.m.

I finished proofreading Frank's first children's story. There were numerous typos but that is par for a first draft. I felt honored that Frank asked me to read it because it shows he values my judgment. It is true that I have my mother proofread my final drafts to ensure perfection. She is a learned teacher and can find overlooked errors. Despite being less than perfect, I was able to do a worthy job of review for Frank. Also, I was blessed to read a very creative story that I believe, if properly illustrated, would capture a child's imagination.

9:20 p.m.

I was called back to work to assist Alex with a mass of paperwork that needed to be completed. Alex becomes stressed and makes too many errors when the work begins to pile up. Tonight, the lieutenant wanted the 90 inmates who were placed on CTQ to be released. Tomorrow is another work day, and for these shut-ins, their four day forced weekend is over.

It is too bad these inmates will not have time to shower before going to work in the morning. Those vocational shops will be rather ripe with unwashed men.

The lost protractor? The cause of the CTQ sequestering? It was found between two desks in the vocational shop. It likely was accidentally pushed off the desk while the inmate was shuffling paper. If the irresponsible inmate is able to keep his position, which is unlikely, hopefully he will be more careful with the implements entrusted to him.

10:30 p.m.

Back in the gym I dropped a letter into the mail box addressed to the Sears Service Center in Sacramento inquiring as to whether they can order parts for my radio. As I did so, the Spirit caused me a pain of guilt. Tommy did not purposely break my radio. I need to forgive him and ask God for forgiveness in placing so much value in a thing.

It is only a stupid radio.

If I receive a response from Sears I will either buy the parts myself or forget the whole thing. I feel better already.

Joel 1:2-3. *Hear this, you elders; listen, all who live in the land. Has anything like this ever happened in your days or in the day of your forefathers? Tell it to you children, and let your children tell it to their children, and their children to the next generation.*

✝ ✝ ✝

Wednesday, May 4, 1994
9:30 a.m.

The light, the giant orb in the sky, it burns, it burns my eyes, and my sense of fashion has gone to H-E-double tooth picks. In all seriousness, could 'they' make uglier eye protection glasses? I left optometry with dilated pupils, flimsy dark eye shades, and a new prescription to correct 20-600 vision. The eye doctor had to be kidding, right? Twenty/six hundred vision? God, I hope I am not going blind.

8:45 p.m.

Code 2, medical emergency, building 10. Officers from other buildings walked to the scene to investigate. Five minutes passed before an MTA with a medical bag strolled across the yard to the building. I hoped the injured or sick one(s) were not critical. Ten minutes passed. The electric stretcher cart cruised silently from the infirmary to the building. It returned to the infirmary carrying an unconscious inmate.

I can understand that subconsciously, if not consciously, medical staff do not give a hoot whether scumbag inmates live or die, but I would have thought they would care about the officers or other free staff. The MTAs do not even run when staff is injured. Was there not an oath of care recited when they became a medical professional? Interesting, I did overhear one MTA tell another, "I'm not paid enough to run." Ah…it was simply a matter of money.

I praise God for my continued good health. Without it not much else matters.

9:15 p.m.

Rumor mill. The Security Squad, the storm troopers, affectionately referred to as the goon squad, is planning to storm into the gym tomorrow, tear it up, take all the cardboard shelves out of the lockers, and basically mangle as much inmate property as possible. Why? Because some jerk-off inmate threw a handball at one of the officers sitting at the officers' station. What a total ass! This inmate obviously does not have the guts to confront the subject of his dislike, but he is willing to destroy all semblance of our relative calm programming in the gym.

Staff put out the word that we inmates should talk to the perpetrator of this act. They stressed, "Don't touch him up," but school him as to the consequences of his retarded actions. Hopefully that will be enough to avoid the dreaded squad.

Regarding the squad, in reality, the officers assigned to these positions are no better or worse toward inmates than regular housing unit officers. They are tasked with investigation into drug and other contraband smuggling, gang activity interdiction, and cause of death review. Essentially, the squad is all about maintaining safety and security, Personally, I appreciate that. It helps me to live linger.

John 14:27. *"Peace I leave with you; my peace I give you. I do not give to you as the world gives. Do not let your hearts be troubled and do not be afraid."*

✝ ✝ ✝

Thursday, May 5, 1994
8:00 a.m.

Ol' Leonard was back from the hole. His shoulders have sag to them and his eyes were ringed with dark circles. He looked like the wind had been let out of his sails. The classification committee placed Leonard on Close B custody to continue the sail trimming. Whether Leonard did what he was accused of, trying to control through blackmail the other child molesters, or not, the hole made its intended impression...only staff controls, we submit.

3:00 p.m.

Apprehensively, I returned to the gym after work. All looked normal, but I still had to open my locker to see if it had been ransacked. Whew. All was well with each item in its place. It is difficult to explain the relief and peace I experience from being left alone. Every time staff searches and destroys my few personal belongings, it is as if I had been raped. I understand and accept the need for security but not abuse. I pray constantly for invisibility. Again, what a relief.

3:30 p.m.

Rule change...again. Inmates must wear only state issued shirts, jeans, and boots to visiting. Personal tennis shoes and Levi's are now prohibited. Would the visiting officers really let me walk out of prison if I showed them my button fly as opposed to the state zippers? I think not.

My state pants were inside out as I taped up the hems on the legs because they were seven inches too long. Even with the makeshift modification I would look tidy because the jeans were new, received after the chow hall fire. My only complaint is they are stiff and constricting, quite uncomfortable in the crotch. Heck, my whole existence is uncomfortable so this is a minor annoyance. And, I would endure this and all discomforts for the enjoyment of a visit from family, friends, or any one. There is probably nothing I would not endure to receive a hug full of love.

Psalm 31:7-8. *I will be glad and rejoice in your love, for you saw my affliction and knew the anguish of my soul. You have not handed me over to the enemy but have set my feet in a spacious place.*

✟ ✟ ✟

Friday, May 6, 1994
12:00 Noon

Rain. Big fat drops that knock bees out of the air. I was hoping for
sun because I wanted to get in a few more games of volleyball and enjoy a few
more laughs before Ed goes home tomorrow. Ed will not come outside in the
rain, and I will miss out on a final good-bye.

9:00 p.m.

The rain continues. Ed will depart in the morning prior to the yard
being opened. Another friend goes home. I am happy for him, depressed for
me. Again, I have to slap myself once or twice to turn my thoughts around and
thank God for the fun times Ed and I spent together. Also, I must never forget
that Jesus is always with me and will not parole until I do.

10:00 p.m.

Propaganda and disinformation in America? The news program *20/20*
aired a segment about weight piles in jails and prisons, *uncovering* how
inmates are getting healthy and in shape on taxpayers' money. What is wrong
with that? Yes, we here at the Creek are staying in shape, but there is an overall
reduction in costs by a decrease in medical due to less violence. Mule Creek's
level of violence reduced by half after our weight piles reopened. As I have
said, exercise reduces stress and allows for the release of pent-up energy and
frustration. I would prefer tax dollars spent on education classes to strengthen
the brain instead of weights to build brawn, but sadly, education has been
determined to be too expensive. Besides, why educate a man; why instill pride
in knowledge; why give the inmate hope for a better life?

When news agencies want a story on any topic, even if the story is
slanted, they can always find one if they dig deep enough, or squint their eyes
to see only what they want, or what they believe will enrage the public for
ratings sake.

With God's help I am able to find a fragrant flower in the crudest
garbage pit. And in contrast, I am sure a little dirt can be scraped from the
corners of a thoroughly scrubbed and disinfected room. Why is it too difficult

to concentrate on and nurture the flowers? When did dirt become so fascinating?

Psalm 5:6. *You destroy those who tell lies; blood thirsty and deceitful men the Lord abhors.*

✞ ✞ ✞

Saturday, May 7, 1994
9:00 a.m.

The rain dampened my thin jacket and weighed down my mood as I walked to and from Building 6 for breakfast. The rain remained but Ed has departed. I would like it to rain on the day I parole. The water would cleanse me as I stepped into freedom…and being manly, the drops on my face would cover the tears of joy and relief of triumph over this insane asylum.

There will be no volleyball today. It is just as well because without Ed there would be one less smile, one less light, to help defeat the darkness, that ever lurking chocolate pudding.

After brushing my teeth I returned to my bunk and pulled the covers over my head. Wake me when it is my time to parole.

11:30 a.m.

Damn. I woke up too soon.

7:00 p.m.

The pudding was still trying to suck me under. I needed to telephone my father to have him cheer me up. During our chat, he told me that he would be at a ground breaking ceremony for a construction project in Barstow next week. Governor Wilson is scheduled to make a speech and my father will be seated near him. I asked my father to get his autograph—on a pardon. I only wish. From his actions, it seems our governor would rather put a bullet in all lifers' heads than let any of us parole and possibly cause him to lose an election if one out of a hundred were to re-offend.

For myself, I will continue praying for my freedom. I feel better now. Thank you, father. Thank you, Father.

2 Corinthians 3:17-18. *Now the Lord is the Spirit, and where the Spirit of the Lord is, there is freedom. And we, who with unveiled faces all reflect the Lord's glory, are being transformed into his likeness with ever increasing glory, which comes from the Lord, who is the Spirit*

✟ ✟ ✟

Sunday, May 8, 1994
MOTHER'S DAY
8:00 a.m.

I telephoned my mother to wish her a wonderful day and to tell her how much I love her. As we spoke I wondered, does a son ever know the woman he calls mother? She is giving, loving, and guides with a gentle hand. I believe a mother tends to blur her true self. She holds memories of all the experiences of a little girl growing up, filled with dreams. Is she ever prepared for the task of mother and wife? We as children too easily forget the dreams our mothers sacrificed to assist us toward our goals. I am struck with awe by my mother's care and devotion to me.

God, let me find the unselfishness needed to give back to my mother, and to others, that unconditional love that the woman I call mother continues to give and has always given to me.

My mother was pleased that I called.

10:00 a.m.

The sun is shining. It will be a glorious day for volleyball but a void will be present by the absence of Ed. Sigh.

11:00 a.m.

The first part of *The Stand* by Stephen King ran its credits across my television screen. Mr. King has come a long way in his fruitful career. Besides writing the book, he wrote the screenplay, and so far, part one was good. I will reserve my final comments until its completion.

I dream of the day that I write well enough to have something produced. It will take a lot of hard work and likely involve many rejections. Hmm…interesting thought. Man rejects man regularly as not good enough; God always accepts man so as to make him good enough.

Proverbs 1:8-9. *Listen, my son, to your father's instruction and do not forsake your mother's teaching. They will be a garland to grace your head and a chain to adorn you neck.*

✝ ✝ ✝

Monday, May 9, 1994
10:30 a.m.

Alarm! Code 3, the chapel? The Rabbi pushed his alarm button because an inmate would not relinquish his identification card. The denial occurred after the inmate asked the Rabbi for toilet paper and was denied. As the inmate exited the chapel he mumbled, "That's just like a Jew." Yes, that was disrespectful, but it did not warrant an emergency response. Disrespectful behavior multiplied by abuse of power can equal tragic results.

Responding staff was not pleased by the cry of wolf.

3:00 p.m.

Work was completed for the day. As I walked out of the Program Office, I paused. To the right was the weight pile; to the left were the gym and my bunk. I should have turned right to exercise but I was not in an energetic mood. I am sitting on a blue funk which is the ledge surrounding the pool of pudding.

A nap sounded preferable at that moment. Zzzz...

8:01 p.m. Our Time

12:01 a.m. Their Time

John Wayne Gacy, the infamous serial killer is dead. Outside the prison a gathered crowd cheered during Gacy's execution. His last words were shouts of innocence. Only God, Gacy, and the victims know for sure, and none are talking.

Can anyone feel satisfaction from Gacy's death? There were more than 10 years of appeals costing the taxpayer millions of dollars to ensure Gacy's rights were upheld so that society could 'legally' kill him. Was it worth it? The prosecutor in the case said Gacy did not suffer enough. What would have been enough to ease the pain of the families of the victims?

Here is a thought: Maybe Gacy should have been given a life sentence instead of the death penalty. It certainly would have cost less and death *is* preferable to life without the possibility of parole. For those who have not walked a prison yard as an inmate, prison is an animated death where pseudo-life clings to a hope of freedom and rebirth. Without that hope there is only a walking death. If our society demands satisfaction, take away hope. Then society can rejoice in killing a man each and every day that he awakes to a horror that does not end.

By the way, who washes the executioner's hands?

Old Law: Leviticus 25:21. *Whoever kills an animal must make restitution, but whoever kills a man must be put to death.*

New Law: Matthew 5:38-39. *"You have heard that it was said, 'Eye for eye, and tooth for tooth.' But I tell you, do not resist an evil person. If someone strikes you on the right check, turn to him the other also."*

✞   ✞   ✞

Tuesday, May 10, 1994
4:00 p.m.

Mail. A letter from my mother, a letter from Madeline in the Philippines, and several pieces of junk mail addressed to Occupant. That would be me. I have a theory that I am still alive so long as I am listed in some computer somewhere. This junk mail proves it. I do exist because computers never lie. Smile. My mother's letter was uplifting, filled with words of love and encouragement. Madeline's was terrifying. What two different worlds she and I live in.

Madeline explained that the company she works for arranged a mandatory participation picnic. On the appointed day, she along with two dozen 20-year oldish girls had only been in this juggled picnic area for a few minutes when a group of 50 plus rebels of the Communist New People's Army appeared out of the dense foliage. They were armed with rifles, hand guns and machetes and were demanding food. Madeline was terrified because the rebels were known for taking conscripts, especially girls, for services beyond cooking and cleaning. Fortunately, after the rebels were fed, they departed the area. The girls ran, fearing the rebels would return

It is difficult to imagine such a frightening scene. Two different worlds. God has abundantly blessed the United States, but distressingly, we as its citizens are tearing it apart by our division, both politically and spiritually.

I believe it is important for Christians to stay strong and hold our moral ground, to be examples for others. The battle is ours if we only engage the enemy instead of pacifying him, remembering always that usually we are our own worst enemies.

It is that speck and plank scenario.

Ephesians 6:10-11. *Finally, be strong in the Lord and in His mighty power. Put on the full armor of God so that you can take your stand against the devil's schemes.*

✝ ✝ ✝

Wednesday, May 11, 1994
10:00 a.m.

Fear is the mind killer; a deep freeze for the soul. A new inmate on orientation status refused to come out of his cell to program among the general population of inmates.

"I'm not safe," he whimpered through the crack in his cell door.

Staff attempted to convince him that he would be safe on this facility. He still refused to come out. The classification committee had no alternative but to send him to the hole. Ex-judges, ex-police officers, ex-CDC employees, child molesters, gang drop outs, and high notoriety cases survive just fine here. All programming - all safe - as long as they mind their own business and remember to employ courtesy (respect) in all their interactions.

I do empathize with this inmate, but it is apparent that he does not know Christ, or God's promise of protection. I, too, was petrified when I first arrived at San Quentin, but I depended on God's word for safety, and He surrounded me with quality people, both inmates and staff. I pray this man will open himself to God so he can receive the peace of mind that I carry with me.

11:30 a.m.

Two months ago while reviewing price invoices for what the CDC paid for each swivel desk lamp, Donna, the other clerks, and I, were shocked by the $75 price tag because Donna had purchased this same model from K-Mart for her home for less than $20.

It is no surprise that California is in dire financial straits. Today we received this quarter's cost breakdown for office supplies. We, actually the taxpayers, were charged $27 for each 500 page ream of copy machine paper. The actual cost of the ream was only $2.50 but between the prison warehouse and our office there is one hell of a markup. As our monthly supplies arrived today we also discovered we were not being credited for the unused supplies that we have been returning. Additionally, we were being charged the full *new* price for file folders that have been recycled and are held together with masking tape.

Someone somewhere is making a lot of money and we can assume the taxpayers are being screwed as always. Please tell me who are the real criminals? I am confused.

4:00 p.m.

Legal mail. My federal appeal has been filed. I received the court stamped copy of my petition with the case number. So it begins.

Ephesians 4:28. *He who has been stealing must steal no longer, but must work, doing something useful with his own hands, that he may have something to share with those in need.*

✠ ✠ ✠

Thursday, May 12, 1994
11:45 a.m.

I took my lunch break on the yard. While I sat eating a bologna sandwich and watching a basketball game of three-on-three, Stephen, a 40 – something Hispanic sat down next to me. Then, as if no time had elapsed from the day we sat together in the infirmary's holding cell, the day of my optometry appointment, he continued his story of medical woe.

Stephen stated that he was poisoned by the prison doctors because the Department of Corrections was attempting to save money by issuing him medication that had been recalled by the manufacturer. Stephen said he went from 230 to 120 pounds and almost died. He was in the infirmary for eight months before the doctors realized it was the medication that was killing him.

Stephen filed a civil suit and after six years of court hearings and mountains of paperwork, he finally won. It was interesting to hear how the state spent more money defending the case than what Stephen originally asked for in damages. I have watched during these years in prison how the state would rather beat you into submission, dragging its feet, and asking for time extensions, instead of admitting wrongdoing and paying a reasonable penalty.

The Attorney General had at his disposal, millions of taxpayers' dollars to spend on a defense, but when the judge ordered the state to pay up, the Attorney General pled inadequate funds. What a strange world this is. It is backward, mixed up, and confused, fighting unnecessary battles. Was it pride or a culture that refuses to publicly admit that prison staff makes errors accidentally or on purpose?

Where was the wisdom that God supposedly blessed our leaders with? I cannot say, but I know everything, and I mean everything, works for the glory of God. I simply do not have the capacity to understand how. Maybe someday.

I thought back to my appointment with the optometrist. In my opinion he was tops. Tops in positive personality and he provided me with a quality examination. He took his time, talked, acted, and treated me like a normal person. When the exam was over, I stepped out of the chair and began searching my pockets for the keys to my long-ago surfer truck. Stupid me! I am an inmate, not a person, but for a moment I felt normal. Ooooh, I got the shivers.

Within all the madness a light was found. Who would believe he was found in a tiny nook examining eyeballs? Come to think about it, Jesus helped the blind to see, too.

Isaiah 55:8-9. *"For my thoughts are not your thoughts, neither are your ways my ways," declares the Lord. "As the heavens are higher than the earth, so are my ways higher than your ways and my thoughts than your thoughts."*

✝ ✝ ✝

Friday, May 13, 1994
7:00 a.m.

The morning of Friday, the 13th. Scary, huh? Naw, it is only another day where I struggle, clinging to hope. I find it strange how myths and fables can take hold and paralyze people. Some cannot do this; others cannot do that—superstition. Ha! Falling for the ol' Satan trap. With God there is only freedom. However, I admit it is difficult, many times impossible to feel free.

3:00 p.m.

I was standing in the classification room making photocopies. Two officers were seated at the large table and updating each other on their old high school friends: where they had moved to; who they had married, and the careers they had undertaken. As I listened, my eyes moistened. I knew nothing of my high school friends. After graduation and college, I went my wrong way and ended up in this never-never land.

Choices I made created the destiny I am living. What a stupid, stupid man I was...*crunch*...paper jam.

4:00 p.m.

Mail. Two letters from the E.T.'s, Ed Thompson and Ellen Turner. Ed made it safely home to Santa Monica and was planning a deep sea fishing trip with his family. Ellen, who I have not heard from in two years, sent me several news articles. I had met Ellen while in San Quentin and we began corresponding. She was part of a tour, not doing time. Ha ha. I was immediately drawn to Ellen's smile, and suffering from the loss of Angela, I hoped that some type of relationship could grow, but nothing materialized. Ellen's few letters grew farther and farther apart.

The news articles that Ellen enclosed featured Chaplain Earl Smith and his work within San Quentin. I miss that man. He and his programs were so innovative and blazing with fire for God. Each time I stepped through those sanctuary doors, the oppressive block walls surrounding my earthly life would tumble down. The Spirit reigned supreme.

Here at the Creek the chapel is dead in comparison to the "Q". At times I feel guilty about complaining about this chapel's inadequacy when I am not trying to light a match to the pews. If I want fire, maybe I should be the one that ignites it. Hmm, food for thought.

Blessings to the E.T.'s for their remembrance of me.

Revelation 3:2, 15-16. *"Wake up! Strengthen what remains and is about to die, for I have not found your deeds complete in the sight of my god. I know your deeds, that you are neither cold nor hot. I wish you were either one or the other. So, because you are lukewarm - neither hot nor cold - I am about to spit you out of my mouth."*

✛ ✛ ✛

Saturday, May 14, 1994
2:00 p.m.

I was in the athletic zone today. Hot! Sizzling! I was king of the concrete beach. In other words, I owned the volleyball court. Ed must have left sprinklings of his spiking magic behind because I dominated. Unstoppable!

The ability to play a sport well is a grand blessing from God. Strength, agility, coordination, health, all are blessings that cannot be bought. Each goes into making up the important ingredients for great sports and a good life. I must pause to take a deep invigorating breath, and revel in this feeling because the zone is a fleeting thing; and if fleeting, it becomes prized, special, something to cherish.

Philippians 4:19-20. *And my god will meet all your needs according to His glorious riches in Christ Jesus. To our God and Father be glory for ever and ever. Amen.*

✛ ✛ ✛

Sunday, May 15, 1994
8:00 p.m.

I am lying on my bunk watching television and thinking about the last several days. Good things and bad occurred but mentally I am remaining on the positive side of the edge. This may sound like an easy thing to do, but it has to be constantly worked on. The other side is a black abyss of depression and potential self-destruction. I have to continually thank God for the small joys that I have in the fabricated world of concrete and steel and not fixate on the things I forfeited in the real one: my fiancée, many years gone; my grandmother and only sister both passing on to be with Jesus; friends who faded away and continued on with their productive lives, and a career that will never be known.

I suppose some, many perhaps, would say, "That's what you deserve," and, "You shouldn't have any moments of happiness." In opposition to their sentiment, I would say they are shortsighted in their beliefs. I would ask them, "What kind of person do they want leaving prison?" Ninety-five plus percent of all inmates will eventually be released. Some will have accepted Jesus, others will not, but all are subject to the same negative environment. Every day I observe inmates who, despite daily brow-beatings, have a positive self-esteem and are working toward beneficial goals. Others who have succumbed, possessing low self-esteem, participate in negative, self-destructive activities. Which group do you think will create more victims after they are released?

Unfortunately, politicians have to be elected. Therefore, they bend to the pressures of the emotional, penologically uneducated public. Being a victim is a tragedy, but today it has become fashionable, influential, and their organizations are financed by the powerful prison guards' association. In the end, the wise but weak leaders are forced to pass emotionally based bad legislation. They are unable to provide the wayward individual the ladder needed to climb out of the deviant life-style he leapt into. If politicians did otherwise, they would be accused being soft on criminals by providing too many *luxuries,* (education, vocations, and mental health) resulting in the demise of their cherished, high-paying, political careers. What will become of us all, especially the victims in waiting?

Still, that abyss draws near, so close, so deep, and my fear of going over the edge into oblivion keeps me looking to Jesus as His lifeline never frays. He is what should become of us all.

11:00 p.m.

The Stand, the made for television movie has concluded. I preferred the book, but it must have been difficult for Mr. King to condense into a few hours that which was written on hundreds of pages.

2 Corinthians 12:9. *But He said to me, "My grace is sufficient for you, for my power is made perfect in weakness." Therefore I will boast all the more gladly about my weakness, so that Christ's power may rest on me.*

✝ ✝ ✝

Monday, May 16, 1994
8:00 a.m.

Good ol' Lieutenant Davenport, a 30-year veteran of Corrections, is going to be absent for a month to take care of his medical needs prior to retiring. His replacement is a female lieutenant. It is not that women cannot do the job, but should they? God graced women with the most important and honorable occupations, and they are motherhood and wife. Nothing is more important than the managing of a household.

The new lieutenant is probably a fine and competent woman, but are the things she buys with her paycheck more important than the love and attention she could be, or should be giving to her family? Does this 40-something woman have a family? Has her rise to power and control over men interfered with her family or how much better could her family unit have been without the demands of the workplace?

Of course there are many factors that may have caused this woman to enter the workforce. The most compelling is the need to feed, clothe and house herself and her children if her husband and father of the children abandoned his responsibilities, but beyond that, a "keeping-up-with-the-Jones'" mentality is questionable.

Who will God bless more, the female chairperson of a Fortune 500 company or the wife and mother who raises a God-fearing, Christ-loving family? It is just a question.

4:00 p.m.

Mail. I received a response from Sears concerning the broken pieces of my radio. They neither have the plastic pieces due to the age of the radio nor do they know where they can be located. As I said before, I realize Tommy did not purposely break my radio. That is why it is called an accident. No one was at fault, except possibly me. If I had stuck to my original plan of listening to my radio and only watching the games, the radio would not have been broken. Sigh. The responsibility was mine.

Titus 2:4. *They can train the younger women to love their husbands and Children, to be self-controlled and pure, to be busy at home, to be kind, and to be subject to their husbands, so that no one will malign the word of God.*

✟ ✟ ✟

Tuesday, May 17, 1994
3:00 p.m.

The mood in the Program Office was upbeat and spirited today. Donna was joking with us inmates, the program administrator was jovial, and the new lieutenant was receptive to our questions of how she wanted to run the facility and our sharing with her as to how it had been running. All the clerks were quite happy. My God, today was a very nice day at work. It was almost worth coming to prison to experience this cooperation and mutual respect between supervisors and subordinates. NOT!

4:00 p.m.

Mail. It was a letter from Charlie who is in Soledad Prison. He has only a few months left on his manslaughter sentence. I have found it a joy to have known him for more than six years since our meeting in San Quentin. What is amazing is that we have been able to keep in contact throughout our transfers to different prisons. Since Charlie's incarceration for DUI motor boat and involuntary manslaughter, he has studied to earn an Associate of Arts degree, and now is only two units from a Bachelor of Arts degree. All this was accomplished while working his prison job as a clerk. He should be very proud of his accomplishment as I am proud of him.

The thing is, Charlie was never a criminal. He had a drinking problem that caused the death of another in a boating accident. It was a tragedy. However, this *down* time has given Charlie the opportunity to become a strong Christian and confront his alcohol problem. His solution is total reliance on the first and abstinence from the second.

I am excited for Charlie as he nears the end of this chapter in his life, and I am hopeful that he can retain his new convictions through Christ and in sobriety.

9:00 p.m.

News Flash! The California Legislature is proposing to cut 130 million dollars from the Department of Corrections' yearly budget. If they do so, how can the legislature expect CDC to manage their 28 prisons, including the four new ones coming online, and the five that have been proposed to be built? They cannot. It is a fiscal impossibility.

"We will have to release the criminals in mass," a spokesperson for the Speaker of the House retorted. In reality, this is just politics at its best, or worst. Budgetary maneuvering and citizens scare tactics so that the public will accept cuts in every other program instead of prisons.

Prisons are more important than health care, education, roads, everything. "Public Safety!" Shout it from the roof tops. The prison monster must grow, and to do so, it must be fed, and the only thing it will eat is our futures. Yum, yum. Good-bye, fiscal soundness. Good-bye, Golden State. Hello, bars and walls.

There will be no cut to the Department of Corrections' budget. Mark my words.

Psalm 147:1. *Praise the Lord. How good it is to sing praises to our God, how pleasant and fitting to praise Him!*

✞ ✞ ✞

Wednesday, May 18, 1994
9:30 a.m.

Alarm! Code 3 in the vocations area. Staff ran toward work change (vocations entrance) as the inmates plopped down on the ground. Well, most staff ran. One out-of-shape, overweight officer waddled as he huffed and puffed from Building 6. This housing unit is the farthest building from vocations. As this officer approached the work change door, he only had one five-inch curb left to hurdle. Viewed in slow motion, his booted foot lifted, but not quite enough. Catching the curb's lip, he stumbled, arms flailing as a splat was imminent, but somewhere among the hoots and howls of inmates, the officer found his footing, avoiding a bumbling, stumbling tumble.

After all the hubbub, the alarm turned out to be false, but the real action then began as staff corralled the once-laughing inmates. Usually hecklers were written up and CTQ'd for the day for their disrespectful behavior and distractions during a code. This time they were only read the riot act, as privately, supervisory staff could see the humor in it. However, at the same time, a need to instill the importance of silence during an alarm was warranted.

10:00 p.m.

I am lying on my bunk contemplating physical dilapidation as I look at my not so taut stomach. No, I am not fat by any measure. I have lost my teenaged muscle tone. I run my fingers over my heightening forehead and then wipe clean my ever-thickening glasses. I am only 33. What is up? These changes are not appreciated. My youth is fading and I have nothing in compensation for the loss: no bank account for the long hours of work; no loving lady to massage my shoulders, and no children to fill a home with laughter.

How could I have been such a fool? The devil did not make me do it, but he sure was the master deceiver. I can only pray that my youth and physical luster is being traded for a bit of wisdom.

Proverbs 2:6. *For the Lord gives wisdom, and from His mouth comes knowledge and understanding.*

✞ ✞ ✞

Thursday, May 19, 1994
9:00 a.m.

A male sergeant was speaking with the female lieutenant in her office. He was commenting on the time he worked at CIM (women's prison) and how he was reprimanded for writing 35 disciplinary reports on women caught in lesbian acts (which is expressly against the rules). He was scolded, saying, "Give 'em a break. They are only seeking affection." Here at the Creek if a man is caught masturbating he is immediately written up, and if he is caught by a female staff, he is given a District Attorney referral for a sex change.

A double standard? Whether a person is doing right or wrong, treat everyone the same. When discrimination occurs, for whatever the reason, it breeds resentment. Treat us all with a firm, kind hand, and you will find that many will seek the path less traveled.

4:30 p.m.

Lockdown. There will be no evening programming, no recreation yard tonight because the SERT team (Special Emergency Response Team) is planning exercises: hostage rescues, riot control tactics, and so on. We inmates tend to make fun of these men in their army fatigues playing para-military games. Hup! Hup! Hup! They march to and fro with zipper-busting pride. However, deep down inside I have a sense of foreboding and fear because these men take their job extremely seriously and appear too eager to play for real their deadly game of subdue, conquer, and kill.

What happened to the ounce of prevention prevents a pound of cure? I am sorry. It is not politically correct to involve inmates in productive and positive activities that would take their minds away from boredom and violence. It appears it is better to show inmates a cocked gun with an itchy finger on the trigger than to give them a book to fill their hearts and minds with dreams and productive aspirations.

The echoes of laughter hide the sobs of sadness.

Galatians 6:9. *Let us not become weary in doing good, for at the proper time we will reap a harvest if we do not give up.*

✝ ✝ ✝

Friday, May 20, 1994
5:00 p.m.

The gym officer called me to the officers' station. I was told to report back to work after chow. There would be no rest for the weary.

5:30 p.m.

Seated at my work desk I waited. The lieutenant had something important for me to type. Time ticked on. Tick tock.

6:00 p.m.

A memorandum? The lieutenant wanted me to type a one page memo that gives approval for inmates to remove one piece of fruit from the chow hall (housing unit) after feeding. What about his clerk? Jeez, ridiculous. I had other plans for the evening. Oh well, I smiled and promptly completed the task in eight minutes. I handed the memo to the lieutenant and rushed back to the gym, my bunk, and the movie, *Backdraft*, that was beginning, and that I had waited all week to watch.

6:30 p.m.

"Watson, report to the Program Office," the loud speaker boomed. What now? I removed my comfy sweats, got dressed in my state blues, and walked back to work, all the while maintaining a strained smile. "I need you to type cc: (carbon copy) to," the lieutenant said. Two names? He wanted me to type two names at the bottom of the memo he had already approved. This was way out ridiculous but I had no choice. It would not be appropriate for me to voice my objection to such a trivial request. A good work assignment was hard to find so I put up with these lame requests, and again, where was his clerk?

As I walked back to the gym I repeated; "I work for God and not man. All would be for the best."

1 Peter 2:18-19. *Slaves, submit yourselves to your master with all respect, not only to those who are good and considerate, but also to those who are harsh. For it is commendable if a man bears up under the pain of unjust suffering because he is conscious of God.*

✝ ✝ ✝

Saturday, May 21, 1994
2:00 p.m.

All day cotton-ball clouds tip-toed across a blue, sun-lit sky. Volleyball was exceptional. The only annoyance was the gun officer in the yard tower. He seemed to have a microphone fetish. On the days that he works it was always the same: talk, talk, talk, talk. Petty orders as the day is long: "Get off the red curb," "Don't sit on the tables," "Move away from the light pole," "One person at the drinking fountain at a time," and so on and so on. All he really accomplished was to raise everyone's stress level. Did this officer know the story of *The Boy Who Cried Wolf?* When it comes time to announce a real emergency, it is likely that no one will hear him because no one listens to what he says anymore. He has become noise that the rest of us have to yell over.

Still, even taking into account Mr. Talk-Talk's annoyance along with my sore toes from jumping and landing on our concrete court, I vote 10 times unanimous that today was a physically active, stress relieving and positive day.

Shh. Do not tell anyone. If word gets out that I am in a good mood, someone will attempt to ruin it.

1 Corinthians 14:33a. *For God is not a God of disorder but of peace.*

✞ ✞ ✞

Sunday, May 22, 1994
3:00 p.m.

Marijuana was discovered in a cell during a random cell search. The two occupants were hauled off to the hole and will do at least another year in prison and will likely be referred to the District Attorney for additional charges. I cannot see the importance of a 45 minute high compared to more time in prison. I would do anything to get out...well, almost anything.

8:30 p.m.

I have been watching the movie *City Slickers*. It was supposed to be a comedy but it depressed me. One character said, "Do you remember the dreams of your youth? Then suddenly you are middle age and you look into the mirror and realize this is as good looking as you will ever get; this is as far as you will ever go; and you look around to realize your life sucks."

My reality is pushing me over the edge again. Please Lord, pull me back. My hope is sinking. My dreams are dissolving. Without dreams I have only despair. In despair there is only death.

I do not believe there is any crime worth this time.

I get it. I truly get it. I have learned my lesson.

Philippians 4:8-9. *Finally, brothers, whatever is true, whatever is noble, whatever is right, whatever is pure, whatever is lovely, whatever is admirable-if anything is excellent or praiseworthy-think about such things. Whatever you have learned or received or heard from me, or seen in me-put it into practice. And the God of peace will be with you.*

✞ ✞ ✞

Monday, May 23, 1994
7:00 p.m.

When was that precise moment we fell out of love and evolved into friends? Mickie, my passionate childhood sweetheart has transformed into a sincere friend. She retains all the endearing qualities, but somewhere along the line has picked up the irritating trait of disappearing from time to time. This is one of those times.

I telephoned Mickie's aunt's house, where she lives, and her aunt informed me that she has not seen Mickie or the children for at least a week. Is Mickie still working? Are the children still attending school? Mickie's actions are irritating because she will not tell anyone where she is going or how she can be reached in case of an emergency.

Mickie has told me she does not want people checking up on her, and because she is an adult, she does not have to check in with anyone. When someone cares for another you worry about them. It is not a matter of checking up on them. It is difficult to care about a selfish and potentially destructive person. I believe I am happily doomed to always care for Mickie because she was my first love, but if I give and give without receiving anything in return, my well will quickly empty.

After fuming for a while, and stomping around in frustration, I thought of God's unending love for me and how He endured my rejection with patience. I am ashamed. I must forgive as God forgives me. And with imperfect patience, I will again express to Mickie that my wish to know her (general) whereabouts is not an attempt to check up on her, but only for peace of mind and her well-being. However, if she feels this imposes on her privacy, I will respect her secrecy.

Matthew 18:21-22. *Then Peter came to Jesus and asked, "Lord, how many times shall I forgive my brother when he sins against me? Up to seven times?" Jesus answered, "I tell you, not seven times, but seventy-seven times."*

✟ ✟ ✟

Tuesday, May 24, 1994
6:00 p.m.

Alarms! Code 3 in the urinals. Not actually in the urinals, but I was using the urinals in the gym when the alarm sounded from building 8. Even though the alarm was somewhere else I am supposed to sit down on the ground regardless of where I may be or what I may be doing. The problem was I was still emptying my bladder. It was rather unnerving to have staff yelling, "Get down! Get down!" And be unable to finish peeing. This was one of prison life's unsettling situations.

Fortunately for me I was only screamed at and not pummeled to the ground with a side-handle baton. Not even staff want to wade into the foam puddles that make up the toilet and urinal area.

11:30 p.m.

Today was the warmest of the year so far, low 90's. No doubt it will get hotter. In summers past, we have suffered through, drenched in sweat, consecutive days above 110 degrees. As the temperature rises, the scramble for fans by inmates and staff intensifies. Several inmates have stopped by my bunk to lust after the cool breeze blowing from the wall vent (swamp cooler).

Hey, these seem to be the same guys that complained about the vent earlier this year because it was too cold. From my observations, inmates take pride in complaining. I, too, fall prey to this malady at times. Too cold, too hot, bugs coming in through the vent, Jeepers, Magee. No one is ever happy here, but I guess that is the goal. This is prison, is it not? But wait a brick yard minute: here is a concept for you; find something, anything to be happy, thankful for, because many exist. Then be grateful for that blessing; however small it may be, because it, too, can be taken away.

Isaiah 58:11. *The Lord will guide you always: He will satisfy your needs in a sun-scorched land and will strengthen your frame. You will be like a well-watered garden, like a spring whose waters never fail.*

☩ ☩ ☩

Wednesday, May 25, 1994
2:30 a.m.

The swamp cooler behind my bunk turned off, waking me. The absence of the drone was deafening. It really chaps my hide when staff turns it off, because through it, comes our only fresh air.

I opened my eyes and it was dark, completely and totally black. All the lights, even the night lights were off. No, I did not go blind. The power must have gone out. Breakfast will be late this morning. So...this is what darkness is like. I have all but forgotten. I am amazed that a prison so new, built in 1987, has so many power failures.

Staff deserved an apology for my unwarranted accusation.

11:00 a.m.

I was in the education bathroom to relieve myself during a break from work. Several other inmates were coaxing a petite transgender into letting them 'get their freak on.' I believe that was an appropriate description for their wants as they eased the transgender into a corner. I could tell by his expression that he was apprehensive by the demands of these four men, but he allowed one of them to massage *his* B cup size breast. While three narrowed the gap between themselves and the transgender, I heard the sound of zippers. The fourth inmate was assigned to 'keep point' (watch for staff) so the others could 'do their thing.' At this point the transgender had no choice in the matter. He would comply.

I flushed and departed, not interested, quite disgusted, and not wanting any part, mind or body of that scene. I am lonely but I will never be that lonely.

It is amazing how the flesh will drive the mind to all sorts of lows to get its fix.

3:00 p.m.

My counselor and I were in a casual discussion that turned to the subject of the parole board. Knowing my case factors, my counselor stated without any emotion, "I don't see how you will ever get a parole date." That was a hard, cold slap in the face. My counselor continued by saying, "There potentially could have been three killings, not just one, and because you have remained disciplinary free with no signs of being a broken man, the parole board will have difficulty seeing a change in you."

What he was telling me was my efforts at being good from day one in prison would work against me. Well, that sucks. And, it may be true that I was neither an addict, nor was I an abused child, but I had a soul so clouded, my character compass so out of whack, that when the sh-- hit the fan, my warped solution was to use a gun. I was broken in the worst way.

Despite my counselor's belief, I will depend on God. He saved my life, my soul, and I truly believe He is saving my freedom for me, too. Unless a person has been saved and understands God's forgiveness he will never know the wondrous blessing of starting over again, of true change.

Man will give me many more cold slaps, but Jesus is always available with a reassuring hug. Praise God.

Genesis 28:15. *"I am with you wherever you go, and I will not leave you until I have done what I have promised you."*

✝ ✝ ✝

Thursday, May 26, 1994
10:15 a.m.

While at work I could not help eavesdropping on a loud conversation between several inmates. They had come out of classification committee and were bad-mouthing staff. They complained because their custody level had been raised and their privileges restricted due to a fight that they were involved in.

How do their little minds work? They physically hurt another person, but they neither feel guilty, nor do they believe there should be any sort of punishment for their wrongdoing. What is worse is these are the types of men under the determinate sentencing law (DSL) who will be paroled, come back, parole again, and come back to prison many times before I, who is under the indeterminate sentencing law (ISL) will ever get a chance to parole.

I am confused.

I understand the great pain I have caused, and look for ways each day to make others' lives better, but I will remain in prison. If you try to figure the wisdom of this system you will go plum crazy.

The system needs to be changed. Someone ask me. I know how; take responsibility for one's offenses; change your behavior, and then freedom should follow. Each step should depend on the inmate, not on the crime committed because we each learn at our own pace.

1:00 p.m.

A planned power outage. I was allowed to leave work early so I came back to the gym to relax and read my *Conde' Nast Traveler* magazine, and then to drift off to sleep when the lights went out.

4:00 p.m.

Three hours? That was more than a nap. Apparently I was more exhausted than I had thought. I have found by listening to my body's needs for food or extra sleep that it helps to keep stress and illness at bay. It is not foolproof, so when stress piles up or I am being cursed by sickness, I have one fail-safe prayer: "Lord, please take this burden from me."

It is a simple, but powerful, prayer and the Lord always takes the burden away. Maybe not immediately, but as long as I do not try to snatch the problem back and solve it myself, He will relieve me of my suffering. Praise God for promises fulfilled.

Psalm 71:8, 15. *My mouth is filled with your praise, declaring your splendor all day long. My mouth will tell of your righteousness, of your salvation all day long, though I know not its measure.*

✝ ✝ ✝

Sunday, May 29, 1994
10:30 a.m.

I received a ducat (pass) last night to report to Receiving and Release. I sat on the wooden bench outside of R&R waiting my turn to pick up ribbons and a daisy wheel for my typewriter and a new pair of headphones. My eyes took in the beauty of the quad area landscaping in front of R&R: finely trimmed green lawn, manicured bushes, and neatly arranged flowers of yellow, orange, white, and red. Dancing butterflies were flitting around while bees alighted in search of the sweet nectar within each flower.

A great amount of planning and work had resulted in pleasure to the eyes. In contrast, there is the walking refuse from society's trash on each of the three facilities. No amount of planning or work is being put into them. It is no surprise the inmates are the way they are. The Beauty and the Beasts.

What a difference, what an obvious lesson, but no one is willing to learn, neither staff, nor inmate. Wait one second. Man may have tended the flowers, but God made them grow. I can tend my own inner garden and through God I will grow. Praise God.

8:34 p.m.

Conflict. I was waiting for my scheduled 8:30 telephone call but the man using the telephone would not get off. He was taking up my time, shortening my call because another man was scheduled after me at 8:45. This was a big dilemma because I could not allow him to stay on the telephone or I would appear weak. Truth be told, a telephone call is not worth getting into a fight over. Nothing is worth violence, but there is this stupid prison etiquette, and I cannot let someone disrespect me or my life will turn to a worse hell as it would be open season on me.

"Hey, partner, you're four minutes into my time,"   I said with confidence and determination. I had raised the stakes, but my mind echoed: "Please hang up." Whew. He said good-bye and hung up, and then apologized. Cool. Status quo was maintained. I hate prison etiquette. Thanks be to God for the courtesy that most inmates show toward each other.

1 Peter 2: 2-3. *Like newborn babies, crave pure spiritual milk, so that by it you may grow up in your salvation, now that you have tasted that the Lord is good.*

✝ ✝ ✝

Monday, May 30, 1994
11:00 a.m.

Lieutenant McMullens, from San Quentin, strolled through the Program Office this morning. He is a big, black, hulk of a man with gnarled knuckles, but with a face that possesses features that could warm the heart of the coldest troll. McMullens is working as a part of an audit team reviewing the Creek's bookkeeping.

My eyes lit up at seeing one of the men who treated me like a human while working for him during my years in San Quentin. McMullens would lay down the law in no uncertain terms to his clerks. Then, when he saw they could toe the line, he treated us like humans, with kindness, concern, and encouraged each of us to find ways to better ourselves. McMullens is a fine model for how Correctional Staff should act.

Unfortunately, McMullens and I were only able to gossip for a few moments, but I was able to ask him to pass along my greetings to Chaplain Smith back at the "Q".

I am grateful that my memories of San Quentin are not only of giant walls and barred cells that stretch forever, but of the fire that was stoked in me for God. Those were wonderful days of spiritual rejuvenation. How strange it sounds to say that any day spent in prison was a good day, but when one is going through God's fire toward a rebirth, one can only praise His name and be thankful for whatever the circumstances.

A warm smile in prison is worth a thousand hugs in the free world. God, please bless Lieutenant McMullens.

Philippians 1:3, 27. *I thank God every time I remember you. Whatever happens, conduct yourselves in a manner worthy of the gospel of Christ. Then, whether I come and see you or only hear about you in my absence, I know that you stand firm in one spirit, contending as one man for the faith of the gospel.*

✝ ✝ ✝

Tuesday, May 31, 1994
5:45 a.m.

I awoke from a dream of Angela as I realized that today is her birthday. It has been more than six years since my last telephone conversation with her. Still, I pray daily for her happiness. In doing so, I try to keep my ego out of my prayers, but occasionally I ask the unanswerable question: does Angela ever think of me or miss me? Today, I wonder who the lucky man is that gets to give Angela her birthday kiss.

Despite the gut-wrenching thought, it was a wonderful dream. No sex was involved. We were in a movie theatre together. I felt her warm hand in mine and smelled the fresh fragrance of her long, black, and silky hair. In the reflected light of the film I saw her smile at me and my heart overflowed with joy. For that moment, however long a dream really is, the world was good and right. Angela was the sun of my summer days. The rays caressing my skin were her gentle touch. Painfully, those days of happiness have ended, and all that I am left with is the burn.

My stomach churns with bile at the thought that I tossed Angela, my love, into someone else's arms. However, because I do love her, I pray that he is good to her because she deserves the very best.

I am solely at fault and fear this wound will never heal. Please keep her safe, Lord, and maybe someday after this waking nightmare ends, I pray to be blessed by at least a gazing glimpse of Angela's form across a busy street, or among a crowd in a shopping mall. If it is your will, Lord.

I do thank you for the dream, God. Rarely can anyone say that the world is right and good, even for the few fleeting moments within a dream.

Isaiah 49: 15-16. *Can a mother forget the baby at her breast and have no compassion on the child she has borne? Though she may forget, I will not forget you. See, I have engraved you on the palm of my hands; your walls are ever before me."*

✞ ✞ ✞

Wednesday, June 1, 1994
8:00 a.m.

A new month and another changing of the guard. The relief female lieutenant's time on our facility has come to an end. I am pleased to report that she used wisdom and tact as well as being very personable. It was apparent that she is from the *old school* of respect and utilization of resources, namely us inmate clerks, in a positive fashion.

The lieutenant's replacement is also female and we clerks are pleased because she, too, is *old school,* or at least that is what we have been told.

It seems that *New and Improved* is not the end-all, be-all of things. Age and wisdom, regardless of a person's gender is a good thing. *Old School* Rocks!

4:00 p.m.

Mail. The officer handing out envelopes of happiness stopped by my bunk. He handed me a letter from Arlene in the Philippines. Short and sweet, the letter, not Arlene...well, actually she is, too. Ha ha. Her nickname is "Apple." How cute. She is preparing for college entrance exams, which I am led to believe is comparable to our high school when using American standards of education levels. Arlene is cute as a button with a bob-cut hair style, a dimple on each cheek, huggable as a doll, and writes letters, short though they may be, filled with wit and humor. I would be happy if our pen-pal relationship continued to grow into something more substantial, but the thousands of miles that separate us is a significant, and in reality, an insurmountable obstacle.

I will leave my desire up to the will of God as He is the only one that can put me together with any lady, close by or far away. Until that happens, I will be thankful for and continue to write encouraging letters.

John 14:8. *"I will not leave you as orphans; I will come to you."*

✞ ✞ ✞

Thursday, June 2, 1994
9:00 a.m.

Office gossip of local/international news. There is a push to remove weight piles from prisons and county jails across the legislative country. It is in response to the media's focus on the few huge men with muscles and no minds. This leash mentality, with the public being led around with a ring in their noses, is a wonderful example of how great masses of people can be inflamed and influenced. I have seen first-hand how the removal of the weight pile actually increased injuries. The use of makeshift weights (water-filled bottles hung from broom sticks) cause injuries requiring medical attention, and violence (physical altercations) doubled due to pent-up stress when the weight pile on our facility temporarily closed.

It may be politically correct to close the weight piles, but line staff that I have spoken with do not want the weights removed because they occupy a large number of inmates for a significant portion of the day. Keeping in mind the overcrowding issue with insufficient jobs, academic, or vocational assignments, which true saying would you prefer: "Busy hands are happy hands" or "Idle hands are the devil's workshop"?

Heel, public, heel!

2:30 p.m.

Nine black inmates were sent to the hole. The administration believes there is a gang conspiracy to intimidate others. Actually, if you dove to the bottom of this sin-filled well, the tarnished coin you would find would be a homosexual relationship.

The gang member who got beat up by the others had been so pleasured by the fleshy lips and plump behind of his lover (cellie) that he decided to leave all his property (food, clothing, radio) to the homosexual upon parole, and not to his homeboys as is customary.

The homeboys were pissed off and thumped him good. Is the homosexual going to the hole, too? No, he/she/it is going after another lonely and weak man. God save us all from the demon that is among us and corrupting our flesh.

9:45 p.m.

Glen is a porter in the gym. He walked up to the officers' station to pick up his identification card at the end of his work shift. The officer, who is not our regular, asked in a mocking tone, what kind of name Sandau was. Glen replied, "German." The officer's response was, "So, you're a fu - - ing Nazi." Glen was stunned by this statement. At the same time, Glen noticed that the officer's last name, stitched on his uniform, was Polish.

Not biting at the bait, Glen turned and stomped over to my bunk to vent his anger. To lighten the moment, we jokingly surmised that this officer possessed a latent inferiority complex due to the Germans kicking the Poles' back sides in the war, oh so long ago. However, on the serious side, it is disturbing when the keeper exhibits less class than the kept.

Colossians 1:13, 18. *For He has rescued us from the dominion of darkness and brought us into the kingdom of the Son He loves. And He is the head of the body, the church. He is the beginning and the firstborn from among the dead so that in everything He might have supremacy.*

✟ ✟ ✟

Friday, June 3, 1994
10:45 a.m.

Achoo! As I walked out of the medical clinic I was relieved that my allergy prescription had been renewed. For some reason, a new policy or procedure, it was renewed by an MTA, not a doctor. I do not mind this change as I know what ails me and I know what medication has been prescribed in the past. Also, I assumed the doctor would review and co-sign all prescription orders at the end of the day. This way the medical staff is able to see more inmates by utilizing MTA's. However, I wonder if a serious medical problem could be missed or misdiagnosed if MTA's are over utilized. Is this use of MTA's a symptom or an attempt at a cure for the inadequate medical care? Hmm . . .

I have said it before but it cannot be emphasized enough. Thank God for my general good health.

11:30 a.m.

Sometimes I have to laugh out loud at the stupid things some of my fellow inmates do. Five inmates were receiving CDC-115's (disciplinary write-ups). They were working out on the weight pile without privilege cards (authorization) and injured themselves. This was where it got sadly laughable. These inmates reported to the medical clinic to have their injuries tended. When each was asked how they hurt themselves, they replied, "On the weight pile." Not too smart, but then rule violations, and the crime(s) that initially brought them to prison, never are.

Anyway, I am confident that these men will be dumbfounded when they are found guilty of the rules violation, and as part of their punishment, are required to pay for their medical care. Will they wonder how they got caught? This is a *macho* giggle moment.

5:00 p.m.

Top of the food chain? Maybe. Top of the intellect chain? Doubtful. I was waiting in the chow hall line, and by their close proximity, I was forced to listen to a group of three inmates heatedly debating who had more rank: prison officers, police officers, or state police? Like it really mattered in the big scheme of things. What was the point? What was the objective of the argument? I certainly could not tell you and probably neither could they. It was an argument for the sake of arguing.

It was just another obtuse moment in another prison day.

1 John 2:21-22. *Dear friends, if our hearts do not condemn us, we have confidence before God and receive from Him anything we ask, because we obey His commands and do what pleases Him.*

✠ ✠ ✠

Saturday, June 4, 1994
8:30 a.m.

The morning wait at the yard gate for the plaza officer was only 30 minutes. Shockingly short. Again, I found myself seated on the Receiving and Release bench, and continued praying as I was in the process of picking up my care package from home that contained food goodies. This is usually a traumatic experience wherein R&R staff can deem items unacceptable, denying them to me, and the items I am allowed to have, even though they come in store-bought sealed bags, are torn open for inspection, causing them to spoil sooner.

My prayers actually started last night when I received my ducat. The first prayer was to be within the first group of 10 inmates. I was number four. Being able to pick up my package early kept me out of the day's heat. Today the temperature was supposed to top 95 degrees. It was never pleasant to sweat rivers while watching my chocolate melt.

My second prayer was for a reasonable officer to search and not destroy my package. Of the two R&R officers working, I was called to the pick-up window by Officer O'Hearn. She is a feisty, red-headed Irish woman who swears with the best of the old-timer prison guards, but she also knows her inmates. I was pleased that it was O'Hearn because she has observed my behavior long enough to know that I pose no threat to the safety and security of the institution. Of course, and for good measure, she was verbally abusive, but in a playful manner. After the gentle search she dumped the entire contents of the shipping box into my pillow case.

Having a full pillow case of goodies reminded me of childhood and Halloween. Thankfully, there were no tricks today. My prayers were answered.

As I turned to leave the pick-up window, O'Hearn leaned over to tell the other R&R officer to tear apart the next package because it belonged to an inmate who constantly tries to smuggle contraband into the prison.

At times in my writing I may give the impression that all staff are lummoxes. This is not the case. As a matter of fact, they are anything but. It is the contradictory system they work within that is stupid and dysfunctional. Line staff, those with boots on the ground, generally know what they are doing and I am grateful that most of them can see Jesus' light coming from within me.

6:00 p.m.

News Flash! The California budget has passed. The Department of Corrections' budget has been *increased* by 9.65 percent. Apparently enough of the populace was scared into allowing the legislators to reduce the educational and health care budgets so that prison spending can continue to grow, grow, GROW!

10:00 p.m.

Despite being pleased with and sated by my care package, I have been feeling an emptiness creep over me today. It is mixed with an unseen weight on my heart, a sense of panic, and a gnawing dread of doom. To remedy this, starting at 8:00 p.m., I read my Bible and listened to several teachings about Christ on my radio. When my cup is low, drained of energy, I can always dip my tarnished ladle into Christ's well. There I am returned sparkling as new and filled.

Being ready to turn in for the night, I can rest my head, knowing that it worked. My spiritual cup overflows with positive hope…and my belly bulges with sweet chocolate. Thank you, Lord. Thank you, mom and dad.

Proverbs 15:29. *The Lord is far from the wicked but He hears the prayer of the righteous.*

✟ ✟ ✟

Sunday, June 5, 1994
2:20 a.m.

A demon dream of epic Steven King proportions: I was wheelchair bound but I knew I could walk and run. The sidewalk I rolled down was in an unfamiliar neighborhood. Distracted, I watched the twilight sky that shimmered with the aurora borealis. Nearing an off kilter, three-story Victorian house I wheeled myself up a handicap ramp that was not there a moment ago, to enter the foyer and a waiting elevator. Following me, a black-cloaked man without a face charged up the ramp. He lunged at me as I frantically pushed the elevator button for the door to close. Incapable of flight, and fearing for my life, I fought the cloaked man as he transformed into a phantasmal beast. Suddenly, the beast vanished. I found myself and the wheelchair lying on the cold elevator floor. "Did I win?" I asked as the elevator door closed. I lied there listening to the hum of electric motors raise the elevator.

As dreams often time do, mine skipped scenes. No continuity. The elevator door opened with me again seated in the chair. I rolled out onto the third story floor. A tea party of jolly, bearded professors was in progress. Then up from between the polished floor boards oozed a tentacled black creature of death. Without mercy it attacked the be-speckled men. Terrified, these men threw themselves out the stained glass windows. I did not witness their impact with the ground but I knew they were dead. Angered by the senseless deaths, I leapt out of the wheelchair and charged the creature. Before I reached it, it fled into the night through the shattered windows. My lips did not move, but the walls shook as my soul screamed, "Weak!" because the creature would not stay and fight.

At that moment my eyes opened. My ears rang with the sound echoing off the wall behind my head. I had groaned the word aloud. My flesh trembled—my spirit within triumphed. I did not fear death for the light of God dwells within me. I knelt in thanks to God for protecting me from Satan's assaults. God knows what I need in advance of tribulations and prepares me through prayers, study, and continued faith in Him. I will always be safe in Christ. With Him I will always triumph.

4:00 p.m.

Today's volleyball, though sweaty under the menacing sun, was mediocre. After my nocturnal battle, this day's competition lost its luster. I retired to my bunk to eat salted peanuts from my care package.

My will cannot be my own, but only yours, Lord.

7:30 p.m.

Alarm! Code 3. Building 8. Four inmates lost control and began fighting. Over what? A domino game? Did one of them cheat? Did one of them get tired of losing? Fortunately, there were no serious injuries, only bruised knuckles and pride. Time in the hole will give each of them time to think. Was the fight really over the game, or something else? Each of us has our own breaking point. How can I judge others' limits, their situation, and their stressors until I have lived in his or her skin?

Deuteronomy 1:30-31. *The Lord your God, who is going before you, will fight for you, as He did for you in Egypt, before your very eyes, and in the desert. There you saw how the Lord your God carried you, as a father carries his son, all the way you went until you reached this place."*

✠ ✠ ✠

Monday, June 6, 1994
3:00 p.m.

Work in the office was slow today, a nice change of pace, so Frank and I sat around reminiscing about our female associations. For worldly men such as we, it was pleasantly surprising that the theme of our discussion was not how great of a womanizer or player we had been, but how our lives were touched, shaped, and our thoughts positively altered by the grace of the different women we had relationships with. I believe the women's liberation movement would put down their weapons after listening to our compliments of the qualities that women possess.

We only wished we did not have to savor memories that were six and seven years old. Time does seem to stop when entering prison, because memories are the measure of time, and rarely is there much to memorialize about the days spent in prison. There are lessons to be learned here, and many inmates do learn them, but the unanswerable question keeps repeating in my mind: When will we be allowed to apply our new found knowledge?

It is the loving touch, warming smile, and intelligent wit of a lady that ranks among the top contenders for what I miss most. Loneliness is a bitch. A hug that is absent is the unbearable punishment for my crimes.

1 John 4:7-8. *Dear friends, let us love one another, for love comes from God. Everyone who loves has been born of God and knows God. Whoever does not love does not know God, because God is love.*

✝ ✝ ✝

Tuesday, June 7, 1994
9:00 a.m.

Sloth causes excessive work. Receiving and Release staff are not allowing inmates who reside in the gym who receive televisions to keep the antennas even though a verbal exception to the No Antenna Rule has been given. "A rule is a rule," they tout. If there is to be a change in the rule, R&R staff wants written verification from the facility program administrator. A verbal one via telephone will not do. It is a C.Y.A. (Cover Your Ass) thing.

The problem or hurdle that has to be overcome is my boss, the program administrator. He has difficulty getting around to the little details of writing memorandums. A big issue he is on top of and that is why Facility B runs as well as it does relative to other prison yards. It is the little, pesky details which he either ignores or fails to find the time to do. I wish he would utilize me more for these things. I can write swell memorandums.

Unfortunately, because my boss did not write one memorandum, he now has to respond to a dozen CDC-602 appeals concerning antennas. It makes for more paperwork that could have been avoided.

9:45 a.m.

Donna was angry because her six and a half hours of overtime will not be paid to her until next month. Staff in the employee pay office was too lazy to pick up the telephone to call and ask Donna if she wanted money or days off as compensation. Instead, they attached a note and sent Donna's overtime slip back to her through the institutional mail. By the time Donna received the slip and note, it was too late to receive the earned funds she was counting on this pay period.

Lack of concern or consideration for others is a too frequent disease that appears to be very hard to cure.

5:00 p.m.

Swede showed me transcripts from his recent parole hearing. One of the board commissioners stated that unless, and until, *Swede* paid restitution to the family of the deceased, *Swede* would not feel remorse. Is this board commissioner saying that *Swede* can only understand loss of life through loss of money? I certainly hope not. Maybe the commissioner misspoke.

The judge that presided over *Swede's* trial refused to fine or institute restitution payments, and within Title 15, the rules governing inmates' behavior, there would be a punishment of 18 months in SHU (Security Housing Unit, the *super* hole) if *Swede* contacts his victim(s) or victim's family and it disturbs them. The commissioner's demand is insane, especially in light of a quote from a member of the victim's family during the hearing: "Our son had it coming. *Swede* should be released."

Ignoring the statement and sentiment by the victim's family member, the commissioner is requiring *Swede* to perform an act that is in violation of the governing rules, or he will not, in the commissioner's eyes, be suitable for parole.

Where have all the wise judges and decision makers from the Bible gone? Too many people sit in judgment seats dispensing verdicts and opinions. Too few have or utilize the wisdom, moral fiber, or divine guidance in their decisions that affect many.

6:00 p.m.

I spoke to my mother on the telephone a few minutes ago. There are only nine days left until she moves to Texas. Where did the time go? It flew by and I was *not* having fun. I am starting to feel panic rise up inside me. I am no mama's boy, but our Christian relationship and emotional support of each other is of great comfort and security to me.

I will be strong for her as this move is a good retirement investment, but I am still nervous. I have depended on our bi and tri-weekly visits for spiritual uplifting. Besides, a mother's hug is irreplaceable, and it could be months, or even years until I see her again. Sons always love their mothers, and because she and I have become more than mother and son, true friends, her departure becomes a double loss. This is going to be difficult.

Lord? Do you hear me calling?

James 1:5-8. *If any of you lacks wisdom, he should ask God, who gives generously to all without finding fault, and it will be given to him. But when he asks, he must believe and not doubt, because he who doubts is like a wave of the sea, blown and tossed by the wind. That man should not think he will receive anything from the Lord; he is a double-minded man, unstable in all he does.*

✢ ✢ ✢

Wednesday, June 8, 1994
11:00 a.m.

Whiffs of fragrant perfume. I breathed deeply with eyes closed and an imagination that ran wild with thoughts of the good ol' days. This is weird to say but the lieutenant smelled heavenly. As she passed our desks she left a hint of powdered spring in her wake. Her perfume brand I dared not ask. In prison it is too personal to inquire as to the scent of a woman. Ooo-wah! It could be deemed as over familiarity and a CDC-115 disciplinary write-up issued.

It was not my fault that under that starched uniform was a woman and that she caused my olfactory senses to tingle. I miss that aroma. I miss all things that make women so special, so alluring, and so lovely. Sigh.

12:30 p.m.

This revelation is to be listed under the stupid file. An inmate appeared before the classification committee today and implicated himself in an unsolved murder in Santa Clara County. Murder is no light or laughing matter, but to readily implicate oneself in front of law officials, and then to be surprised when you are placed in handcuffs and taken to the hole pending investigation is not only stupid but laughable. I wonder if this inmate's guilt got the best of him and this was his way of coming clean, of beginning the process of paying for his offenses against society. Sadly, as I know only too well, causing the death of another is a debt that can never be paid, but one must try.

6:00 p.m.

"When I die and they lay me to rest I'm going
To go to the place that's the best
I'm going to go where I can rest.
I'm going to go up to the Spirit in the sky.
That's where I'm gonna go when I die.
Gonna go up to the Spirit in the sky."

"Look at me. I'm roller skating, Ma. I'm roller skating!" are the words I said aloud to that classic song by Norman Greenbaum.

There are not too many things better than a good ol' rock 'n' roll station and the memories it brings to mind, that being high school and roller skating on the weekends in the San Fernando Valley. Yes, I was a valley boy in the 1970's, in the midst of young romance, kissing soft lips, and fondling teenage skin in the back of my 1931 Model A pickup. It was all so new, so innocent, and wonderful. Youth rocks!

Wait. This year is my 15th year high school reunion. Maybe, just maybe if I send a letter to the organizer of the reunion, he or she would read it or post it at the reunion. With luck, some of my old friends may write to me.

How humiliating. I do not want pity, only a little compassion, some understanding and maybe a few words of encouragement. Glen recently said, during one of our Bible studies, that it is my responsibility to reach out because no one can reach in unless they know I am here. It is a long shot, but I will swallow my pride and write the letter.

Romans 8:24-25. *For in this hope we were saved. But hope that is seen is no hope at all. Who hopes for what he already has? But if we hope for what we do not yet have, we wait for it patiently.*

✝ ✝ ✝

Thursday, June 9, 1994
9:00 a.m.

Inmate Cooper was escorted to the hole. He claimed he was being sexually harassed by a staff member who wanted sex from him. That is an interesting and not unheard of story, but usually it is told by female inmates about male guards. In a men's prison, there would be too many willing inmates unless it was a male guard demanding *favors*.

Word on the yard has it that Cooper is paroling soon, within a month, and he is fearful that someone will carry out the $15,000 contract that was placed on his life.

Cooper was charged and convicted of manslaughter for the molestation-killing of a 7-year-old girl. During the trial, Cooper stated that she fell from the 40-foot water tower. Doubt it. That crime should have been charged as felony murder. Unconfirmed rumors have it Cooper had an accomplice that he testified against to earn a reduced sentence. Whatever the case, he is going home soon and has decided to hide in the hole until then. We call it a 'PC' (protective custody) move. Has Cooper reformed? Has he rehabilitated himself? We will find out soon enough, or actually the next little girl Cooper passes on the street will find out.

1:00 p.m.

Today was a day for deviants. Old man Lewis, convicted of molesting his daughter and granddaughter, with only two years of his five year sentence left to serve, was given a bed move to live in the gym with the rest of us privileged men. Did he enter this cavernous cube? No, he ran to the sergeant to say his safety would be jeopardized. Lewis was allowed to remain in his cell.

It is an unusual twist that those who are the most disturbed, or have the most disturbing cases get the best treatment, yet no treatment for their sicknesses.

Thankfully, Lewis is not my problem. He is society's problem because Lewis is going to be free soon and he has told me the Bible allows a father to marry his daughter and use her as he pleases. I am sorry, but I simply cannot find that passage in *my* Bible.

6:00 p.m.

Whew. A pleasant change of human pace. Little *Ray-Ray,* a jolly dwarf-Mexican roly-poly W.C. Fields look-alike, with a toothless smile resides in the first bunk as one enters the gym. *Ray-Ray* has lived most of his 50-odd years behind one prison wall or another on both sides of the U.S.-Mexico border. Theft of this or that is his crime of opportunity. If an item is left unattended, *Ray-Ray* can't resist, especially if the item is a bicycle. *Ray-Ray* loves bicycles. I believe *Ray-Ray's* affinity for bicycles is because he can't see over the dashboard of an automobile and he wouldn't be caught dead using a booster seat.

Ray-Ray has said he never steals in prison but only when he's on the street. Hmm…go figure. I find it difficult to reconcile *Ray-Ray's* criminal behavior with his attitude. He is, for the most part a good man, although his caricature in movement and speech could put off some people.

Ray-Ray is one of the many people I am glad to see each day. He is a person, as some would say, who keeps it real. Too many of us live behind a facade. *Ray-Ray* is refreshing. He may be unique in his physical attributes, dare I say peculiar, but he makes this pressure cooker bearable by his positive outlook and demeanor.

Criminal acts, a weakness that overshadows a positive character.

Leviticus 18:5-6, 17. *"Keep my decrees and laws, for the man who obeys them will live by them. I am the Lord." "No one is to approach any close relative to have sexual relations. I am the Lord." " Do not have sexual relations with both a woman and her daughter. Do not have sexual relations with either her son's daughter or her daughter's daughter; they are her close relatives. This is wickedness."*

✞ ✞ ✞

Friday, June 10, 1994
3:00 p.m.

It is hot; very HOT. A scorching 105 degree day where through the shimmering heat the concrete buildings appear to melt, but sadly, they are as solid as ever. After returning from work I lied on my bunk wearing only boxer shorts. The stifling air in the gym proved it was not intended to house the living. A slight breeze from the swamp cooler behind me tingled my sweat-covered skin. A distant portable floor fan osculated attempting impotently to move the heavy air.

Water. That was what I needed to wet my lips. I trudged past other glazed and prone bodies toward the over-burdened fountain. The sound of buzzing increased. The fountain, the showers, the stopped-up sinks, and musty urinal and toilets were covered with big, black, buzzing flies. Hungry Blue-bellies that inflict nasty bites and will fight any daring swatter swarmed the area. My thirst instantly dried up, lost in revulsion. I returned to my bunk and lied back down. Drip, drip, drip went my sweat.

4:00 p.m.

Legal mail. I was not pleased to have to put my clothes back on, to face the over-heated and blazing sun, to go to the Program Office where legal mail is distributed. I was pleased to receive notice that the federal court ordered the State's Attorney General to answer my petition within 30 days.

As Sherlock Holmes would say to Dr. Watson, "The game is afoot."

6:00 p.m.

"Get on your bunks for chow release. No one's going to eat until you're all seated on your bunks," shouted Herr Fuehrer. Officer Bartels has returned from his temporary re-assignment. Every inmate in the gym hates him. As I have said, I feel sorry for him. Officer Bartels runs an authoritarian program which combined with today's oppressive heat is raising the stress in the gym to an unbearable level. Unfortunately for us inmates, Bartels does not violate any rules in his heavy-handed management so there is no way to put him in check. On the surface, the gym appears to run in an orderly fashion, but underneath it is a seething cauldron waiting to explode. I pray often for Officer Bartels' safety. One day he may push an inmate, who believes he has nothing to lose, too far.

An inmate told Bartels that one day he would be found in the gun tower with his brains blown out, having committed suicide from being wound too tight. Bartels was pissed, handcuffed the inmate, and escorted him to the sergeant's office for counseling. Bartels wanted to write the inmate up, but was unable to because the inmate only made an observation concerning Bartels' mental stability and did not actually threaten him.

I fear it is going to be a long hot summer.

Romans 12:21. *Do not be overcome by evil, but overcome evil with good.*

✞ ✞ ✞

Saturday, June 11, 1994
6:45 a.m.

As I walked the track to breakfast I breathed deeply the coolness of the morning. It was sweet. We have begun eating our meals in the vocations' mini dining hall. Actually, only the gym inmates are eating there. The inmates living in cells are still fed in their housing units. It seems the inmates housed in the gym have another advantage over inmates housed in the buildings. Besides easier access to phones, our food will be served hot.

Mornings are always difficult for me because day after day I have to accept that I am still in prison. Because of this I prefer to wake up slowly. The advantage of being half awake is that it usually makes breakfast (this morning it was French toast) taste better as I view it through one sleepy eye. My taste buds work on the theory of: if I cannot see it, it will not taste bad.

The group I was walking with, like me, was dragging their feet, so we had to wait outside the vocations building entrance until the line inside the chow hall shortened.

Alarm! Code 3 came from the vocations' chow hall. The other inmates and I plopped down on the ground as responding staff from the buildings rushed in, batons at the ready. The alarm turned out to be false, thank you very much. The alarm jolted me awake and I was forced to use two eyes to consume my meal. That did not help to start my day.

2:00 p.m.

The volleyball games were mediocre today. Lately I have been saddled with less experienced players on my team. We may not win very often, but I hoped God would be pleased that I have been trying to help them and be supportive of those with less ability. Truth be told, I do not care much about winning anymore. It is how I play the game that matters, and of course, there is God's larger picture that I am trying to keep my focus on. Character trumps trophies.

Galatians 6:2, 10. *Carry each other's burdens, and in this way you will fulfill the law of Christ. Therefore, as we have opportunity, let us do good to all people, especially to those who belong to the family of believers.*

✝ ✝ ✝

Sunday, June 12, 1994
9:00 a.m.

I needed a haircut and as *Ray-Ray* is the barber in the gym I asked him to do it. He has done a fine job in the past so I was confident he would do so again. Maybe I was not clear in my explanations. When I said, "Short" I did not mean Boot Camp short. I meant trimmed. I suppose it will save wear on the teeth of my comb and it will be cooler for the summer so long as I wear a baseball cap. If I forget, yeow-sa! Burnt scalp for sure.

It is true that hair does not make the man, and as mine continues to recede, I am grateful that my self-esteem and upbeat personality will be able to make up for the loss.

6:15 p.m.

I placed an open letter to my classmates, Class of '79, into the gym's mail box. It is always difficult to explain the why and how of my incarceration. It is a shame-filled experience...as it should be.

Will anyone write to me? Only God knows.

9:30 p.m.

Emergency count! Apparently someone is missing. My bladder is on the verge of exploding but I have to remain on my bunk until the count clears. We are not allowed to get up or move about even though all the inmates in the locked gym are present and accounted for. Very kindergarten but that is the steadfast rule.

"No exceptions!" shouted Officer Bartels.

10:15 p.m.

"Count is clear," the loud speaker announced. Thank God because I could only twist my legs around so many times. I've got to run.

The missing inmate was located hiding in an empty cell in a building other than that which he was assigned to. What was he thinking? Or was he at all? Inmates do the strangest things with no foreseeable or advantageous results. I do hope he is now comfy in his new surroundings—the hole.

10:30 p.m.

What is this? A whisper of breath across my perspiring skin? The breeze coming in through the air vent behind my bunk seems to have finally increased enough to tease me. I am still hot, still sticking to my sheets, but with this light wind I will hopefully get a better night's sleep. I will need all my strength to handle the jokes made at my expense over my new hair style, if stubby porcupine quills can be considered *style*.

Luke 21: 17-19. *All men will hate you because of me. But not a hair on your head will perish. By standing firm you will gain life."*

✟ ✟ ✟

Monday, June 13, 1994
6:00 a.m.

Shocking News Flash. Every television station is reporting on the brutal killings of football star O.J. Simpson's ex-wife Nicole and her friend Ron Goldman that occurred last night. The police are focusing on O.J. as a potential suspect. Speculation, defenders, detractors, on whether the *Juice* could have or would have done it, and of course, why is rampant on the television and within the gym.

Isn't anyone concerned with the children who were in the home during the killings and what about the parents of Nicole and Ron? They seem to be an afterthought.

Tragedy on every level.

9:00 a.m.

After the water fountain gossip and theorizing about O.J. and his possible connection to the killings of Nicole and Ron, the focus turned to my lack of hair style. The names kept rolling off my co-workers' tongues: skin head, Telly Savalas, Yul Brynner, Gomer Pile, John Luke Picard. My new do is the day's novelty, but fortunately my many years of verbal assaults from swim team coaches toughened the hide.

John Luke Picard, I liked that one best. He has class. However, if I were a free man I would lean toward Yul Brynner because, if Hollywood rumors are to be believed, he was a ladies' man and always able to please. Yes, I can dream, can't I? Regardless of any alias that attaches, I am starting to like my no hassle short hair because it accentuates my perfectly formed and manly ears. Ha ha.

11:00 a.m.

The other second watch clerks worked on the disciplinary reports written by staff on; the inmates who were involved in the conspiracy/threats (homosexual thing) and who were sent to the hole. Originally there were 13 CDC-115 disciplinary reports, 92 CDC-1030 Confidential Notices, and assorted associated memorandums.

Frustratingly, old man Payne and Brian, the third watch clerks who were responsible for the original typing of all these appeared not to take pride in their work as all the reports had to be redone. There were too many mistakes. Added to the typos was the confusing way the sergeant put the (incident) package together and then conveniently for him, he left for vacation. This was not a good thing.

I asked Donna to call Payne and Brian in to help figure the mess out because they were the clerks that the sergeant explained it to. With their arrival I was able to back away from the mess and allow them free reign because, in my opinion, too many clerks spoil the report.

7:30 p.m.

The Abyss—the movie. Over the dark edge, falling, fearful, towards what? In the film it was toward beauty and intelligence beyond comprehension and imagination. In real life we all must take that unknown step, or leap of faith. When we do, we too will find beauty. We will find God; loving, caring, forgiving, but at the same time, demanding in regards to His laws. There are none so tough that we will be defeated; we only have to love the Spirit more than the flesh.

Great movie. God and I are working toward a great life.

Ephesians 2:4-5. *But because of His great love for us, God, who is rich in mercy, made us alive with Christ even when we were dead in transgressions— it is by grace you have been saved.*

✟ ✟ ✟

Tuesday, June 14, 1994
8:00 a.m.

We have a new female sergeant working on our facility. She has been temporarily assigned while the regular sergeant (he left the incident package mess) is on vacation. What a small world. What a coincidence. This sergeant attended the same junior high and high school as Frank. Her major function then was as the pass-around girl who spent many evenings on her back playing the part of night depository for Frank and his football team buddies.

Needless to say, she is now the one on top, at least in authority, but she appeared embarrassed by having to work in close proximity to Frank due to their history. She is in her early thirties, and not wearing a wedding band, so I assume she is single or at least unmarried. Unfortunately for her, 15 years later, and probably forever, she will be stigmatized by those who know of her past as a woman of little discretion, and because of it no man will seriously consider her for a permanent relationship.

This is distressing because it does not allow for change, and she does seem to be a nice person. However, our pasts, whether illegal or immoral, are hard to outdistance. We can be thankful that God forgives *and* forgets our sins so we can be new in our hearts and minds, and go forward to a bright future in His eyes. All God requires is that we believe in His Son, Christ, and ask for forgiveness. This world would be a wonderful place if humans were willing to offer the same compassion and mercy as God.

John 4: 16-18, Hebrews 13:4. *He told her, "Go, call your husband and come back." "I have no husband," she replied. Jesus said to her, "You are right when you say you have no husband. The fact is, you have had five husbands, and the man you now have is not your husband. What you have said is quite true." Marriage should be honored by all, and the marriage bed kept pure, for God will judge the adulterer and all the sexually immoral.*

✠   ✠   ✠

Wednesday, June 15, 1994
9:00 a.m.

Was I surprised? Not really. All those conspiracy reports came back to me. Three dozen 1030 Confidential Reports were not completed properly and there were still too many typing mistakes within the CDC-115 write-ups. I smiled to myself and tried not to be prideful, but it felt good that the lieutenant gave them to me to correct, and I was able to do so on the first attempt.

Was it a lack of pride in their work or an inability to fully comprehend the process that kept the other clerks from properly completing the task? This I do not know, but I am thankful that God has blessed me with the brain cells required to accomplish the work assigned to me.

10:00 a.m.

The *very* Basic Education instructor, Mr. Carreon, again, came into the Program Office to ask me how certain functions on his typewriter worked. Mr. Carreon is horse-faced, squat-bodied, and wears 1950's style suits that reek of his three-pack a day cigarette habit. His timidity is only surpassed by his fear that everyone is out to get him, to force him to retire. From any angle, Mr. Carreon is a burnt out old guy who has given up on everything, and now only passes time while checking the shadows for spies. I believe he would make a perfect stereotypical inmate as he, like many inmates, believes there is a conspiracy against him.

Mr. Carreon bugs me constantly, whether it is about his typewriter, report writing, class roster, or supplies, which interrupts my regular assignments. Christ is a tough example to live up to, but I believe it is good to have lofty goals.

6:30 p.m.

Entering the gym I tore off my clothes as I headed first for my bunk to deposit them, and then to the showers. I returned from sitting on the Receiving and Release bench for two hours, baking in the sun, fully dressed, and a panting breath away from expiring. One hundred plus degrees sucks. Are these books worth it? You bet they are. I did lose the CDC-602 appeal requesting packages be opened to see what is in them before they are mistakenly returned for coming from an unauthorized vendor, but that will never deter me from obtaining books. Quality reading is a blessing and whatever I have to go through to acquire them I will.

Reading is fundamental.

I took a shower prior to work this morning, one after work, one in my own sweat, and again prior to lying on my bunk…to begin glistening again.

Aaauugghh!!! All this heat and not a sandy beach in sight!

Romans 12:16. *Live in harmony with one another. Do not be proud, but be willing to associate with people of low position. Do not be conceited.*

✝ ✝ ✝

Thursday, June 16, 1994
6:30 a.m.

The early morning news, a human interest story: a woman and her infant were traveling the mountain highway from Sacramento, California to Reno, Nevada. When they did not arrive at their destination, family members filed a missing person's report. Five days later, several motorists reported seeing a naked woman walking along a stretch of mountainous road leading toward Reno. A highway patrolman was dispatched to investigate. He stopped and got out of his vehicle and began walking along the shoulder of the road where the woman had been sighted. There he found an infant's shoe near the shoulder's edge. Upon further investigation, this officer discovered the wreckage of a car far down the ravine. The car was smashed, shattered, totaled. The missing mother was inside the car, dead. The infant was naked and curled up next to the mother, still alive, but in critical condition.

Was it the spirit of the mother who walked the road naked? A clothed woman would have drawn little attention. How did the infant's shoe get to the top of the ravine? Can there be any doubt that angels exist? My body trembles with fear and excitement knowing the truth. God loves his children and will do whatever He can to ensure their survival. Praise God for the angels.

5:00 p.m.

The dinner menu stated beef stew with vegetables. I was near the end of the line, the last of many inmates to be served, as the line server scraped gravy from the bottom of the pan to pour over my rice. There was no beef and no vegetables. I brought this absence to the attention of the line officer who replied, "You got a full scoop. Take it or have a seat without it. You're holding up the line," he grunted. I sat down without dinner.

Prior to releasing the inmates from the vocations' chow hall, the sergeant appeared and I was able to explain why I did not have a tray. When the sergeant asked the line officer about my claim, the line officer stated, "He got a full scoop." I fully agreed, but it was only gravy. I asked the officer to state whether be observed any meat or vegetables in the full scoop. He refused to answer, then stated again, "You got a full scoop." It was apparent by the sergeant's sour expression that he knew the officer was wrong by the way he avoided the question. I wanted to say to this hulk of a man: "No matter how many muscles you pile on that squat body of yours, and no matter how many times you avoid the question, I will be right, and you suck." However, discretion is always the wisest choice when living in a world where I have no power so I remained silent, sat down, and composed in my head a CDC-602 appeal that would request that this officer be instructed to observe quality as well as quantity.

When the inmates were released from the vocations' mini chow hall I walked back to the gym where I prepared a Top Ramen soup dinner. There was no meat or vegetables in it either.

Luke 4:10-12. *For it is written: "He will command his angels concerning you to guard you carefully; they will lift you up in their hands, so that you will not strike your foot against a stone."*

✞ ✞ ✞

Friday, June 17, 1994
7:30 p.m.

Tonight was the last visit with my mother and her husband, Walt, for many months to come. Next week they pack up and move to Texas. My mother cried but I kept a stiff upper lip. I am going to miss her dearly. I pray the move will be a positive and prosperous adventure for them. I know her leaving will not hit me hard for several weeks as the absence of our visits multiply. I will have to keep extra busy and try to patiently wait for a letter confirming their safe arrival.

Please, God, bless us all with your strength and love.

8:30 p.m.

I entered the gym to notice all the inmates and staff glued to the televisions. "The Juice is loose!" A news reporter exclaimed. As I previously mentioned, O.J. Simpson, star of football and television, was detained and questioned concerning the brutal stabbing, slashing, and killing of his ex-wife Nicole, and her friend, Ron Goldman. It is a shocking, bloody tragedy. This morning a warrant for O.J.'s arrest was issued, and he was supposed to turn himself in, but he was a no-show. O.J. is now a fugitive. His whereabouts are unknown. This is a strange turn of events that, in the eyes of the public, make him look guilty.

Has another American hero fallen?

9:30 p.m.

O.J. was spotted in a white Ford Bronco that was driving on one of many Los Angeles freeways. He was pursued in a low speed chase by a dozen law enforcement vehicles and several helicopters. News footage showed hundreds of people lining overpasses cheering and holding up signs in support of O.J. (so much for guilty sentiment).

In the Bronco with O.J. and speaking over a cellular telephone, O.J.'s friend (Al Cowling) informed the police dispatch that O.J. was in possession of a gun, was pointing it at his own head, and only wanted to go home to call his mother.

No matter how old we get, when trouble comes, it is always our parents that we seek solace from. O.J. Simpson's illustrious road appears to have come to an unalterable end. I have to hold back tears for the many victims, the families, the children, and neighbors who live near the crime scene, and I can understand the terror of the judicial process, the loss of freedom, that O.J. will be facing. For O.J. though, he will also face the scrutiny of a world-wide media circus. I do not know which will be worse for O.J.

For me, it is the pain I caused to many.

10:00 p.m.

O.J. reached his home, and after negotiations, he surrendered. He was allowed to use the restroom, telephone his mother, and he drank some orange juice. O.J. is no longer a fugitive. He is now a captive. From a mansion in Brentwood to a tiny cell on suicide watch, that difference alone is enough to put a person into shock.

O.J.'s only prospects for sanity are to reach down deep for all the strength he can muster and to reach out for peace in Christ. Hell on earth has begun for O.J. Simpson.

2 Timothy 1:3, 5. *I thank God, whom I serve, as my forefathers did, with a clear conscience, as night and day I constantly remember you in my prayers. I have been reminded of your sincere faith, which first lived in your grandmother Lois and your mother Eunice and, I am persuaded, now live in you also.*

✞ ✞ ✞

Saturday, June 18, 1994
6:00 p.m.

Reality Check. Pettiness quotient.

After returning from the evening chow I discovered that my night curtains had been torn down and confiscated by the gym officer during a random search of my bunk area. I started to get pissed off, but I realized that in the grand scheme of things, this was a silly thing to be upset about, so I shook my head and sighed at the inconvenience.

As I have previously stated, at night the lights in the gym are only dimmed so we have been (sort of) allowed to hang towels or sheets next to our heads from the upper bunk to block the light. It is easier to sleep and as long as the first watch officers can see our bodies they do not harass us.

Admittedly, this practice of hanging curtains is against the rules so the confiscating officer had every right to do so. It is only an inconvenience for me because I have to round up another spare set of sheets. This was also a good lesson to remind myself that no matter how good a rapport I believe I have with staff, I am still a lowly inmate who is required to follow *all* the rules.

Ecclesiastes 7:9. *Do not be quickly provoked in your spirit, for anger resides in the lap of fools.*

✝ ✝ ✝

Sunday, June 19, 1994
FATHER'S DAY
7:30 p.m.

Ten lifetimes of thanks to God would never be enough because I have been truly blessed in having a wonderful father. I know I disappointed him by my actions that caused me to come to prison. How terribly disgraced he must have felt. All those years of careful nurturing, guidance, and preparation must have been questioned by my wanton disregard for his teachings. Fortunately for me, among my father's many enviable traits is his ability to forgive. This has allowed me to move forward and again seek his guidance that I so desperately need.

I telephoned him and also sent a Father's Day card. I would have loved to do more, but as I have little money and cannot go to visit him, my words of love and concern for his welfare will have to do. Even though my words are from my heart, they are inadequate to express my love, appreciation, and gratitude.

I look around the gym to see so many men without a father or whose father holds animosity toward them. I have such a warm feeling of security when I think of mine. No, he is not perfect, but I love him just the way he is. I pray the Lord will allow me to regain my freedom before my father passes away so that I can spend some quality time with him.

In the meantime I will do everything in my power to show my father that I appreciate his love and that I am listening to his teachings.

Proverbs 4:1-5. *Listen, my sons, to a father's instruction, pay attention and gain understanding. I give you sound learning, so do not forsake my teaching. When I was a boy in my father's house, still tender, and an only child of my mother, he taught me and said, "Lay hold of my words with all your heart; keep my commands and you will live. Get wisdom, get understanding; do not forget my words or swerve from them."*

✝ ✝ ✝

Monday, June 20, 1994
3:00 p.m.

Spencer, a good friend, fellow volleyball player, and walking-around-the-track companion, asked me if I would be his best man in his upcoming wedding. My heart was touched and I felt honored.

Though I suspect many free people feel differently, especially victims of crime, it is important for family ties to be encouraged while a person is in prison. If a man has something and someone to look forward to upon release, he programs better. He is more likely to seek opportunities to better himself and is less likely to re-offend. Detractors of prison marriages cite the high divorce rate among inmates but fail to take note of the similar rate among free people.

Love, marriage, and family; we need more of them. They need to be strengthened and encouraged, and someday I would like to be the one that says, "I do."

4:00 p.m.

Timing is everything and it is sometimes amazing, if not a cool coincidence.

Mail. I received a letter from Arlene today and in it she 'jokingly' asked if I would marry her. My interest and loneliness was piqued. I accept that she was kidding, but I will playfully test the waters in my next letter to her to see just how much of her question really was a joke. I will also do a lot of praying to ask God if I should pursue Arlene in this fashion. I am excited about the prospect but scared to be rejected. Also, for me, marriage is a forever thing, a total commitment, and a life-time act of giving.

5:00 p.m.

A week has passed since I mailed my letter to the high school reunion committee. Did it arrive? Did they laugh? Did they throw it away? Or will my letter be posted or read? Will anyone respond? Only time will tell.

Genesis 2:24. *For this reason a man will leave his father and mother and be united to his wife, and they will become one flesh.*

✞ ✞ ✞

Tuesday, June 21, 1994
5:45 a.m.

Alarm! Alarm! Code 3? Nope, just my Casio watch sounding off. Casio, it is the preferred watch of a criminal because you can read the time in the dark while on a caper and then set the alarm to sound on your release date after you have been convicted. Ha ha.

Today's alarm was only to wake me up, bummer. The problem I am having this morning is I cannot remember what day today is. Monday? Tuesday? Wednesday? Seriously. I concentrate harder but the answer does not come to me. I do not believe I am losing my mind, it is just that at times each day looks and feels the same as every other one.

When I go to sleep at night my mind is able to conjure up a beautiful place. I am relaxing on a classic, wooden, sailing ketch at anchor off the shore of a palm tree lined beach. A cool tropical breeze soothes my sun-warmed skin. The transparent water allows viewing into a wet world of multi-colored creatures and quietude only dreamed of during waking hours. These comforting visions come easier each night. They are my own personal escapes; a withdrawing to a better more tranquil world.

Some psychiatrists might say, "Greg, you are not dealing with your world, your reality." As a matter of fact I am dealing quite well. I leave it as much as possible; through travel brochures, *Sailing* and *Islands* magazines, novels, and creative writing of my own. I figure that if I am not allowed to physically live a wonderful life, I will dream up one of my own and go there as often as my wandering mind will allow.

Who cares what day it is?

5:00 p.m.

The hypocrisy of it all. Miss I'm-So-Perfect, Officer Wynon, who with a vengeance and pleasure harasses inmates for the most minor infractions, tonight in front of 150 inmates in the vacations' chow hall, and strictly against the rules, leaned against the wall and ate three ice creams. These desserts were purchased by the taxpayers and meant solely for inmate consumption.

What have we learned today, children? That if you have the power you can break the rules with impunity while punishing others beneath you for the same or other minor rule infractions.

Officer Wynon is our role model?

Revelation 21:1, 4. *Then I saw a new heaven and a new earth, for the first heaven and first earth had passed away, and there was no longer any sea. He will wipe every tear from their eyes. There will be no more death or mourning or crying or pain, for the old order of things has passed away.*

✞ ✞ ✞

Wednesday, June 22, 1994
10:30 a.m.

Facility A inmates jumped off. Three shots were fired in two separate violent incidents. They may have only been fist fights, but they were vicious, and seemingly unstoppable. It is frightening to me when anger and passion override reason and the only drive that fuels a man is to inflict great pain and to kill.

The fights were eventually stopped by responding staff, and fortunately only one was struck by the streaking bullets. Bruised, battered, and bleeding, the inmates may be, and the swelling may take days to go down, but there are no permanent injuries or disfigurement.

I am very grateful to be housed within Facility B. Even though there are daily fights, rarely do they escalate to full on brouhahas, let alone the necessity for gun fire. The joke among staff is it is safer to live on B yard than to live on the streets. This is kind of distressing because there seems to be validity to this statement if one were to concentrate solely on the daily news programs that splash mayhem and murder across the television screen.

3:00 p.m.

Work has been completed for the day. Time to relax. What have we here? On my bunk was a brown paper bag, a lunch sack. In it I found two oranges and a note. A love note? It was a joke, right? Read for yourself and decide.

Hello My Friend,
I truly pray that this letter would reach you happy and well. I know that this letter will be a shock if not a surprise, but you have truly been on my mind and I just had to petition this letter to you because I truly want to know where you are coming from, and I hope that I can get to know you, and hopefully we can sit and talk.

You are a very special and unique person and that is why I find myself writing, and I mean no disrespect—but understanding is the best thing in a world and this is what I want from you...

Yes I can say I like you, but I want and need to know the true person that has my attention and I would not be the for-real person that I am if I did not try to reach you this way — for I have too much respect for you to confront you in front of other people — for I can keep a secret, and our business is only for us.

I hope that you will not be alarmed or hurt. I mean you no harm. I just have "love" and "friendship" for you if you want to mesh with me. For I am always here for you.

I hope that you will know who this letter is from, but if not— then wear only one sock on your left foot to the shower tonight, and I will have the right one. That way I will know that you are not hurt or upset, and I will show, but if not—I will never know, as I will never try to reach you anymore on this matter.

No. I did not wear the sock to the shower out of curiosity. I shared the note with several friends who got a good laugh out of it. They wanted me to wear one sock so they could find out who wrote the note. I did not have the courage or desire. I could live without ever knowing who my secret admirer was. If I could only make that kind of positive impression on a woman, my life would be fulfilled.

9:00 p.m.

News! O.J. Simpson was present for his evidentiary hearing. A bailiff informed O.J. that he did not have to attend if he did not want to. O.J. was overheard to say, "I'll do anything to get out of that cell." I know what he means. Looking at him in the court room was like looking into a mirror of me many years ago. His face was drawn and pasty from the stress. I know he is still in shock and will be for a long time.

I sometimes wonder if I still am.

Leviticus 18:22. *"Do not lie with a man as one lies with a woman; that is detestable."*

✟ ✟ ✟

Thursday, June 23, 1994
8:00 a.m.

STUPID! Incredibly stupid! Why did I not wait for Donna? All I do is tell people how fortunate and blessed I am to work in the Program Office. I am trusted, and for the most part, treated with a small measure of respect and dignity.

So what did I do? I will tell you what I did. I tried to make personal photocopies on the photocopy machine. That is strictly forbidden without prior approval. Donna was late to work this morning, and instead of being patient and waiting for her to arrive and receive permission and sign the trust withdrawal form, I made the copies.

Yes, I got caught. The program administrator and relief lieutenant are upset and displeased. I feel as if I am going to vomit. Not only am I probably fired, but I feel terrible that I betrayed my supervisors' trust.

I have followed the rules and worked hard for so long, and then in a split second, my impatience and poor judgment has ruined what semblance of an existence I have.

The lieutenant asked me into her office, requesting that I explain my actions. My only saving grace was to admit my guilt and ask that my past four years of superb service be counted for something. I apologized and told her that I will harbor no ill feelings against staff for any action they take. The lieutenant will make her recommendation to the program administrator as to my fate. I will not like it and would prefer a flogging or the rack to the disappointment etched in their faces.

What a stupid, stupid thing for me to do.

2:00 p.m.

The program administrator returned from a meeting off the facility. The lieutenant entered the program administrator's office and conferred for 10 minutes, and then she exited his office. The lieutenant stated to me that she would be right back and at that time would inform me of their decision.

God, please help me not to puke all over my desk. I hated waiting for the jury's verdict. Just let the ax fall.

3:00 p.m.

My work day ended and I prepared to return to the gym. The program administrator was in his office but the lieutenant had not returned. I did not know if I should continue to wait or leave. I asked the program administrator if he wanted me to stay. He said, "No."

I dragged my sorry butt back to the gym to meet my workout partner. We walked to the weight pile and I tried but I could not mentally handle working out.

Why was I so stressed out? It was only a measly prison job. Why did I care so much? I cared because it comes down to trust, and I gave prison officials a reason to smugly say, "See, he is just like the rest. You can't trust any inmate."

And I let God down, too.

4:00 p.m.

No Mail. The absence of a letter of love punctuated a disastrous day that I and I alone created. What a stupid, stupid man I am.

1 John 1:9-10. *If we confess our sins, He is faithful and just and will forgive us our sins and purify us from all unrighteousness. If we claim we have not sinned, we make Him out to be a liar and His word has not place in our lives.*

✝ ✝ ✝

Friday, June 24, 1994
6:00 a.m.

There were no sweet dreams, not much sleep at all, as I lie sweating on my bunk. The sweating had nothing to do with the heat either. It was all mental anguish.

9:15 a.m.

The moment of judgment arrived with the waving of the lieutenant's hand, summoning me into her office. Calmly she said, "After speaking with Donna regarding your photocopy privileges, and a review of your C-File, the program administrator and I have decided to split the difference with you. We are not going to write you up but you are fired."

And there was the ax.

Damn. There went my pay, my air conditioned office, and my quiet place to write creatively. All lost over a couple of 10 cent photocopies. I could not decide whether to scream in anguish or cry…so instead I thanked the lieutenant and apologized again. Justice will always prevail in prison. There is little room for mercy because that is considered weakness. However, I admit that not being written up was a blessing.

So what did I do next? I finished out my day, completing each assigned task to the best of my ability. I may have stumbled, but the last impression I left was one of gratitude and pride in my work.

Psalm 62:5-6. *Find rest, O my soul, in God alone, my hope comes from Him. He alone is my rock and my salvation: He is my fortress, I will not be shaken.*

✦ ✦ ✦

Saturday, June 25, 1994
9:00 a.m.

The word rolled across our yard like shock waves after a nuclear explosion: the king clerk dethroned himself.

I was not surprised by this rapid sharing of information, but what I was surprised by is the support and encouragement I am receiving, not only from inmates, but from staff as well. I have had three job offers already. I guess I am not too bad of a guy after all. Yes, I made an error in judgment, and I will continue to work on that part of my character, but I do have a few redeeming qualities. My spirits are lifting. Now I have to choose between the gym, plumbing or welding clerk positions.

Decisions, decisions, decisions—make it count.

2:00 p.m.

Bible fellowship. Among the many condolences from my friends during Bible study over the loss of my job, I thanked them, and reminded them that I was my own undoing, not staff. It was a good lesson in remaining vigilant—never waiver in being steadfast.

Ron updated us on his son's legal situation. Joel is still in the county jail. There has been talk of a plea agreement to a manslaughter charge if Joel accepts responsibility and pleads guilty. So far Joel is unwilling to do so.

A hardened heart is difficult to reason with.

10:30 p.m.

The last two days have been an emotional roller-coaster, and to it I add thinking of and praying for Mickie to my mental mix. Today was her birthday. Last week I mailed a birthday card to her. I filled it with words of heartfelt care and encouragement. I have been getting the impression that Mickie is drifting away. Is it a busy-in-the-world thing, or is she moving on? Only time will tell. Regardless, she will always be in my heart and in my prayers.

Happy Birthday, Mickie, and sweet dreams.

John 14:13-14. *And I will do whatever you ask in my name, so that the Son may bring glory to the Father. You may ask me for anything in my name, and I will do it.*

✞ ✞ ✞

Sunday, June 26, 1994
9:30 a.m.

I had an excellent visit with my father, his wife, JoAnne, and our close friend and family attorney, Linda May Stone. The visit was upbeat even though the swarming flies were biting and the room temperature was in the mid 90's. It was very uncomfortable sitting on the vinyl-covered seats and sweating, but as I had not seen my father since Christmas, there was nothing I would not endure.

I did not tell them of my job loss and mental deficiencies when it came to decision making. Hey, I am in prison. I am obviously not perfect, and there was no reason to depress the happy mood.

In addition to visiting me, my father, JoAnne, and Linda May were going to attend a wildlife art show in Sacramento that featured wildfowl decoy carving and painting. Carving duck decoys have been a gratifying hobby for both my father and me. When I was in San Quentin I carved one and two-inch duck lapel pins. After painting them, I thought they were quite lifelike, and others must have agreed, because they sold quickly in the prison handicraft shop.

It is a shame there is no handicraft program here at the Creek.

2:30 p.m.

Where did that precious time go? It seemed the visit had just started, but before I knew it we were giving each other those farewell hugs. A few moments of pleasure, good conversation, and lip-smacking tidbits from the vending machine, and then POW! The visit was over. I shuffled back to my nightmare while my father, JoAnne, and Linda May began their long drive back to San Diego.

I really hate prison, but I am so grateful that dad was willing to drive the 18 hour round trip. That is love.

Only 13 more years until I go before the parole board. I hope I am judged on who I am becoming and not on the political whims of a governor, even if he or she is doing what he or she believes is right.

Damn. I really wanted to go home with my father.

11:00 p.m.

El Sid, the four hour movie starring Charleton Heston and Sophia Loren is a historical epic about Spain and the clashes between the Christians and Muslims. There was breathtaking cinematography, a cast of thousands, and the story was of a man who could have been king, but desired only to be a noble servant.

God, I could have been great, but I fell so far. Can I ever rise above this self-dug mud pit to lead the hearts and minds of men toward honorable goals? Or has our society decayed to the point that bureaucracy would kill a king? I have the stirrings of potential greatness beneath my skin, but the weakness of the flesh and the fear in my heart of retaliation by the *system* prevents me from standing up and realizing my goals. I need to cast off these doubts and give them all over to you, God. I need to allow you, my Lord, to guide my heart and my steps.

It is very difficult to be a noble servant.

Philippians 3:12-14. *Not that I have already obtained all this, or have already been made perfect, but I press on to take hold of that for which Christ Jesus took hold for me. Brothers, I do not consider myself yet to have taken hold of it. But one thing I do: Forgetting what is behind and straining toward what is ahead, I press on toward the goal to win the prize for which God has called me heavenward in Christ Jesus.*

✝ ✝ ✝

Monday, June 27, 1994
7:00 a.m.

I did not receive a ducat un-assigning me from my job last night so I reported for my normal duties in the Program Office. I know that I have been fired, but the rules state that I must report until I am officially notified by ducat.

9:00 a.m.

Staff, especially the program administrator appeared to be a teensy bit uncomfortable by my presence, but I acted my same old self: happy, cordial, and I continued to provide quality work. I knew I was out, but I would go out with class and dignity.

After I finished with the daily morning paperwork, Frank and I bounced writing ideas off each other for the children's story he continues to work on. Besides our brainstorming sessions I would miss Frank's daily wit and sarcasm.

I learned that Officer Johnson had taken my work change slip to the inmate assignment office. I had decided this morning to accept the relief clerk position in the gym. The staff in the gym wants me, and to be wanted for my attributes, the good ones, felt good. Besides, it would be a short commute.

2:00 p.m.

Frank's work day ended, and as he was leaving I could tell by his solemn demeanor that he was disheartened by my demise. Unfortunately, we guys have difficulty expressing these types of emotions in words, but Frank's nod and crooked smile said it all.

3:00 p.m.

The battery operated clock on the wall struck three. It signaled the end of my work day and the end of my dynasty. Staff and the other clerks will survive without me. I was only a cog in the massive wheel that is the Department of Corrections. However, they will never forget me. Sigh.

9:00 p.m.

It is official. I was handed my reassignment ducat. I am now the relief clerk for the gym. A new adventure begins tomorrow. A new determination is within me to toe that line. On the positive side, I can say my mistakes are getting smaller.

I vow: Never again.

Proverbs 16:3, 26. *Commit to the Lord whatever you do, and your plans will succeed. The laborer's appetite works for him; his hunger drives him on.*

✝ ✝ ✝

Tuesday, June 28, 1994
8:00 a.m.

It is the first morning of my new job as relief clerk in the gym. I did not have to travel far because the desk is only 40 feet from my bunk. The second watch gym officer, Officer Mann, and the second watch clerk, gave me the low-down as to my duties. This job will be a cakewalk in comparison to the responsibilities in the Program Office.

Four days a week I am a clerk and one day I am an 'extra' which means I do nothing. When I do something, the something includes: keeping the housing rosters up-to-date; logging in and out locker combination locks and laundry bags when inmates are assigned and unassigned to the gym, and typing the housing supply order forms. I can certainly handle that, and it just so happens that today is my 'extra' day so I am sitting on my bunk.

What to do? What to do? I will catch up on some correspondence. I have to write letters to receive them. I average writing three to receiving one. At least I get that precious, precious one.

10:00 a.m.

Something was definitely wrong. I looked up from my bunk, questioningly. No noise. The gym was peaceful. I am in shock. I had no idea the week days were in such contrast to the evenings and weekends when the gym reverberates like a Super Bowl stadium. Eighty percent of the gym inmates are presently at their assignments or have gone to the recreation yard. The televisions are turned off and the temperature is, for the moment, in the moderate range of 75 degrees. I shake my head in disbelief at this luxury. I suddenly realized that I, too, am at peace, and that the stress has been washed away by the silence. Shh...maybe good would come out of my photocopying disaster.

God works wonders when I trust in Him.

2:00 p.m.

The mob is returning. Vocations has released its inmates and along with them comes *Lurch*. He bunks under Brian. I am not sure why people call him *Lurch*. He is in his late 60's, very tall at 6'6", but he reminds me more of one of those drunken pirates wobbling back and forth on wine kegs in the Disneyland ride Pirates of the Caribbean.

I would not describe *Lurch* as a bad guy or even one with mental problems. It is that he has been incarcerated too long and his mind has turned to mush. Thirty-three years behind walls can do that to a person. *Lurch's* annoying trait comes from his tendency to be in everyone's business, and to mother to perceived needs, regardless of their existence.

If I were to act too buddy-buddy with *Lurch* he would want to take me under his wing, and I would not get a moment of peace. I believe *Lurch's* annoying traits are manifestations of being lonely. If he finds a willing listener he will talk as much as he can because he may not find another receptive ear for months. *Lurch* appears to be one of the lost boys without spiritual direction. The Spirit within is moving me to accept *Lurch's* motherly irritations, befriend him, and direct *Lurch* toward God's love.

Lurch will always find a friend in Jesus.

James 1:17. *Every good and perfect gift is from above, coming down from the Father of the heavenly lights, who does not change like shifting shadows.*

✝ ✝ ✝

Wednesday, June 29, 1994
10:00 a.m.

Today is my day off. As if I needed it because I have worked so very hard this week. NOT! Regardless, I decided to sleep in. I traded breakfast of boiled eggs for several extra hours cocooned under the covers of my bunk. I could get used to that, but no, I needed to get up and get myself outside into the fresh air and bright sun to exercise my muscles.

12:00 Noon

I completed a very strenuous bar routine, which causes blood to rush to my head, but I do not believe my workout was the source of my dizziness. I believe the allergy medicine is either too strong or simply wrong for my system. I fear it is those drug prescribing MTA's because what I am taking, the color and shape of the pills are different from last year's.

5:00 p.m.

I am stoned to the bone. No more of that medication for me. I need to go to dinner but everything seems to be in a hazy-daze, and lying on my bunk my muscles do not want to cooperate. Wow. Look at all the pretty colors. I am confident that many inmates on this yard would pay big money for this feeling, but I do not like it at all.

6:30 p.m.

Dinner ended an hour ago. I managed to get up but the food did not help. I am still not of this world. I would have preferred to remain in the gym but I had made an appointment with *Whiz*. His building was slow to release so I had to stand, sweating in the 95 degree heat, watching the water mirages shimmer off the asphalt track.

Whiz is a legal beagle, affectionately referred to as a 'jail house lawyer'. He has given me suggestions and procedural guidance for the filing of my federal appeal. Our meeting was a 'touch base' to keep him up-to-date. As I am in the waiting stage, *Whiz* and I shook hands, and then went our separate ways, he to another client and me back to the gym.

6:45 p.m.

Back in the gym, which was not much below 90 degrees, I tried to process *Whiz's* words: "Do not get your hopes up, even though your issue of the witness fleeing the country, which denied you the opportunity to cross examine his preliminary hearing statements should be enough for a reversal." I would, under normal circumstances, be depressed by *Whiz's* remarks, but I am too stoned. Maybe the numbing of emotions, the ability to hide from this horrible reality is why inmates get drunk and high as often as possible.

11:45 p.m.

The allergy drugs finally wore off. The pretty colors have faded to prison gray; the dizzying numbness has dissipated to allow me to feel *Whiz's* words as a stab at my hope, and my ears are inundated by the gym inmates' deafening noise even at the late hour.

What a contrast. Stoned is a world of pretty illusions. Sober is a drab reality of despair.

Always there are choices as to how to live one's life.

I flushed the remaining pills down the toilet. I do not like being out of it, mentally or physically, even if it means I have to face my miseries stone cold sober. It is only fair because my many victims must do so as well.

Isaiah 28:7. *And these also stagger from wine and reel from beer: Priests and prophets stagger from beer and are befuddled with wine; they reel from beer, they stagger when seeing visions, they stumble when rendering decisions.*

✝ ✝ ✝

Thursday, June 30, 1994
5:30 a.m.

Applause? It is too early. Did Officer Bartels work a double which included first watch? No, the inmates clapped last night at 10:30 when he departed. Oh, I see. Scabby-gay Scott is transferring to another institution this morning. We will never have to see him or observe his distasteful habits again. I pity the next man who has to sleep on Scabby-gay's mattress.

It is unfortunate that the abuse Scabby-gay is subjected to is, for the most part, unwarranted, because he is not a terrible person. He does not steal.

He does not snitch. Besides turning people off by his consumption of bodily fluids and excretions, his only other annoyance is his propensity to embellish. When telling stories, he constantly name drops famous people as his associates, but in all likelihood, none of them would accept his collect phone calls.

I have tried to be nice to Scott, though I realize I did not do a very good job because of peer pressure, and for that I am ashamed. I am always aware, and in fear of failing the angels who are sent in disguises to test us. I know at times I am not as hospitable as I should be, but as I want to please God, I have to work harder to befriend the mental or physical lepers, regardless of the ick factor, or what others may think.

All Day
(In The World)

Welcome to the *big* show. Satellite trucks, miles of cable, and reporters speaking a dozen languages. It is the spectacle of worldwide television broadcasting. Total coverage from beginning to end of O.J. Simpson' preliminary hearing. Vultures at a carcass, all shouting: "Tell us of the stab wounds." "Were the victims nude?" "Stay tuned for photographs of the bloody crime scene."

How deplorable our society is, but then, maybe, just maybe the spotlight will shine on the twists and turns of the criminal justice system and the district attorneys who shout, "Hallowed ground!" but can never wipe the stains from their own sullied hands. Oprah, move over. It is parlor tricks and criminal high-jinx time.

Here is the question: Though it is O.J. Simpson's constitutional rights that have to be protected, as he is the man who could lose his freedom, if not his life, if convicted of a double homicide, in the end, after the media goes away, will Nicole and Ron be remembered by anyone other than their families?

John 3:19, 21. *This is the verdict: Light has come into the world, but men loved darkness instead of light because their deeds were evil. But whoever lives by the truth comes into the light, so that it may be seen plainly that what he has done has been done through God."*

✝ ✝ ✝

Friday, July 1, 1994
6:00 a.m.

Another departure from the Mule Creek family. This time it is Glen, but he is going home, not transferring to another institution as Scabby-gay Scott did.

Glen is a good ol' boy with a heart as big as his many muscles. I would describe Glen as a friendly peacock with thick Italian hair that is impossible to run a comb through. I have often wished that I still possessed a full mane of hair.

Hands were shaken and well wishes passed back and forth. I always become depressed when a friend goes home. Will Glen be back? Will he re-offend? It is difficult to say for sure. Glen does have a strong, supportive family to return to, which is more than many of the solitary souls who walk out of these steel gates. But; yes there is a but. Glen has an addiction to drugs. He has been clean and sober for 6 ½ years, but will those old tingles return if his life on the streets becomes difficult? Will the desire to escape reality overwhelm him? Has it sunk into Glen's skull that his next offense, any offense, will bring down on him the dreaded Three Strikes & You're Out life sentence?

I pray he will remain free. No tingle is worth this walking death.

8:00 a.m. – 2:00 p.m.

Today really began my first day on the job. There was little to do. However, I did carry paperwork to my old work site. The mood in the Program Office had changed. It was no longer upbeat. I am confident that this is only a temporary thing, but there was an evident gloom, and unsettling quiet. My light was being missed. Sorry, I meant to say, Christ's light from within me was being missed.

I missed them, too.

5:00 p.m.

Uh-oh. Beef stew with vegetables for dinner. What a surprise. I was ladled big chunks of beef, potatoes, and carrots. A *real* beef stew over mushy noodles. Magnifique? Not really - a little bland.

I have yet to reach a conclusion on my 'full scoop' CDC-602 appeal. It is pending review at the second level and this is where the process slows down. The original offending officer's written reply to my appeal was: You got a full scoop.

No duh.

1 Corinthians 10:13. *No temptation has seized you except what is common to man. And God is faithful; He will not let you be tempted beyond what you can bear. But when you are temped, He will also provide a way out so that you can stand up under it.*

✞ ✞ ✞

Saturday, July 2, 1994
10:00 a.m.

My supervisor, Officer Mann, age 45, is an anomaly. He wears a smile; is respectful, and filled with a generous Christian spirit. Jesus' light, which shines from Officer Mann is blinding.

Officer Mann is extremely pleased that I chose to work for him because, as he said, "I haven't had a clerk that could type or spell in months." These were very flattering words but as of yet I have not done much of anything. Go figure?

At present, I am sitting on my bunk fighting the Sand Man. A few minutes ago I peered out the gym door. I saw the downside to my job. It is having to work on Saturdays and only being able to watch my friends play volleyball. They were joyfully spiking that white ball.

Wish I were with them. Wish I was anywhere but in prison.

I am trying to think positively, and even though I dug myself another emotional hole, I will look for the bright spot that is God's goodness. It is very difficult to find any in prison, but they do exist. One of them is Officer Mann.

Proverbs 17:22. *A cheerful heart is good medicine, but a crushed spirit dries up the bones.*

✞ ✞ ✞

Sunday, July 3, 1994
1:00 p.m.

My relief clerk position has RDO's (regular days off) of Wednesdays and Thursdays, which means I work both Saturdays and Sundays. Fortunately, Saturdays I am off by 2:00 p.m. so I will not miss Bible fellowship, and Sundays and Mondays I work third watch, beginning at 2:00 p.m., so my mornings are open (I would have said: my mornings are *free* but that stretches the truth).

Yesterday, as I watched my friends playing volleyball, I ached to be part of their revelry. Today, I felt as though I was with children in a concrete sand box. Five hours of bickering lips and argumentative tongues. Over what? Lousy line calls? Net infractions? Double hits? Come on, folks. Volleyball is a game. What is the big deal? More than once I have thought these games were not worth the trouble, but I cherish the exercise, the challenge to improve, and on good days, the camaraderie.

Alarm! Code 3 in the Program Office? False alarm. Responding staff, including a female officer walked back to their posts. A disrespectful inmate cat-called something about the curve of her backside. The offending inmate was identified, handcuffed, and led away. I always wonder why it is that staff, many who rarely show professional or leadership qualities, expect convicted felons to behave like gentlemen. Rather hypocritical because, at times, staff acts in ways that are far from gentlemanly or lady-like.

This double standard causes inmates to hate staff. I never used to hate or even dislike anyone until I came to prison. I need help with this ill feeling that only poisons me. I know just where to turn, God.

5:00 p.m.

While seated at my desk next to the officers' station, Officer Palamino and I talked about our previous occupations, and come to find out, both he and I used to manage restaurants. What do you know? We are more alike than different.

The topic of restaurants brought back fond memories of the Italian Cottage in Chico, California. There were good friends, tasty food, and fun with hard work thrown in...and Angela. This is where we first met. This is where I lost my heart. It happily drowned in her pools of sparkling root-beer eyes.

Now and again my dreams are of Angela. In them I am watching her from a distance. She pauses in her daily routine. Her eyes have a far-away gaze. She is thinking of me and the good times we shared of laughter, and love. The moment passes and Angela returns to what she was doing; living her life. When I am awake, reality's cold whisper tells me she is happily married with children and does not give me a passing thought. This is what I pray for, for her happiness, but still my guts twist until I am sick. Angela should have been my wife, having my children, and loving me, but I was not worthy.

Tears well up. I need to think of something else.

Psalm 37:27-28. *Turn from evil and do good; then you will dwell in the land forever. For the Lord loves the just and will not forsake His faithful ones.*

✝ ✝ ✝

Monday, July 4, 1994
FOURTH OF JULY

A day to celebrate freedom and independence. Well, others may be celebrating, but it is difficult for me because I have neither. My father told me in a letter that he is planning to visit our old neighborhood in Laguna Hills today. The Laguna Hills neighborhood was a terrific place to live because, besides the caring neighbors, each 4th of July a block party is held with surfing in the morning, softball at noon, volleyball in the afternoon, and a barbecue with fireworks at night. Those were the days of joyful and carefree laughter. Those were my friends. Those are the people whom I have not heard from in half a decade. They are not uncaring people. I am just out of sight and out of mind.

2:00 p.m.

I am exhausted and my toes are sore after six hours of volleyball. The first four were uneventful but the last two were exceptional. These last two hours I played two-on-two games with Ron, Spencer, and *Fast* Eddie. All are experienced players which made for spectacular saves and spikes, plenty of laughter, and best of all, NO ARGUMENTS.

I have become aware that the arguments occur more often when the *trucks* (not-so-good-players) join in. To our good fortune the *trucks* made themselves scarce after lunch. Even though the games were great, they did not make up for the absence of surfing, softball, barbecue, fireworks, and most importantly, family, but thankfully I was blessed with sharing today with new friends.

9:30 p.m.

"Hello?" It was my sweet mother's voice echoing across the miles. I finally got through to her in Texas. I may have awakened her, as they are two hours ahead of us making it 11:30 her time, but she was happy to hear from me. I was relieved to know they were safe and sound in their new home.

9:40 p.m.

CLICK! Damn! The jerk-off officer in the tower turned the telephone off five minutes early, and he did so without giving any warning. He did not give me a chance to say good-bye to my mother. Where is the courtesy? Another great role model. Another moment to punctuate the fact that I am in prison.

Regardless of the rudeness, thank you Lord for the mercies.

Isaiah 61:1. *The Spirit of the Sovereign Lord is on me, because the Lord has anointed me to preach good news to the poor. He has sent me to bind up the brokenhearted, to proclaim freedom for the captives and release from darkness for the prisoners.*

✞ ✞ ✞

Tuesday, July 5, 1994
11:00 a.m.

Today is my 'extra' day at work. This means there are two clerks to do nothing, but because I am the relief clerk I do the 'extra' nothings that come up. I don't get paid in my position but I still do the best job of nothing that I can. What was that? My bunk and book are calling for me? It is a tough job but someone has to do it.

1:00 p.m.

I started having difficulty concentrating on my spy book because that No-Control-Over-My-Life panic began to envelope me. I feel as if I have no purpose and I am being prevented from being productive. I want to go, go, go, and do, do, do something that will make a difference, but everywhere I turn there is a rule, regulation, or law to prevent me. This is not a new feeling, only more intense since losing my job in the Program Office. At least in there I could show the decision makers that I was valuable. Yeah, right, I showed them. Now I can show no one anything. My life is a leaf on the stagnant pond. I am going nowhere and it stinks.

The answer to my panic is, of course, God. I am confident from past experience that He will answer my calls for help. Though what I need to ask for, I am at a loss to put into words. I am too blind to see where I need to direct my attention. At times like this I remind myself to allow the Spirit within me to make my plea.

Keeping the focus on God brings me peace, even if I cannot explain it fully, calming my panic, and allowing me to be patient in waiting for God's divine guidance.

1 John 4:18. *There is no fear in love. But perfect love drives out fear, because fear has to do with punishment. The one who fears is not made perfect in love.*

✟ ✟ ✟

Wednesday, July 6, 1994
12:00 Noon

So far so good this morning. Emotionally I am feeling strong and upbeat. I wrote five letters to pen-pals, two who are in other prisons, and three who reside in countries around the world: South Korea and the Philippines. I constantly thank God for the postal system with all its diligent employees working to carry letters to and from distant locations.

The mail is a lifeline to the world; a tether that I hang onto for specks of real world reality. However, it can be a double-edged sword. If I receive mail, I am thrilled and uplifted. If I do not, my stomach churns with emptiness, a feeling of being abandoned. This unease should never occur because I have my friends and an extensive family who strenuously promise me, or my father, that they will write, but the majority never seems to find the time to put pen to paper. A small card with the words "Thinking of You" would mean the world to me.

I am; however, exceedingly thankful for the letters I do receive because many inmates never receive any, but do they write?

2:00 p.m.

As I sat on my bunk listening to an oldies rock station, the song *The Lion Sleeps Tonight,* with its classic repeating verse *A-Wee-Mo-Way* played. It brought to mind pleasant memories of roller skating and Mickie. I mulled over Mickie's image in my mind—lovely.   Her birthday of June 25th, and her receipt of my card came and went, but I have received no reply.

It makes me sad that she seems to have moved on. We, who were so important to each other for so many years, now appear not to matter to her anymore. Fine, I am not the center of her world. I never expected to be, but our 18-year friendship means a great deal to me. Mickie is always pleased when I telephone or write, but her letters to me have dwindled to almost nothing. Is not a friendship based on a two-way thing? It is difficult to continuously empty my cup in support of her and never be replenished.

I am probably getting an inkling of how God feels a lot of the time. He gives and gives and not often does He receive the praise and glory He deserves.

I suspect relationships mean so much to me because prison prevents or kills most of them.

In Mickie's defense, I can only see the world from my point of view. Her view, though she is free, may be far more difficult than I can imagine. I will be forever grateful for whatever she is willing and able to offer me. Maybe *that* is true friendship?

Jeremiah 31:3. *The Lord appeared to us in the past, saying: "I have loved you with an everlasting love; I have drawn you with loving-kindness."*

✟ ✟ ✟

Thursday, July 7, 1994
9:00 a.m.

Yard Officer Hardy came into the gym to see me this morning, and though it is my day off, he asked if I would exercise my fingers and utilize my vocabulary for him in the form of typing a memorandum. He stated: "You're the only clerk around that can do it right." That is not true but it was a wonderful compliment. Of course I performed the work requested with excellence. It is heartwarming to know that line staff working in the trenches still view me as worthy.

10:00 a.m.

New Flash! Moments ago the judge in the O.J. Simpson case ruled that the evidence collected in and around O.J.'s house and property was admissible even though no search warrant was secured.

The old adage that a home is one's castle lost another buttress. It is neither the guilty I seek to protect, nor were our Founding Fathers seeking protection for the guilty, but for the *presumed* innocent.

Sanctuary! Sanctuary! Are there any left? Only in God's house.

6:00 p.m.

More negative propaganda concerning inmates' rights. A news broadcast focused on several inmates who were suing the state for financial compensation. It is true, the media found several frivolous cases as examples of abuse. However, are there not frivolous cases filed by free people? How about the lady who sued McDonald's because her hot coffee burned her? She did order *hot* coffee, did she not?

The majority of law suits filed against the Department of Corrections are valid and could easily be considered as proof of criminal acts by state employees, if the act had not been perpetrated on the incarcerated. Please do not take my word for it. Ask any of the jurors who in the past have granted large sums of money to inmates who have sued. Or, here is a better one. Contact your political representative and ask him or her how many millions of dollars the state budgets each year in preparation for payouts to inmates for the illegal acts done to them.

To me, the irritating aspect of these civil suits is that the taxpayer is required to pay the settlement, not the offending state-employed doctor, officer, or administrator who was found guilty. That is what needs to be changed, not the ability of the inmate to seek legal redress for the wrongs perpetrated against him.

Heck, even dogs have the Humane Society protecting them. Who looks out for those behind these walls?

Psalm 3:3, 6. *But you are a shield around me, O Lord; you bestow glory on me and lift up my head. I will not fear the tens of thousands drawn up against me on every side.*

✟ ✟ ✟

Friday, July 8, 1994
9:00 a.m.

I strolled to the Program Office to deliver paperwork for the officers in the gym. While I was there, Frank told me that Robert, Mr. Plagiarist, the forger of a counselor's name, and defrauder, who was fired a year and a half ago from the Program Office has been working in the office with the goal of securing the job left vacant by me.

Frank and Brian are stunned and Donna is disillusioned. Out of earshot of the other staff I mentioned to Donna, in a joking manner, that it appears that plagiarism, forgery, and fraud are lesser on the offense scale than unauthorized photo copies. Donna shook her head and started to laugh, then as if realizing it would be showing disrespect and a lack of loyalty to her boss, she turned on an emotional dime, got angry, and ordered me out of the office.

I exited the Program Office feeling sorry for Donna. At her core, she is a nice person but a prisoner to her job and the meager wage it pays. If only she were a Christian. Maybe then she would have the courage and confidence to seek employment elsewhere, where her talents would be appreciated and appropriately compensated.

1 Timothy 6:17-18. *Command those who are rich in this present world not to be arrogant nor to put their hope in wealth, which is so uncertain, but to put their hope in God, who richly provides us with everything for our enjoyment. Command them to do good, to be rich in deeds, and to be generous and willing to share.*

✟ ✟ ✟

Saturday, July 9, 1994
12:00 Noon

Brian returned to the gym from the Program Office to eat his lunch. While he devoured his peanut butter and jelly sandwich he told me that *Don*

Dario is asserting presumed power as the de facto program administrator's clerk. This is not a wise thing to do. Subtle is the name of the game in prison.

I chuckled to myself. I envisioned what would be the *Clash of the Titans* if Robert were assigned to the vacant clerk's position, because he is an obnoxious S.O.B, and with *Don* Dario's new-found assertiveness, stand back and watch the battle axes fly. And what about Terri? Remember Teri with an "i"? Well she/he/it has interviewed for the job in the Program Office, too. What a menagerie of candidates staff has to choose from.

2:00 p.m.

Pant-Pant. It is hot. I mean no birds flying, grass browning before my eyes hot, but we conduct our Bible fellowship at this time so before I stepped out the gym door I prayed that God would send a breeze while we sat under His sun. I always feel so blessed to be part of this group of men because it is comforting to know they pray for me and will listen without judgment as each of us talk through our problems, concerns, and worries, and then give them up to God in prayer. Together we are a thread of sanity weaved with strength by God's love within a quilt of madness.

9:00 p.m.

Tonight my high school buddies are gathered for the reunion. Together they will raise toasts to the passage of time, celebrate enduring friendships, and shake their booties possibly to everyone's favorite music— disco. Hey, it is the class of '79. But on a somber note, did anyone there read my letter? Is anyone concerned with my plight?

Acts 2:1, 42. *When the day of Pentecost came, they were all together in one place. They devoted themselves to the apostles' teachings and to the fellowship, to the breaking of bread and to prayer.*

✞ ✞ ✞

Sunday, July 10, 1994
6:00 p.m.

The local Public Broadcasting Station aired the *Migration of the Monarch Butterfly*. Incredible, Mexico to Canada and back in one year, but taking four generations to complete the journey. At their nesting site, 9,000 feet up in the Mexican mountains, hundreds of millions of orange and black Monarchs blanket the ground and trees.

This mass of insects brought a smile to my face with memories of my sister, Julie. She loved bugs of all types, marveling at God's varied creatures. Whether they crawled, crept, jumped, or flew, Julie would watch and play with them for hours. Someday I would like to take Julie's daughter, Jenna, to this land of butterflies as a tribute to the remembrance of her mother.

If it is God's will.

1 Thessalonians 5:16-18. *Be joyful always, pray continually; give thanks in all circumstances, for this is God's will for you in Christ Jesus.*

✝ ✝ ✝

Monday, July 11, 1994
6:00 a.m.

As I walked into the chow hall (vocations) this morning, Officer Johnson told me she had spoken with the dining hall officer (not the one I had a 'full scoop' issue with), and he is going to call me in for a job interview for the lead clerk position. I was really touched by Officer Johnson's efforts on my behalf, but I graciously declined. One of the requirements for working in the chow hall, due to having access to knives and other metal implements, is I would have to strip-out (get naked) every day for searches as I exit work. I do not have the internal strength for that humiliation. My new job in the gym is peaceful and I need that at this point in my prison career.

2:00 p.m.

Howard, a gym dweller, stopped by to tell me that an old friend of his named Rick Stevens, who used to be the lead singer for the Tower of Power until his arrest for a triple murder, has been recruited from Facility A to be the new program administrator's clerk on our yard.

After a warm reunion of friends, Rick was surprised to learn from Howard that he was housed in the gym. Howard replied, "You'll be living there soon, too." Rick laughed and said that he would not have to live in the gym because, "I've got juice with my new P.A. job." Howard smiled and said this is not an old school prison yard where quality clerks have 'juice' (influence). This is Facility B, and the last program administrator's clerk has been living in the gym for over half a year. Howard related to me that Rick literally gulped at the reality check.

I wish Rick the very best in his new position

Romans 5:1-2. Therefore, since we have been justified through faith, we have peace with God through our Lord Jesus Christ, through whom we have gained access by faith into this grace in which we now stand. And we rejoice in the hope of the glory of God.

✝ ✝ ✝

Tuesday, July 12, 1994
3:00 p.m.

Have you ever lived in a place for so long that it seemed that you knew everyone? It is very comforting to know all the key inmates on this facility, but it is more important that they know me as a solid, stand-up, no B.S. guy. This provides me with security, and a measure of protection, because if something out of the ordinary were to happen I would be given the benefit of the doubt.

The only problem, and it is really not a problem, is I am obliged to say, "Hello," "What's up?" "How ya doing?" etc. etc. every few steps that I walk, everywhere I walk. I imagine myself as a parrot, walking along repeating these words, but courtesy and acknowledgment is the key to survival in this society.

Besides, they are my friends and associates, and I do care about how they are doing.

6:00 p.m.

As required when the recreation yard is closed, to enter the library I waited on the volley ball court. I needed another novel to read. Mr. Microphone is again in the yard tower making his presence known. When the yard is closed, the inmates walking to the Med-Call line at the clinic window are required to stay on the track surrounding the field to get there.

One inmate, Mr. White, who is in his late 60's exited building 9. His head was bandaged, he walked with a severe limp and from his pained facial expression he appeared to be in agony. White's injuries were caused by a fall, so he says, down the building's metal stairs.

Instead of walking the third of a mile around the track to the clinic, Mr. White cut across the field. Mr. Microphone, who apparently was lobotomized, removing all humane sensitiveness, began screaming into the microphone, repeatedly ordering White to go back and walk the track.

Mr. White, in a pain induced haze, continued to limp across the field. Receiving no compliance, Mr. Microphone radioed for assistance from the three officers who were monitoring the Med-Call line, with the apparent hope that they would subdue White's act of insurrection. When these three common sense officers looked to see who was hobbling across the field, and the severe medical condition he was in, they stared up at Mr. Microphone with disgust and waved him off.

It is not only the inmates who get tired of, and who ignore, poor ol' frustrated Mr. Microphone, but fellow officers.   Hmm…could Mr. Microphone's behavior be wrong?

1 John 1:7. *But if we walk in the light, as He is in the light, we have fellowship with one another, and the blood of Jesus, His Son, purifies us from all sin.*

✝ ✝ ✝

Wednesday, July 13, 1994
7:15 p.m.

The doppelganger of O. J. Simpson visited my father's home. Not a spirit but a flesh and bones double who threatened a re-enactment of the crime. I am disturbed by what my father shared with me over the telephone. My brother-in-law, who lives in a condominium that my father owns in Santa Monica, has been dating a woman who is separated from her husband. Her husband, who does not want to share his wife, found out where my brother-in-law lives. He climbed over the fence into the swimming pool area where my brother-in-law and niece were playing. He threatened to kill both of them if my brother-in-law did not stop seeing his wife.

I cannot imagine how terrifying the confrontation must have been for my niece who is four.

The police were called, but because the husband had left by the time the police arrived, they could only take a report. Please O Lord, my family needs heavenly intercession and protection. I will also pray that wisdom prevails. First, that the husband will calm down, and second, that my brother-in-law will reconsider his adulterous relationship with the woman, if only for the safety of his daughter.

11:45 p.m.

The threat on the lives of my family has me tossing and turning. Sleep will not come. I do my best to trust in God to keep my family safe, so that is not the overriding reason for my distress. My dis-ease, heightened by today's events, is my daily struggle with the horror that I inflicted on the family of my victim. They did not deserve the wrenching pain of a loved one lost to violence. I wish there was a way they could know how sorry I am, but really, would that lessen their pain? I doubt it. I can only pray that God will help my victims find peace.

1 Samuel 2:9. *He will guard the feet of His saints, but the wicked will be silenced in darkness. "It is not by strength that one prevails; those who oppose the Lord will be shattered."*

✝ ✝ ✝

Thursday, July 14, 1994
3:00 p.m.

I made a nauseating mistake. I stayed in the relative cool of the gym (75 degrees) all morning and then I went outside into the 103 degree heat to lift weights. Back in the gym, I keep looking to see if there is an open toilet in case I have to vomit. My muscles are not sore or overly tired. It is my dizzy head and a queasy stomach that is doing flip-flops. Could it be heat stroke? Naw, just poor planning. Tomorrow I will have to go outside an hour earlier to better acclimate my body to the excessive temperature. Hopefully that will help.

6:00 p.m.

News Flash! An inmate who is incarcerated in a prison in Vacaville has served 15 years and is now eligible for parole. In addition to being a model inmate, he presented a letter of acceptance from a medical school to the parole board.

Unfortunately for the inmate, the family of his victim along with several victim rights' groups protested his release. This exertion of pressure on the parole board commissioners did the trick because the inmate was denied parole.

My heart goes out to the victim's family for their loss, their pain and suffering, but they need to find a way to forgive this man so they too can be free and go forward with their lives. Remember, forgiveness does not mean acceptance of the wrong doings. It is an empowering act by the forgiver, proclaiming that the offender will no longer have influence over the victim.

If an inmate is showing he can be a functional person in society, exhibits remorse, and has proven over the years that he is able to follow rules, I believe he should be released. Why must he remain a burden to society?

"In God We Trust" and "One Nation Under God" are this nation's mottos; therefore we need to live as God commands. The Bible says: "If you cannot forgive others of their trespass, how can I (God) forgive you?"

I will pray for this family and the commissioners who sit on the board with the hope that their hearts and eyes can be opened to these important words, and realize the joy of pain removed when the words "I forgive you" are spoken.

Hebrews 8:12. *"For I will forgive their wickedness and will remember their sins no more."*

✝ ✝ ✝

Friday, July 15, 1994
9:00 a.m.

Can you believe it? I actually worked this morning. I typed and delivered bed assignment changes and made photocopies of forms for the gym. While I was in the Program Office, I stopped by the CCII's (head counselor's) office wherein I found Mr. Carter busily working. Mr. Carter gave me a compliment, saying that since my departure, his daily reports have been screwed up, and he has been unable to keep track of the incoming inmates' caseloads. My head did swell ever so slightly by his unsolicited accolade.

11:00 a.m.

Brian returned to the gym for lunch and told me that Mr. Carter was upset during a staff meeting. Apparently, Mr. Carter exclaimed: "I can't find a fu - - ing thing since Watson's termination."

My diligence is paying off in strange ways. I am being remembered for the good things I accomplished; the smooth operation and dissemination of accurate paperwork, not my indiscretion.

4:00 p.m.

Legal mail. It is the response from the Attorney General to my federal petition. Very brief. In four pages, he summarized the case, the dates of state appeals, and concluded with a request for dismissal based on delay. Not a single word about the merits of my legal claim. The A.G.'s tactic is to have my petition dismissed on a procedural ground without having the court rule on my constitutional right to confront my accuser.

Damn! Did I wait too long?

My next step is to file a reply (traverse) stating why I am not too late.

Isaiah 32:17. *The fruit of the righteousness will be peace, the effect of righteousness will be quietness and confidence forever.*

✝ ✝ ✝

Saturday, July 16, 1994
3:00 p.m.

Bible fellowship on the yard. Our group faithfully continues to bare its soul to God, while sharing our problems with each other for support and our blessings for celebration.

Alarm! Code 3, the gym? I always get a scary, sick feeling inside whenever an alarm is sounded. The bone-jarring buzz means someone is intentionally hurting another.

All the inmates were seated on the ground as staff ran to the gym, their side-handle batons at the ready. A gym officer stepped out the door to wave off responding staff.

Thank you, God. All was well in the cube. One of the gym officers accidentally bumped the alarm button against his desk.

Even though, all was well, my nerves and queasy stomach took 20 minutes to settle down. I hate alarms. I hate violence. I pray for continued protection for myself, for this group of men, and that God's hand of peace would rest on this facility.

Psalm 34:3-4. *Glorify the Lord with me; let us exalt His name together. I sought the Lord, and He answered me; He delivered me from all my fears.*

✝ ✝ ✝

Sunday, July 17, 1994
10:00 a.m.

New York; not the city, the man. Dave is his birth name. He is six feet, five-inches, with a bubbly personality, and just too dang handsome for one person. He was busted for a multi-million dollar jewelry heist. Nope, the jewels were never recovered. *New York* will be released January of 1995 and at age 35 he says his days of thievery are finished as his retirement is secure.

Occasionally, *New York* plays volleyball with us, and due to his lack of skill, he is given a lot of unwarranted grief by the other little-bit-better players. *New York* does his best and is fun to be around. That is all *I* ask. *New York* takes all the guff in stride, and I need to remind myself to thank him for his tolerance of the other players' inconsiderate behavior. *New York* is becoming more skilled all the time, but as maturity goes, he is far ahead of many of the other players.

2:30 p.m.

Dinner will be late tonight. An inmate was brutally stabbed on the back dock of Facility C's main kitchen where all facilities receive their food. The individual chow halls only re-heat and serve.

Both Facility A and C are locked down. Why Facility A, too? Facility A experienced several Hispanic gang altercations (North vs. South). This caused staff to lock down the facility to prevent escalation.

How terrible. How sad. We must learn to love in spite of other people's actions or our own learned prejudices. We may look and act different, but we are the same. We are all God's children.

4:00 p.m.

Surf doggy-dog! *North Shore,* the movie.   Spellbinding surfing sequences. God, you know how much I miss surfing. The adrenaline rushing through my veins as I would drop down a wave whose glassy face exceeded 20 feet would keep me high for a week. I once told Angela that a good day of surfing was better than sex, however, never better than love. She was offended. To prove my point, after squeezing her curvaceous figure into a spare wet suit of mine, she lied on my surfboard. She then held onto my leash as I towed her out through the shore breakers. Turning Angela so she faced the beach, I told her to hang on and do not try to stand up. A modest two-footer swelled and I gave her board a shove. The wave did the rest. It gently lifted Angela, and then as it broke, the crashing white water thrust her forward, jetting her toward the shallows.

All I heard were screams and shrieks.

I caught the next wave to catch up to Angela who by then was standing thigh deep in the receding water. The first words past her mile-wide grin were: "We are never having sex again."

Angela understood, and oh, did we laugh.

Sigh. But now, I am so empty, needing to be rejuvenated by the salty seas and cool water splashing on my skin. When will I return to it? When can my senses soar on watery wings? When? When? When? When? When?

I must hang on.

Ezekiel 11:19-20. *I will give them an undivided heart and put a new spirit in them; I will remove from them their heart of stone and give them a heart of flesh. Then they will follow my decrees and be careful to keep my laws. They will be my people, and I will be their God.*

✟ ✟ ✟

Monday, July 18, 1994
2:00 p.m.

Today is my father's birthday. How I wish I could be with him; to take him to dinner, and to embrace him with a big loving hug. Being without a dime to my name and not able to afford even a birthday card, let alone a gift, all I could do was to call collect to tell him that I love him. I know he appreciated my call, but my father does so much for me that the words, "I love you," are inadequate.   Actions always speak louder than words so I must continue to work toward my freedom by staying on the narrow path of good behavior and addressing my prayers to God.   To walk out of prison would be the greatest gift I could give my father.

6:30 p.m.

And what of this Nick Taylor, an old, crusty, hermit-looking man with gray whiskers and missing teeth. However, his looks do not define him.

I was relaxing on my bunk as this disheveled man approached.   Nick commented enviously on the air coming from the vent behind me.   Yes.   It is hot in the gym tonight.   The thermometer on the wall reads 84 degrees.

Nick is in prison on a violation of the rules of parole.   He has three months left to serve.   Nick and I started talking and he said he is a securities broker for some big people in Hollywood. Nick was upset by all the injustice he has seen while serving his sentence for drunk driving.   "Welcome to the club," I said with a smile.   Nick has written several articles on the criminal justice and incarceration system and wants me to read them, as he believes my point of view as a lifer would be insightful.

That was either a compliment or Nick views me as another one of the poor bastards who is stuck in the grinding mill.   Who knows, maybe both. Either/or, Nick tells an interesting story, and he is another one I can add to my acquaintance list.

Exodus 20:12. *"Honor you father and your mother, so that you may live long in the land the Lord your God is giving you."*

✞ ✞ ✞

Tuesday, July 19, 1994
9:15 a.m.

Whether one is an inmate or a staff member it is never wise to call names.   An officer, corn-fed and uppity, called a Mexican inmate, "A little wetback," as the inmate passed by on the yard.

Surprise! Surprise!

Springing like a tight coil, the Mexican had the officer on the ground and was applying a death grip to his air passage.   So quick and almost fatal, but fortunately for both, as usual, other inmates backed away from the area, and another yard officer observed the incident. He ran to the assault and pulled the Mexican off the stunned officer before any permanent damage or injury occurred.

Did corn-fed learn his name-calling lesson? Only time will tell. Will the staff in the hole brutally beat this Mexican to a pulp for assaulting a fellow officer? We will have to listen for screams in the night.

Never, never, ever touch one of the Department of Corrections' finest.

2:30 p.m.

Bang! Bang! Shots fired. This has not been a good day for the forces of peace and harmony. Two black inmates were *slinging it* (fighting furiously). Staff ran to pull the combatants apart but they got tossed to the side. That pissed them off. The tower officer fired warning shots. The warriors ceased fighting and allowed staff to handcuff them. Fortunately no one but the combatants were injured and they only suffered bruised knuckles and fat lips. Two more inmates were off to spend time in the hole.

I bet a dollar to a donut that the clerks in the Program Office are swamped with reports and lock-up orders. I'm glad I'm not working in there now.

Titus 3:3-5a. *At one time we too were foolish, disobedient, deceived and enslaved by all kinds of passions and pleasures. We live in malice and envy, being hated and hating one another. But when the kindness and love of God our savior appeared, He saved us, not because of righteous things we had done, but because of His mercy.*

✞ ✞ ✞

Wednesday, July 20, 1994
6:30 a.m.

I slept like a hibernating polar bear. Slumber undisturbed is a treasure more valuable than King Solomon's mine. The reason I am so wealthy is that *Wolf* is on a family visit so there are no squeaks, shakes, shudders, or banging from the upper bunk. Sleep deprivation is a form of torture, and though *Wolf* is a good bunkie, he is a restless sleeper. I have one more night of riches and I will be grateful as an angel smiled upon by God for it.

2:30 p.m.

The three amigos. Not the movie, but *Swede,* Howard and I. All lifers. The discussion? What else? O.J. Simpson and class injustice. It has been announced that the district attorney in his case may not seek the death penalty if O.J. is convicted. You can bet your sweet bippy that if any one of us three nobodies had killed these two people, we would be facing the death penalty.

Hells-bells, in my case only one person died and the district attorney told the judge she was saddened that she could not request the death penalty. What kind of person is disappointed when they cannot facilitate the death of another?

We three amigos are devastated that a life was taken during our criminal acts. Are the district attorneys devastated when they succeed in acquiring the death penalty for someone? It is more likely they celebrate their brilliant performances acted out before their juries, while basking in the will of the People.

Some will. Sorry people.

Hebrews 10:30. *For we know Him who said, "It is mine to avenge; I will repay," and again, "The Lord will judge His people."*

✝ ✝ ✝

Thursday, July 21, 1994
4:00 p.m.

Mail! Because of this letter from Madeline, I will be running and running, lifting, pushing and pulling, exercising until I drop in a pool of sweat. In her letter she wrote that her purse was snatched while she was walking home from work. The Philippines is a dangerous place, too. Her two week paycheck along with my photograph was stolen. She was more upset by the loss of the photograph than she was over her paycheck. Does this girl know how to touch my heart or what? I have 30 days until my next canteen draw to change these few pounds of fat into muscle. At canteen I will purchase a photo ducat, if funds are available, and smile for the camera. I know I can do it, convert the flab to muscle, and I will look marvelous. Maybe I am a little vain, but I want to put my best self forward.

8:00 p.m.

A ducat? For what? Oh, it is a job interview for tomorrow in the Associate Warden's conference room, Central Core. Wow. That is big time. Am I excited? You bet. I wonder what the job is. Obviously someone somewhere believes I am a good clerk or is it for a porter's (janitor) position? No thanks to that. Been there, done that.

I admit I am extremely curious about tomorrow's interview and I will have to think carefully about the pros and cons of working under and around administrators again. I do not know if I want to subject myself to the stress that comes along with it.

Deuteronomy 30:9. *Then the Lord your God will make you most prosperous in all work of your hands and in the fruit of your womb, the young of your livestock and the crops of your land. The Lord will again delight in you and make you prosperous, just as He delighted in your fathers.*

✞ ✞ ✞

Friday, July 22, 1994
9:20 a.m.

STATE OF CALIFORNIA	DEPARTMENT OF CORRECTIONS	
INMATE PASS	CDC 129 (7/88)	
INMATE'S NAME WATSON	CDC # D-67547	HOUSING # BG-167
ISSUED BY	DATE:	PASS FROM:
PASS TO: A.W. CONF. RM.	DATE:	TIME: 0930
REASON: JOB INTERVIEW		
ARRIVAL TIME: VOID DURING	RECORDED BY:	
DEPART TO: WORK TIME:	RECORDED BY:	

In ten minutes I will be escorted to the Central Core where all the answers to my career questions will be revealed.

10:30 a.m.

The position I was interviewed for was the Associate Warden's clerk position. The secretary who interviewed me said she had heard great things about me from Donna. Donna? The same Donna who kicked me out of the Program Office? You could have knocked me over with a feather. I will have to send her a thank you note. People sure can surprise me at times.

The interview went well even though I was giggling inside. Fired from the Program Administrator clerk position, which was entirely my fault, to be desired by his supervisor. Is that an interesting turn of events or what? In the end I declined their generous offer as the hours would be long and would not afford me the time I need for creative writing, exercising, and reading.

Many people may believe prison is strictly for punishment, and that it is, but I also believe it should be a place to change and prepare for one's release. Working for an administrator may be status within the prison but it will not help me to pay bills after I am released.

I explained my reasoning to the secretary and she appreciated my honesty and understood my thinking. I exited the interview feeling positive. I chose what was right for me and did not fall into the temptation of status, which is only fleeting.

I am learning, Lord.

Proverbs 3:3-4. *Let love and faithfulness never leave you; bind them around your neck, write them on the tablet of your heart. Then you will win favor and a good name in the sight of God and man.*

✝ ✝ ✝

Saturday, July 23, 1994
10:00 a.m.

Alarm! Code 3. The altercation was between an inmate and an officer but who assaulted who? Officer Aldridge, a cussing-degrading staff member who constantly jokes at inmates' expense pushed his alarm button as a huge Hispanic inmate angrily walked toward him. Threatening Staff? Attempted assault? If so, then why is the inmate not going to the hole?

12:30 p.m.

Officer Aldridge has been escorted off the prison grounds. The truth has surfaced. Aldridge was the instigator of the incident. Will he be fired, suspended, or merely reprimanded? Whatever the end results, a message was sent. If staff pushes inmates verbally they will have to answer for it.

Sometimes those in authority do seek the truth, and despite pressure to ignore it, a wrong is righted.

6:00 p.m.

Two long weeks of wondering; fourteen dragging days has passed since my high school reunion was held. I have not received a single letter from my old classmates. Was my letter to them read? I do not know. Am I disappointed? Very much. I do not hate them for not writing, but it shows me how separated I am from the world, and once separated, always alone.

Where is the compassion for a fallen friend? I do not seek a hand out, only a hand to hold while pulling myself up.

Romans 8:38-39. *For I am convinced that neither death nor life, neither angels nor demons, neither the present nor the future, nor any powers, neither height nor depth, nor anything else in all creation, will be able to separate us from the love of God that is in Christ Jesus our Lord.*

✞ ✞ ✞

Sunday, July 24, 1994
7:30 p.m.

Nothing is wrong that I can pinpoint but I feel miserable. No one has mistreated me today. No new inconvenient rules have been posted. My sadness is not caused by anything specific. It's caused by the weight of prison life. The drab gray walls, faded blue clothes, and the bland food served day after day. They add up to mountains of gloom that would cause even the great Hercules to hunch over.

I maintain a smile on my face to show others God's strength in me, and my faith in Him, but God knows the tears are flowing inside. I am so tired of giving to Caesar. I desperately want to live a normal life. I want to be happy. Am I asking too much?

8:30 p.m.

I telephoned my father for a cheering up and boy did he do a great job. First, simply hearing his strong and encouraging voice did wonders. Then, secondly, he told me that through our family attorney, he met a movie/television producer, who as a favor, would review and critique one of my scripts. Wow!

My father asked which script he should send. I thought for a moment and then replied, "Pacific Moon." He thought that was a good choice.

Yes, I am feeling much better. Hope combined with opportunity is awesome.

Thanks, God.

1 Peter 4:12-13. *Dear friends, do not be surprised at the painful trial you are suffering, as though something strange were happening to you. But rejoice that you participate in the sufferings of Christ, so that you may be overjoyed when His glory is revealed.*

☩ ☩ ☩

Monday, July 25, 1994
11:00 a.m.

Eleven o'clock! I slept through breakfast and half the day. I am dizzy and not feeling well, physically speaking. It is depressing to get sick in prison. No one is here to take care of me. I can only lie on my bunk and suffer. Yesterdays' mental roller coaster has changed into physical ailments. Maybe a steaming shower will help my aching body. Too bad for me, the water is only lukewarm. Sigh.

12:00 p.m.

I am still woozy but not as groggy headed. Sitting on my bunk I notice how worn my sweat bottoms have become. There are holes in the knees and seams unraveling. I have owned them for 4 ½ years. I suppose they have served their purpose well but I am not ready to give up on them yet. *Swede* has a sewing needle, and I have dental floss, so if I can see to thread the tiny hole I will stitch closed the accumulating air vents.

1:30 p.m.

There, that is much better. I am no Susie Homemaker but the holes are repaired and the seams should last a year or two more. No one can accuse me of not being frugal but it is out of personal necessity. Sure, I could call home and ask that my parents purchase and put another pair of sweats in my next care package. They would happily do so, but as I am responsible for my incarceration and inability to earn a living, my parents should not have to constantly dig into their pockets. Besides, it is not their money that I need. It is their love and they give all they have. Being clothed in love makes me the best dressed man around.

2 Corinthians 9:8. *And God is able to make all grace abound to you, so that in all things at all times; having all that you need, you will abound in every good work.*

☦ ☦ ☦

Tuesday, July 26, 1994
7:00 a.m.

Today is my 'extra' day again and I will not have much of anything to do. That is okay as I am still in need of recuperative rest. I am feeling a little better. My muscles and joints do not ache as much, and so I thank God for His healing touch. However, to be quiet and continue to concentrate on God is what I am still in need of for both physical and mental recovery.

11:00 a.m.

Forty-five days have passed with not a letter or card from Mickie. I attempted to telephone her aunt's home where Mickie was last living but no one answers. I miss her. Does she care? I often wonder what is happening in her life.

Without communication, how am I supposed to know what prayers she needs?

3:00 p.m.

I have finished reading Nick's political writings. They are very impressive. He used many fancy words. A reader would never know that the author was subject to that which he wrote about as it was done objectively, clinically. Nick could be what he said he was, a learned man with a drinking problem. What a relief. I am not surprised by my initial cynicism of Nick's claims or any inmate who tells me what they are or who they were on the street. I try to be trusting, but so many games are played in here with so many egos puffing themselves up, that it becomes difficult at times to distinguish the bull from the sh--.

9:00 p.m.

The third watch officer who passes out the re-route mail handed me a ducat for a job change. Starting tomorrow I will officially be the second watch gym clerk. My predecessor wanted to work in the chow hall, where as he put it: "I can get my grub on." It is true that those inmates who work in the chow hall eat better than those of us who only funnel through. The food is the same, but when one makes his own individual meal, it is done with care, and the portions are larger.

I chuckled at the timing of the job change. My new job starts tomorrow which is Wednesday, and as the relief clerk, it would have been my day off. Oh well, I do not mind because I need the money, even if the second watch clerk's position only receives 18 cents per hour. It will pay for postage stamps, greeting cards, and a photo ducat.

11:30 p.m.

The Public Broadcasting Station showcased a documentary on the making of Francis Ford Coppola's *Apocalypse Now*. The absolute hell he endured to create that masterpiece was horrendous. Filmed in the Philippines, there were conflicts with rebels, bouts of malaria among cast and crew, substantial cost overruns, rumors of drug addictions on the set, and Marlon Brando's penchant for unpredictability all conspired against the epic coming to fruition. In spite of the obstacles, Coppola pulled it off. I have a new and deeper respect and admiration for the film and its genius creator.

Throughout my life there have been three films that I relate to the different aspects of my personality. *Apocalypse Now* reflects the darker side wherein lies confusion, horror, and the evil that lurks within all men. *Romeo and Juliet* hold my heart with romance, where love is worth any and all sacrifice. And finally, *Excalibur:* the character Lancelot to be specific. He was not a perfect knight, but his honor, his word, and trustworthiness meant everything to him, as they do to me.

And what about the Holy Grail that the knights of old sought after? To me it is the quest for God. God is everything and a part of me. There are many sides to a castle and all are required to be strong if it is to stand against attackers. There are also many parts to a man and he who knows his character will not flail in the darkness or be defeated by the enemies that come against him.

1 Corinthians 33:15. *Do not be misled; "Bad Company corrupts good character."*

✝ ✝ ✝

Wednesday, July 27, 1994
10:00 a.m.

Oh God. A knife in the heart pierces so deeply, so painfully. Can the whole world hear my anguished scream?

"I am so happy for you," I said to Mickie.

Honor sucks.

My telephone conversation with Mickie has ended. Her musical voice tore at the fabric of my ears as another door of hope, of a special love, has slammed closed. She purposely had not been in contact with me because she did not know how to tell me that she is getting married. Married? I did not know she was dating anyone.

He is a Christian and a carpenter. How ironic, a Christian carpenter. Though my feeling of loss is overwhelming, my honest joy for her is present, too. I cannot give Mickie the things she needs or desires from behind bars so I am content to know that God has blessed her with a good man. A carpenter named Steve.

Mickie asked if I was okay. Sure, I am fine. I am always fine. God and me, we will get by. So, God, when will it be my turn to love and to be held? Mickie wants to stay in contact and has told Steve about our long friendship. Friends are supposed to outlive everything. I will have to be satisfied to be a supportive friend.

Does anyone have a heart-shaped bandage?

4:00 p.m.

July 21, 1994

Mr. Gregory Barnes Watson

Dear Mr. Watson,

Three thousand, nine hundred and thirty-four entry scripts -- a roomful of words wishing to be transformed into movies. By virtue of the sheer numbers you have to know that the 1994 Nicholl Fellowships competition was rather spirited. Over six months have passed since the arrival of the initial entry, and, finally, we've made our decisions. Unfortunately, DREAMTIME was not one of the 206 entries selected to advance into the Quarterfinal Round of the 1994 Nicholl Fellowships in Screenwriting.

As your script was read twice but didn't receive high enough scores to advance, I'll remind you that the reading of screenplays is an extremely subjective matter. The lack of success here may have little bearing on a sale elsewhere. A judge new to this year's competition offered this opinion: "These scripts are better than those I'm reading at [xyz Productions]." Clearly, there were a great many good scripts entered, and not all of them advanced into the next round. At least one "reject" sold recently. It would not surprise me if others have sold as well.

To tell you something about the process: we read each script once (yes, even those that were out of format); 1,600 scripts, after receiving a positive evaluation, garnered a second read. We read 170 with a disparity between scores a third time. We totaled the top two scores, resulting in the selection of the quarterfinalists. The system is arbitrary, but it is also fair and scrupulous.

In January of next year we'll send you a 1995 application form, which will include a list of the winners of the 1994 Fellowships.

Best of luck with all your future endeavors.

Sincerely,

Greg Beal
Program Coordinator
Nicholl Fellowships in Screenwriting

Mail. The result of the Nicholl Fellowship for screenwriting has been decided. Damn. My script *Dreamtime* did not win. I had such high hopes as I believe it is a great story of Australian adventure. No overnight sensation for me.

It is time again to place my plastic bucket which I use as a stool, upside down, in front of my bunk, and begin squeezing out those creative juices. Sigh.

7:30 p.m.

Officer Bartels searched my envelope and scanned each page of my reply (traverse) to the Attorney General's request to have my petition dismissed. After sealing and signing the envelope addressed to the federal court, Officer Bartels said, "Good luck," and he meant it.

As I have said, people always surprise me.

Ephesians 5:22, 25. Wives submit to your husbands as to the Lord. Husbands love your wives, just as Christ loves the church and gave Himself up for her.

✝ ✝ ✝

Thursday, July 28, 1994
2:45 a.m.

Sleep is not coming. I know Mickie was never mine, but the pain of my loss of her as more than a friend is great. The death of a hope, of a dream is equally painful as if the sparkling diamond that was real in your hand crumbled to dust.

Plastic pillows do not easily absorb tears.

9:30 a.m.

The inmates on this yard are changing. Facility A is being converted to a level IV (higher security) from its current level III. Because Facility B is a level II and III, the counselors have been swapping inmates so their custody level matches the facility.

About two dozen trouble makers who thought they could hide here on Facility B received a rude awakening. Their property was rolled up and they were packed off to Facility A this morning. What one reaps, sooner or later, that is what they will have to sow.

12:30 p.m.

I was, for the briefest moment, able to ignore the pain in my heart, finding distraction, if not contentment. Leaning against my locker, sitting on a five gallon plastic bucket, and watching a captivating movie on television, I was at peace until my counselor walked by on his way to his office. Seeing my level of relaxation, he commented, "What a life."

I am not sure how he intended his comment but despair set in like fog on San Francisco's bay. "This is not a life, you idiot," vibrates in my head from the shriek I dare not let out. I hang on by my finger tips and through God's grace. I have no one to hold; no special love and no social activities to enrich my soul except for volleyball and Bible fellowship.

Free people, righteous people, want inmates to suffer. Congratulations. They are getting what they want, but they have no idea of how much I am suffering. My body may again be healthy, and the occasional snippet of peace may pass my way, but my mind is constantly tortured by the daily depravity that is incalculable.

6:00 p.m.

News Flash! Legislative and Executive law making.

Trust?! The Inmate Welfare Fund is supposed to be a pooled trust account wherein inmates are forced to pay a 10% surcharge for everything purchased, from shampoo to radios. This money, this trust fund, was created for use toward the inmates' welfare, i.e. programs, especially for indigent inmates.

For many years the Department of Corrections has been utilizing (stealing in my opinion) this money for their own political gains through seemingly appropriate legislative bills and accounting procedures. Example: Correctional Officers did not used to be peace officers and their requests to become such was voted down by the other California peace officers associations until the Department of Corrections gave a 20 million dollar loan (no interest) to the Highway Patrol. It was not surprising that at the next voting the correctional officers became peace officers. Where did the money come from? Did it come from the prison guards' association? Hell no, it came from the Inmate Welfare Fund. No crime? No foul?

Recently good ol' make 'em suffer Governor Pete Wilson signed a bill into law that allows county jails and state prisons to legally use the trust funds for any purpose they want. Administrators say there is 40 million dollars statewide and they do not know how to use it. Here is a suggestion: education for the illiterates, intensive counseling for molesters, rapists, drug addicts, and classes to raise victim awareness and criminal forgiveness. Ask any inmate what he needs to become a viable society member and he will give you a list.

State Representative Andal said he wants to take all the money and place it in the general state fund because inmates should pay their own way. How the heck are we supposed to do that when inmates' wages begin at zero, which is the vast majority, to near one dollar, which is the tiniest minority. No one is getting rich working for prison wages and the money we do have for amenities comes from our families.

Can we face the truth? It is easy for those in power to attack those who cannot fight back, let alone are prohibited from voting. Again, ask us what we need, if you care. And, Mr. Andal, you too would be surprised, but by asking, it would acknowledge that we are more than just animals; more than boxes to be wedged into a shelf and forgotten. Discouragingly, from all your actions, Mr. Andal, it is apparent that you are not interested in seeking the human, only kicking the caged dog.

Hebrews 13:17. *Obey your leaders and submit to their authority. They keep watch over you as men who must give an account. Obey them so that their work will be a joy, not a burden, for that would be of no advantage to you.*

✝ ✝ ✝

Friday, July 29, 1994
11:00 a.m.

Well, so much for rising early as I crawled out of my bunk with the morning almost gone. It was my day off, but I had planned to spryly rise at 8:00 a.m., make a couple of quick telephone calls, and then exercise and read. However, it seems my body had other plans and said to itself, "Rest," and it obeyed. My mind now has the desire to be non-productive and it's suggesting, rather strongly, after I shower and shave, that I sit back and watch numbing no-purpose television talk shows. My name must have been changed sometime during the night to slug-mister lie-about.

3:00 p.m.

Twitching and antsy muscles. Enough was enough. My body finally said, "Workout." As I walked toward the weight pile I stopped in front of the Program Office to speak with ex-Tower of Power singer Rick Stevens. Apparently Frank told Rick about my creative writing (screenplay) attempts and Rick believes he may be able to get them reviewed for production consideration. Also, Rick may want me to write his story.

Rick was a Rock 'n Roll star until drugs and kidnap killings placed him on death row. Then in 1972 Rick was given a reprieve from the gas chamber when the California Supreme Court abolished the death penalty, ruling it to be cruel and unusual. Since that day Rick has begun a new life and has attempted to be productive and an asset to his community even though it is limited to a prison community.

I am flattered that Rick would consider me to write his story, but at that moment I was late for a date, so we decided to discuss the project later.

Coleman, my workout partner would be annoyed, jokingly so, if I was tardy for our exercise routine. "A strong body promotes a strong mind," is Coleman's motto.

8:30 p.m.

Hot and heavy, back and forth, volley, spike and point. The evening game of volleyball was exhilarating, but anything good in prison cannot last. Over the loudspeakers came, "Yard recall." It was not yet 9:00 p.m. What a bummer. Another emergency count. I have to get on my bunk to be counted.

One…two…three…

10:30 p.m.

Two hours later and my sweat has dried, leaving salt rings on my skin. What is up with this count? One of the advantages of being housed in the gym is it is easier to 'bird bath' (bathe in the sink). Even though the showers are out-of-bounds after the evening count, I can use the large tub sink to soap up and rinse off. If I were in a regular housing unit with cells, bird bathing is more difficult because the cell sink is a tiny wash basin, and water splashes everywhere, getting the bunk and personal property wet.

Generally, the count clears within 25 minutes. Maybe someone really did leave without permission.

10:30 p.m.

"Count is clear," blares from the gym speakers. Finally! Now I can get up and go to the bathroom, bird bath, and brush my teeth for bed. It's true that I only rose at 11:00 a.m., so I should not be tired, but even on a relatively good day; the heavy burden of my criminal past is an emotionally exhaustive yoke.

Will it ever lift, Lord? As I ask this question, I realize it should not. The pain I inflicted on my victims will never end so why should I be granted relief?

11:25 p.m.

The line to use the tub sink stretched 18 deep with inmates who had the same idea. However, with patience and only a few jostles, I finally reached the sink to remove the salty crust. Waiting 50 minutes to use the sink when a dozen showers are four feet away is crazy-nuts, but rules are rules and must be followed. If they are not - anarchy.

Isaiah 30:15. *This is what the sovereign Lord, the Holy One of Israel says: "In repentance and rest is your salvation, in quietness and trust is your strength."*

✝ ✝ ✝

Saturday, July 30, 1994
8:00 a.m.

Feeling that I needed some cheering up, I telephoned both my mother in Texas and my father in San Diego. To hear caring and encouraging voices does wonders. While speaking with my father, I learned that my grandfather is visiting him and he and I were able to speak for a few minutes. The conversation was rather stilted because I found that I did not have much to say to him. This was only the third time in nearly eight years that he and I have talked to each other. I used to write cards and send letters to my cousins, aunts, uncles, and grandparents, but because I never received any replies I finally gave up. It is sad when one has nothing to say to a relative. I always believed we were a close family.

Maybe it is another one of those out of sight, out of mind things.

9:00 p.m.

Brian returned from work with horror stories about his co-workers. Alex is afraid of making mistakes on the paperwork he is being asked to process but he is too timid to ask questions; *Don* Dario is making too many typos as he tries to speed type through his work instead of taking the necessary time to be accurate, and Donna declared today that the clerks must learn each other's duties, because after I departed, no one knew the magnitude and variety of tasks I accomplished without being asked on a daily, weekly, and monthly basis.

The fallout continues.

Brian did share one bright spot and that is Rick. He has a positive personality, is fitting in well with both the inmates and staff, and work-wise, he appears to be able to handle what is given to him to process. So all is not chaos.

Malachi 4:6a. *"He will turn the hearts of the fathers to their children, and the hearts of their children to their fathers."*

✝ ✝ ✝

Sunday, July 31, 1994
8:30 a.m.

A new volleyball recruit, *BMW.* We call him *B* for short. He is a 20-year-old, muscular black youngster with a likable personality. Besides his good nature, *B* can serve and spike the ball like a bullet shot from a high-powered rifle. The funny thing is he has a problem with putting his arms together to bump pass the ball because his muscles are too darn big. I am glad *B* has come by to play, and I hope that he continues to do so because he is an asset to our games and uplifting to our attitudes.

10:00 a.m.

Through our discussions during our exercises, Coleman shared with me that he has a son named Greg. Coleman has been writing to a family friend and discussing Greg's excessive drug use, depression, and his own fear that Greg might do something crazy and harmful to himself and others.

This morning, Lieutenant Davenport summoned Coleman into his office to discuss me, Greg. Staff was concerned, after reading Coleman's letters that the loss of my job in the Program Office had caused me to go off the deep end. Fortunately for me, Coleman was able to clear up the confusion about the 'Greg's,' but it does make me more aware of the close scrutiny our correspondence receives.

There is no privacy - none. We are all open wounds without salve.

On a less touchy-feely note, staff was trying to find out where 'Greg' was getting the drugs from.

8:00 p.m.

Yard recall. Again! This is past becoming annoying. Twice in almost as many nights. The legislature needs to pass a law forbidding people on the streets from wearing blue jeans because when someone with blue jeans is seen walking anywhere near the prison we have to stop and count.

8:30 p.m.

Waiting...waiting...waiting on our bunks for count to clear.
Twiddle my fingers.
Twiddle my fingers.
Wait one super hero minute. Who was that caped crusader? Yes, I believe it was him. The ever elusive BUNK MAN comes to rescue us.

For the briefest of moments, an inmate leapt up to stand on top of one of the double bunks. He had applied white cream to his face and drawn a large letter B on his chest. He had a towel for a cape and was wearing only white boxer shorts. Bunk Man jumped up and down on the squeaky bed springs, and shouted, "Never fear because the bouncing Bunk Man is here." Then in a flash, the caped crusader, who had sworn to defeat boredom wherever it may be found, vanished from atop the bunk to the cheers and applause of all, staff included.

Humor and spontaneity: what a pleasant interlude.

9:10 p.m.

Count cleared.

Proverbs 14:13. *Even in laughter the heart may ache, and joy may end in grief.*

✝ ✝ ✝

Monday, August 1, 1994
8:00 a.m.

Maybe I was a glutton for punishment, but I was compelled to telephone Mickie. Mostly I wanted to reassure her and myself that our friendship can and will continue. Our conversation was constructive with only a few awkward silences. The lightness and music of Mickie's voice revealed to me how happy she is and I admit that is what I have always prayed for, so I cannot be a hypocrite. I have to be aware of what I ask of God because He does answer my prayers, but not always in the manner that is most appealing to me.

Father knows best.

2:00 p.m.

Lost soul, lost mind. I was walking around the track to breathe in some fresh air and exercise the legs. Near the *going home* gate (Plaza Gate), a 4'10" Hispanic inmate was standing, apparently waiting for the gate to open. This was wishful thinking, because Officer Fairbanks and a sergeant were trying to explain to the non-English speaking inmate that he cannot stand by the gate, and that he needed to return to the main yard area. They were being frustrated by the inmate's blank stare and inability to comprehend. After several minutes the inmate walked a dozen yards with staff, then abruptly turned and ran back toward the locked gate.

Like a caged, frightened animal, this inmate could not understand his fate. Officer Fairbanks, the sergeant, and two additional staff who arrived to assist, attempted to place handcuffs on the inmate to return him to his cell. The gunman in the nearby tower readied his rifle to shoot if a struggle broke out and staff was assaulted. Officer Fairbanks reached out, and with surprising gentleness slowly turned the boxed-in inmate around. The trembling creature did not resist allowing Officer Fairbanks to handcuff him. Unfortunately that was only one example of a growing number of mentally disturbed inmates who are being held captive within the Department of Corrections, but who should be in a patient treatment center. I am not saying that mental illness should excuse criminal activity, but being locked in prison cannot help reform a person whose brain is not functioning properly.

And before I forget, praise goes to Officer Fairbanks for the gentle manner in which he handled and restrained that terrified man.

Psalm 31:4-5. *Free me from the trap that is set for me, for you are my refuge. Into your hands I commit my spirit; redeem me, O Lord, the God of truth.*

☦ ☦ ☦

Tuesday, August 2, 1994
3:30 p.m.

Ah… a good stretch after a long run helps to lengthen muscles that are pumped to the max.

Coleman has become my steady exercise partner. He is amazing. At 20 years my senior, he can squat, bench press, and curl far heavier weights than I. Where I outdo him is in dips, pull-ups, and jogging laps around the track. I admit I have a weight advantage by 35 pounds less, so in reality, Coleman keeps up with me just fine. At 6'2", his ex-marine physique is imposing, but it is his mind, both creative and business sense that I admire most.

Sadly, Coleman is serving a 15-year to life sentence for second degree murder. He has served more than 10 as an exemplary inmate. Will Coleman ever receive a parole date from the board commissioners? Only time will tell.

Together, Coleman and I have been doing well sticking to our exercise routine. This dedication has caused my shoulders, neck, and back muscles to become extremely sore, but boy-o-boy, are they growing. To relieve the soreness I would give almost anything to have a caring woman's soothing fingers massage and knead my back and shoulders. Besides reducing the aches and pains of muscles that have been overworked, my spirit would be enriched by the touch of feminine hands.

At times, it is as if I cannot catch my breath from the lack of human touch. I understand why newborn babies die if not held. I may have muscles, strong arms for hugs, but without love, without a caring person to hug me in return, what is the point?

Luke 18:15-16. *People were also bringing babies to Jesus to have Him touch them. When the disciples saw this, they rebuked them. But Jesus called the children to Him and said, "Let little children come to me, and do not hinder them, for the kingdom of God belongs to such as these."*

✝ ✝ ✝

Wednesday, August 3, 1994
3:00 p.m.

A sweaty, brow-dripping three mile run was the remedy to clear my head, release the physical pent-up energy, and reduce the mental stress of life behind bars...sort of. While walking around the track to cool down and catch my breath, *Don* Dario approached me in an agitated state, and handed his work supervisor's report to me.

A work supervisor's report (CDC-101) is a report card given every three months and details an inmate's work performance. An example of one of mine is below.

STATE OF CALIFORNIA CDC 101 (Rev. 4/82)		**WORK SUPERVISOR'S REPORT**		DEPARTMENT OF CORRECTIONS	
GRADES	GRADE			GRADE	
1 = Exceptional	1	A. Demonstrated Skill and Knowledge		1	F. Teamwork and Participation
2 = Above Average	1	B. Attitude Toward Fellow Inmates and Workers		1	G. Learning Ability
3 = Satisfactory	1	C. Attitude To Supervisors and Staff		1	H. Use of Tools and Equipment
4 = Below Average	1	D. Interest in Assigned Work		1	I. Quality of Work
5 = Unsatisfactory	1	E. Effort Displayed in Assigned Work		1	J. Quantity of Work
PAY STATUS: From $		To $	From Job No.	To Job No.	
Total No. Hours Assigned		Total No. Hours Worked		LENGTH OF SUPERVISION	
SUBJECT ASSIGNED TO	DATE ASSIGNED	ACTUAL WORK CONSISTS OF:		PERIOD COVERED BY REPORT	
P.A. CLERK	04/10/91	CLERICAL		06/30/93 - 02/28/94	
RECOMMEND FOR: ☐ REASSIGNMENT	☒ RETAIN	☐ PAY INCREASE	☐ PAY DECREASE	INMATE'S INITIALS	
COMMENTS (IF MORE SPACE REQUIRED, USE REVERSE SIDE): Watson continues to do an excellent job and has always shown respect to his supervisor and co-workers.					
SUPERVISOR	H. ANDERSON		WORK DETAIL PROGRAM OFFICE	ETHNICITY WHITE	
INMATE'S NAME WATSON, GREG		NUMBER D-67547	INSTITUTION MCSP	DATE 03/01/94	

Donna checked threes and fours on *Don* Dario's. Ones are excellent and fives are unsatisfactory. *Don* Dario was upset and understandably so. He does work hard and believes he should have received higher marks. However, *Don* Dario seems to have forgotten he has to be reminded often about details of processing reports, and his typing errors cannot be overlooked, but still, those were rather harsh marks.

Fortunately for *Don* Dario, he is not a lifer and those reports mean little if nothing, except to his ego. I told him that even with his few faults he is number one in my book. Why? Because he has always treated me kindly and tries hard. A smile crossed *Don* Dario's wrinkled face.

Everyone, even in their current state of imperfection needs affirmation. God bless *Don* Dario.

Proverbs 11:27. *He who seeks good finds goodwill, but evil comes to him who searches for it.*

✝ ✝ ✝

Thursday, August 4, 1994
4:00 p.m.

Mail. Letters. A lot of them. One from *Bull,* one from Ed, one from Mary and Beck (my mother's pseudo aunt and uncle), and one from Jennifer. Jennifer? Oh Lord, is it? It is! Jennifer from high school. I received a response from my high school reunion. Jennifer enclosed with her letter a photograph, actually two. One was of her class photograph and one of her now.

1979   1994

Jennifer and I attended high school together, but it was only when we worked together at a local Italian restaurant called Petrocelli's that we became good friends, and even dated several times. Jennifer was a class act, so beautiful, slender and blond, and though I hold a preference for brunettes, Jennifer was a special lady. Among the many uplifting words to me she shared in her letter is that she has been married for 14 years.

I will write her immediately and I can honestly say that I am a bit envious of her long relationship with her husband. Not that he has it with her but that I miss being in one myself. Together, they live in the small town of Grass Valley. It is 45 minutes from here via winding roads. I hope with all my heart that in time they will want to come for a visit or I will be offered the opportunity to telephone.

I am so, so happy. A walking on tippy toes happy. It was worth opening my heart and reaching out because my gesture was rewarded. An interesting note is Jennifer wrote that she is a Christian. Why I am not surprised?

Thank you, God. Thank you, Jennifer.

Oh, and not to ignore the other letters I received today, they were terrific, too. I was blessed today.

6:30 p.m.

While I wrote to Jennifer, I sat on my bucket at my bunk with her photographs beside the pad of paper. Several inmates, as they walked by, stopped to ask if the lady in the photographs was my special girl. She certainly is special but not my girl in that sense. One man who stopped for a few minutes to chat is named Alamean. As we talked he learned that I was a lifer, a 34-years to life, lifer, and he could not fathom spending that length of time in prison. I told him I am a Christian and each day God blesses me more than I deserve. I may still be in prison and may have to "Pay Caesar what is Caesar's" by doing all the time, but God will make my time worthwhile if I obey His commands and listen daily to the Spirit.

I readily admitted that I hate every moment in prison but I still try to be God's light. I knew Alamean was a Muslim so I added, "No matter what you choose to call Him: God, Allah, Jehovah, or Spirit Father, He is the one and only God. If we praise Him and ask for guidance He will always help us."

Alamean shook my hand and was pleased that this Christian did not condemn or attempt to convert his Muslim beliefs. Even if I do not fully agree with a person's beliefs, I try to enlighten them by example. This is the way Jesus did it.

Matthew 12:34b-35, 37. *"For out of the overflow of the heart the mouth speaks. The good man brings good things out of the good stored up in him, and the evil man brings evil things out of the evil stored in him. For by your words you will be acquitted, and by your words you will be condemned."*

✞ ✞ ✞

Friday, August 5, 1994
6:00 a.m.

I awoke from gliding on the pillory wings of a giant jellyfish. I have not had many good dreams since my incarceration but last night's made up for quite a few bad ones. I was soaring across the bluest of skies on an airborne jellyfish. We were flying over lush green orchards brimming with sweet-smelling oranges, nectarines, and pears; over undulating breeze-blown grass plains, and rugged mountains with swift-flowing streams that sparkled as they cascaded over mile-high cliffs. I was higher than a kite could ever reach and happy to be me.

The only difference between last night's dream and all the other nightmares was the receipt of Jennifer's letter. It takes so little to brighten my life. I suspect my joy in this renewed friendship is double-fold because of the loss of the hope of a *special* love between myself and Mickie.

Hmm...this must be that door closing, window opening policy that God offers His children...if we will only be patient.

Big smile.

I will give extra thanks to God for touching Jennifer's heart and filling mine with joy.

Psalm 48:1. *Great is the Lord, and most worthy of praise, in the city of our God, His holy mountain.*

✞ ✞ ✞

Saturday, August 6, 1994
8:00 a.m.

After telephone conversations with my mother and father I always say to myself: I have the greatest parents, my mother for her nurturing and kindness, and my father for his strength and guidance. They are two wonderful examples of what people of loving character should be.

At the mobile home park in Texas, my mother is not only the landlord, but is becoming a social worker, a light for God, for the elderly poor who reside there. Among her many kind deeds, my mother has helped an elderly blind man to receive aid so his electricity would not be shut off. It took many hours of her time, as well as several trips to the aid office, but it was what she believed God wanted. The Spirit touched her and she moved with it.

As for my father, whenever I need advice or assistance, I know he will do whatever he can for me. This has always been a comfort, like a soft mattress to fall back on. I would be utterly lost without it.

I have been truly blessed.

Joshua 22:5. *"But be very careful to keep the commandment and law that Moses the servant of the Lord gave you: to love the Lord your God, to walk in all His ways, to obey His commands, to hold fast to Him and to serve Him with all your heart and all your soul."*

✟ ✟ ✟

Sunday, August 7, 1994
2:30 p.m.

Paul, fortyish, with triple-thick glasses, who is an obsessive analyst, stopped by to talk politics. Augh!

Pete Wilson or Kathleen Brown, who will be the next California governor and which of them, will be more likely to parole lifers? This is the current question that Paul ponders and worries about, searching each poll, and reviewing every political news article he can lay his hands on. Paul has served 19 years of a 7-year to life sentence. Too, too long.

After an hour of patient listening I finally told Paul that the whole political process was not worth worrying over because we cannot vote and politicians traditionally pick on those who cannot defend themselves. Then I had a wonderful opportunity to share the peace I cling to in my heart because of God's love for me. Not to diminish each day that we suffer in prison, but we in prison must learn to be content with our station in life. Through Jesus' love even prison affords us opportunities. For me, it is who I can help and what example am I setting. Together, these make for days where the work is never ending, but joy-filled.

I explained that God is our Father and He wants us to be happy in this world, but He is more concerned with our eternal life and spiritual well-being. We must pray to contentment. We must work for God's glory, and when the time is right, His divine time, the gates to prison will spring open, and we will have the physical freedom we seek. If however, the gates to the physical prison never open, we can still revel in the freedom that the Spirit makes available to us now.

Paul thanked me for talking, really talking to him because he had been stressed out and my words made sense. I invited Paul to our weekly fellowship and will remind him again this Saturday. I believe Paul would be an asset to our group and be able to gain comfort and knowledge from it.

Whenever I am afforded the opportunity to speak of Christ's work, in my life, to another, my insides light up with His spiritual fire. It is a unique tingling feeling. What a rush! Thank you Lord for this time, to share You with a friend in need.

Psalm 29:11. *The Lord gives strength to His people; the Lord blesses His people with peace.*

✟ ✟ ✟

Monday, August 8, 1994
7:00 a.m.

Lost in space, definitely in time. While waiting for breakfast, three inmates seated on nearby bunks were transfixed by the children's string game Cat's Cradle. They twisted and turned, weaved and knotted the long circle of string with the giggles of preschoolers in a Romper Room setting. A mind, what a terrible thing to lose.

5:30 p.m.

"Helter Skelter," said the news anchor. Twenty-five years ago the animalistic killings of the Manson murders took place in Los Angeles. Today the family members of several of the victims were interviewed. They each complained how they are still victims because each year they have to attend the parole hearing of those convicted of the crimes and re-live the horror.

I neither speak for others, nor would I try to diminish the terrible loss felt by the families, but would their outlook, their mental health be better, more positive if they were able to forgive? Then they could go forward with their lives, leaving the decision to parole to the board of commissioners. The heinous nature of the Manson murders would not be viewed as any less if the family members were not present during the hearings.

The Manson murderers may or may not be the best example, but are the followers of Manson 25 years ago the same people today? I am certainly not the same person who was involved in the crimes that brought me to prison and that was less than eight years ago. I doubt that those who were involved in the Manson killings are the same people either, assuming they have asked the Lord into their lives.

I do believe in freedom of the press as a cornerstone of this country, but lately the media has become an instrument for manipulation, sound-biting panic in the public. There seem to be fewer facts spoken by anchor persons, and in their place, adjectives of drama, as if the public needs to be told how to feel about any given topic.

Does anyone remember Saul who became Paul? He was a vicious hunter-killer of Christians. Then by circumstance he was converted and became one of God's greatest preachers and teachers. Now I ask myself: has anyone really talked with, not to or at, the men and women who committed those "Helter Skelter" crimes? Probably not. It would not be politically correct. How can we as a society survive if we are unable to forgive transgressions? How can we live with ourselves, let alone others, if we harbor hate? Allow God His glory to turn evil to good and sorrow to joy.

Luke 18:9-14. *To some who were confident of their own righteousness and looked down on everybody else, Jesus told this parable: "Two men went up to the temple to pray, one a Pharisee and the other a tax collector. The Pharisee stood up and prayed about himself: 'God, I thank you that I am not like the other men-robbers, evildoers, adulterers-or even like this tax collector. I fast twice a week and give a tenth of all I get.' "But the tax collector stood at a distance. He would not even look up to heaven, but beat his breast and said, 'God, have mercy on me, a sinner.' "I tell you that this man, rather than the other, went home justified before God. For everyone who exalts himself will be humbled, and he who humbles himself will be exalted."*

✞ ✞ ✞

Tuesday, August 9, 1994
10:00 a.m.

Exercising my mind as I read and learn about hunting and fishing along the Chesapeake Bay during the turn of the 20th century. It is refreshing to be propelled to another time and place. Learning becomes an addiction. Once hooked, knowledge is a rush that no Twelve Step Group can cure.

3:00 p.m.

Exercising the body. A good balance in one's life is very important. Keeping the body fit by jogging and weight training helps to facilitate another addiction - learning. A healthy body helps to facilitate a healthy mind.

4:00 p.m.

Mail. Arlene has replied to my letter where I inquired about her joking marriage proposal. She mentioned nothing about the subject of matrimony. That is a depressing omission even though the letter was sweet.

10:00 p.m.

The Quest for Butch and Sundance, a Public Broadcasting Station special. What really happened to them and their remains? We all have seen Redford and Newman's movie and how they ran out of the building in Peru to meet their doom by a hail storm of bullets from the Peruvian Army. In reality, these bandits did not have the guts to stand up and face their punishment. One of the bandits shot his partner in the face and then turned the gun on himself. A murder-suicide. Not a very glamorous, romantic, or heroic ending. It is not surprising that Hollywood changed it.

In my own case, people who find out are amazed that I turned myself in—twice—knowing full well the amount of time I would face if convicted. Though honestly I did not believe I would be convicted. Surprise! Surprise! Regardless, there comes a time when each of us has to stand up and take responsibility. I finally did what was right and since that day my heart and mind continue to have a brighter, more hopeful outlook. There have been and will continue to be many hard days, but I fight always for victory over the deceiving voice that says I was a fool. I was a fool to turn away from the teachings of my parents and of God. Standing up for what *is* right and for God, I feel His Spirit in my heart and this gives me comfort and strength to take each step in the right direction.

Scientists still have not found Butch or Sundance's remains, so I guess you could say their bodies still elude capture by man, but their souls cannot elude God.

Will they stand up then?

John 14:15-17. *"If you love me, you will obey what I command. And I will ask the Father, and He will give you another Counselor to be with you forever— the Spirit of truth. The world cannot accept Him, because it neither sees Him nor knows Him. But you know Him, for He lives with you and will be in you."*

✟   ✟   ✟

Wednesday, August 10, 1994
7:00 a.m.

Breakfast conversation: The California Department of Corrections' Olympics. This is where Correctional Peace Officers use vacation time to compete in various sporting activities against officers from other prisons to enhance their *esprit de corps*. This year, the sport that was by far the most popular was boxing. The unfortunate thing was it did not occur in a ring. During a baseball game between Mule Creek's and Folsom's prison officers, a brawl broke out, and apparently continued until officers from another prison arrived to break it up. So much for role models! I wonder if their title as 'Peace Officers' should be re-examined?

This violent incident, which is not an uncommon occurrence between staff members in the prison's parking lot, should be an eye-opener. If these men will fight each other, men who are employed to protect society against violence, it is not a wonder that some of them treat inmates with cruelty.

We all need God's love and compassion. Remember, baseball is only a game, and we are all God's children.

Romans 3:22-24. *The righteousness from God comes through faith in Jesus Christ to all who believe. There is not a difference, for all have sinned and fall short of the glory of God, and are justified freely by His grace through the redemption that came by Christ Jesus.*

✟ ✟ ✟

Thursday, August 11, 1994
A Full Day of Discussions

If I had my choice, I would be perfectly content to walk the track, sit on my bunk, and be introspective…alone. Quietude is what I call it. There may be shouts of chaos all around me, but I am peaceful, having found an inner contentment in contemplation of Christ and in seeking ways for self-improvement.

Rarely am I able to obtain these moments.

As I walked around the track today I looked up and there was God, pictured as a soft, opal sky, highlighted with wispy, snow-white clouds that were stroked by a Master's brush. Normally I would have filled my lungs deeply and smiled, knowing His Spirit is within me and all around me. This was not to be one of those days, let alone an uninterrupted moment. Everyone I passed, or tried to pass, Brian, Leonard, Alamean, Howard, Coleman, *Chief,* and *Swede* brought forth frustrating discussions of political intrigue in Washington D.C., that being President Clinton's crime bill, the California governor's race, and how each of these inmates would run the prisons if they were given the opportunity.

In return for my patient listening I received a splitting headache from all the negativity. Too many words of doom and gloom. The conclusion of each conversation was that those in charge do not know what they are doing. This is a misguided statement because *they* do know what they are doing. We (inmates and many free people) neither like it nor do we understand it. It does seem that public appointed officials are only out for themselves and are not willing to make the hard, unpopular, belt-tightening decisions required for society's long-term good, and for God's sake.

No man is an island because we each affect the other by our actions. It, as in crime, education, the infrastructure, health care, and every issue can be fixed. We only need to stop and seek a role model that will never lead us astray for the benefit of the few without thinking of the many. He is easy to find. Just look up, look up, and take that needed deep breath.

I can feel Him.

I can see Him.

Can You?

I may be viewed as a wretched criminal, but I still see hope reflected in the eyes of those who are forced to shoulder all the woes of society whether they are free or incarcerated. If we can have faith so can everyone.

Some days are for seeking that which is within, and other days are for speaking one's mind, but only if we are using Jesus' words.

I still have a headache but my heart is at peace.

Psalm 73:16-17a. *When I tried to understand all this, it was oppressive to me till I entered the sanctuary of God.*

✝ ✝ ✝

Friday, August 12, 1994
10:00 a.m.

I observed Alex, with shoulders slumped, walking back from Receiving and Release. He was called to transpack his property because he is being transferred to Old Folsom. He told me last night that he is scared to go. I suppose he has a right to be. The unknown is always frightening, but added to that, Alex is in his 70's, and he is not physically or mentally strong.

These characteristics make Alex a prime target for predators. However, I am hoping, for Alex's sake, that staff at Old Folsom have removed the majority of the worst abusers of the weak and have sent them to reside in New Folsom (higher security prison). Regardless of what the situation may be, Alex will have the opportunity to experience a real *follow the inmate code* prison.

Respect!
Respect!
Respect!
Translation: Courtesy

I wish safety for Alex and I will be praying on his behalf because Alex has all the glibly plausible excuses for not acknowledging God. However, as Alex now prepares to enter a temple of doom, he may re-think his less than logical reasoning.

2:00 p.m.

Lifting weights with Coleman and feeling fine. Then, as a tornado descending on Kansas to destroy our day, Bill, double lifer, storms over and said that the weights and bench we were using were his, and he demanded that Coleman and I leave.

Excuse me?!

For one thing, Coleman and I gathered the weights and blankets (for padding the metal bench) from around the weight pile. Secondly, there was no indication, such as a water bottle or inmate identification card on the bench to indicate that anyone was saving the area.

Coleman and I tried to explain this to Bill, Mr. Puffed-Up, Mr. I-May-Be-Short-But-I-Got-More-Muscles-Than-Brains, but he began shaking and his eyes glossed over. Suddenly, Bill grabbed the bench press bar and rushed me with it. I was more surprised than afraid because if I had chosen to I could have downed him or caved in his face with a single, unpreventable blow. It is not that I am rough and tough but both Bill's hands were holding the bar so he could not protect himself. Instead, I simply backed away and said, "You've got no class."

I was angry. Not that Bill took the weights but because his actions endangered our lives. When a fight breaks out on the weight pile the tower officer shoots first and then asks questions later. There are too many potential weapons lying about. Even if we had not gotten shot, my 7½ years of 'clean time' would have been ruined with a write-up for fighting. And for what? A few piddly pieces of iron that Bill, after all that posturing, did not use? I have goals and the main one is to be free again. To prove I am worthy of that freedom I can and will show that I will never use violence to solve a problem. Nothing in prison is worth jeopardizing that goal; not pride, not what other inmates may think of me, and especially not for ignorant, immature displays of macho possessiveness.

The laughable thing is it took only about two minutes for Coleman and I to gather another bar, weights, and a bench that was unoccupied. All were readily available.

Always focus on the goal.

1 Corinthians 9:26-27. *Therefore I do not run like a man running aimlessly; I do not fight like a man beating the air. No, I beat my body and make it my slave so that after I have preached to others, I myself will not be disqualified for the prize.*

✞ ✞ ✞

Saturday, August 13, 1994
10:00 a.m.

Coleman stopped by my bunk to say that Bill tried to apologize to him for his inappropriate behavior on the weight pile yesterday. Coleman would not accept it because Bill's friends have been going around telling others that Bill faced down Coleman and Watson. Some might say we lost face. Others, those of a higher order, know that our restraint will allow us to go home one day, to live a wonderful life, and Bill, if he continues with his violent tendencies, will remain behind and can have all the weights he wants.

3:00 p.m.

Bible study and fellowship. We discussed societies' versus inmates' views and perceptions on the heinousness of different crimes. Inmates view rape and child molesting as the worst kind of crime because they are perpetrated against victims who are weaker than the assailant. At the other end of the bar, a person who kills out of passion, for greed, or in the defense of themselves can be understood, and their acts, usually a one-time event, can be analyzed by the offender to prevent the situation from ever occurring again. Unfortunately, rapists and molesters have a mental illness that is not being treated, if it even can be. Society views it in the reverse and enacts laws to punish offenders to fit their beliefs. As a fellowship group, we would like to see each category of crime and the circumstances surrounding it viewed individually, and not lumped together for sentencing purposes. Judges need the discretion to impose a sentence that best fits the offender, the offense, and the effect the crime has had on the community.

After the mandated punishment for the offenses, I believe it comes down to, which type of person would you want living next door to you? Probably, no type of ex-offender and that is understandable, but the fact is, the majority of all offenders will eventually be released. It then becomes an issue of trust. Would you trust a person with an untreated mental disorder or one who has had a one-time abhorrent behavior?

Our Bible fellowship group's discussion was passionate with many sides expressing their opinions, but when it was concluded, we prayed and praised God that we could disagree on minor points, but agree in Christian brotherhood and fellowship.

10:00 p.m.

I wondered all day if Bill would come by to ask my forgiveness. If he did, would I accept his apology? My prideful self wants to spit in his face, but if he is mature enough to humble himself and ask, it is my responsibility to shake his hand and accept.

I want to please God and be an example of His teachings for Bill.

1 Corinthians 12:12-13. *The body is a unit, though it is made up of many parts; and though all its parts are many, they form one body. So it is with Christ. For we were all baptized by one Spirit into one body...whether Jews or Greeks, slave or free...and we were all given the one Spirit to drink.*

✝ ✝ ✝

Sunday, August 14, 1994
11:30 a.m.

Fight! Fight! Fight! Three Code 3's so far this morning and it is not yet lunch time. There must be something in the air and not just summer pollen. The Lord said, "We must master our emotions," but in prison it seems that to lose face is to lose one's self-image. I would think getting into a fight has the greater potential for losing one's self image by have one's face rearranged.

3:00 p.m.

Who would have thought? Nick Taylor has offered to represent my creative writing after he is released. Hmm... Interesting offer. He may look like a scruffy hermit in here, but on the street I can picture him as a suit-wearing shark of a businessman.

In my pursuit for an agent I have sent out more than 150 query letters and have not received a single positive response. Has God brought one to my bunk? Nick said he would meet with my father to draft the needed contracts as soon as he is released. This is an exciting possibility, however, I have learned to thank God for what appears to be a blessing, but to temper my enthusiasm until it comes to fruition.

Job 36:1. *If they obey and serve Him, they will spend the rest of their days in prosperity and their years in contentment.*

✟ ✟ ✟

Monday, August 15, 1994
8:00 p.m.

It is a hard addiction to break but I am doing it. The addiction I speak of is television. I check *Swede's* T.V. Guide and unless there is something worthwhile on I am not going to turn on my set. If we counted the hours we sat numbing our minds in front of the television we would be shocked at the quantity. Instead, I will listen to the radio, read, work on legal and creative writing, and study my Bible. At the moment, however, I am re-reading a letter my father sent me where he included photographs of his cowboy party. He is looking dapper in a black hat, shirt, pants, and silver string tie. Dapper yes, though John Wayne he is not. However, I can picture him riding the range on a vast cattle ranch and singing, "Oh Montana, your wide open plains call my name." Ha ha.

8:15 p.m.

Mr. Hancock walked by my bunk wearing a stretched, muscle tank top with more holes in it than Saddam Hussein's palace. Hancock is a squat, muscle-bound man whose grimace could freeze a flame, but whose smile and handshake brings friendship and security. These two extremes come from years as a lifer battling wannabe tough guys while clinging to a spark of love for friends and family.

I pulled Hancock aside and said, "Hey. What's the deal?" I then scrounged in my foot locker for a new tank top and gave it to him. "Here. Make yourself presentable." Hancock looked like a deer in a car's headlights. His eyes were wide with surprise, but the upturn at the corner of his mouth showed delight, pleasure, and shock because I wanted nothing in return. I told him, "It's called a gift." Yes, a rare thing I prison, but if we searched mythology we could find hints of a kind act or two behind bars.

I saw an opportunity to share and I received as much pleasure in giving as Hancock did in receiving. I only wish I had more to give more often.

Luke 6:38. *"Give and it will be given to you. A good measure, pressed down, shaken together and running over, will be poured into your lap. For with the measure you use, it will be measured to you."*

✢ ✢ ✢

Tuesday, August 16, 1994
9:00 a.m.

Adoption! It's not all it's cracked up to be. Yes, I am the clerk, but that does not mean I know everything about paroles, work time credits, consecutive sentencing, or the trust office. The perception is that since I wear glasses and I sit behind a typewriter that I am all knowing, all seeing, and at the least the master of all that surrounds me...I only wish.

With this erroneous perception in mind, there are always one or two orphaned men who cling to my cerebral strings wanting advice about the most obscure things. It's a pain in the you-know-what, but then I think about God and laugh to myself. I am confident that I am a pain in His you-know-what, too. So I smile, adopting another confused soul, and do my best to direct him to what he seeks.

11:00 a.m.

Officer Mann summoned me to the podium and then sent me to the infirmary to pick up my new glasses. A needed gift from my parents and not paid for by the taxpayers. It was a time to celebrate because I would now be able to see clearly again.

Stupid, forgetful me. I walked to the plaza gate wearing my personal Levi's jeans. Inmates are not allowed to wear Levi's off the yard. Why? What is the difference? I do not know. The state jeans look identical to Levi's. The only difference is one is zippered and the other is button-fly.

I had to turn around and go back to the gym, change pants, and then the plaza officer would escort me to the infirmary to pick up my new spectacles. I am beginning to be fearful of the degree to which my vision has deteriorated since my incarceration. When I first came to prison I could read without glasses, needing them only to see long distances. Now, I have to wear them to read and write. To me, this is becoming a significant disability. At this point I will not be able to surf because I would not be able to see the approaching waves.

There is laser surgery but I am not sure it has advanced enough for me to be confident in its success. I guess I will cross that swell when I have the opportunity to paddle over it.

8:30 p.m.

Alarms! Code 3. Building 8.

9:35 p.m.

Code 4. Resume normal program. That was an extremely long code. Thankfully I was seated on my bunk and not stuck sitting on the concrete floor or in the toilet area.

Word has it there was a vicious brawl over the use of the telephones. I wonder if it was worth it. A little courtesy would have resolved the problem. Instead, no one in building 8 will be using the telephones, and they will not be allowed out of their cells. It's lockdown time for them…but hopefully only for the night.

Matthew 8:16b-17. *And He drove out the spirits with a word and healed all the sick. This was to fulfill what was spoken through the prophet Isaiah: "He took up our infirmities and carried our diseases."*

✝ ✝ ✝

Wednesday, August 17, 1994
4:00 p.m.

Mail.

Beck and Mary Shelton
1944 - 1994

Love is of God
In whom we live
And more
And have our being
Together.

Fifty years of marriage. That deserves a double Wow! Wow! In this day and age of throw-away relationships, this feat is incredible and praiseworthy. Beck and Mary have been a part of my outside Christian support group with letters of encouragement. Even though I am in California and they live in Washington State, they make me feel close with their friendship, love and prayers on my behalf.

I thank God for Beck and Mary's example of God as the center in a relationship, especially in a marriage commitment, and how with Him it can work and thrive. There are no promises of Yellow Brick Roads or Happily Ever After, but the beauty of God's pairing can be more than enough to overcome all obstacles.

Happy Anniversary Beck and Mary. Thank you for sharing God's love with me.

5:30 p.m.

Tonight's dinner conversation revolved around the state senate's passing of a bill to remove all weight lifting equipment from California's prisons and jails. I do hope this is only election hype and poking at the perceived bear that is caged behind correctional walls. However, if such a bill is signed by the governor, when testosterone-filled men begin to overload with stress, they will no longer have the weight pile to release it in a positive and safe fashion. It is likely these inmates, who see no other alternative such as prayer or meditation, will turn on each other and on staff. If I were not in the middle of this scary place, it would be humorous to watch as our legislative leaders continue to press the gas pedal toward the floor as they steer a course rapidly toward the inevitable brick wall.

Unwittingly, most of the public have rings in their noses and have forgotten the prime directive: Question Authority.

Proverbs 5:18-19. *May your fountain be blessed, and may you rejoice in the wife of your youth. A loving doe, a graceful deer—may her breasts satisfy you always, may you ever be captivated by her love.*

✞ ✞ ✞

Thursday, August 18, 1994
5:30 p.m.

Officer Palomino, a chunky, Hispanic officer with a needle-thin mustache, is easily fed up with many of the institution's senseless regulations for inmates and staff, and at times shows a flippant side. Defiance? Tonight, as he stood in a corner of the chow hall monitoring feeding, Palomino donned a paper serving hat that he pushed down to his bushy eyebrows. His starched collar was turned up Elvis style, and he had his bright-green and reflective, bug-eye glasses on. With his uniform sleeves rolled up to show U.S. Navy tattoos, he crossed his hairy arms to take a superior-than-thou stance. His face was a faux grimace.

Slowly, heads turned in his direction—silence and then ruckus laughter from all the inmates broke out. No one was laughing at Officer Palomino. We were all laughing with him. The oh-so-proper third-watch sergeant and lieutenant were not as pleased, but who cared? No one cared. Those that did have swallowed too much Department of Corrections' propaganda...not an ounce of humor left in their bones.

The evening meal was a huge success, the entertainment portion that is, because we all needed the laugh. Thank you, Officer Palomino, for showing us your human side to remind all that we are in this soup together.

Proverbs 15:13a, 15b. *A happy heart makes the face cheerful. The cheerful heart has continual feast.*

✝ ✝ ✝

Friday, August 19, 1994
9:00 a.m.

Wolf is meeting with his attorney to prepare, once again, for facing the parole board. He has appeared several times before but has been denied each time for a variety of reasons: he failed to report to work on two occasions, needs vocational upgrade, his letter of apology to the family was not remorseful enough, and last year, the board members harped on how *Wolf's* children must feel about their father being in prison. In addition they recommended that *Wolf* cut off his beard and get a haircut. What in the name of all things does the length of one's hair have to do with suitability for parole and the public's safety? Absolutely nothing! Say it again, "Absolutely nothing." *Wolf* is always clean and well groomed, only groomed long.

Could it be that Governor Wilson's promise not to allow lifers out on his watch has the parole board searching for something, anything, no matter how minute to deny a parole date? I obviously have no special, mind-reading powers, but really, whose safety is the parole board looking out for? Is it the taxpayers' personal safety or Governor Wilson's political safety?

Wolf continues to study to increase his knowledge in the field of automobile repair which was his vocation prior to incarceration. In addition, *Wolf* is attempting to learn more about God and Christ through correspondence

Bible courses. I know that both of these subjects give him comfort and strength. I pray that one day *Wolf* will receive a parole date.

10:15 p.m.

Big Sigh – Today was Mickie's big day. She spoke her vows to a Christian carpenter named Steve. I want to be filled with joy for Mickie, but my feelings of loss, of being left behind are too overwhelming at this moment. In time, in hindsight, and with God's grace I will be grateful that Mickie has found a wonderful man to appreciate and care for her. In the meantime, I will focus on being the best, supportive friend that I can be. Mickie certainly deserves that from me. Prison sucks.

2 Peter 3:18. *But grow in the grace and knowledge of your Lord and Savior Jesus Christ. To Him glory both now and forever. Amen!*

✟ ✟ ✟

Saturday, August 20, 1994
1:00 p.m.

Volleyball. I love it but it may be time to leave it. The players' immaturity and useless bickering with, "You don't know how to play the game," and "You don't know what the c$%"* you're talking about," is wearing thin on my nerves and ruining the joy of the game. I believe I can find something better to occupy my time where the participants treat each other with more courtesy.

What may be bothering me is several of these mouthy men claim to be Christians. The majority of the time they act it, but competition brings out the worst in them. Their actions are not a good example for those who are watching Christ's followers.

I do my best to always remember that God and His Son Jesus are too often judged by the behavior of their followers.

2 Timothy 2:24-25. *And the Lord's servant must not quarrel; instead, he must be kind to everyone, able to teach, not resentful. Those who oppose him must gently instruct, in the hope that God will grant them repentance leading them to knowledge of the truth, and that they will come to their senses and escape from the trap of the devil, who has taken them captive to do his will.*

✝ ✝ ✝

Sunday, August 2, 1994
6:00 p.m.

Sergeant…I mean Lieutenant Jasper is working Facility B tonight and stopped by the gym on his rounds. I spoke with him for a few minutes, and the first subject he inquired into was how my family was doing. He had met my mother in the visiting room one evening.

Among the cold darkness of prison a warm light shines within this recently promoted man. Even though we only spoke for a few moments, Lieutenant Jasper was able to show his concern for me, an inmate. Yes, he is staff, and supposed to be the enemy, but he is a good man who is greatly respected and who I have been blessed to cross paths with.

11:45 p.m.

Bummer. I do not know why but I woke from a wonderful dream. I was a secret agent working *closely* with a beautiful, dark-haired, scantily-clad Asian lady in Indo-China. We were swimming in the warm, ocean waters when a patrol boat of an enemy government captured us. We were convincing in our story of simple tourists frolicking in the water while on vacation for them to let us go. We quickly made our escape across a stormy sea in a sleek, high-powered boat.

As the wind slapped my face I could smell the salt air and feel the jarring bumps as the boat raced across the swells to the safety of a secluded island. My knees went weak as my companion ran her slender fingers and then her arms around my waist to draw me close. The heat of her body and breath as she gently kissed my neck intoxicated me.

For a dreamscape moment I was alive. My senses tingled with excitement and freedom. Now I am awake. My reality is a stinking room of snoring men.

1 Corinthians 15:22-23. *For as in Adam all die, so in Christ all will be made alive. But each in his own turn: Christ, the first fruits; then when He comes, those who belong to Him.*

✝ ✝ ✝

Monday, August 22, 1994
10:00 a.m.

Attitude of tact is everything. Jeez, do these people know anything about tact? Gym staff requested that I go to the Program Office to pick up the menu. While I was waiting for a copy to be made, Donna, bi-polar Donna, came out of her office and asked, no, dare I say, demanded to know if I had permission from the sergeant to be there. "No," I replied. "I was instructed by the gym officer." Donna proceed to tell me in that special tone that some women use when asserting themselves, that if I came into the office again without the sergeant's approval I would receive a disciplinary write-up. I smiled, seething inside, thanked her for informing me, turned and departed.

Brrr. The wind is blowing cold today.

10:30 a.m.

Back in the gym I explained to Officer Mann what had happened to me and he stated that he, too, had been chewed out this morning by the sergeant for signing in and out at the same time. Technically, staff is not supposed to do that but it has been allowed for many years. Officer Mann was annoyed at being treated like a child instead of receiving a polite instruction as to the change in the informal policy.

"Welcome to the club," I said. We both shook our heads to ponder the $10,000 question: How did we get here?

Until staff learns to approach inmates and co-workers with a measure of courtesy they will neither reduce the level of hate by inmates nor increase morale among peers.

Who trains these people? Who should train me?

4:00 p.m.

Legal mail. With each word I read, the judicial blade drew more blood. CASE DISMISSED. The magistrate judge of the federal district court agreed with the attorney general that too much time had elapsed since my state court filings. Basically, I am procedurally barred and no ruling on the merits of the case was given. The only recourse is to file objections and pray that the judge over the magistrate will reverse the decision.

Today has not gone well. Come to think of it, these last few days have been difficult to keep a smile on my face. I think I will go to bed early. Maybe I will meet up with that Asian spy.

Romans 13:3-4. *For rulers hold no terror for those who do right, but for those who do wrong. Do you want to be free from fear of the one in authority? They do what is right and he will commend you. For he is God's servant to do you good. But if you do wrong, be afraid, for he does not bear the sword for nothing. He is God's servant and agent to bring punishment on the wrong doer.*

✝ ✝ ✝

Tuesday, August 23, 1994
5:10 a.m.

There were no dream escapes last night to whisk me off to exciting and blood-pumping adventures. My long, long, night was filled with reality: thick walls, razor-wire topped fences, men with guns, and hatred. This is not going to be the life that God had planned for me. What a stupid, stupid man I am. Sigh.

8:30 a.m.

Peculiarities, eccentricities, oddities, and, "I just do not like him," attitudes. Prejudice? Fear? Hatred? Maybe, but in my eyes these are excuses equaling lost opportunities. I may not like a person's crime, the way he dresses, or his expression in body painting, but each man has a story. And from each story, a lesson can be learned and a value gained.

I will use Nick Taylor as an example. He is a scruffy hermit who is not much to look at, but he has a brain to be envied. Maybe it is because he and I think along the same lines when it comes to politics. Ha ha. Mr. Taylor paroled this morning, and as I have stated, he has offered to show my scripts to several people he knows in the film industry...for a percentage of any sale of course. Hey, business is business.

If this comes to pass, then my God-taught openness will have paid off and a miracle worked. All I need is a break. That is if my writing is good enough. Awaiting judgment raises a stomach-churning fear of inadequacy. I have no excuses because I chose this field of endeavor out of egotistical belief that I have compelling stories that others would want to watch unfold on the silver screen. It is time to put up the product and shut up while value is added or taken away.

I thank you, Lord, for bringing Mr. Taylor and I together.

10:00 a.m.

Cadets on patrol. Fear-filled eyes walk in tight packs of brown. Men and women, fresh-faced, and starched from preparation in the academy, walk with correctional stiffness while being escorted by a prison officer. Jumpy? That they are! Their heads have been filled with terror propaganda of the evil that lurks in the hearts and minds of every inmate. These cadets remind me of a virgin I once knew. She was nervous, apprehensive, but wanting, yearning for the experience; waiting for the pain, and the alarm that would come.

That is what the cadets do.

That is what the inmates do.

Wait and wait some more.

Isaiah 54:14. *In righteousness you will be established: Tyranny will be far from you; you will have nothing to fear. Terror will be far removed; it will not come near you.*

✟ ✟ ✟

Wednesday, August 24, 1994
9:30 a.m.

If ignorance is bliss, then is insanity heaven? Fortunately or unfortunately I will never know, but the youngster, pimple-faced and pony tailed, playing tennis on the volleyball court could give a dissertation on being out of touch. He has no ball, no racket, and no opponent, but it does appear from his antics that he is winning and getting a good workout.

The first question that causes my head to pound is why is this young man in a prison? The second question is does he know he is in prison? If not, I am not going to wake him to the nightmare. Insanity is another form of escape.

1:30 p.m.

Lurch, our Caribbean pirate, went to his parole board hearing this morning and was denied a parole date. He has served 33 years on a 7-year to life sentence. I believe it is time for him to go home.

"Help, Mr. Wizard," is Yertle the Turtle's cry.

The only person who spoke against *Lurch* at the hearing was the mother of the deceased. It seems logical except she was involved in the original criminal conspiracy that led to her son's death. At the trial she received immunity to testify against Lurch. There seems to be something wrong with that. This woman was as guilty, as responsible for her son's death as *Lurch,* but she has remained free all these years, and is preventing *Lurch* from regaining his freedom. Am I the only one that has a bad taste in his mouth? Am I missing some point?

4:00 p.m.

And the Two
Shall become one....
The honor of your presence is requested
At the marriage of
Hanna------
To
Paul------
On
Saturday, the twenty-fourth of September
Nineteen hundred and ninety-four
At one o'clock in the afternoon
Thibold Community Center
Vista, California

Mail. Another announcement. This time it includes an invitation. My cousin Hanna is getting married. Mickie was married last Friday and Beck and Mary recently celebrated their 50th wedding anniversary. Lives go on except mine. If life is a play, I have not only been placed in the audience, but in the nose bleed section, way, way, way back from the action. It is very difficult to continually watch the happiness of others and be supportive. I know Jesus wants me to be; therefore, I am trying my best. I do appreciate the announcements because it shows me I am thought of. Another double-edged sword slices my heart. It cuts out the loneliness but stings with the pain of separation.

It is all about missing family, or those who are like family, and admitting that my suffering is self-inflicted does not help. This is especially so because it swings wide the door that is always ajar in my heart for the pain, the suffering, and the permanent separation I caused when I took a life.

The pain of separation that the family of the person whom I killed will always trump my own, as it should be, and so it is, when I sink lower and lower, that they come to mind, and I endure simply to be a witness to say, "Do not do as I did, but only as Jesus teaches." Jesus saves in more ways than one.

1 Corinthians 13:2. *If I have the gift of prophesy and can fathom all mysteries and all knowledge, and if I have faith that can move mountains, but have not love, I am nothing.*

✝ ✝ ✝

Thursday, August 25, 1994
7:00 a.m.

"Come here! Demands *Two-Guns*. Six feet six inches of black muscle stacked on a 60-year old frame whose voice stole the blues from B.B. King. Every morning *Two-Guns* sits at the first table inside the gym with his catcher's mitt hand out, "Come here! Give me something, anything. Let's talk." If you are not going to eat something from your lunch sack you give it to *Two-Guns*.

If you do not know him well you would feel pressured, but all you have to say is "Good morning," and walk on by. Does he eat the week's supply of food he receives each morning? Heck no. *Two-Guns* passes the food out to inmates who did not go to breakfast. Remember, if you do not make the

trek to the chow hall for breakfast, you do not receive a lunch. "Come here!"
echoes within the concrete cube. I love his method and generosity.

9:00 p.m.

That is something I do not see every day. Usually an inmate is
handcuffed and escorted out of the gym. Tonight, as half a dozen inmates
grudgingly move in, one of them was in handcuffs and escorted in and, then
un-cuffed. Staff did not want to do the paperwork to lock him up, so with the
belief that if they physically plop the uncooperative inmate in the gym, he will
admit defeat, and be resigned to the situation. So far so good.

Whiskered Darryl was one of the unlucky souls to move in tonight. He
is 'Mr. Rogers' with a fuzzy, not quite full beard even though he is 72. He is
slender, quiet, and contemplative with a smile and a warm handshake. What
the devil could a grandfatherly man like that have done to deserve prison?
Regardless, it will be nice to have another Christian in the gym to increase the
Spirit's light. Each man brings his own candle to – "Let it shine. Let it shine."

Romans 6:23. *For the wages of sin is death, but the gift of God is eternal life
in Christ Jesus our Lord.*

✝ ✝ ✝

Friday, August 26, 1994
11:00 a.m.

Racial equality! Shout it from the bunk tops. A black inmate who
moved into the gym yesterday is upset because he wants a wall bunk, but
unlike everyone else, he does not want to wait his turn. Instead, he starts racial
tensions because the whites have two more wall bunks than the blacks. He
wants these bunks changed, removing the whites from these bunks, and
replacing them with blacks. Well, my inciting friend, there are almost 20 more
whites living in the gym than blacks.

"Oh, that is unfair, too," he cries.

The problem originates with the black inmates themselves. Not
enough of them who are housed in Facility B have remained disciplinary free
to reduce their points to a level II classification, and thereby making them
eligible for gym housing. Some of the write-ups are on purpose so they do not
have to move into the gym. Overall, the prison itself has an equal number of

each race of inmates. And because the prison makes its money by the number of inmates it houses, it will fill the empty bunks in the gym with any inmate, regardless of race, when he becomes eligible.

The inciting black inmate says he is going to file an appeal (CDC-602) on this issue because more whites, a total of four get to use their own televisions by living next to the wall which has electrical outlets. I pointed out that staff view televisions as a privilege. They will also agree that this is an issue of racial tension that could lead to violence. To solve it they will take away all the televisions. I asked him to think carefully about those ramifications. He is going home in less than 39 days and the televisions would be taken away from mostly lifers.

After some contemplation he realized the seniority system that has been in place for over a year will suffice, even if it does mean he will not be assigned to a wall bunk in the time he has left. A very wise choice, but still, his actions have stirred up a hornets' nest.

Think. Think of the forest, not only your own tree before you grind your ax.

2 Timothy 3:2-5. *People will be lovers of themselves, lovers of money, boastful, proud, abusive, disobedient to their parents, ungrateful, unholy, without love, unforgiving, slanderous, without self-control, brutal, not lovers of good, treacherous, rash, conceited, lovers of pleasure rather than lovers of God—having a form of godliness but denying its power. Have nothing to do with them.*

☩　☩　☩

Saturday, August 27, 1994
7:00 p.m.

Teri with an 'i' is at it again. He/she/it is dancing and singing in the chapel in front of the 4'x 4' yard window. Inmates are stopping on the track, laughing and jeering. I have to say that I feel sorry for Teri because she/he/it obviously is insecure and constantly in need of attention, even if it is of the negative kind.

I would have thought that it took courage for Teri to make the public statement that 'he' is a 'she.' If this were the case, be at peace, and refrain from being a spectacle, or in the eyes of his/her/its audience—a clown.

9:00 p.m.

Slowly *it* has been enveloping me all day. Depression. Usually I revel in it, make it my friend, and then snuggle under my covers to sleep it away. However, today's emotional pudding has more despair swirling through it, and I have been experiencing those 'missing out' blues. I try to pick myself up by reminding myself that I am a much better person now. Then to put the final painful touch on my downward emotions, Angela's lost caress creeps across my goose-pimpled skin. I want to scream; "When? When will I be free again? How will I ever get back on the wonderful Merry-Go-Round of life?"

Tonight is going to be a long, lonely night.

Psalm 145:18-19. *The Lord is near to all who call on Him, to all who call on Him in truth, He fulfills the desires of those who fear Him; He hears their cry and saves them.*

✟ ✟ ✟

Sunday, August 28, 1994
4:30 a.m.

Jesus, help me. I shiver awake from a terrible nightmare wherein I am fighting an intangible creature called self-doubt. Doubt about my writing, about surviving prison with an ounce of sanity, about everything. I remind myself as I stare at the bunk above me that I am a champion and have succeeded in everything I have ever attempted: sports, education and business. I will reign victorious over this incarceration. I have to. The alternative is oblivion in this un-world of contradictions and irrelevancies.

10:00 a.m.

I can only hold my breath and other things for so long. I have to use the commode but to do so I have to overcome the stench and crowd. Eight men seated in a row facing the butts of other men 2 ½ feet away as they, too, relieve themselves at the urinals. There is no peace even for a bodily function.

2:00 p.m.

King Arthur and Sir Lancelot, a myth? I think not. At least they exist in my heart. I am nurturing a comeback with tinglings of greatness that signal I am honorable and worthy. I sought neither Merlin for advice, nor a magic potion, but Christ in prayer for peace and renewal. I must be quite a burden for the Lord as I am always calling His Name, and rarely am I able to give anything in return except praise, appreciation, and love.

I am comforted to know that these simple acts of praise, appreciation, and love are all that God wants from us, His children. Thanks again, Lord. Please, no more nightmares.

Luke 10:17-19. *The seventy-two returned with joy and said, "Lord, even the demons submit to us in your name." He replied, "I saw Satan fall like lightning from heaven. I have given you authority to trample on snakes and scorpions and to overcome all the power of the enemy; nothing will harm you."*

✝ ✝ ✝

Monday, August 29, 1994
8:00 p.m.

I am in bed choking on chocolate pudding again. I almost made it out of depression valley, but I slipped, and kept on sliding. My flesh is so susceptible to unseen emotions that I cannot define, to mood swings for unknown reasons. I want to go far, far away, and dream of a better day. If I had a mirror, I know I would look so damn pitiful and this only makes the depression worse. My poor little light flickers. I dare not think of the good life that I lost, that I forfeited in the free world. If I do, the grasping abyss will pull me down beyond the Spirit's rescuing love.

There is no good in this night.

John 1:12-13. *Yet to all who received Him, to those who believed in His name, He gave the right to become children of God—children born not of natural descent, nor of human decision or a husband's will, but born of God.*

✝ ✝ ✝

Tuesday, August 30, 1994
9:30 a.m.

Is there life, intelligent life, out there? In the cosmos? No, in politics.
We have gotten to the point where laws supersede intended goals. As I was
exercising on the weight pile, I watched an officer step outside of his building
to comply with the new No Smoking law. This was good, but also bad because
it left the building floor partially unguarded. If someone, an inmate or an
officer, were to be assaulted, the question of where the other officer was would
have to be answered. Let us educate not legislate.

12:00 Noon

News Flash! The well-thought-through Three Strikes & You're Out
law is claiming another hardened criminal. A man, on a dare, stole several
slices of pizza from children at a beach party in Southern California. He is
now facing a life sentence in prison. The judge has no other choice. Yes, good
point. This was the man's third crime, but does the punishment to the offender
and cost to the taxpayer fit the crime?

6:00 p.m.

And me? Emotionally I am on the mend, stitch by frayed stitch. I
looked around this bunk-crammed, have-to-save-yourself gym, shook my head,
and then had a good sob into my plastic pillow. It was good letting go, but I
still need a hug, but as God is in me, He is helping me to do better. However,
if anyone is moved by God to contact the governor for me, please let him know
that I am ready to go home, because I truly, truly have learned my lesson and
have been punished enough.

Proverbs 9:9-10. *Instruct a wise man and he will be wiser still; teach a
righteous man and it will add to his learning. "The fear of the Lord is the
beginning of wisdom, and knowledge of the Holy One is understanding."*

✟ ✟ ✟

Wednesday, August 31, 1994
8:00 a.m.

Before the work call and yard unlock, *Chief, Dusty, Wolf,* and Ramirez are in the corner near their bunks. They are laughing, teasing, tickling, and goofing around. Basically they are having fun but I find their revelry more irritating than interesting. They are adults caught in a child's time warp called prison. They are not growing or maturing as they would if they were on the street. They are stagnating. Maybe I am too serious. Maybe it is harder for me to find a lot of humor in here. I know God wants me to be joyful and satisfied with my station in life but I am miserable. It is difficult to smile when one's insides are churning with burning bile that is created by sadness. I truly wish and pray that I, too, could find more things to laugh about, but the burden I carry for my criminal acts against others weighs far too heavy on my heart.

1:30 p.m.

The program administrator told Howard, who shared with me, that our showers will be closing for up to five days for repairs. For longer than anyone living in the gym can remember, the tiles have been falling off the walls and peeling up from the floor. The standing water under the loose tiles breeds mold and other undesirable microbes that stink. If these repairs do come to pass, I will be grateful. Though my question is: has staff figured out where the 160 inmates who live in the gym are going to shower during the down days? Or will we? That is to be seen.

4:00 p.m.

No mail. What is everyone doing out there? I know. They are trying to survive, too.

1 Corinthians 13:11-12. *When I was a child, I talked like a child; I thought like a child, I reasoned like a child. When I became a man, I put my childish ways behind me. Now we see but a poor reflection as in a mirror; then we shall see face to face. Now I know in part; then I shall know fully, even as I am fully known.*

✝ ✝ ✝

Thursday, September 1, 1994
5:00 a.m.

I was shattered awake as symbolisms of my life flashed before my eyes. While driving a custom-painted monster-engine Volkswagen bug along a forested mountain road I spotted a brown-eyed lady standing in the rain and hitchhiking. I picked her up and quickly realized from our conversation that she was feisty and full of youthful energy. I immediately became enamored. It was love at first sight for both of us. I saw in her eyes that she cared for me and trusted me to take control of our lives. Faster and faster I drove on the darkening and slick road that was becoming wetter with an increasing downpour. I knew I could not see. I could not safely negotiate the turns. Ignoring the danger I kept going, clutching the steering wheel, and driving with white knuckles. I sped faster and faster until I lost control and crashed hearing screams and tearing metal.

After the explosive crash, the world was eerily quiet. I blinked my eyes to clearly see what I had done. The young woman and I were still alive but her legs had been severed. I tried to console her while carrying her dismembered body away from the wreck, but her pain was unbearable. I looked around but there was no hope of finding help.

I had driven my love to a place of destruction. Worse still was the look of trust betrayed in those brown eyes that streamed with tears.

This may have only been a movie created by my mind, but the truth of it stabbed at my heart for the pain I caused those who trusted and loved me. Will I ever heal? Will they ever heal? Will the pain ever stop hurting? Where is that lovely brown-eyed lady now? Has she forgiven me? Can I forgive myself?

What a shitty way to start the day.

12:00 Noon

Rosa Parks, the courageous black woman who ignited the civil rights movement, was attacked in her home by a young black man who was trying to steal from her. How soon triumphs are forgotten. If not for Ms. Parks' success and the successes of other brave civil rights leaders, this young man would not have been handcuffed and read his rights. More likely he would have been beaten, shot, and hung, especially if he had attacked a white woman.

I weep for our youth and pray that something can be done to turn their negative attitudes and destructive ways around. How humiliating it must have been for Ms. Parks to accept the fact that she had been beaten by one for whom she had risked her own life for to ensure a brighter future.

4:00 p.m.

Mail. A letter from Weila. It is filled with encouragement and prayers for my safety and happiness. I realize that many free people, friends and relatives, past and present, think of me during their day, but the extra effort of a letter such as this one means so much to me. Words on a page may not be able to replace a hug, but they come close. Thank you Weila, and thank you God, for inspiring her to write.

6:45 p.m.

Officer Ryan (not the usual gym officer) searched and sealed my legal mail containing my objections to the Magistrate's ruling. Officer Ryan's snide comment to his partner was, "Such a waste of time." As I dropped the envelope into the mail box I knew he was referring to having to search and seal legal mail. At the same time I wondered, I hoped his words were not an ominous premonition.

My future now lies in the judge's hands...and God's of course...but that 'free will' thing messes up a lot of us.

2 Timothy 2:22-23. *Flee the evil desires of youth, and pursue righteousness, faith, love and peace, along with those who call on the Lord out of a pure heart. Don't have anything to do with foolish and stupid arguments, because you know they produce quarrels.*

✝ ✝ ✝

Friday, September 2, 1994
8:00 a.m.

Today is my day off so I chose to sleep through breakfast. What a pleasant change from yesterday's nightmare as today I awoke with a warm, comforted feeling. In my dream I was held and soothed by Mickie. We were riding speckled, brown and white horses, and had stopped to take in the expansive vista of a deep green valley surrounded by towering, snow–capped mountain peaks. I felt the chill, a slight shiver of the Sierra breeze and then the comfort of Mickie as she reached out to embrace me. It was an enduring love within our friendship that swam through my veins, recharging my empty, left-behind heart, and allowing my soul to be touched with her feelings of care.

It cannot be normal to seek sleep and pray for dreams to sustain myself. To live for illusions and to dread the wakefulness of morning is certainly a sign of an unhealthy life.

Yes! It is prison.

11:00 a.m.

"Don't shoot!" That crazy little Hispanic slipped through the first security gate between buildings 9 and 10 while the garbage truck was picking up the trash. He ran and ran and ran and then leapt onto the second fence and began pushing apart the concertina wire. Fortunately the electrification between the two perimeter fences was not turned on.

The yard staff, who were shouting to the tower officer not to shoot, pulled the little guy down, handcuffed him, and then trotted him off to the hole. That poor, befuddled, little man should be in a hospital, not a prison, because he does not understand what is happening to him. He only understands that he is caged and wants to be free.

Hmm…maybe he is not crazy after all.

3:00 p.m.

Only an hour into the Labor Day visiting and it is over, cancelled, terminated. A bullet was *allegedly* found near a sidewalk leading to the visiting room. This sidewalk is located outside the security area where no inmate has access to, but inside an area where visitors must pass through a metal detector to access. It is unlikely that the bullet, if it exists, came from a visitor, but more likely from a staff member returning from the shooting range. The prison administrators have determined this to be an emergency situation and have locked down the entire prison.

8:00 p.m.

A memorandum has been posted in the gym. To summarize: inmates will not use the telephones, will not shower, and there will be no visiting until further notice. Actually, this is not unexpected. Rarely, in my years here at the Creek, has a Labor Day weekend gone by that we were not locked down. A coincidence? A conspiracy? Well, half the staff need the overtime and the other half want to go on vacation. It is not difficult to figure out what is happening. I am only saying it the way it appears.

On all sides I am surrounded by angry inmates whose families were told to come back tomorrow to visit. With the inmates unable to use the telephones to call home to inform their family members not to travel to visit, in some cases, several hundred miles, because the visits have been cancelled for the entire weekend, great expense and time will be wasted for nothing.

Is it surprising that inmates view staff as the cold-hearted enemy?

10:00 p.m.

20/20, a news program? Tonight it was not impartial. A man, a pastor, in Topeka, Kansas is being vilified. He preaches that the gay lifestyle leads to death. He calls gay men sodomites. The gay coalition does not like it. The pastor also preaches that if a woman commits adultery once or a thousand times, and is not repentant, that she is a Jesabelian whore. Woman in the community do not like it. Sorry, but both commentaries are in the Bible. Is the pastor wrong for boldly preaching the Word as it is written?

Our country is bending over so far (no pun intended) to be accepting of everyone that we have become afraid to stand up and say, "No, that is wrong." Barbara Walters, the correspondent on this story, wants to know why the government cannot pass a law to prevent this pastor from speaking out and offending others. Well, Barbara, there is this pesky thing called the Constitution and the First Amendment. It is what allows you to do your job, but maybe that ought to be prevented, too.

We should follow Christ's example. He hates the sin but loves the sinner. If we claim to be a Christian, we should not persecute sinners, in this hot-button case, homosexuals and adulterers, but these acts should not be encouraged either. We should neither support legislation or behavior that would promote or allow these activities, or legislation that would criminalize it. These acts are moral determinations where faith and one's belief comes into play. Again, educate. Do not legislate.

It is disturbing to me that man cannot see plainly that the Holy Bible calls homosexuality "detestable" and adultery "wicked" (Lev. 18:20; 20:13; 1 Cor. 6:9). In the Old Testament, men and women caught in these acts were put to death (Lev. 20:10; Dt. 22:22) In the New Testament, having sinned without repentance is death everlasting. Our spiritual leaders are commanded by scripture to wake up those who stray from the straight and narrow path and guide them (with love) to repentance and salvation. No physical harm should come to a sinner in this world, but do not encourage activities that lead to eternal separation from God.

This pastor from Topeka should be lauded, not made out to be a hate-monger. It is with God's love that he speaks the truth. Prayerfully, some may hear, and this world and what lay beyond will be heaven for them.

John 15:20-21. *"Remember the words I spoke to you: 'No servant is greater than his master.' If they persecute me, they will persecute you also. If they obeyed my teaching, they will obey yours also. They will treat you this way because of my name, for they do not know the One who sent me."*

✟ ✟ ✟

Saturday, September 3, 1994
11:00 a.m.

My brain screams with anguish as my balled fists shake with frustration. Where is their sensitivity? Where is their humanity? How can *human* officers treat *human* inmates with such malice?

The recreation yard being closed, all 160 gym inmates were required to sit on the hard, asphalt basketball court. From 7:00 a.m. until 10:45 a.m. we sat under the glaring sun while staff searched the entire gym, our bed areas, and personal property. When we were allowed back inside, I discovered to my painful horror the damage staff inflicted. Could a tornado have caused more destruction? My bedding was tossed into a ball. My locker shelves have been torn out. My neatly arranged papers, files, books, and toiletries have been strewn about and thrown back in. And...Aauugghh!! The antenna to my television has been broken off.

Why? Why? Why was this necessary? Oh, right, a bullet was found outside the inmate perimeter.

I could file a CDC appeal but how do I prove that the antenna was not already broken? It would be my convicted felon's word against a righteous peace officer's word. I am screwed...for the rest of my life. How the fu—ing hell can people treat me and others this way? How am I supposed to learn to love humanity if the representatives of humanity rarely show it? If God's Spirit was not in me, the devil surrounding me would surely win.

2:00 p.m.

Inmates, including me, are still cleaning up and trying to salvage their shredded pittance of property—three hours later.

No showers! Why? They are right there, empty, but unavailable. What seems to be the problem? I have not done anything wrong. Why am I being persecuted for some alleged bullet discovery, which as I believe, was probably dropped by a staff member? Will this madness ever end? Does society ever forgive? What is wrong with us, all of us? And who is responsible?

I am responsible. It all started with me.

4:00 p.m.

Mail. Really? It's Saturday. Is the mail room getting too far behind again? Regardless, I got a double-up. Two letters. The first was from Bonnie and Rod. Bonnie shared her concerns about her son, Jeff, who has been leading a wild life. She is afraid that trouble lies ahead for him and asked if I would keep him in prayer. Of course!

The second letter was from Jennifer. She had been reminiscing since our reunion by mail and had gone back through our school's year book. She photocopied and enclosed a page where I wrote my sentiment.

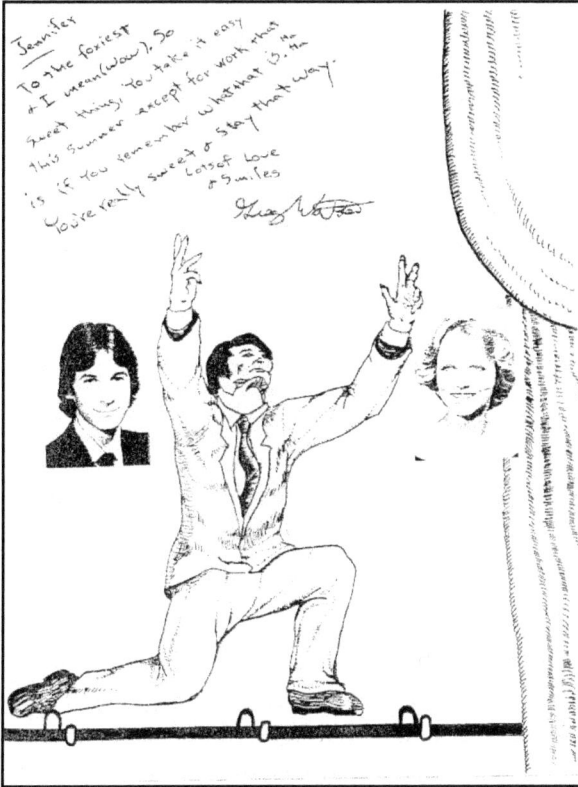

Yes siree, I had a crush on Jennifer.

Jennifer spoke fondly of our Senior Follies where I brought down the house as the closing act, dressed as Alice Cooper and lip syncing to *School's Out.*

Both letters were wonderful and appreciated.

The morning started terribly but the day ended terrifically. Thank you, Bonnie and Rod, Jennifer, and God.

Ephesians 4:31-32. *Get rid of all bitterness, rage and anger, brawling and slander, along with every form of malice. Be kind and compassionate to one another, forgiving each other, just as in Christ God forgave you.*

✝ ✝ ✝

Sunday, September 4, 1994
8:00 a.m.

Still stressed, unnerved and on edge. That proverbial knife could cut the hate and tension ebbing and flowing across the rows of bunks. Its cause is a stew, its ingredients made up of being shut-in, unable to call family, no visiting, no showers, and the abusive search that revealed nothing.

For me, yesterday's surprise letters helped to shake off the correctional assertiveness. Today, I need to divert my mind. I could attempt some creative writing, but my thoughts swirl, which do not allow for a stream of thought worthy of the ink I would expend. What's that? No, pillow, you are not soft, but I could try. Maybe I can sleep this lockdown away.

2:15 p.m.

I awoke dripping in sweat. It is hot, stuffy, and uncomfortably sticky, but I'm more relaxed. Wow! Four hours of sleep. My brain and body needed to shed the built up stress.

2:20 p.m.

Announcement: "Showers are open." Thank God. However, it will be a while until I can delight in the wet refreshment of cascading water because there are 160 inmates and only 12 showers. Hopefully, after dinner the showers will contain only a scarce number of men, because I don't enjoy bathing cheek-to-cheek, so to speak.

8:00 p.m.

Ah...I am clean, refreshed, and my spirit has found its equilibrium. I'm thinking that I will read for a while. Let me see what the Good Book has in store for me tonight. Ezekiel is appropriate.

Ezekiel 36:25. *"I will sprinkle clean water on you, and you will be clean; I will cleanse you from all your impurities and from all your idols."*

✝ ✝ ✝

Monday, September 5, 1994
LABOR DAY

My eyelids are opening to another day; still locked down, and still no telephone usage. My parents have no way of knowing why I have not called them and I do know they worry when I do not make a scheduled call. I am bored but I do not feel like writing letters, reading, or watching the titillating television talk shows (which I have sworn off doing). Happy Labor Day to me.

8:00 p.m.

Television football. God, I hate it. The gym sounds like 80,000 coked–up fanatics all screaming their spastic heads off. All these wannabe jerk-off jocks rooting for the 49ers or the Raiders. Jeez, get a life, guys. I am not a snob with my Public Broadcasting Station programs, but get a grip and expand your horizons, and SHUT UP!

What is worse than the rooting for is the argument of 'my' team is better…" Fights often ensue from a false assertion of 'my' team. These teams are not owned by any of these inmates; though a casual observer would assume otherwise by watching the over-the-top display of aggression to the point of violence in the name of their team.

Football is a business where talented men make boatloads of money. I say, "Enjoy it if you want to but it *ain't* that serious."

I feel as though I am slowly going bonkers. There must be a lesson here for me to learn, Lord, or you would not subject me to this insanity. Oh, that's right. You did not place me here, I did. Sigh.

Hebrews 12:1. *Therefore, since we are surrounded by such a great cloud of witnesses, let us throw off everything that hinders and the sin that so easily entangles, and let us run with perseverance the race marked out for us.*

✜ ✜ ✜

Tuesday, September 6, 1994
9:30 a.m.

Still locked down. Still no telephones but the showers are a blessing. I am starting to feel like a cave dweller; a wingless bat in a giant, hollow, concrete cavern of batty blue convicts. Squeak, squeak.

12:00 p.m.

News Flash! A federal court judge has ruled that Governor Wilson's revoking of life prisoners' paroles and parole dates without cause is illegal. A small light in the vast darkness. Truth among the many lies. A voice of good sounding out to stop the evil. These inmates have served their prescribed time, and should be allowed to be a community asset, not solely a drain on tax coffers by further incarceration. It is unfortunate that their victims cannot be brought back, but the perpetrators of these offenses do have to live with that tragedy for the rest of their lives. The families of the victims, who are victims themselves, cannot be compensated or made whole for their loss, but we do need to strive for healing in whatever form is possible, or we are all doomed to continual loss.

4:00 p.m.

Mail. It is a letter from my cousin. Hanna writes about her wedding plans. Reading about them and her excitement is a mixed bag of emotions for me. I am happy to be a part of her thoughts that the ache of missing out on life, love, and my own happiness is soothed. If I cannot be an actor in the play of life, I am at least pleased to be given a program.

5:30 p.m.

As I walked back from the chow hall, I noticed white strings cutting the grass area into segments and quadrants, but they only covered half the recreation yard. It appears to me that the other half still needs to be searched with metal detectors. I can assume it will be a minimum of two more days of shut-in-ship.

James 5:7-8. *Be patient, then, brothers, until the Lord's coming. See how the farmer waits for the land to yield its valuable crop and how patient he is for the autumn and spring rains. You too, be patient and stand firm, because the Lord's coming is near.*

✝ ✝ ✝

Wednesday, September 7, 1994
8:00 a.m.

Still on lockdown!

9:00 a.m.

My friend *B.C.*, who has been in prison for 19 years appeared before his *impartial* parole board today. Two of the three commissioners had had children killed, and one of the two, Mr. Baker, his son was killed by Richard Alton Harris. Mr. Baker stated, after viewing Richard Alton Harris' execution in San Quentin, that, "If I were on the parole board, I'd never let any of them go." Yessiree, that is an impartial commissioner. *B.C.* was denied a parole date.

3:00 p.m.

"Yard recall. Emergency count," blared from the loud speakers. What? How can the yard be recalled if all the inmates are locked down? There is no logical answer to that question.

Okay, we are all seated on our bunks for count. Waiting...

3:35 p.m.

"Count is clear," is announced. The inmates get off their bunks to use the restroom.

"Back on your bunks for alarm check," is shouted from the officers' station. Here comes the daily eardrum bursting...

BUUUUUUZZZZZ!!!!

4:00 p.m.

Mail. A lifeline. An encouraging letter from my mother. Perfect timing because my rise-above-it-all battery was dangerously low and her loving words help to recharge it. Thank you.

Oprah. Yes, I watched her show today. I learned that I am not a progressive thinking person. Why? Because I do not accept the acts of those who choose to live a homosexual lifestyle. I do accept and care for the individual, but I condemn, as the Lord has, the gay way of life. What is up,

Oprah? What is up, America? Have we been so contaminated that we no longer know right from wrong? Pray. Pray hard for the confused and satisfiers of the flesh, for their reward is neither in heaven, nor is it with God.

Someone needs to stand up and speak out for God's way of life. That someone must be me, and hopefully, eventually, it will be everyone.

Philemon 1:7a. *Your love has given me great joy and encouragement.*

✝ ✝ ✝

Thursday, September 8, 1994
12:01 a.m.

"Resume normal program," resounds from the speakers, waking everyone who was sleeping, me included. So, we are off lockdown. Yeah, team! It is back to relative normalcy and sleep.

9:30 a.m.

I telephoned my father and he was pleased to finally hear from me. He said Nick Taylor did call. I am so relieved. It had been a week since Mr. Taylor paroled and I was beginning to wonder if he would keep his word. Thanks, God. I hope Mr. Taylor and I can get moving on this representation biz so that my years of creative writing can begin to pay off. Yes, I still need to exercise patience. I hate patience. It is so slow. Ha ha.

12:00 Noon

An officer whom I have known for several years walked into the gym from the recreation yard. He strolled up to my desk and dropped a zip-locked barbecue chicken breast into the trash can next to my desk. He smiled at me and said, "You will take care of that, won't you?" I grinned back and said, "Right away, sir." Yummy. My taste buds came alive with the tangy, home-cooked barbecue chicken. I loved it, and appreciated his kind gesture with all my heart, but what a sight I must have been. Look how far I have fallen; taking food out of the trash. How sad is that?

3:00 p.m.

I was going to exercise to re-acquaint my muscles with the weights but I am too darn busy. Due to the lockdown there were no inmates moved into the gym but inmates still transferred and paroled out. To make up for lost time, staff moved 10 inmates in, including *Don* Dario. Needless to say there is a lot of paperwork. Actually, I am not complaining because I thrive on busy. Busy keeps my mind occupied, focused on a task, and not on prison. I will exercise tomorrow as it is likely that I will still be here.

7:00 p.m.

I tried to telephone my mother to let her know that I am okay, but the line was busy, and then no one answered. I will have to wait until Saturday morning as it is getting late in Texas.

8:00 p.m.

While walking along one of the bunk aisles in this human storage room, I caught the eye of some tough-faced youngster. I smiled and for a moment he smiled back. There, in that instant I saw and knew the true good character of the person God intended that young man to be. The moment quickly passed. The façade of the man he thinks his homeboys expect him to be returned. I saw it though, and I know it is there, only hidden. Now how to hold that moment, to instill into him the strength and courage to be the man God intended? That is the question the Department of Corrections should be asking itself.

2 Peter 1:19. *And we have the word of the prophets made more certain, and you will do well to pay attention to it, as to a light shining in a dark place, until the day dawns and the morning star rises in your hearts.*

✢ ✢ ✢

Friday, September 9, 1994
10:00 a.m.

A relaxing day. An experience that occurs too infrequently and treasured more than can adequately be expressed. I am going to pause. I closed my eyes as a breeze tickles the hair on my arms. Reclining on my bunk, I savored this moment.

12:00 Noon

News Flash! Governor Wilson signed a bill into law to give first time child molesters and rapists life sentences. Wow! Unbelievable! Please do not get me wrong. I have no love lost for men who commit these types of crimes, but there is too much leeway for false accusations by custody-battling couples and women who have been scorned by not-so-loving lovers.

I do not want molesters or rapists on the street any more than I want non-repentant murderers set free, but this new law is another knee-jerk reaction. It is not a solution to society's ills. This emotional law will do one thing, and that is, it will bolster popularity points and secure votes for Governor Wilson's re-election. Give us what we need, not what we want, Governor Wilson. Lead us along a fruitful path, not headlong down a dead end alley.

9:00 p.m.

I previously said I would not play volleyball anymore, but I was weak and played this evening. It was A-Okay. My skill level was off due to my not having played in a while, but there were no arguments, only encouragements, so that made the evening emotionally enjoyable. Also, God's multi-colored sunset was a spectacular touch to close out an A-Okay day.

1 Timothy 1:8-10. *We know that the law is good if one uses it properly. We also know the law is made not for the righteous but for lawbreakers and rebels, the ungodly and sinful, the unholy and irreligious; for those who kill their fathers or mothers, for murderers, for adulterers and perverts, for slave traders and liars and perjurers—and whatever else is contrary to the sound doctrine.*

✟ ✟ ✟

Saturday, September 10, 1994
10:30 a.m.

Violence: child against child. Prayers for the children. I was talking to Mario; a Mexican, lickety-split runner, runner, runner. He and I encourage each other with our individual jogging. He was telling me that his niece was no longer paralyzed, but that she is still blind, and the bullet could not safely be removed from her brain.

What?! She, Mario's niece was *that* 13-year-old girl who was shot by a 14-year-old boy in a drive by? I was stunned. I had seen the news broadcast several days ago but the victim did not have a name, face, or family for me to attach a personal touch of pain to. It was a sad story but one of an unknown child. Some other neighborhood. Now it was my friend's family. A child-relative of a man I knew and could personally witness the pain and concern on his face.

God, what is happening to the children? Where did so many of them slip through morality's fingers? Many prayers are needed. Many prayers I beseech you with, oh God. Help her and help them all.

3:00 p.m.

An answered prayer. Our fellowship group has been praying for Ron's grandmother. We were asking God to help her regain her mental faculties so Ron's mother could communicate with her and that mother would recognize daughter.

Finally, after six months, and all glory to God, during the last trip that Ron's mother made to Ron's grandmother's Alzheimer's care facility, she was able to recognize her daughter. Mother and daughter were able to have closure on several unresolved and troublesome issues. Both are now at peace and once again our prayers have been answered. His glory, God's glory cannot be denied. Only His healing hand could have restored this aged grandmother's coherence for the duration of the visit. Thank you, God, for your kindness and mercy.

Matthew 8:8, 13. *The centurion replied, "Lord, I do not deserve to have you come under my roof. But just say the word, and my servant will be healed." Then Jesus said to the centurion, "Go! It will be done just as you believed it would." And his servant was healed at that very hour.*

✟ ✟ ✟

Sunday, September 11, 1994
9:00 p.m.

Which is the illusion? Prison or the place in one's mind? I know I am in prison, but my aspirations and concept of who I am, as well as the glory of God within do not mesh. I feel and think like a sprinter poised in the starting blocks: Waiting, muscles tense, heart rate increasing, waiting for the starter's gun to begin life anew in the world.

It is a wonderful feeling of hope that is in constant clash with worldly realities. I have been tentatively denied in the federal court; the governor is not likely to pardon me; and I have 13 years, until 2007, when I appear before my first parole board.

Am I in complete denial of the impossible and horrific situation that I am in, or is God's grace so magnificent that my hope and faith have risen above reality to a wondrous anticipation of things to come? Is it only hope beating futilely at despair, or is my hope built on example after example of Christ's daily blessings in my life? I believe the latter. God's love is sufficient and wonderful.

Ephesians 1:18-21. *I pray also that the eyes of your heart may be enlightened in order that you may know the hope to which He has called you, the riches of His glorious inheritance in the saints, and His incomparably great power for us who believe. That power is like the working of His mighty strength which He exerted in Christ when He raised him from the dead and seated him at His right hand in the heavenly realms, far above all the rule and authority, power and dominion, and every title that can be given, not only in the present age but also in the one to come.*

✟ ✟ ✟

Monday, September 12, 1994
5:27 a.m.

Shake, rattle, and roll, and no, I am not on an epileptic roller coaster. EARTHQUAKE!!! I am wide awake but confused. If the roof was to fall in I am not sure I would know what to do, let alone where to go. Where to go? Hell's bells, the doors are all locked. There is nowhere to go.

Holy moly! It was a 6.2 on the jiggle meter. That was much more than a little tumbler. Fortunately, the cracks in the gym's concrete walls widened only a fraction of an inch. Cracks?! Get me out of here. I am thoroughly amazed that we are allowed to be housed in this sinking, sagging, hotel of penal punitiveness. Who builds a foundation on slipping clay? If the walls and roof come crumbling down and we all die, no one will care except our families. Likely some politician will exclaim, "Good riddance." There will be at least one exception. God! He will care. Sometimes if the light is just right, and I am not wearing my glasses, I believe I can see angels holding up the gym walls. If only one soul is saved is not all the effort worth it? Jesus believes so.

7:00 p.m.

"Yard recall," echoes. What? Oh, the lights have gone out. Another evening inside.

7:37 p.m.

Lights. Camera. Action. Well, the lights are back on at last.

9:00 p.m.

News Flash! Governor Wilson has signed the bill limiting or removing the weight training areas from all California prisons. I am sure that will have a direct effect on street crime. NOT! Oh, that is right, the election is drawing near and our governor needs to kick a few more muzzled dogs to bolster his ineptitude concerning the state's lagging economy, falling education scores, crumbling infrastructure, and growing homelessness. When all else fails to impress, shout, "Tough on crime."

Fearfully, I foresee a future of increased violent incidents in the prison, as did occur when the weight pile was previously closed. Shame, shame, Governor Wilson: wasted time and effort on nonsensical laws for personal gain. Where is your public interest?

When was the last time a 7/11 was strong-armed (robbed) by a man flexing his biceps?

Luke 15:6b-7. *"'Rejoice with me; I have found my lost sheep.' I tell you that in the same way there will be more rejoicing in heaven over one sinner who repents than over ninety-nine persons who do not need to repent."*

✟ ✟ ✟

Tuesday, September 13, 1994
9:00 a.m.

In addition to my few minutes of clerk work each day, on Tuesdays, which is our facility's inspection day, I acquired the task of cleaning the raised officers' station. Sweep, mop, sponge-dust, and straighten up. It is not too difficult, not too taxing, and I barely break a sweat. I can handle it.

Ten minutes later the work is accomplished and I am off to...

9:30 a.m.

...my photo-op. Madeline wanted another photograph of me because her last one was stolen along with her purse. I am pleased to report that the photograph turned out handsomely, but that is not unexpected. Hey, look at the subject matter. Ha ha. Seriously though, I usually blink at the flash, causing my eyes to appear closed, but this time I managed to stay wide-eyed. I will enclose this photograph with a lengthy letter covering my many ups and downs since I last wrote along with wishing her my best. Madeline is a true pen-pal blessing.

4:00 p.m.

Mail. Pieces and parts, all that was left of the letter my mother sent to me. It was torn, mangled, and stapled to hold the four pieces limply together. It was trashed and unreadable, worthless. A handwritten note on what was left of the envelope stated the letter had been received at the institution in the destroyed condition.

Really? I think otherwise. I have it on good authority and personal experience that when mail is mangled by the U.S. Post Office they attach an adhesive stamp to the letter apologizing for the damage.

There are times that I wonder if a self-appointed persecutor in the institution's mail room sees my last name and confuses me with Charles "Tex" Watson. Charles tends to receive a significant amount of grief from staff. Or, does the mail room person destroy in-coming mail at random? There are too many judges in this world who wrongly believe they are doing good by doing evil to others who have, in the past, done evil themselves.

I have no idea what my mother's letter said, though contradicting what I said above, the letter was not worthless. I know it was filled with love for me. I am blessed and thankful.

9:00 p.m.

A graduation ducat? For tomorrow? For what?

Luke 6:37. *"Do not judge and you will not be judged. Do not condemn, and you will not be condemned. Forgive, and you will be forgiven."*

✝ ✝ ✝

Wednesday, September 14, 1994
9:15 – 11:15 a.m

| STATE OF CALIFORNIA | DEPARTMENT OF CORRECTIONS |
| INMATE PASS | CDC 129 (7/88) |

INMATE'S NAME: WATSON CDC #: D-67547 HOUSING #: BG-167
ISSUED BY:
PASS TO: Facility "B" Visiting   TIME: 0915
REASON: GRADUATION
DEPART TO: TIME: 10 50 RECORDED BY:

Very interesting. It was a graduation ceremony for completing my tutoring class. What a good idea. Certificates and diplomas for education and vocational achievements were also being presented. The visiting room was rearranged with rows of chairs. There were proud and enthusiastic speakers, and for many of these inmates, this was the first time they had ever been recognized for anything except wrong doings. The attending teachers and inmates applauded each inmate when he walked up to receive his certificate or diploma for attaining his set goal. Well almost everyone applauded.

The obese and slovenly figure of our associate warden sat prominently in the front row, legs spread wide, glaring annoyed at the procession. Not once did he applaud or show signs of approval for the inmates' achievements. Any glory or esteem that I or these men felt was immediately sucked away by his scorn-filled eyes. We knew we could all die right there and he would not give a damn. His job is suppression and containment. To be in a room full of achievers goes against his goals.

There is a broad consensus among many unenlightened staff that an educated and goal-oriented inmate is to be feared. He must be crushed by all available means. Why? Because this type of inmate will question authority with a properly formatted sentence.

2:00 p.m.

I knew something bad was missing. *Mr. Stress* walked in at shift change. Officer Bartels has returned. He has been absent for two, almost three weeks. Since Officer Bartels' departure the gym has settled into a moderately stress-free, smoothly-run, almost honor dorm-type of living quarters. There were no megaphones with needless announcements and no clapping and shouting inmates upon his departure. Mutual respect and courtesy, for the most part, between the staff and inmates. A palatable détente.

Officer Bartels stated to me that the lack of discipline in the gym was proof that he had been absent. I replied, "That is one opinion." I mentioned that there had been no need for disciplinary 115 write-ups for misbehavior. Officer Bartels did not appreciate my point of view and said, "Life's a bitch. I'm back." I bowed my head, shaking it with sadness.

1 John 2:9. *Anyone who claims to be in the light but hates his brother is still in the darkness.*

✝ ✝ ✝

Thursday, September 15, 1994
9:50 p.m.

Today was another one of those rare days; pleasant, peaceful, and contemplative. It was like a coffee commercial with a twist. The sun's rays warmed my skin as I jogged the track with ease. The four code 3 alarms were false activations. My bed area and property were not one of the six randomly searched. The creative juices were flowing into my current story and the dinner conversation over spaghetti was about positive topics.

After a day like this, all I can do is marvel at God's grace while in my prayers I give Him all the glory. For what? Nothing special happened. This may be true, but considering all the evil surrounding me in here, and all the evil surrounding my family as they go through their daily lives on the street, to have nothing happen *is* special. To be able to lay my head on my pillow without anxiety almost guarantees a slumber filled with magical dreams.

Can anyone ask for more? Certainly not me.

Job 10:12. *You gave me life and showed me kindness, and in your providence watched over my spirit.*

✝ ✝ ✝

Friday, September 16, 1994
10:00 a.m.

Mario stopped by my bunk to inform me that his niece is seeing colors and can distinguish shapes. A miracle? Could it be? Praise God. Our prayers seem to be answered in the affirmative for her continuing recovery. No one knows if she will regain full sight but this news is a wonderful start. Maybe she would have regained the shapes and colors without our prayers, but we did not want to take a stupid chance like that.

Our humble fellowship group has had many prayers answered over the years since we have been praying together. It is comforting to us to know the Lord does not distinguish or discriminate between prayers from the righteous or from sinners. He loves us both equally.

1:20 p.m.

Gentle persuasion toward self-discipline. *Smiley,* a 22-year-old Hispanic ex-gang member stopped by my bunk. His face was filled with worry. He received his classification chrono that indicated he was being placed on the transfer list to a higher security level prison. The reason for this is his many disciplinary write-ups for fighting, making pruno, and tattooing. He tells me he is afraid of being sent back to a hard core prison. It would have been too easy for me to say, "Well, you deserve what's happening to you because you screwed around, received write-ups, and because you act like a bad ass you're being sent to a prison with other bad asses." Instead, I gave him some suggestions that may help to keep him here especially since he only has seven months left to serve on his sentence. I also told *Smiley* that this would be a good time to prove his worth, to show staff that he can restrain himself, and not cause them, and ultimately himself, more trouble. *Smiley* agreed with me and thanked me for listening.

Though there are many examples of where staff falls short in their professionalism, I will never hesitate to give credit to the administration for their attempt to create a prison atmosphere where an inmate can, if he chooses to, concentrate on self-improvement. For this I will be forever grateful. It is unfortunate that many inmates do not see the blessing that is being offered them and continue to spend their time in non-productive activities.

I will keep *Smiley* in my prayers that regardless of where he ends up, that he will be safe and learn self-discipline.

7:10 p.m.

As I walked around the track this evening I discovered that I was the first to wish Ron a Happy Birthday. His eyes lit up. It is only a small thing, but to remember one's occasions, I believe shows you care, and I do. Sure, accuse me of being a sentimental fool, but darn it, people are important. If we each took a little more time to look for the good things and always remember our friends, family, and be considerate to strangers, there would be fewer people acting out in negative ways for attention.

A birthday. It may be just another day in prison with no presents and no cake, but a smile and a handshake; that I can give.

Romans 15:5-6. *May God who gives endurance and encouragement give you a spirit of unity among yourselves as you follow Christ Jesus, so that with one heart and mouth you may glorify the God and Father of our Lord Jesus Christ.*

✞ ✞ ✞

Saturday, September 17, 1994
9:00 a.m.

The power in the gym will be turned off for an undetermined length of time; thus no lights. The electricians are working in the main chow hall. Remember the chow hall? Many months ago it burned. It appears that someone is finally beginning to work on it. I will not wager a guess as to how long the cleaning and refurbishing will take. I mean, it is a state-run project.

We gym inmates have been given a choice. Oh, I love choices. We can either sit on our bunks in the dark or venture outside. If we go outside we will stay there until the power is back on. No unlocks.

Decisions. Decisions. Decisions.

Ah…outside.

12:00 Noon

The lights are still out and I am still on the recreation yard.

1:00 p.m.

The lights are still out and I am still on the recreation yard.

2:00 p.m.

The lights are still out. Enough already. My tan is sufficient. I am hungry. I want my sack lunch that sits on my locker inside the darkened gym. Even though the sack only contains a thinly sliced piece of bologna, graham crackers, and bread, it is enough to fill the void.

2:35 p.m.

At last. Some man said, "Let there be light." Unlock is announced and the gym's door swings wide to allow many sun-burnt and hungry inmates inside. – Scarf, Scarf, Scarf – My grandmother was right. If I am made to wait long enough, anything will taste good. Ha ha.

7:00 p.m.

I cannot believe it. Again, some jerk-off cut the tension nylon rope out of the top of the volleyball net. The thief or thieves unwind the rope to make small shower bags for carrying soap, shampoo, and other toiletries. –Scrounge, Scrounge, Scrounge – Eureka! The yard officer was helpful in locating some thick twine for us to make temporary repairs on the net. I would love to catch the person or persons who are stealing the rope. Actually, this third destruction of the net does not say much for the observational abilities of the tower officer. What else is he missing?

7:45 p.m.

After 45 minutes of engineering ingenuity we produced a net that worked. The games proceeded with positive encouragement, leaving the negativity that the thief tried to instill behind us.

Psalm 145:5-6. *They will speak of the glorious splendor of your majesty, and I will meditate on your wonderful works. They will tell of the power of your awesome works, and I will proclaim your great deeds.*

✞ ✞ ✞

Sunday, September 18, 1994
6:45 a.m.

New officers. New rules. Walking to breakfast they bellowed, "Hands in your pockets...single file...stay to the right." Hey, buddy; this is not a level V prison. We are level II. Yes, half of us are convicted murderers, but we have earned our low level custody by staying out of trouble. Stop harassing us, especially so early in the morning. Geez Louise.

Subdue and submit. They subdue and we submit. I do not think so and if staff believes it they are fools. We may conform, temporarily, but no man submits permanently. Actually, all these rule changes and idiotic demands build our strength of character. For some, the character of evil; for others, including myself, it is the character of Christ. These officers may temporarily subdue me but I only submit to God. Simply stated, God is always the same. I can count on Him always. I can never count on man. No one should. Man will always disappoint.

10:10 a.m.

As I sit on my bunk I realize that the only disadvantage to its location in the gym is the proximity to the telephones. I am constantly subjected to the abusive dialogue and vulgar language that too many of these men use in a false belief that it is effective communication.

1:30 p.m.

Unbelievable! The same man has been on the telephone for 3 1/2 hours. He has been berating either his wife or girlfriend for the majority of the time and she is paying for repeated collect call charges. Not trying to, but forced to listen to too many of these types of one-sided telephone conversations, it saddens me that so many women accept this abuse. I have to ask: Are these women so insecure and have nothing going for them that they will sit idly and take it? Ladies, catch a clue, you do not have to subject yourself to abuse. DO NOT ACCEPT THE COLLECT CALLS!!!! Each of you is precious, regardless of what you are being told, and you should never be treated in this manner. And men, if you treat your lady this way, you are missing out on the best part of a woman. Lift her up and watch her shine for you.

Acts 5:29. *Peter and the other apostles replied: "We must obey God rather than men!"*

✝ ✝ ✝

Monday, September 19, 1994
4:30 a.m.

"Attention all housing units. Count is clear. Count is clear." Thank you very much for waking me. Stupid loud speakers were turned to full volume. If the officers in Central Control have to be awake, then all the inmates should be, too.

5:15 a.m.

The gym's bright lights flash on. "Prepare for chow release. Prepare for chow." Damn idiots. Chow is between 6:30 and 7:15 a.m. not 5:15 a.m. Oh, I see. The officer on the podium is laughing. Yeah, he thinks it is funny, but the on-coming staff who now have to deal with 160 angry, pissed-off inmates whose sleep has been interrupted several times during the night are not laughing. Sleep is the only time we can legally escape, so when that is disturbed, our stress rises, and the day becomes more unbearable.

4:00 p.m.

Mail. A letter from Charlie. Perfect timing. I needed cheering up after a day of stressed out men and interrupted sleep. Charlie will be paroling from Soledad prison in a couple of weeks and I wish him well. He has been a terrific Christian friend and loyal correspondent. How I wish I were going home, too. I have been feeling as though I am sliding down a black, greased tunnel into the bowels of the nether world. Will I ever get out?

Despair has a heavy hand.

I sometimes wish the Lord would take me away in my sleep. Unfortunately, I believe I will survive to fight each and every dreaded day of this waking death. On top of that, God has instilled in me a drive to succeed which is in constant battle with my deprived flesh that just wants to give up. My spirit keeps trying to be productive and positive but most of the time it is a no-win situation. At times it seems that no one really wants a felon to change, let alone succeed.

Actually, I should clarify. There are rules on rules created to corral the inmate/parolee so it is inevitable that he fails and either re-offends or his parole is violated for a technical reason and he is returned to prison. A technical violation can be as simple as using a cheese cutting knife in the living room while eating cheese and crackers during a sporting event on television. The citizens of this state should not be surprised that more than seven out of ten parolees return to prison. I have no doubt that all these hundreds of rules were well thought out and intended to protect society but are they when the result is failure? Is there not a way to lift up the parolee with opportunities for success instead of weighing him down with burdens that he cannot overcome?

For me, and for right now, I focus on surviving this character-building crap one day at a time. Just one step at a time, always moving forward...

AAAAAUUUUUUUGGGGGGHHHHHH.....!!!!

Can you hear me, Lord? I know you can. There are many blessings to be thankful for: friends, family, health, a sort of sound mind, and inspiring dreams. And, as long as the dream for a future, being productive and free, is alive then so am I.

Believe it or not the letter from Charlie did cheer me up. Every so often a bit of ranting is needed.

9:00 p.m.

The third watch sergeant came into the gym so I took the opportunity to ask him if he could, in passing, ask the first watch (4:30 a.m.) crew to not announce "Count is clear" over the gym's loud speaker system. It is unnecessary because the same announcement is made via radio transmission and all staff is equipped with one. The sergeant replied that the Central Control sergeant would "Blow him off," and that I should file an appeal.

File paperwork? With a straight face I said, "So there is not much cooperation among staff?"

"No, we work just fine together," was his retort.

The sergeant's defensive side quickly came out and it was obvious that he would not do anything. His final reply was, "You have to realize that staff doesn't give a damn whether you get any sleep."

That said it all.

1 Corinthians 4:10b-13. *We are fools for Christ, but you are so wise in Christ. We are weak but You are strong! You are honored, we are dishonored! To this very hour we go hungry and thirsty, we are in rags, we are brutally treated, and we are homeless. We work hard with our hands. When we are cursed, we bless; when we are persecuted, we endure it; when we are slandered, we answer kindly. Up to this moment we have become the scum of the earth, the refuse of the world.*

✟ ✟ ✟

Tuesday, September 20, 1994
12:00 Noon

News Flash! A young, black man who killed a manager of a Kentucky Fried Chicken store holds his breath. He has been convicted of the crime and the district attorney is pushing the jury to come back with the death penalty. I have to ask myself: "Self, is the fact that he stole $1,700 make his crime more heinous than O.J. Simpson's alleged killing of two people, and therefore he warrants the death penalty, while O.J. Simpson does not?" Why is it we can execute a no-name but we cannot kill a rich American hero? It seems like one of these two black defendants is getting the short end of the judicial stick. Maybe the Kentucky Fried Chicken defendant could not afford a longer stick.

5:00 p.m.

Meat loaf for dinner; I thoroughly enjoyed it. Why? Because the meat loaf was store bought. It was perfectly proportioned, equal size for all, and the cooks were only required to heat it. That left little room for ruin or error. Served with rice as a side dish, and cherry jello for dessert, it was a hot and filling meal. Boy-o-boy my taste buds must really be dead.

7:30 p.m.

Smitty stopped by my bunk. His request to transfer to San Quentin was denied because San Quentin no longer accepts inmates convicted of execution-style killings. It is a strange new law. There are numerous inmates, including my friend Mo, who are convicted of multiple murders, and they are housed in San Quentin, but Smitty who only killed one person cannot be. I guess what is important to the rule makers is not the number of people one kills but how the killing is committed.

I am confused.

Smitty has been disciplinary free for more than 12 years and is only asking to be housed in an institution that is closer to his wife and children. I am sad for Smitty, but pleased for me. He is a good friend and I would miss him if he transferred. Maybe next year the policy will change and Smitty will have another opportunity. If I were a betting man I would wager in Smitty's favor because policies and rules change as often as we are allowed to change our underwear.

Proverbs 29:7, 14. *The righteous care about justice for the poor, but the wicked have no such concern. If a king judges the poor with fairness, his throne will always be secure.*

☥ ☥ ☥

Wednesday, September 21, 1994
7:00 p.m.

I do not know where it came from but my ol' joker's side ran wild this evening. To quote a well-used phrase: "I danced with the sinners and cried with the saints." What a grand and rare feeling. Joking, teasing, and laughing with fellow murderers.

Unbelievable.

Bizarro world.

Men being men, we shared long-forgotten humorous stories of beach parties, dances, cruising in custom cars, and friendships. We accept each other, white, black, and Hispanic, based on the character we have developed and on our word. There is nothing else. Smiles all around tonight. It has been a pleasant evening in this here cube of a domicile.

This is the old me, the good-natured, laughing Greg; light-hearted and witty. Yes, I can still crack 'em up. I have been in fear that this joy had vanished forever because too seldom do I see his happy man in the mirror.

Symbolically, I beat my chest and shout inwardly: I am still alive.

10:00 p.m.

The television program *48 Hours* focused on the American soldiers in Haiti and how they prepared for this mission. Praise God, as yet not one has been killed. Film footage showed the soldiers' wives, tears in their eyes, as their husbands boarded ships for deployment.

My heart aches for that kind of love. I will never get over the pain I witnessed in Angela's eyes when I turned myself in to the sheriff's office. She did not know if we would ever hold each other again. As it happened, I was convicted. It would have been better that I were dead. A widow is treated more kindly than a lover of a convicted murderer.

I constantly pray that with God's blessing I will one day meet another lady who will find me worthy of a love with the kind of passion that Angela possessed. I believe I have learned how to love; totally, absolutely, and without judgment. Angela taught me through her pain, and God has taught me through His mercy and discipline.

I pray the wives' tears turn to joy on their husbands safe return.

Six years later, have you stopped crying, Angela? Time is supposed to heal all wounds. Painfully, my heart still bleeds for you.

Tonight's dreams will be a mixture of today's joys and life's sorrows.

Genesis 29:20. *So Jacob served seven years to get Rachel, but they seemed like only a few days to him because of his love for her.*

✟ ✟ ✟

Thursday, September 22, 1994
9:30 a.m.

It is fall cleaning time. A very tall lift-type, scissors platform on wheels has been brought into the gym. The inmate porters are using it to clean the lights, pipes, nooks and crannies in the ceiling of the gym. The porters are standing on a wobbly platform 40 feet in the air; way too high for me. I would have to respectfully beg to decline if I were a porter.

The gym resembles a haunted house. All the bunks are covered with draped sheets. Large globs of dust splash from their disturbed resting places to spread out like a foggy London night. I am not sure that anything is being cleaned. It looks more like a case of move the dust from one place to another. Cough, cough. I have to get the heck out of here.

10:00 a.m.

Before the dust storm began I read a new memorandum while posting it for all to see. Suspiciously, the administration has decided, at least for the time being, to keep the weight pile open on a privilege basis, despite the new law against weight training areas in prisons. Oh no, say it is not so. I agree with something they are doing. Actually, everything in prison should be on a privilege system. Praise the good behavior and punish the bad. Do not punish everyone for the acts of one or two. That only breeds animosity.

12:00 Noon

Muscles tight and sore. I always feel better after a strenuous workout, and I can see the stress leaving the faces of the men on the yard after their workouts. Weights are a great mental therapy. Concentration on the exercises clears the mind of stress and usually wipes away any evil intentions that may have been simmering.

Though I feel physically good, it felt weird to be breaking the law even with the consent of the administration. I have been dutifully following every rule (excluding the photocopy blunder), regulation, and law since turning myself in, in 1986, that doing something, anything against an edict grates against my soul.

4:00 p.m.

Legal mail? Oh, a letter from my trial attorney. It is a follow-up on my request for police reports. His letter provided me with several good chuckles. I had asked in my letter to him if he had had any contact with my ex-business partner. He replied, "Gladly, no. I have not heard from that Judas in a number of years." He also mentioned that the district attorney in my case had retired, though not from advanced age. To quote him: "She was such a sweet Lady. *NOT!*" His emphasis. A little levity always helps to raise the spirit.

I am fortunate to have gained a friend and not just a paid legal counsel.

Matthew 23:26. *"Blind Pharisee! First clean the inside of the cup and dish, and then the outside also will be clean."*

Friday, September 23, 1994
8:30 a.m.

Zzzzzz... Bang! What the...? It is that damn scissors lift. The porters thought it would be funny to ram it into my bunk while I was sleeping. I guess it is my cue to get up and get out of here. Breathing in who-knows-what is not my idea of a healthy way to spend my day. With luck, they will finish today.

11:15 a.m.

"Watson, out of the gym, report to the Program Office," the yard speaker announced. That is a curiosity.

11:30 a.m.

My organizational skills were missed. The originals for the yard crew inventory tool sheets were missing. I explained where I had always kept them, but seeing the re-organization of the shelves since my departure, those files have either been thrown away or permanently misplaced. Faded copies still exist but they are in such poor condition that a new original will have to be made. The dreaded look on Rick's face at that prospect showed how hopeful he was that I would somehow locate the originals that took me hours to type. "Good luck," I said with sincerity. Rick sighed.

3:00 p.m.

I am in the gym. The door to the back dock, which is adjacent to the chow hall, has been opened to help in airing out the gym of the free-floating dust particles. A free-person contractor pushing a wheelbarrow full of wet insulation passed by the door on his way to a dumpster. He is working on cleaning and repairing the chow hall. On his trip back to the chow hall I asked him how long until it will be ready for use. He replied, "About three months." That is remarkably quick. Despite the longer walk in the heat and rain, I prefer eating in the vocations dining hall. It is smaller, quieter, and the food is served hot. The last reason is a real luxury.

1 Corinthians 8:8. *But food does not bring us near to God; we are no worse if we do not eat, and not better if we do.*

✝ ✝ ✝

Saturday, September 24, 1994
8:00 a.m.

Whoosh! This week flew by and I believe I can safely say that it was a good week. Is that even possible? Or politically correct to say? To use the word good while *in* prison? My inner spirit has been climbing the feel-good ladder, step-by-step, each day and I am pleased to give praise to God for the much needed break in my constant battle against depression.

10:00 a.m.

I spoke to my mother on the telephone. Both she and Walt are doing well in their mobile home park venture, but at the same time, they are struggling with all the refurbishing that each neglected unit requires. I pray with all my heart that God will bless them with an adequate windfall so they can get over the financial hump of empty units while each are being repaired.

As children I believe we all want to help our parents any way we can. Not only because they have done so much for us, but because we, I, love them and want to honor them.

For the time being my prayers will have to be sufficient. C'mon, God, kick with some prosperity blessings.

5:00 p.m.

The pass-around female sergeant was supervising in the chow hall tonight. I noticed an interesting trait of hers. She would not, or was unable to maintain eye contact with the inmates or other staff when talking to them. Is it fear? Is it inadequacy? How about insecurity? I am not a body language expert but it is a thought-provoking observation.

In life, and especially in this setting, I believe it is important to never show weakness. Stare down your monster. Show no fear.

8:00 p.m.

Volleyball was fair with a comfortable temperature of 85 degrees. Above, there was a heavy cloud cover, and below, swirling around us was a cooling breeze. I was hoping for high-quality games because one of our 'truck' players paroled today, but another one materialized to take his unskilled place. What? Did we look like we were having too much fun? Drip-drop.

Drip-drop?

Rain? Rain.

I dig the rain. It is difficult for me to see through water-streaked glasses but I still enjoy the rain's wet refreshment. To breathe in deeply, smelling the cleansed air, sans pollen, is delicious. Unfortunately, the concrete slab we play on becomes soap slippery, so we agreed to postpone our games until another, dryer, safer time.

Fall rains—love 'em.

Romans 15:13. *May the God of hope fill you with all joy and peace as you trust Him, so that you may overflow with hope by the power of the Holy Spirit.*

✠ ✠ ✠

Sunday, September 25, 1994
1:15, 2:22, 3:50, 4:11, 5:28 a.m.

Very disturbing! I kept waking from nightmares of killer elephants rampaging through my high school town of Yuba City, California. With tears in my eyes I had to shoot in an attempt to kill them to save my school mates, but they would not die. The bullets were absorbed into the huge bodies with no affect.

In my entire life, no demon, and no menacing animal, no evil person have I ever been able to vanquish (kill) in my dreams. Now there is one for the psychoanalyst. Where did the nightmare come from? Last night on the evening news there was film footage of an out-of-control elephant in Hawaii stomping its handler to death. That, plus watching the bloody shooting and killing of the elephant by the police on the tropical street traumatized me more than I realized.

Brrr…what an unnerving way to start my day.

8:45 a.m.

I was sitting on my bunk writing when Dusty summoned me to his bunk area. Robert was standing there with him. Robert informed me that he has been re-assigned to work in the Program Office. He asked me if I would like for him to recommend me for his old position, the clerk's position in the kitchen. I thanked Robert but declined. I am satisfied with the job I presently have and I could not be paid enough to return to a cloistered position such as the kitchen clerk's would be.

Those are the first words in many months that Robert and I have exchanged since his book plagiarism and attempt to defraud Aaron and his wife. It was strange, but maybe, since Robert seems unable to directly ask for forgiveness, that this was his way of doing so. I will have to pray and ask for Christ's guidance.

11:15 a.m.

That was the face of an unhappy man. I watched as Rick Stevens pushed a laundry cart filled with his property into the gym. "The fix wasn't in," he woefully stated. I smiled, happy to have him join us, and replied that living in the cube has several advantages to cell living. Rick eyed me suspiciously. It will take Rick a couple of restless nights to get used to having so many people around him at all times, but he will adapt. We all do. There is simply no other positive choice.

9:00 p.m.

20/20 news program was doing a segment on American businessmen in Russia and the problems they are having with the Russian mafia. As I am privy to the fact that Robert is writing a story about the Russian mafia, I used this as my opening. I walked to Robert's bunk and informed him about the topic of the *20/20* program. He was genuinely pleased. The proverbial ice appears to be breaking. A good tit for a thoughtful tat. I will always be wary of his writing credibility but I can accept him for who he is—a human being.

Christ loves Robert. I am supposed to, too.

1 Peter 3:8-9. *Finally, all of you, live in harmony with one another; be sympathetic, love as brothers, be compassionate and humble. Do not repay evil with evil or insult with insult, but with blessing, because to this you were called so that you may inherit a blessing.*

✟ ✟ ✟

Monday, September 26, 1994
11:15 a.m.

A peaceful morning shattered by knuckles against cheek bone. The unnerving sound reminds me of hitting a flopping fish against the railing of a bass boat. Three Hispanics were quietly playing Monopoly. Without any warning they stood up and began pummeling each other. There were no shouts, no screams containing vulgarities, and no posturing. Simple battle royal.

No Alarm? No code 3?

From behind the combatants, Officer Blakewood, Marine extraordinaire, baton drawn to strike, ordered them to the ground. The brawlers continued, falling against a nearby bunk. Its occupant scrambled out of the way. Again, Blakewood bellowed his order. Having fallen to the ground and exhausted, they complied. Still no alarm. None needed. All was under control.

"You move and you get the stick," shouted Blakewood. I would remain still if I were them.

On the officers' station, Officer Mann telephoned for escort officers. These battling boys will now be confined to cells, likely in the hole. Bummer, now I will have to do paperwork moving these men out and others in. Bunks do not stay empty in the cube. I do not mind as it is my job, but what I do mind is these men, who still cannot control themselves, will be released back into society long before me. Even worse, they will re-offend, leaving more victims in their wake.

4:00 p.m.

Mail? Yes and no. Junk mail. I have to giggle even though it is less than manly. Though I am buried deep in the chasm of a penitentiary, junk mail still finds me. The packet I received contains teasers for hotel accommodations in the Sonora desert close to 12 world-class golf courses; scuba diving in the Bahamas; and snow skiing vacations in the mountains of Colorado. I suppose I should be pleased. I am not truly dead or too far gone into the abyss so long as my name remains on someone's mailing list.

7:00 p.m.

Oh for the love of a washing machine. I am tired of washing my jeans and shirts while taking a shower. The problem is the soap. Being naturally slippery, as I scrub the pants against the tile wall, the soap jumps out of my hand and skims across the floor.

Nope. I do not bend over to retrieve it. I always carry a spare as I have learned to think ahead. There are consequences both small and great if I do not focus on my actions and inactions.

I do miss that warm, soft feeling of comfy 501's right out of the dryer. Ooooh, feel that fit.

Romans 8:9. *You, however, are controlled not by the sinful nature but by the Spirit, if the Spirit of God lives in you. And if anyone does not have the Spirit of Christ, he does not belong to Christ.*

✞ ✞ ✞

Tuesday, September 27, 1994
8:15 a.m.

As I walked back into the gym after delivering bed moves to the Program Office, Officer Mann informed me that the lieutenant wanted to see me. I wondered what he wanted. It is like being called to the principal's office, only the consequences can be far worse. I cannot think of anything I have done wrong, but in this environment, conspiracies abound. Am I paranoid? No. I just do not like surprises.

9:30 a.m.

I am stunned, honored, and redeemed. Lieutenant Davenport has offered me my old job back in the Program Office. He said he had a long conversation with the program administrator and the program administrator admitted that he was wrong in relieving me of my duties over such a trivial indiscretion. They would like for me to consider returning. Wow. Praise God.

Also, after reviewing Robert's central file, and trying to find a new clerk among the inmates on the facility, no one was found to be qualified or acceptable. The lieutenant stated that he has been unable to get his work accomplished in a timely fashion due to the new clerk's organizational shortcomings.

I would like to believe my acknowledgment of making a mistake, a lapse in judgment, accepting responsibility in a positive manner, and not speaking ill of staff's dismissal of me helped my case. I could use the extra $12 a month, but, yes, there is a but. I enjoy my assignment in the gym and the staff there took me in, so to speak, when I was cast out. I do not believe it would be right to abandon them. I believe in loyalty. Most of all there is little stress working for the officers in the cube. That by itself is a major plus.

I asked the lieutenant when he was planning to retire. "In December," was his reply. Hmm...another boss. An unknown element. "Can I think it over, pray on it today, and then give you my answer tomorrow?" I asked. He said, "That will be fine."

Decisions. Decisions. This is unreal. Time to pray.

7:00 p.m.

I spoke with my father on the telephone. He said that Hanna's wedding was beautiful but too old fashioned for him. Very curious. Apparently the pastor made comments indicating the wife is to obey her husband and the husband is to be the spiritual head of the family. What is wrong with that? Maybe the pastor needed to elaborate the point by saying that the wife is to obey the husband, and the husband is to be as Christ was for the church, a servant. Christ came to serve and ultimately gave up his fleshly life for us and the church. This is the responsibility of a man, a husband toward his wife. To sacrifice for her.

They are heavy words but old fashioned? I think not, though they have apparently gone out of style. Could that be why there are so many divorces?

I say, good for you Hanna, and good for your husband Paul. Live as God intended and be happy. God is forever and I will pray that your marriage will be, too.

Psalm 35:27. *May those who delight in my vindication shout for joy and gladness; may they always say, "The Lord be exalted, who delights in the well-being of his servant."*

✛ ✛ ✛

Wednesday, September 28, 1994
8:10 a.m.

As I waited outside the lieutenant's office to give him my answer, the program administer exited his office and greeted me with a warm, "Good morning." Interesting! Likewise, Donna, who has been warm and cold to me since my departure gave me a welcoming smile and a good-to-see-you, "Hello." The lieutenant waved me in.

I graciously declined the job offer.

Lieutenant Davenport was visibly and verbally disappointed. He was hoping that I would retake the helm to ease the office back into smooth waters. Yes, I am paraphrasing. I sincerely thanked him for the offer and for confronting the program administrator on my behalf. I also wished him a wonderful upcoming retirement and praised him for his respectful and humanistic attitude toward inmates. His leadership style has become rarer as the old guard retires. He will be dearly missed.

Why did I decide against accepting the position? Simple! Faith in myself and in God. I want to become a screenwriter and the office position would take up too much time, energy, and my stress level would rise again. My position as gym clerk may not be as prestigious in the eyes of other inmates, or as financially rewarding, but my creative time between inmate intakes has a value far beyond money and perceived power. Besides, I have been redeemed by their offer, and I do not need to prove my worth.

My true craft is in creative writing, and dedication to it will garner excellence, prosperity, and in the end, freedom. Maybe not physical freedom, but mental freedom.

Officer Mann and the other gym officers were shocked and pleased that I turned down the offer.

12:00 Noon

BOOM! BOOM! BOOM! Thunder and lightning on an eardrum shattering scale. The lights in the gym are flickering as the rain bounces off the pavement to meet other wet projectiles. Can you dig it?! The awesome power of nature. Or, is it a perfect game being bowled by the cloud dwellers? This is the first significant rain of the season and it sends electrified chills up and down my spine. The air has a musty smell that at least for the moment overrides the stink from the urinals. The ground steams as it sucks up the moist elixir. The small black birds dance about as they take their first bath of the winter season. The departure of summer is given a fine fanfare of electric strobe lights and stomping of giants. It is a magnificent show.

10:00 p.m.

I got up from my bunk for a final trip of the evening to the rest room. I am in a surreal, giddy mood. Earlier I succumbed to the comic allure of the mind-numbing boob tube. What the heck. I deserve a laugh or two, maybe even three, and the sitcoms were in great form. As I returned from the fly-bombardier sector I observed half a dozen men, Asian-squatting, in the far corner of the gym. They were passing around Buglar-brand rollies.

This is a game the inmates and staff play in this No Smoking housing unit. The staff pretends not to know the gym is on fire and the inmates pretend they are getting away with something. It is hide and not seek by the adults in this bizarre world of Corrections.

10:10 p.m.

Ah...fresh sheets to comfort touch-starved flesh; the swoosh of air from the vent over my head; and I imagine I am sailing the deep blue South Pacific Seas. Another day has ended. Another prayer of thanks. More praise for a life which, measured good against evil, is better than the district attorney would prefer. More prayers for a life I can only hope for on the far side of the barbed wire and thick walls. I closed my eyes as consciousness dissolves and I am swallowed by blackness that tonight hides no monsters.

Proverbs 14:23. *All hard work brings a profit, but mere talk leads only to poverty.*

☦ ☦ ☦

Thursday, September 29, 1994
8:00 a.m.

A blissful morning. No bed moves into the cube or among its residents. Is everyone happy with their bunkie? I doubt it, but for the moment no one has requested to move. I am relaxing with my last tea bag. Three more weeks until I can go to the canteen. Groan. Unlike most inmates, I never got into the habit of drinking 'mud,' though I am surprised by the large number of inmates who do drink tea. There must be a bit of European left in us or maybe it's that we wish we were in jolly ol' England instead of in prison.

Wolf and the third watch gym clerk, Carpenter, are bitchin' about snitches. "Why do they rat us out for smoking, tattooing, making pruno, or whatever? Why don't they mind their own business? Do the rats feel a sense of power? Staff doesn't like 'em and it's a dangerous game they're playing. They might get socked-up."

My thoughts on snitches. Well, I believe God wants us to concentrate on ourselves and worry less about what others are doing. It is that speck-plank-eye thing.

4:00 p.m.

Legal mail. I received from the Ventura Superior Court clerk several reports, letters of support and condemnation, and court documents that I had requested as I was missing them from my files. I skipped the boring reports and got right to the letters. The condemning ones, a total of two, were interesting as they were not from my victims but from their family members in Argentina. They did not know me and did not know of the drug business the victims were involved in. I tossed them aside. The good ones, 23 to be exact, touched me deeply; especially the one from Pastor Peters.

I had met Pastor Peters while out on bail and living with Angela in San Diego. Angela had called a telephone number on a church flier that was placed on our apartment door. I had given my life to Jesus while in county jail, but I was still not thrilled by having a visit from a minister. For one, we were living together out of marriage, and two, facing the upcoming murder trial was all I could handle.

Then Pastor Peters arrived. There was no judgment on our living situation and he did not flinch upon hearing of my trial. Needless to say,

Angela and I began attending his church. And though we remained living together, we ceased having sex. Talk about the Spirit overcoming the flesh, because Angela and I were a passionate pair, but we wanted to please God more than ourselves.

Several months later, my ex-business partner, after providing evidence to a police investigator, became paranoid and began to fear for his safety. He told the police of his fear and the court ordered my bail be increased to a million dollars. Not being able to come anywhere close to paying the increase, the court gave me three days to turn myself in *again*.

I telephoned Pastor Peters and asked if I could be baptized before returning to jail. It was bad timing. The church baptismal was under renovation but he asked me to call him back in a couple hours. That evening he informed me that an elderly couple in his congregation had offered their swimming pool. I accepted.

Under twinkling stars and witnessed by Angela, Pastor Peters and his wife, and the gracious couple who opened their home to strangers, I was baptized. I saw lights. I felt the spiritual rush. I was filled with His strength.

I will never forget that night or Pastor Peter's going the extra mile for me. It has been six years and far too long since I have written to him. The Spirit is moving me and I will answer. There have been plenty of changes to report but thankfully the constant remains—God.

Mark 1:10-11. *As Jesus was coming up out of the water, He saw heaven being torn open and the spirit descending on Him like a dove. And a voice came from heaven; "You are my Son, whom I love; with You I am well pleased."*

✞ ✞ ✞

Friday, September 30, 1994
9:30 a.m.

News Flash! End of the world. End of the world? Says who? A televangelist says so: "After decades of intensive Bible study I have concluded that Christ is coming back today and the end of the world has begun." I suppose I should pack my bags, and then cheer when I vanish in a twinkle of an eye, screwing up the 4:00 p.m. count. I will get right to stuffing my pillow case. NOT!

Jesus will come as a thief in the night. That is what *my* Bible studies have taught me. That is what I believe. So if He comes as a thief in the night, we will not know when that is. Sure, there will be signs foretelling his arrival, but as Christ Himself said, "Only the Father knows." So in my immodest opinion, relax, take it easy, but be prepared. Seek redemption through Christ; seek peace among your brothers and sisters; and live your life, regardless of what it may hold for you.

However, for me, it would be terrific if Jesus did come today because I would not have to go through another day in prison. Unfortunately, Jesus did say that we each should pay to Caesar what is Caesar's, and if in His eyes my debt is not paid, I may be here a while.

6:00 p.m.

Insensitivity and unprofessionalism. This irks me to no end. Every morning and evening after breakfast and dinner, a great number of inmates report to the Med-Call line at the Facility B clinic to receive their psychotropic medication. Yes, there are a lot mentally disturbed individuals in prison. Anyway, tonight, the officer who announced Med-Call thought he was a comedian as he did so in the following manner: "Listen up. All psychos, drug addicts, depressants, nut balls and pill-poppers; now is the time to trot out to the pill line. C'mon, mooo-ve along in an orderly catatonic state. Last call; the pretty colored pills wait."

It is bad enough that prison is used in place of mental hospitals, but labeling, and then deriving humor from a person's mental deficiencies is unnecessary. What a jerk.

8:00 p.m.

Revenge can be sweet when served with a cold volley ball. This evening Mr. This-Is-My-Workout-Bench stepped onto the court to join the opposing team. A crooked, slightly evil smile crossed my lips because this is my court. This is where I dominate. "Heads Up!" I shouted as the game began. It was 'D.T.' (designated target) time. My teammate set the ball perfectly for me. Spike. Pow! Pealed his cap. A ricochet off Bill's forehead. I can be very accurate with my spikes and it is all part of the game. I chuckled to myself.

Side out.

It was my turn to serve. Two steps, toss the ball into the air, a leap and—Thwack! Zooooom—a chest shot that left the word Spalding imprinted on Bill's skin. "Where're you going?" I called out as Mr. This-Is-My-Workout Bench left the court. "Is Bill quitting?" I asked a teammate.

Volleyball, it is a great game.

Romans 12:20-21. *On the contrary: "If your enemy is hungry, feed him; if he is thirsty, give him something to drink. In doing this, you will heap burning coals on his head." Do not be overcome by evil, but overcome evil with good.*

✞ ✞ ✞

Saturday, October 1, 1994
6:00 a.m.

Surprise. Surprise. I am still here and there has not been widespread vanishing of people (Christians) from all over the world. I will have to assume Jesus was not paying attention to the schedule the televangelist set for Him. Actually I am sure Jesus was paying close attention because teachers of the Word are held to a higher standard, so says The Book.

Well, as I am still here I suppose I should prepare for breakfast. The menu says waffles. More appropriately they should be called Frisbees.

So when are you coming, Jesus? I am really, really, tired of this place.

11:00 a.m.

Straining, grunting, and pulling on the pull-up bar. Exercising. Feeling good. Feeling Strong. Ouch! My right lat muscle. Did I strain something? I was pulling hard to get that last rep but it should not have hurt that much. Damn, this sucks. At least it was my last set. Hopefully taking an Ibuprofen and two days off I will be okay. God has always blessed me with a quick-healing body. Hopefully this blessing will continue.

3:00 p.m.

Bible fellowship. Chastisement. My Christian brethren did not believe my 'spikeful' behavior toward Bill was appropriate. In my defense, weak though it was, I said, "Hey, he was the one that almost got me shot. And besides, he did not know I purposefully spiked the volleyball at him." Okay, okay, God knew. Okay, Okay, that is not the way Jesus would have acted. Okay, Okay, I was wrong.

I hate being a Christian at times. It takes all the fun out of revenge.
Although, being a Christian also takes the bile out of hate, and makes
forgiveness easier and joyful. It is good to be chastised by caring friends.

4:00 p.m.

September has come and gone without a word, a letter, or a visit from
cousin Penny as she promised. So many promises un-kept; so many roads
paved with good intentions. I am not angry with her. I am only disappointed
because I miss her, her hugs and smiles, and each time hope is dashed it is
harder to brush the dust from my knees. Thankfully, Jesus is always here to
give me a hand back up. I have promised myself that I will never break my
word because I know how it feels to be overlooked and forgotten.
    It hurts.

2 Peter 2:1. *But there were also false prophets among the people, just as there*
will be false teachers among you. They will secretly introduce destructive
heresies, even denying the sovereign Lord who bought them—bringing swift
destruction on themselves.

✞ ✞ ✞

Sunday, October 2, 1994
8:00 a.m.

Discouragement. I spoke with my father. He received a letter from the
movie producer whom I had sent my latest script, *Pacific Moon*. The producer
did not like it. "Seen it. Been done. The female lead was too demure for the
90's," was his reply. Okay, it was constructive criticism which I accept, but
she was a Filipino virgin of strict Catholic upbringing, not a California trollop.
I am bummed but I will not let one rejection cause me to quit. I have put too,
too, too, too many hours of brain-racking into my writing to stop because of his
or anyone's rejection. I am sure there will be many more. I will also hang
onto the closing words of the producer which were, "And then again, I could
be all wrong.   This is just my opinion." Needless to say, he is not going to
push the script to the studio he is affiliated with.
    Besides that bit of news, my father is alone this week because JoAnne
is in Colorado. JoAnne's aunt is dying and JoAnne has taken her mother to
visit her. My father felt pangs of loneliness and was thinking of how I must

feel. It was a nice empathic thought, but to try to contrast his momentary feelings of loneliness to my years of, "Hello is anyone there?' is like placing a single grain of salt on the tip of the tongue, compared to an overflowing gulp of curdled milk that is sour and chunk-filled. No comparison, although I do appreciate my father's thoughts, and I do know he does everything in his power to ease my isolation.

12:00 Noon

Encouragement. I spoke with my mother. She believes as I do, but it is helpful to hear, that God would not have blessed me with stories if they were not meant to be shared. I do hope this is His will. In addition to sharing my stories, I would enjoy helping those in need, family and friends, with the proceeds from a sale of a script, and of course to have a small nest egg available when I am released—if I am ever released.

Well, a writer writes and I need to and must continue. My friends and family believe in me, and I in God, so I will someday, some way, and some-how succeed.

10:00 p.m.

Plodding along in my plastic slippers to the urinals before bed revealed a friend in trouble. Darryl, who is allergic to sulfur, was vomiting uncontrollably, and close to passing into unconsciousness due to inmates inconsiderately smoking cigarettes around him. Another friend, Giles, was by Darryl's side so I was off to notify the first watch officer. Surprisingly and compassionately the officer took Darryl's illness seriously. The officer telephoned medical staff, and then after waiting 15 minutes, decided to escort Darryl to the infirmary himself.

Illness, and the inattention medical personnel give to it is at a crisis level. I cannot compare how inmates are treated compared to others around the country, or how much money is spent on care, but whatever it is, the usual lackadaisical attitude to what appears to staff to be inmates that are hypochondriacs only magnifies the problem. Is it too difficult or onerous to examine an ailing man before assuming he is faking? What does that cost except a little time?

I thanked and praised the officer for helping a man in need. This officer was a small light, a ray of human kindness, and truly a man touched by Christ's Spirit of compassion.

I will sleep easier knowing Darryl is at least under medical observation.

Colossians 1:29. *To this end I labor, struggling with all His energy, which so powerfully works in me.*

✝ ✝ ✝

Monday, October 3, 1994
2:00 p.m.

Bored...Bored...Bored... The library is closed. No books. Bored... Bored... Bored... I keep looking into my locker for something to do—nothing interests me. I am not tired so I do not feel like taking a nap. Open. Close. Open. Close. It is not a refrigerator. It is a locker. There is nothing in it to eat and nothing to do. My television calls but I refuse to watch the crappy talk shows that come on at this hour and get caught up in their immoral discussion of, "Who's my baby's daddy?" I do not want to write letters because at the moment I have nothing positive to say. I do not feel like writing anything creative as my bored mind is a mush of blah; nothing exciting. No stimulation. God, I am so bored.

Thank you, Lord, for the boredom.

4:00 p.m.

Mail. A postcard. Southern California Ed sent me a "Thinking of you," note on a postcard that pictures two extremely endowed ladies wearing skimpy-skimpy swim suits and cavorting on a white sand beach. Love it. Hate it. I am grateful to be remembered, and the ladies are lovely, but oh how I miss *it; it* being life among the free and happy. I am slipping over the dark edge again. I need a hug. Anyone? Anyone?

6:00 p.m.

I dined with *Chicken* George this evening. That man can pick bones so clean that a vulture would starve. It is obvious that his nickname is derived from his preferred entrée and not from any deficiencies in bravery. George was for many years of his life a powerful leader of the Mexican gang called the Texas Syndicate. Now in his mid-fifties with snow-capped hair, and after dreaming of his own assassination, George has become a Christian with a sense of humor that leaves every listener with a bellyache from deep, rolling laughter.

Due to the dream, George was able to thwart the assassination attempt, and with Jesus' Spirit with him, he was able to leave his gang behind to serve as an example of Christ's power to change lives.

Smacking his lips and laughing infectiously, "Oh, so finger-licking good." George told me that when he dies he wants to be buried under a chicken coop in homage to the birds that brought him so much tasty pleasure during his lifetime.

As delicately as I could say the words, I replied, "But won't the chickens crap all over you?" "Yep," he said, and with a knowing smile. "It's just a vessel. Don't matter what's on the outside. It's my insides that matter to God. Besides, maybe my body will be fed on by worms, growing fat for the next generation of chickens to enjoy. It's only fair."

What a character that *Chicken* George is and what a new creature in Christ he has become.

How much time does *Chicken* George have left to serve? He has served 22 years and has 19 more until he sits before a parole board. Will he make it? If it is God's will.

8:00 p.m.

I gave up again. I walked away between volleys. All I wanted was a couple of pleasant games of volleyball to end the day. But no, the *Children of the Corn* started quarreling again.

Face down on my bunk I rupture the eardrum of my plastic pillow as I scream with frustration for a lover's ear. I do not want sex. I want her to listen to me. I want her to care about me; to cry with me, to hold me, to love me.

9:00 p.m.

God, help me.

2 Samuel 22:28-29. *You save the humble, but your eyes are on the haughty to bring them low. You are my lamp, O Lord; the Lord turns my darkness into light.*

✝ ✝ ✝

Tuesday, October 4, 1994
8:00 a.m.

There is a super-secret staff meeting in progress. No inmates have been allowed to go to their work assignments. No inmates are on the recreation yard. There is no inmate movement, period. If I were a conspiratorial, woe-is-me, thinking kind of guy I would have to believe that us inmates are in for it again. What new rule, regulation, or policy has been created and is being explained to staff to further repress us? Only time will tell.

10:00 a.m.

The meeting is over and staff is not talking. Not a good indication of things to come because usually staff is eager to share what goes on in their super-secret meetings.

10:15 a.m.

We are back to normal program with inmates off to work, out to the yard, and moving into the gym. And, within the gym, staff has decided to move Rob, the freeway killer's assistant, from the back corner to up front so he can be under their protective eyes. The 'Good Woods' (tough white boys), have been putting out their cigarettes on Rob's bunk and threatening him.

First off, there should be no smoking in the building, and second, we are back to the speck-plank-eye thing. No one is here for kicking kittens. If *they* do not like someone's crime, oh well, get over it, and set an example of how to act. They should not play judge and executioner just because they can gang up on someone. They should remember that there will always be someone bigger, stronger, tougher, and more dangerous.

How do they want to be judged?

11:30 a.m.

Look at the wall of rain and hear that rumbling thunder. Flicker goes the lights. Will they go out? This is the second heavy downpour of the season. I love it. I have nice snuggle memories that were created in front of a crackling fireplace with a special lady when I was attending college in Chico, California. This was before I met and fell head over heels for Angela. I can still smell her hair. It was scented with essence of lavender and its silkiness would tickle my skin. Ho-boy. Living on memories is not only pathetic but it is like trying to gain weight solely by the aroma of a candy bar.

2:45 p.m.

It is still raining buckets and barrels. How much water can be carried by an ocean of clouds? There will be no exercising today. It is probably for the best because there is still a twinge in the muscles I strained. Another day off won't hurt, and it will help with the healing.

3:30 p.m.

Announcement: "Per the watch commander there will be no night yard." What a bunch of weenies. Are they afraid the lights will go out? Probably. Or, is it that yard staff does not want to stand in the rain watching the die-hards walk the track and exercise? Hmm? It's a coin toss.

10:00 p.m.

I am feeling a touch better tonight. For some people, if they are feeling down and blue, rain makes it worse for them. For me, the rain is a release for my emotions as well as being uplifting. Each drop is an angel tear for me. Believing that God cares enough to have His angels cry for me lifts my spirit and fills my well of hope. Sure, it may be egotistical, illogical, and ignores the cycle of evaporation and precipitation, but it does not change the fact that God loves me and I feel better
Thank you, Lord, and good night.

1 Timothy 1:16. *But for that very reason I was shown mercy so that in me, the worst of sinners, Christ Jesus might display His unlimited patience as an example for those who would believe in Him and receive eternal life.*

✝ ✝ ✝

Wednesday, October 5, 1994
7:00 a.m.

No rain. No booming bowling balls or stomping giants. The sky is scattered with long wisps of clouds with their under-bellies on fire from the rising sun. Beautiful, Lord, beautiful. My walk to and from breakfast, breathing freshly washed, crisp air made up for the cold scrambled eggs and untoasted toast.

10:15 a.m.

Darryl returned from the infirmary. I was beginning to wonder how he was fairing. Since his name had not shown up on the DMS (Daily Movement Sheet) going to an outside hospital, or a worse place, I was at a loss for information.

Darryl thanked me for my part in his rescue, and shared his treatment of a shot, an oxygen mask, and being prescribed an inhaler. Darryl asked medical staff if he could be reassigned to a cell for medical reasons; i.e. his cell would be smoke free. The doctor's reply was: "The gym *is* a no smoking building."

5:00 p.m.

On my way back from evening chow I stopped by the Program Office to procure forms that several inmates had requested and that we were out of in the gym. When I returned with them, the inmates were appreciative. It is a terrific feeling to be able to assist others who cannot, or do not have access to, or know how to locate what they are seeking. It was a simple gesture requiring only a small effort but the rewards were immense, both from the inmates who thanked me profusely, and from God who blesses good work.

8:30 p.m.

A new addition to the gym; a very inconsiderate inmate was slapping and banging his hand on the steel table as he was playing an interminably long game of dominoes. Apparently he is under the impression that there is no one else in the gym. Finally, after too, too many bangs that echoed back and forth across this giant cube, I got off my bunk and shouted at the top of my lungs to "Knock it the fu-- off." Everyone in the gym stopped and looked in my direction, including the officers perched atop their station, which the shout was actually intended for. If staff did their job and kept the jerk-offs in line, inmates would not have to get in each other's faces.

The result? The inconsiderate inmate stopped his annoying pounding. I truly despise rude and inconsiderate people.

Acts 20:35. *"In everything I did, I showed you that by this kind of hard work we must help the weak, remembering the words the Lord Jesus himself said: "It is more blessed to give than to receive."*

✟ ✟ ✟

Thursday, October 6, 1994
8:00 a.m.

Another round of telephone fussing. "If you haven't signed up, you cannot use it, and they will be turned off," spouts the relief officer who is not a regular, but filling in for one of our full-time staff who is on vacation.

In the gym there are hours that go by where the telephones are not being used, especially in the morning when the majority of gym inmates are at their work assignments. If no one is using the telephones, it is a good time to have an unhurried, not limited to 15 minutes, quiet conversation with a family member or friend.

A common sense thought is that the administration should encourage telephone usage because they receive a kickback from the telephone company. Oops. My mistake. It is called a user fee for granting the contract to install telephone service for the inmates' usage. You see, we have to call collect, the most expensive way, and we are not given a choice of long distance providers. I believe it is called a monopoly. It is also called against the law unless you are the law.

I may be frustrated at the moment, but in several weeks this relief officer will be gone, and we will return to 'things as usual.' I must remind myself to take several deep breaths and use a small amount of patience when I see a resource being underutilized, or in this case - wasted.

3:00 p.m.

Coleman has had a rough day at work. He is the lead inmate plumber for the prison. He told me that he is not in the mood to work out this afternoon, but I convinced him it would be good for him. To exercise the body; to speed up the heart; to increase blood circulation to the brain relieves stress, and will allow a person to better deal with any and all situations.

Coleman's problem? A childish co-worker believes he is not getting as many perks as Coleman. Therefore, this co-worker is going to snitch-off his boss, the free man plumber, for bringing in personal equipment for the apprentices to learn on and to fix. I do not see how this antagonistic action is going to get him more perks.

Feelings of envy built on feelings of jealousy and lack of self-worth lead to destruction. Rise up, man. Seek God's wonderful blessings and know how valuable you are, even if presently you are not as high on the perk ladder as you think you should be. Rise up!

What are the perks that Coleman is receiving? The use of the boss' microwave and coffee from a coffee maker that uses grounds, not instant.

So sad. So petty.

9:45 p.m.

Chief, who works in the kitchen, asked if I was going to chow in the morning. He tells me, "It will be hash (from a can – the good kind), an egg, and fried potatoes." Usually, Friday's breakfast consists of dried cake and soupy oatmeal so I sleep in as it is my Saturday. Friendship, thinking of others, and care; these simple things or lack of can bring people together or separate them.

Thanks, *Chief,* for letting me know of the change.

Thanks, God, for friends.

1 Timothy 6:4-5b. *He is conceited and understands nothing. He has an unhealthy interest in controversies and quarrels about words that result in envy, strife, malicious talk, evil suspicions and constant friction between men of corrupt minds.*

✝ ✝ ✝

Friday, October 7, 1994
10:00 a.m.

I browsed through a smut magazine this morning. Yeow-za! There sure are beautiful women out there. However, with the turn of each page, the smiling faces looking at me and contorted bodies enticing me was more torture than it was pleasurable. It was like living next door to a chocolate factory and only being allowed to smell the sweet delights. Having tasted the real McCoy, a photograph of a nameless woman is a poor substitute. I would rather be surfing.

4:00 p.m.

No mail. Bummer.

7:00 p.m.

I am either a sucker for punishment or I am a hopeful idiot. Several of the volleyball players asked if I would come out and play tonight. I am not up to it; I do not want to...but okay. I am dreading the likelihood of arguments.

9:00 p.m.

Count time. Officer Bartels stands by my bunk while Officer King walks the row counting inmates. I started to laugh inside as I almost said, "Officer Bartels, could you bring me a glass of water?" I felt like a child being checked on by an evil orphanage ward matron. Count time: a serious act of juvenile proportions. At least that is how it makes me feel.

Come to think of it, I am thirsty. Ha ha.

Romans 1:24. *Therefore God gave them over in the sinful desires of their hearts to sexual impurity for the degrading of their bodies with one another.*

✟ ✟ ✟

Saturday, October 8, 1994
5:00 a.m.

Every night after I have prayed with extra earnest for God to get me out of prison, I have had a nightmare in which my ex-partner plays a role. In the dream I am out on parole and he either sets me up or lies to the police to get me re-incarcerated. This makes me wonder if God is trying to tell me something. Maybe God is keeping me safe *imprisoned* until Marc is no longer a threat to my freedom. They are terrible dreams of helpless panic filled with stress that makes my waking a mixture of relief and dread.

3:00 p.m.

Alarms! Code 3. A fight in the yard. A black and a Hispanic. The Hispanic appears to be okay but his adversary wearing the white tee shirt is covered in the sacrificial red of punch. Not a fist punch but a Cool-Aid punch. Thankfully, this is a case of looking worse than it is. Code 4. Resume normal program.

Our Bible fellowship of seven continued after the interruption. We prayed for Dusty's brother-in-law who has cancer and is slipping. He has fought the good fight, but the treatments are not working and the disease is taking its toll. In situations like this, we pray for recovery, but also if it is his time to return to God that God take him quickly without further suffering.

As a Christian, I look forward to the death of my flesh because it is the reuniting of my spirit with my Father, Almighty God.

Besides our prayers for Dusty's brother-in-law, the majority of our fellowship time was taken up with condolences for Ron and prayers for his son, Joel. Joel remained steadfast in his claim of innocence, refusing to plead guilty to a manslaughter charge for the death of his girlfriend's child, so he was put on trial. Ron found out Thursday night that Joel was convicted of 2nd degree murder.

Sentencing will be in 30 days. Sadly, the only term the judge can give Joel is 15-years to life. Ron, of course, is devastated. As a father he blames himself, though rationally he knows it is not his fault. That is what fathers do. They blame themselves because they love their children and wonder what they could have done differently. The answer is nothing.

Our advice to Ron is to love his son regardless.

That is what our Father in heaven does for us.

That is what my father on earth has done for me.

7:30 p.m.

Bunk chat. Howard tells me that while I was outside, the maintenance staff came into the gym to replace the large, half-moon shaped mirror that hangs over the showers. That is cool for the maintenance folks because they will receive extra pay for working Saturday. This three foot mirror is angled so that staff can observe the inmates taking showers from their station. There is *no* privacy in prison. Anyway, the mirror had fallen from its perch, shattering as it hit the floor, and came close to the inmates who were using the showers.

One of the maintenance workers, while watching the other two install the mirror, told Howard that it had been decided that they were not going to repair the loose and missing tiles in the shower area because it would cost too much and the gym is only temporary housing. Then he jokingly said, "The gym may remain open in perpetuity but each inmate housed here is only temporary."

As Howard shared this information with me we both shook our heads while laughing our *we're screwed again* laugh.

1 Corinthians 15:55-57. *"Where, O death is your victory? Where, O death is your sting?" The sting of death is sin, and the power of sin is the law. But thanks be to God! He gives us the victory through our Lord Jesus Christ.*

✝ ✝ ✝

Sunday, October 9, 1994
11:00 a.m.

Respect. Can you say this word? Do you understand its true meaning? Translated for the lay person it means consideration for others. But no, we have these jerk-offs who somehow have the idea that all the occupants in the gym want to play along with their concept that television football is a participation sport. Well, many do not, and it isn't. So...

SHUT THE HELL UP!

Shouting, yelling, and arguing to hear their own lame view of this play or that official call is sure a sign of "Hey, I'm a nobody. Won't someone pay attention to me?"

4:00 p.m.

I was walking toward the officer's station wearing my boxer shorts and tee shirt. Officer Wynon, female, asked where I was going. Well, I was going to read the menu that is posted on the bulletin board in front of the officers' station, but realizing my semi-clad muscular body was stirring her animal lust for me, I said, "To the restroom."

I had momentarily spaced the fact that inmates are not allowed to walk around in our living quarters wearing boxer shorts and a tee shirt. This is a men's prison, is it not? If female staff are offended or stirred by the sight of a man in his underwear, maybe these women should get a job in a women's prison. And, as a side thought based on a recent controversy, I do not believe female reporters should be allowed in men's locker rooms or visa-versa. Am I old fashioned? Or is it that I simply get irritated when a person who takes a job as a pooper scooper, complains because it's a crappy job.

I was flattered by her discomfort. It must mean I am still handsome. Ha ha . My ego still lives.

Genesis 2:25. *The man and his wife were both naked, and they felt no shame.*

✟ ✟ ✟

Monday, October 10, 1994
COLUMBUS DAY
8:00 a.m.

A day of celebration, at least in our grand ol' U.S. of A. Time tends to reveal all truths. Christopher Columbus is credited with discovering America. However, he never set foot on what became known as the United States, and by golly, it had already been discovered as there were people living here and in the land where Columbus planted Spain's flag. Do you remember the original inhabitants? Columbus named them Indians, despite the fact they all had names of their own. They had been here for thousands of years prior to Columbus' footfall. Even though we discredit Columbus for certain feats we do have to give him credit for two things. The first, he sailed into the unknown, which makes him an incredibly brave man, and second, on arriving, in God's name, he and his crew slew whole cultures with a metal sword for an instant death, and with erect penises for a slow, but assured demise through disease.

Should we celebrate or mourn Columbus' accomplishments? We should remember and learn. Exploration should be with a light foot, thinking always of how our entrance will upset a balance already in place.

7:00 p.m.

What's this? A new Public Broadcasting Station program called *Future Quest.* It was well produced and graphically eye appealing. The program contained interviews, thoughts, and speculations on what our future will be like. Hey, "The future is where we will spend the rest of our lives," was the thread that tied the guests together. There were many thought-provoking comments by physicists, authors of science fiction books, poets, comedians, and by men of New Age thinking. All the speakers were in agreement that what we choose (decide) to do right now will determine the direction of our future, individually, and as a whole.

I see several problems: where is God in all this future talk? What are our choices based on? How will we judge our decisions? The answer is obvious to me. For a successful future we need to judge everything we decide to do by God's perfection and Jesus' examples. This is the only choice for prudent avenues for all mankind to follow. Many people will say that we have difficult choices to make. Really? Is doing right difficult? Is following God's and man's laws difficult? I say, "No." Having to deal with the consequences of not obeying, that is difficult. Trust me.

I admit there will be situations that arise that could be described as a gray area where a decision doesn't fit neatly into a box designed by God or man. This is where prayer is important. For within prayer, the Spirit will direct the choice, and all will be made clear.

7:30 p.m.

Ring... Ring... Ring... Finally, someone answers. Steve? It was Mickie's husband. He and I had a slightly awkward but pleasant conversation at first, and then he turned the telephone over to Mickie. Steve sounded like a wonderful man with strong Christian views. He is the kind of man that Mickie needs and deserves and who I pray will work with her to create a happy home. I specifically wanted to begin a friendship-relationship with Steve so there would be no misconceptions regarding my intentions with Mickie, his wife. Mickie and I had a wonderful past, and now, together, Steve and Mickie have the potential for a wonderful future. I want to be an asset as a Christian friend, not a suspect for marital friction.

It sucks being honorable but it is what God demands. It is an easy choice to make.

Proverbs 6:22-23. *When you walk they will guide you; when you sleep, they will watch over you; when you wake, they will speak to you. For these commands are a lamp, this teaching is a light, and the corrections of discipline are the way of life.*

✛ ✛ ✛

Tuesday, October 11, 1994
6:30 a.m.

What a wonderful restful night's sleep. *Wolf* is again on his family visit so there are no shakes, rattles, squeaks, or rolls as I try to sleep. And, there was no conflicting aura from having another person that is not family sleeping in close proximity. My life's spirit was at peace; no static and no interruptions. I am not saying *Wolf* is static, but he is neither my wife nor a family member; therefore, we are not as one. We are two entities trying to slumber within 2 ½ feet of each other. It is not an easy thing to do. *Wolf* may be getting sex, but I am getting a peaceful sleep. I know I am getting the better part of the deal.

8:30 a.m.

Cleaning the officers' station; my weekly contribution to the housing inspection clean-up effort. Sweep, mop, and then straighten. It takes about 15 minutes and then I can resume relaxing, reading the magazine articles that my father occasionally sends me. The articles are about duck decoy carvers and waterfowl hunters of yesteryear. They are colorful characters that used what I would call weapons of mass destruction to put food on the tables. Hmm... There may be a story here.

God, I really appreciate this job assignment. Thank you for turning a mistake on my part into a blessing.

11:45 a.m.

Ron, who has draftsman skills, dropped off plans he drew for new volleyball poles. The poles would be bolted to the ground and utilize ¼ inch steel cable as net supports. Currently, the poles are cemented into tires that can be moved. This plan would also eliminate the ongoing problem with the nylon tension rope being stolen. I typed the memorandum requesting permission for the welding shop to construct and install it; a very proper looking proposal. This is what I call teamwork.

12:30 p.m.

I turned the pole proposal into the sergeant who turned it over to the lieutenant. Both thought the proposal was a reasonable request as it would better secure the poles and prevent theft. The lieutenant promised to discuss it with the program administrator, and then let me know of the decision to approve or deny. I hope it will be approved because with the cable controlling the net tension, it will keep the net from sagging.

There are so many positive and productive projects and activities that could be accomplished if inmates and staff were to work together and listen to each other.

Okay. Okay. Maybe I am a dreamer. But again, staff is not the enemy. Most of the time, the enemy is the man in the mirror.

10:00 p.m.

While saying my nightly prayers I received a chill throughout my body. I contemplated the fact that I am a convicted murderer. It is unsettling to realize that society has lumped me in with the Jeffrey Dahmer-Ted Bundy-Juan Corona types and, in their vengeance-filled frenzy, would probably enjoy watching a Pay-Preview special as I choked on gas pellets in San Quentin's chamber of death. Needless to say, my belief and hope for a miracle release any time soon is wavering. This looks to be a long haul chapter...a true life sentence.

Fortunately, underlining this icy horror is a peace in the belief and trust in Jesus. I smile as His warmth embraces me. I will be okay. Today was a good day. Thank you, Lord.

John 8:34-36. *Jesus replied, "I tell you the truth, everyone who sins is a slave to sin. Now a slave has no permanent place in the family, but a son belongs forever. So if the Son sets you free, you will be free indeed."*

✞ ✞ ✞

Wednesday, October 12, 1994
4:30 a.m.

Darryl transferred this morning. I was surprised when his name was called because I was unaware that he had been put up for transfer and he had not mentioned it. All things considered, Darryl needed a change of scenery...for his own safety. What I learned recently was that he had been filing 602 appeals concerning inmates smoking in the gym. That sounds reasonable especially with his severe allergies, but it is still telling on a fellow inmate. Telling was unwise enough but Darryl was also naming specific inmates in his appeals. Not smart at all and certainly not a life-sustaining activity. As a precursor to physical retaliation, inmates have been putting cigarette butts and ashes in Darrel's bed, some still lit. That is not an easy or healthy way to do time.

Darryl forgot that he is wearing blue and is an inmate. He is not wearing green as does the staff. Let them be the police. I do not advocate looking the other way when crime is committed (rules violated). In fact, it is our duty to join neighborhood watches and be another pair of eyes for the good of the neighborhood and to assist the police, but that is when we are free. While in prison, my duty is to set an example for others to follow; to show others, inmates and staff alike, the benefits of following the rules regardless of whether they are inconvenient. God has placed authority over us all and we are to obey. When we do, the blessings will follow.

By ratting out other inmates you only place yourself in danger, and by not living another day, how would you spread His word?

4:00 p.m.

Mail. Only junk mail and no word back from Nick Taylor. The absence of any correspondence to me or follow-up telephone calls to my father from him gives me the feeling that I was conned. I was raised to trust and respect my elders, but I was taken advantage of. I always thought that as one matures chronologically, they shed the games of childhood, and learned to speak with an honest tongue. I am learning that this is not always the case, and I need to discern the spirits of others with a more critical eye. I forgive Nick for his deception and for getting my hopes up because a liar always loses in the end.

I will start sending query letters including my script synopses to agencies again.

8:00 p.m.

Nights in the cube are becoming chilly with the winter season upon us, but also because the heaters have yet to be turned on. The Hispanic inmate in the bunk across from me, a 5'2" border brother (one who snuck into the country), who keeps to himself most of the time, is under his covers with a sheet wrapped around his head, Arabian Nights style, for warmth as he reads a Spanish novel.

Bingo! Brotherly love.

I dug into my locker for the extra knit beanie that I have been saving for no particular reason. I got up and asked, using broken Spanish, if he needed a beanie. His eyes lit up as if I had offered him an embrace from Selena. He may have received a warm head in the exchange but I received a warm heart. Thanks for the opportunity, Lord.

10:00 p.m.

This is very scary. I have a feeling of well-being as I hold back giggles caused by the comedy show that I am watching. I quickly look to the right and then to the left to be sure no one is watching me. If others, those who prescribe to the theory of "misery loves company," know I am in a good mood they will certainly want to spoil it. Shh...we'll keep this between me and God.

Isaiah 2:12, 22. *The Lord Almighty has a day in store for all the proud and lofty, for all that is exalted and they will be humbled. Stop trusting in man, who has but a breath in his nostrils. Of what account is he?*

✟ ✟ ✟

Thursday, October 13, 1994
9:30 a.m.

Seated at my desk, I have been busy typing memorandums, work orders for the lights that have gone out, and request for office supplies. Normally, because the majority of inmates are at work, in education classes, or have gone out to the recreation yard, the cube is quiet in the morning. Today is not a normal day. Two vocabulary-challenged, 20-year-olds who are caricature cut-outs of toothless trailer park punks who should be in school, have pulled an all-nighter, struggling to play Scrabble. I am not an aficionado of the game, but at least I have a reasonable grasp of commonly used words. After sitting through an hour and a half of their annoying arguments over this word or that word I interrupted their gutter banter to inform then that 'honker' *is* a word. It is a term for a goose or one that honks. Please, guys, read the dictionary.

Ignorance, too bad it's not painful. Well, actually it is for those who are subjected to it.

4:00 p.m.

Legal mail. The return address on the envelope reads: U.S. District Court. This is it. This is the answer that will determine where I will reside. The officer who processed my envelope ripped open the end and stared inside to determine whether or not contraband was within, and without care or concern to the magnitude of the contents, handed it to me while calling, "Next."

I walked out of the Program Office and returned to my bunk where I now sit. The brown envelope lay atop my blanket. It is only shredded wood and ink, but the symbols imprinted on its surface have supernatural power to bring elation or to crush dreams.

I reach for the envelope while saying a prayer, surprising myself in that I ask God for strength instead of freedom. Maturity? Prognosticating? Surrendering to God's will? I flipped over the cover page, skipped the introduction, and got to the meat. Quoting the judge: "This court adopts in full the findings and recommendations of the magistrate. This case is dismissed." Sigh, sigh.

The chaos of the cube has muted in my mind. All I allow myself to hear is the whoosh of air through the vent, as I cling to my illusion that it is wind off waves crashing on a sun-splashed beach.

Alarm! Code 3, gym. Two inmates are fighting over who will use the toilet next.

Reality. I will have to deal with it for a long, long time.

4:30 p.m. – 6:30 p.m.

"Stay on your bunks!" the officer shouts for the umpteenth time. This has been a long and tiresome count, not that I have anywhere to go; however, dinner will become an overcooked chicken patty tonight. How hard is it to count? One, two, three... Hurry up will-ya? I have to use the restroom.

8:30 p.m.

Not being in the mood to do anything, I gave in and watched a comedy on television. I did not find any humor in it. The sitcom was about funeral arrangements for a deceased parent. In fact it made me tremble and well-up with tears at the thought of losing my parents. They are my rock, my lifeline through strength, prayer, and encouragement. I need them as much as I need air to breathe. This is of course because God has blessed us with being close. I tell them that I love them as often as possible but it never seems to be adequate for what is in my heart.

My parents may express a difference of opinion, as long as I am in prison, and likely for as long as I live, I will feel my failure and shame. In my parents and God's eyes, I am not a failure because I have turned my life and daily activities over to Jesus, but I am ashamed because I squandered my freedom by attempting shortcuts that caused the loss of life of another human being. And though I ask for many things in Christ, there are only two things that I really desire equally. I want the pain I caused to be soothed and for my parents to still be living when I am finally set free. With today's judicial hammer nailing the door shut, I will be incarcerated for many years to come, so to have my parents still living if I am ever released would be a miracle.

In the *mean*time, which prison is, I will thank you and praise you, Lord, for keeping my parents safe, healthy, and prospering. I know you are all I am supposed to need, Lord, but I want my parents, too. I hope you can understand.

10:30 p.m.

Today has been difficult, to say the least, with a door slammed shut, but as I listen to my radio, Fleetwood Mac's *Don't Stop Thinking About Tomorrow* plays, encouraging me. I believe God will open a window some day and likely in a way that will surprise me. I will think about tomorrow while remembering my blessings of good health, family and friends.

I would say, "Good night," but I would be lying.

1 Peter 2:15. *For it is God's will that by doing good you should silence the ignorant talk of foolish men.*

✞ ✞ ✞

Friday, October 14, 1994
7:00 a.m.

I know I will be hungry later because skipping breakfast deprives me of a sack lunch, but regardless of what my head tells me of God's blessing to come, my heart is swimming in thick pudding. I have no energy to get up. Today is my Saturday so I choose to be sucked under. With prayer, hopefully dreamless sleep will come.

12:00 Noon

While crawling out from under my covers, the relief clerk, who cannot type a lick, came by my bunk. With a distressed look on his face, he informed me that I was needed earlier because seven, wow, count them, seven inmates were moved into the gym. Due to his lack of digital dexterity he panicked, messed up the roster and bed cards, and looked incompetent in front of our supervisors, the gym officers. Too bad - so sad. He should not try to be what he is not. I am not going to do extra work in order to cover for his deception. Maybe if he practiced typing during slow times, which are many, instead of playing cards, his skills would improve. Priorities.

3:30 p.m.

Exercising to drive away the pudding blues. Alarms! Code 3. Besides the interruption of having to sit in the dirt with a cold wind blowing dust into my eyes and reddening my checks, what I find puzzling about this alarm is that it is located in the laundry exchange room. There is no one in there at this time because the laundry room closed at 3:00 p.m. Phantom inmates? Ghostly staff? Only the shadow knows. Code 4. Resume normal program.

4:00 p.m.

Mail. A letter from Weila in the Philippines. She is a sweet girl who works incredibly hard trying to get out from under her deprived situation. She never knew her father; there is no supportive family; she has only the most basic of education; and therefore has to accept menial jobs that pay close to nothing. Even with all these odds against Weila, it does not deter her because she has a strong faith in God. She believes that if she continues to work hard she will be able to afford the schooling she needs to rise out of her poverty.

In comparison, we in this country have it easy. Too many Americans believe that having only one car or having only one color television is poverty. We have everything we need to succeed and yet we complain. I had everything and yet I was not satisfied. Shame! Shame!

6:30 p.m.

The California gubernatorial debate. Politicians bellowing their mantra:
"I'm tough on crime."
"I'm tough on crime."
Really? What does that prove, that they don't have the solutions to crime or how to change the lives of those incarcerated? Eight out of ten inmates in this *tough on crime* state fail and return to prison. I can only ask the question: Is tough on crime the solution?

Acts 11:23. *When he arrived and saw the evidence of the grace of God, he was glad and encouraged them all to remain true to the Lord with all their hearts.*

✛ ✛ ✛

Saturday, October 15, 1994
9:00 a.m.

Still, I am the trusting soul, or is stupid a better description because I am going to give *Ray-Ray* another chance at *trimming* my hair. Clearly, so there would be no miscommunication, I said, "Just a quarter inch, Ray. That's all. I do not want to look like a skinhead again."

9:20 a.m.

Buzzzzzzzz… Not too shabby. Okay, *Ray-Ray,* you have redeemed yourself in my barber shop eyes. What is the cost of a hair cut in prison? It's anywhere between two 20 cent Top Ramen soups and a pack of Camel cigarettes. For me? Nothing. *Ray-Ray* and I are friends, but I do occasionally tip him or any other barber I use with a candy bar. Sweet incentive helps to induce quality work…most of the time.

10:00 a.m.

I walked by *Wolf* as he is now seated in *Ray-Ray's* barber chair after returning from his family visit. *Ray-Ray's* trimmer is struggling because *Wolf* has requested that his long locks and wild beard be seared. *Wolf* is appearing before the parole board later this month, and due to the board commissioner's negative comments about his hair, it is being sacrificed. I wonder if this is necessary. Will *Wolf* be less dangerous with short hair? The suit may make the man, but really, isn't what is inside more important?

Let's face one fact. *Wolf* will never work for IBM. He is an auto mechanic and the length of his hair is less important than his wrenching abilities. Unfortunately, *Wolf* must play the parole board game and jump through hoops that free people could neither obtain nor stand for. Oh, I forgot, *Wolf* and the rest of us are animals in training. NOT! But because freedom is all important to each of us and our families, when the board says, "Jump," we'll ask, "How high?"

For the reader who may take from my less than sterling comments regarding the Board of Prison Terms that I hold it in contempt, I apologize. The members of the board are pillars of the community, and as such, have been recognized and appointed by the governor. As previously remarked on, the governor has stated on the record that no lifers will be paroled. The governor is the commissioners' boss who has secured for them an appointment that pays in excess of $100,000 per year plus expenses. Would you go against your boss's wishes and risk being removed, of losing this income? And as stated by at least one commissioner, he, too, would never let any lifer out.

I have no doubt that many hundreds of lifers who appear before the board are legitimately found unsuitable because their in-prison acts of violence warrant being denied parole. For this, the commissioners should be applauded for keeping the public safe. However, at the other end of the spectrum there are as many, if not more men and women who should be paroled, but for political reasons, they are not.

I don't blame the commissioners. I blame myself first for subjecting myself to their judgment; second, I blame Willie Horton, the east coast felon and poster child for politicians using crime and criminals to be elected; and third, I blame the politicians for failing to have the courage to lead their constituents with the truth.

The system has morphed from a procedure to return the rehabilitated back into society to one where very smart, creative, and self-interested wordsmiths have unashamedly locked the door on 99.8% of all who come knocking.

Thank God for Jesus' policy.

11:00 a.m.

The wind is blustery today. It is rushing hither and yonder with wild abandon. Swooossh. If I were out on the yard and opened my coat I could be lifted, Mr. Mary Poppins style up and over the fences. Stop it. I cannot think that way. Swooossh. Sparks flash and dance along the power pole lines. Pow! The lights are out in the gym. The only beam-size lights, narrow and inadequate, come from wall-mounted battery pack lights over the officers' station.

Hang on. Wait for it. Wait...the emergency generators will kick on...they will immediately kick on. "Hello?"

"Everyone sit on your bunks!" The officers shout from their station because the loud speakers do not work without power.

C'mon, generator, kick on. Who built this place?

12:00 Noon

Still waiting.

Why is it that when staff attempt politeness and ask certain inmates to sit on their bunks, these inmates say, "Sure," but continue to walk around, and or do whatever the hell they feel like? If they cannot or will not learn to follow the rules in prison, how can society expect them to do so when they are released? I can understand why inmates are viewed as cutting their own throats.

Damn it, there are exceptions. Compared to those running around while only passing unchanged through prison on two and three year stints; I sit obediently on my bunk while serving life. What is wrong with this picture? Again, maybe Joe Public should look at the individual man and not the conviction to determine who is released and when. It's a thought.

I also understand why staff gives up trying to be polite because from their point of view it does not work. I wish they, too, would look closer. Many inmates are seated on their bunks.

12:15 p.m.

Lights on! The power must have been restored because the emergency generators did not kick on.

4:30 p.m.

Count time. Blink…darkness. Out go the lights. Dinner will be late tonight.

6:15 p.m.

I am pleasantly surprised. We ate in the chow hall. The lights came on a half hour ago, but from past experience, because there was no power in the kitchen for a good portion of the day, I assumed we would be eating cold sandwiches on our bunks. Happily, it was three-time warmed burgers. They were cooking with gas. God bless that blue flame. Rubber burgers are always preferred to cardboard-tasting sandwiches; a better chew factor.

7:00 p.m.

No recreation yard tonight. Too windy. Too risky. Swoooossh.

1 Samuel 15:22-23. *But Samuel replied: "Does the Lord delight in burnt offerings and sacrifices as much as in obeying the voice of the Lord? To obey is better than sacrifice, and to heed is better than the fat of rams. For rebellion is like the sin of divination, and arrogance like the evil of idolatry. Because you have rejected the word of the Lord, He has rejected you as king."*

✟ ✟ ✟

Sunday, October 16, 1994
9:00 p.m.

Stillness both inside and out. No swooshing wind. No code 3's. No inmates shouting. No yard birds chirping. The entire day was in a quiet, contemplative, and reflective mood. It was the calm after the storm. This is a dangerous state for me because my mind could turn my emotions to either smiles or tears. Fearing the direction my wondering thoughts could take me I retreated to my center and found Christ's Spirit. I found that I am already filled with His love and comforted as I meditate on His soothing vision. I see Jesus both as a man who suffered, barefoot and hungry in the wilderness, and as ascended, brilliant in white robe among the clouds. I inhale deeply. It is the scorched dust of the desert Holy Land and the pure fragrance of sanctification that overwhelms my senses. Christ is here with me. I am safe, which allows both smiles and tears to take me, to release the pent-up stress from disappointing days past. I am being prepared to face another night on a too narrow bunk, and tomorrow, which will bring...

I'm not going to think about what tomorrow will bring. For now, I am simply going to inhale.

Psalm 23:1-4. *The Lord is my shepherd; I shall not be in want. He makes me lie down in green pastures, He leads me beside quiet waters, and He restores my soul. He guides me in paths of righteousness for His Name's sake. Even though I walk through the valley of the shadow of death, I will fear no evil, for You are with me; Your rod and Your staff, they comfort me.*

✝ ✝ ✝

Monday, October 17, 1994
6:45 a.m.

On the way to breakfast, Brian said I scared him because I looked too happy too early in the morning. I began to reply with something sarcastic, but knowing it was last night's close communion with God, I said, "Mornings are the worst for me, but because God made this day for me, I believe I have an obligation to do my best to meet it with a smile." Realizing I was serious, Brian thought about what I had said, and halfway through breakfast he looked at me and asked, "It ain't easy, is it?"

"Nope," I said with heaviness in my voice.

Taking another bite of his toast, Brian smiled and mumbled, "Thanks for being honest."

6:35 a.m.

On the walk back from breakfast, as I passed the Program Office, Lieutenant Davenport, who was standing in the doorway, motioned for me to come in. Stepping into his office I learned three things.

The Lieutenant informed me that the associate warden denied the proposal for modifying the volleyball poles. His reason was the proposed ¼ inch cable could be used as a whip to injure staff or other inmates.

Bummer.

The Lieutenant next informed me that he would be retiring next week instead of at the end of the year. He was taking the rest of the time off, using his built up vacation and personal days.

Bummer.

The Lieutenant then stood up and stretched his hand out to shake mine, which is the rarest of gestures because staff and inmates never touch each other, and then he stunned me by using my first name, saying, "Greg, I've witnessed the good in you. Cling to that and don't let this place grind you down. I believe you will make it out of here."

Wow!

3:00 p.m.

Scarcity breeds ingenuity. My $18 per month paycheck does not allow me to splurge on tennis shoes and I don't like to beg too often of family and friends so I attempt to make each pair last one year. I have been pleased with the fit and feel of my Nike's, but the cushion sole has taken a beating with the many miles I jog, and is disintegrating. A large hole has developed in the bottom of each shoe. This is not good with three months left until January, my one year goal. However, a solution was found with the help of an unnamed friend. I obtained through the inmate underground a tube of rubber caulking. I squeezed the caulking into the gap and "Tallyho!" I'm off and running again. Big smile.

6:45 p.m.

News Flash! The nightly news anchor spoke of heavy flooding and several deaths in south-eastern Texas. That is where my mother lives, though exactly where in south-eastern Texas; what towns were affected the anchor did not say. I cannot wait for the weekend call. I dialed. One ring... Two rings... Three rings... Come on. Answer. Please.

"Hello, mom?" Whew. The streams have been rising and their street is flooded but their house is elevated enough and should not be affected. Mom said, "We are soggy, but not swamped."

Thanks, God. Your protective hand is always there.

5:00 p.m.

Salmonella casserole. The menu states Salmon Casserole. If I was Joe Public I would be upset if inmates, convicted scumbags, were eating 'salmon' casserole. That is until I saw, got a whiff of, and was forced to eat it or go hungry. Then I would cheer, knowing that the punishment does fit the crime.

After vomiting, and then brushing my teeth, I fixed a Top Ramen soup - ol' reliable.

Jeremiah 21:12, 14. *O house of David, this is what the Lord says: "Administer justice every morning; rescue from the hand of his oppressor the one who has been robbed, or my wrath will break out and burn like fire because of the evil you have done—burn with no one to quench it. I will punish you as your deeds deserve, declares the Lord."*

✟ ✟ ✟

Tuesday, October 18, 1994
8:00 a.m.

"Yard call. If you're going to the yard, get out!" shouted Officer Lane while opening the gym door.

Standing in front of the gym during the unlock, I breathed in fresh air of what looks to be a beautiful, clear, and mild day. Alarms! Code 3. I sat my butt down on the cold concrete curb as staff, side-handle batons at the ready, ran by. "Oh my," I whispered to myself as a not seen before and petite female sergeant pumped her firm legs with the muscled cheeks of her rear moving back and forth…WAKE UP. I have been in prison *way* too long if I start thinking that a staff member is attractive. Well, actually, that one was cute. However, it is dangerous to think about staff in any way except as untouchables. A man's thoughts can lead to actions. Any action or interaction between an inmate and a female staff can only end in disaster for the inmate.

Despite the dangerous thoughts, it was a pleasant view, and reminded me of many lovely, bikini-clad beach babes of days gone by. I can still hear their laughter and see the heat radiating off their bronze skin. Sniffle.

Code 4. False alarm. Resume normal program. Back into the cube. Time to type and process bed moves. Good-bye for now ladies. Reality bites.

3:30 p.m.

A planned power outage in the cube so the electricians can work on the chow hall. Because it is darker in here than usual I attempted to take a nap. Thinking otherwise, several idiot inmates felt the urge to make loud animal sounds and shout derogatory comments toward staff. Why? They would not do it with the lights on so why prove their cowardice and do it under cover of darkness? These juvenile acts are not only disrespectful and serve no purpose, but it annoys staff, and they will 'catch an attitude' (rightly so) and the rest of the evening will be hell. People, grow up!

4:00 p.m.

Mail. What's this? My mail was returned due to insufficient postage? That's a crock. I sent it 4th class and the third stamp, open your eyes mail room staff, is a one dollar stamp, not 29 cents. My mail out will now be delayed two days. I am surrounded by incompetence. No. I take that back. I am surrounded by many, who for whatever reason, fail to perform their duties in a diligent manner.

4:30 p.m.

Whew. I have calmed down. In reflection, I have been fortunate with my mail. In-coming and out-going, there have been few irritations over the years and I would have to say that 95% of my correspondence has reached its destination. The figure is more than good. I will attach another stamp and chalk it up to life in the big house.

4:45 p.m.

No telephone sign-ups today; thus, no telephone usage tomorrow. See, staff got even. Never poke the bear.

Numbers 15:39. *You will have these tassels to look at and so you will remember all the commands of the Lord, that you may obey them and not prostitute yourselves by going after the lusts of you own hearts and eyes.*

✞ ✞ ✞

Wednesday, October 19, 1994
ALL DAY

Nothing and good!

Nothing was what I was able to do: not work, no yard, no telephones, no showers. Nothing and no reason were given by staff for the deprivations.

Did I mention no mail?

Still, I felt good emotionally. This positive feeling is always scary because what goes up sooner (especially in prison) than later goes down. In spite of, or despite the inevitable fall, I am grateful for God lifting my spirit during this 'stay in the gym and remain on your bunk' day.

Psalm 150:1-2, 6. *Praise the Lord. Praise God in His sanctuary; praise Him in His mighty heavens. Praise Him for His acts of power; praise Him for His surpassing greatness. Let everything that has breath praise the Lord. Praise the Lord.*

✝ ✝ ✝

Thursday, October 20, 1994
8:30 a.m.

Mornings in the cube during the week are as peaceful as it gets. I can think clearly. I am able to open my mind without the mental filters futilely trying to screen out the barrage of music in a variety of languages; the talk-talk filled with negativity and profanity; the blaring televisions; the splashing showers and toilet flushes; the telephone bickering and cheers and shouts over card games.

Serenity; it is not only a feminine hygiene product. It is a state of mind treasured beyond all the gold in this freaked-out world that I reside in. It is the *ah*...from unbuttoning your pants after a stomach-gorging Thanks-giving dinner.

10:00 a.m.

I stopped by Howard's bunk to talk. He pinched a nerve which makes it difficult to breathe, let alone bend at the waist to get up and move about. We spoke about his pain for a few moments and then ended on the subject of inmate overcrowding; how the California penal system is eating itself, as well as the seemingly cold-blooded killings that we see daily on the evening news.

Appraising his own guilt and after 25 years in prison for two murders, Howard is able to say without hesitation that if anyone deserved the death penalty it would have been him. The young couple Howard killed were innocent tourists. Howard wanted money for his drug habit and eating their hearts was a tribute to Satan. Fortunately, time and experience changes everyone who is looking for it. From my interaction with Howard, he is not the same person he described who committed those crimes.

During this last quarter century, Howard has become clean and sober (going on 22 years). He has educated himself by receiving not only his G.E.D. but his four-year college degree in business through correspondence courses paid for by his family. Howard has completed numerous self-help and self-examination courses to understand why he succumbed to the escapism of drugs and the suffering he caused many. It would seem time to give Howard the opportunity to be an asset to and not a continual drain on society's resources. Unfortunately, I do not have that power to influence those who possess the power to make that decision. And, as certain sectors of society prefer to punish into infinity, it is unlikely that Howard will ever be released. I can only sympathize with Howard's situation and pray for a change in society's belief system.

I wonder if they will ever let me go.

11:45 a.m.

I only had to wait 45 minutes in the laundry line to pick up my new winter jacket. New to me; not new as in never been worn as it obviously has been by the frayed hem and threadbare elbows. Putting it on, I am reminded of a summer windbreaker because this so-called winter jacket does not have a liner, only a nylon shell. Thinking ahead, I was smart enough to request one that is four sizes too big so I will be able to put the shell over my old, heavy-duty, and moderately warm jacket. The old jacket style is no longer being issued because it is too expensive to produce. I believe the word to describe the older jacket is quality. Together, old and new, I should be comfy so long as I remain out of the rain because neither is waterproof.

I was also given a new, truly new, knit beanie to replace the one I gave to my Hispanic neighbor. I did ask for a pair of canvas, lace-up shoes but because I have a pair of leather boots the laundry supervisor would not give them to me. I thought that was kind of stingy. Oh, sorry. I forgot. This *ain't* Burger King.

9:00 p.m.

Occasionally I get weak and watch the television sitcom *Mad About You*. It is, in my opinion, a wonderful show with a loving, happily-married couple who playfully tease each other concerning the daily situations that arise in life and in marriage.

The aspect of the show that always touches my heart is this couple is always available for each other. They have a willingness to listen when the other needs a compassionate ear even if it is in a comedic way. There may be differences in their characters because they are individuals, but their love and commitment to each other and their desire to put the other first are their utmost priorities.

I ache for the undivided attention of a lover's caring ears to listen to me. All the ladies I have ever known on the street have moved on, gotten married, gone forward, and are living lives independent of mine. It has been a painful loss for me because I miss them all so much. Each was very special. And even more cruel, as the dagger of despair plunges deep into my body, I know it is my own hands that thrust it. Each of these ladies had promised me forever, but I was too busy, too occupied with seeking the next wild escapade to realize that any one of them would have been the ultimate in life's adventures.

It sucks not being able to blame someone else.

2 Corinthians 5:17. *Therefore, if anyone is in Christ, he is a new creature; the old has gone, the new has come!*

✟ ✟ ✟

Friday, October 21, 1994
7:50 a.m.

I rushed out of the gym at the yard unlock to be one of the first in line for canteen. I was number three, after two yard crew workers who had been outside since 7:00 a.m. The procedure for running the canteen is as slow as snails. If I am not among the first I will have to wait hours.

Buildings 6 through 10 unlocked several minutes after the gym. With their release, dozens of inmates ran across the yard to begin forming a line behind me. While reviewing my list of items I wished to purchase... "Oh Shoot!" I realized I brought the wrong identification card. I needed my red privilege card. It indicates I have a job and I am allowed to go to canteen during the week. Without my red card I will not be allowed to turn in my list until Saturday. I looked toward the gym. Thank God, the gym's door was still open.

I ran, lickety-split, back to the gym, grabbed my red card, and dashed back.

Back in line I was 30-something and my hope for a brief wait had vanished. Then three, four, and then the majority of waiting inmates who witnessed my dash back and forth, said, "Go ahead. You were before me." I was stunned, but not to silence, as I profusely thanked each man for his kindness. Maybe because I did not demand my position I was elevated to it? I don't know but it is something I'll have to think about.

9:45 a.m.

I glanced at my watch as I saw the canteen man waddle onto the yard. He was supposed to open the canteen at 8:00 a.m. It must be liberating to have a job paid for by the inmates' purchases, but not be accountable to them.

10:20 a.m.

While my $15 worth of soups, stamps, envelopes, and shampoo were being thrown at me through the 5"x10" canteen window slot, I thought of the lost privilege of simply walking into a 7/11, picking my desire off a shelf, and purchasing it. That easy life is long gone. Two hours and twenty minutes wait for this month's ration. Not bad. Heck, I could have been number 30.

3:30 p.m.

Coleman and I were walking around the track after an invigorating workout. We were talking about our families and I mentioned the passing of my sister, Julie, and how I am comforted by her acceptance of Jesus prior to her death. I still become upset by the insensitive and miscommunication; the way staff gave me the message—telling me at two in the morning that my mother had died.

Coleman said that as friends it is good to talk about these things. He shared his pain over the loss of both his parents and grandfather since he has been in prison. In my mind I flashed back to my prayers for someone to talk with - my wish for a caring ear. Unrealistically, I asked for a curvaceous brunette in her early 30's, but a balding 50-year-old filled the same need; someone to share and understand my pain.

God answers even if it is in unexpected ways. I need to remember to be patient and keep my eyes open for answered prayers.

Proverbs 25:6-7. Do not exalt yourself in the King's presence, and do not claim a place among great men; it is better for him to say to you, "Come up here," then for him to humiliate you before a nobleman.

✟ ✟ ✟

Saturday, October 22, 1994
9:00 a.m.

I've showered, shaved, and put on my cleanest un-pressed state blues, clothes that is. Now it's all about waiting.

11:10 a.m.

Watching the minute hand clicking away is painful because each is a minute that I won't be able to spend with my father and JoAnne. I expected them at 9:00 am. Each visit is precious, and as it has been more than four months since my last visit, my last hug, I am anxious for their safe arrival. Besides having an uninterrupted conversation without beeps and recordings and without staff listening in on our telephone conversation, it is a type of freedom that is difficult to explain.

11:28 a.m.

"Watson. Visit," the glorious words echo across the cube from the speaker mounted above the officers' station.

3:00 p.m.

Love—dang, it felt good. Felt wonderful in fact. Felt like life worth living. During the visit I asked my father if they were going to Yuba City after our visit to see relatives, and he replied, "No, we came up solely to visit with you." Does that make me feel special or what? An eight-hour drive each direction for only a 3 ½ hour visit in a crowded and noisy room. Not many parents would do that for their wayward child.

The reason they were late, their usual arrival time being 9:00 a.m., was due to a dead battery. Dad and JoAnne had driven halfway from San Diego last night and stayed in a hotel. This morning, after rising, they entered their car, turned the ignition key and CLICK. Nothing. A dead battery. Dad called AAA so their car could be towed to a nearby service station where they purchased a new battery…ALL FOR ME.

Our conversation was spirited. We talked of family, friends, financial opportunities, my creative writing, their decoy carving and painting, frustrations, disappointment with the court's ruling, and hope for a better future. Then, as with all good things, this visit had to end. They exited through the doorway to freedom and I passed through the door where I was stripped naked and my body cavities checked for hidden contraband. It is humiliating but worth it for the two hugs, the smiles, and caring words. It is always painful to say good-bye at the end of a visit. However, if I think about it, the pain is only proportional to the love we share.

Please protect them on their travels home, Lord. They have a long drive home.

4:00 p.m.

No mail on Saturdays. Many years have passed since mail was delivered on Saturdays in prison. It is a budget-staffing thing. And come to think of it, it has also been a long time since Arlene last wrote to me. I had been wondering how long she would write because she is a bit young for me, or is it that I am a bit old for her?

Many wonderful pen-pals have lightened my days throughout these years of incarceration but after a year or two the majority vanishes. I suppose it sinks in that I am stuck here and the thrill of writing to a prisoner wears off. The thing that has always bothered me is the abrupt endings to their correspondence. One minute all is fine and dandy, and the next minute, well, there is no next minute. This abrupt, no reason why, ending always leaves me worried. Are they okay? I will write several more times explaining that it is okay to move on, but please let me know you are safe and healthy. I am a human being. I care. I care a lot. Sometimes I wonder if I care too much.

In my mind I will admit abandonment and say good-bye to Arlene as I have for the others who have written and stopped before her. My heart, being grateful for their correspondence, will forever keep each of them in prayer for a wonderful life.

I sometimes wonder if God is passing me from one caring person to another to keep me company. However, as I have said, it would be easier on my worrying if each would have had the courage to say good-bye when their time was up.

Matthew 7:9-11. *Which of you, if his son asks for bread, will give him a stone? Or if he asks for a fish, will give him a snake? If you, then, though you are evil, know how to give gifts to your children, how much more your Father in heaven will give good gifts to those who ask Him!"*

✝ ✝ ✝

Sunday, October 23, 1994
10:00 a.m.

Setting the record straight. A vocational instructor escorted his visitor-guest into the gym on a tour of the institution. I was seated at my desk and was asked several questions about the living conditions.

Oh, boy. Speech time. But seriously, I enjoyed enlightening the gentlemen about the facts of prison living, both what was wrong and right. I believe a balanced presentation lends more credibility and I don't sound like a whining inmate. We spoke for 25 minutes, and then they thanked me, and departed. It was obvious they both appreciated the candor and came away with a better understanding of prison conditions and what the taxpayer was not getting for his money.

I will pray they will spread the word, because through truth, positive and worthwhile changes can occur.

6:00 p.m.

I telephoned my father to make sure he and JoAnne arrived safely home. No one answered.

7:00 p.m.

Ring… Ring… Ring… "Hello?" Yes, home and safe. "You stopped off where?"

Click.

What the H-E- double toothpicks is going on here? Why was the telephone turned off? The wires are crossing with a telephone in building 10 so staff decided to turn off both phones. It would have been courteous to either break in on our conversation to inform us or allow the conversation to conclude. Very rude. Maybe as an inmate I have "nothing coming" as some staff are often heard saying, but my family deserves to be treated with a tad bit of courtesy.

7:30 p.m.

Officer Garcia stopped by my bunk while I was fuming over the disconnect. He apologized for not giving me the chance to say good-bye to my father. I accepted his apology and thanked him for his unusual understanding. I have great respect and admiration for anyone who apologizes. In my eyes this is an act of strength and confidence in one's character. If I was wearing a hat it would be off to Officer Garcia.

8:00 p.m.

"Hello, it's me again." I was given the opportunity to use another telephone to call my father and explain what had occurred. To talk with him was stress relieving, but it cost several more dollars simply to say good-bye, and to let him know that we here at the Creek had not been nuked.

11:30 p.m.

I say it's my 'winter' allergies that are causing my eyes to water but really it is this Demi Moore and Patrick Swayze movie. One of the last lines of dialogue in *Ghost* as the character Sam is ascending to heaven is: "It's so wonderful. The love, you take it with you." After wiping away the tears I think to myself that the statement was obvious. Of course you take the love with you. You are returning the love to its source – God.

I pray I someday will be able to write a love story as moving as *Ghost*. I will sleep cozy tonight.

1 John 4:16. *And so we know and rely on the love God has for us. God is love. Whoever lives in love lives in God, and God in him.*

✟ ✟ ✟

Monday, October 24, 1994
9:00 a.m.

"We know what an E.K.G. is…an electrocardiogram. So what is an E.G.G.?... An egg." Yuck, yuck. That was an officer's joke; a relief officer to replace Officer Mann who is taking a personal day. The joke may have been super lame, but I will never complain because if staff is joking around they are not terrorizing. I can summon a belly laugh to encourage this behavior any time.

2:15 p.m.

I knocked on the door at the back of the gym and then entered Mr. May's, my counselor's office, to ask him a question about some books I want to order. Mr. May is relatively new in his position as a CCI (Correctional Counselor I). My previous counselor, Mr. Burton, who last year was taken out of his office in a wheel chair, never returned. Thankfully he didn't die, but he took an indefinite medical leave. Hopefully, along with an improving health, his attitude and work ethic will improve.

After entering Mr. May's office I ended up staying almost an hour discussing the cultural and ethnic trends in society and how they spill over into prison. Mr. May is a very intelligent man who pulls no punches. There is no sugar coating his beliefs. I can understand why certain inmates, inmates that have screwed up and are subject to Mr. May's scrutiny, would not like him, but that's the bed they made. For me, when not being slapped with the harsh reality of how my crimes will be viewed by the parole board, I can appreciate Mr. May's insight and stimulating conversation.

As I exited his office, I shook my head in disbelief. For a moment I had a flashback to normalcy and the theoretical debates of my college years which stretched and formed my malleable mind.

And I did get the answers to my original question; policy change. Books are required to be soft cover. Hard bound covers will be cut off.

Ecclesiastes 7:11-12. *Wisdom, like an inheritance, is a good thing and benefits those who see the sun. Wisdom is a shelter, but the advantage of knowledge is this: That wisdom preserves the life of its possessor.*

✝ ✝ ✝

Tuesday, October 25, 1994
7:00 a.m.

S.O.S. (Sh-- on a shingle – or for the colloquially uninitiated, biscuits and gravy). It's one of my favorite breakfasts. Hot, mildly spicy and filling. A stomach that is full helps the heart to beat strong and the mind to be quick witted. This morning the entrée was true to form but I had to wait one spoiled milk moment. My milk carton was dated 10-20-1994 and the smell was retch-worthy. "Oh, Miss, Miss," like a kindergartener I raised my hand to attract the attention of Officer Blake. I informed her of the expired date, and bingo, I was given new milk.

Then the monkey-see, monkey-do began. Other inmates began standing and shouting as they, too, wanted new milk. The difference was they had already consumed theirs. Sorry, pal. You are out of luck. Then, like feces-throwing simians in the zoo, they got belligerent. Stupid inmates. That negative behavior never garners favor from staff. The strange thing about being monkey stupid is that when it breaks out it is like a virulent virus—too many are infected.

I sat quietly eating while the ruckus grew louder and louder until the sergeant entered the chow hall and banged his baton on a metal table. Chow was over.

11:00 a.m.

My heart flutters as the female relief officer in the gym playfully teased me with the delicious-smelling eggplant casserole that she prepared and brought in for her lunch. I knew she was not flirting in a sexual way but it was good for my ego to have the feminine attention.

Fresh herbs and spices, plump vegetables from her garden, cooking, and the taste-bud explosion of consuming a meal prepared with care. We talked of it all as my mouth watered.

I am *not* an animal. I *am* human. God did magnificent work when He created women. They are what is the very best in our species and I had forgotten how enjoyable it is to have a normal conversation with one.

4:00 p.m.

Mail. It was a brief but wonderful Thinking of You card from Jennifer with her telephone number and the words: Call Me, eloquently written inside. Lights, bells, and whistles went off in my head—a lifeline to the world. A huge smile stretched across my face.

6:45 p.m.

Jennifer answered with the same musical voice I remembered. Our conversation was spirited and I learned she works at a retail store, but she is considering branching out, maybe into Mary-Kay cosmetics. Jennifer spoke fondly of her husband and loved being married, but wished he were a Christian. Our 15 minutes ended too quickly but Jennifer made me promise to call again soon. Of course, is tomorrow too soon?

9:00 p.m.

Smitty stopped by my bunk with his latest magazine article on the dangers of ATM's (automatic teller machines) and the crimes associated with them. It was well written and made me a believer. I will never use one again. Smitty asked me to use my most critical eye to proof-read the article for errors and make any suggestions before he mails it to the editor of the purchasing publication.

After reading it carefully twice, I found several typos but nothing that was glaringly wrong. It was an informative article and I received a great feeling of worth that Smitty sought out my advice and critique.

Smitty shared with me that he is receiving $400 for the article; a fortune in my mind. What is Smitty using the funds for? He is sending it all to his daughter for her to help with her baby, Smitty's grandchild. Isn't that what fathers (grandfathers) do?

10:15 p.m.

Count has cleared; the lights have been dimmed; and I laid my head back next to the blowing vent. A moment's reflection and I reviewed a good, no a great day. Surprise! Time for prayers and praise to the Provider above. Good night.

Psalm 68:3. *But may the righteous be glad and rejoice before God; and may they be happy and joyful.*

✟ ✟ ✟

Wednesday, October 26, 1994
11:00 a.m.

Busy. Busy. Busy. Eleven, can you count them? I processed 11 new inmates into the gym. As with all jobs, it was hectic at first, making sure I added and deleted all the right names in the three different log books, the two card files, and the roster board that hangs behind the officers' station. It seems simple enough and doesn't take too much time but there are combination locks, laundry bags (two each), pillows, property cards, and trust withdrawal slips for each incoming inmate to receive and sign. Basically my job is one of memory.

After the paperwork is completed, the wait begins. The inmates are notified in their buildings, their work, or education assignments, or on the recreation yard, and lacking joy at their new housing arrangements, they stall as long as possible, but eventually they trickle in. "Sign the forms, please," I said again and again. With my duties complete, I relax. Difficult in the beginning, simple in the present. Practice, repetition, and attention to detail.

3:55 p.m.

Awakened from a nap by the loud speakers that orders me: "Watson, report to the counselor's office."

Mr. May informed me that I would be going to classification committee tomorrow and asked me where did I want to go?

My mind screamed, *Tell him.* I said, "I only want to go home."

Mr. May smiled at the joke. *I* wasn't kidding. Mr. May then said, "CSR (Classification Specialist Representative) will want to transfer you to a level II prison because you have level I points." As a lifer, level II is the lowest security level that I can be housed in. "I thought the gym was a level II?" I said, questioning. Mr. May explained that the gym is only sort-of a level II. It's temporary housing.

I pondered this: I could ask to go back to San Quentin because it is now a level II, I have friends there, and I believe Chaplain Smith is still there. I could also ask to be transferred to San Luis Obispo because it has a history of providing programs for inmates to improve themselves. But, I am situated and I hate moving. There's the packing, the shackles and hassles of the bus ride, and I don't know what either prison will or will not allow concerning personal property. I don't want to give up my typewriter because I am trying to become a real, earn-a-living writer. I am trying to prove I can be an asset to society. I am trying to prove that I am suitable to be released one day.

The old saying, "It's the devil you know," popped into my head. For all the things that are wrong with this prison; for all the irritating, non-professional staff that make my daily life miserable; there have been moments of joy and blessings. The majority of staff are good, honest, hard–working men and women doing a difficult job. I have made friends and have created a positive reputation—both invaluable. And, it is unlikely another prison will be significantly better than the Creek.

I asked Mr. May if he would request a level override for me to remain here. He replied, "I will try."

7:30 p.m.

Worried, I said in the telephone conversation with my father, "It's out of our hands. What they decide for me I'll make the best of it." My father, always wanting me to know that he is in my corner, replied, "It doesn't matter where they send you. We'll visit you there." My father's words are said in a voice that leaves no room for doubt that he loves me and will always be available when I need him. His last words, simple, but comforting, were, "Call whenever you need to talk."

A million "I love you's" could not equal that.

9:00 p.m.

"Watson, ducat," the gym officer announced. I accepted my ducat for tomorrow's UCC at 10:00 a.m. Okay, it is time to trust. God, your will is my will, I repeat to myself, and I trust you to place me where I can serve you best. But…if you don't mind me asking, "Please, let me stay here!"

11:20 p.m.

Tossing and turning. Worry. Worry. Worry. God, I pray for the faith of a mustard seed. You've proved yourself time and again to me, but my stupid nerves will not settle down. Fear is the mind killer, the destroyer of reason. The unknown is where fear breeds and I know the devil dances to spite God's protection and blessings.

I have come so far in my walk with Jesus, but at times I feel as the newborn trying to waddle on unsteady legs. This is a lifelong journey.

Matthew 26:39. *Going a little farther, he fell with his face to the ground and prayed, "My Father, if it is possible, may this cup be taken from me. Yet not as I will, but as You will."*

✞   ✞   ✞

Thursday, October 27, 1994
7:00 a.m.

While walking back from a breakfast of two boiled eggs, toast, and juice, Sergeant Martinez, who I've known for three years, stopped me on the track to inform me that I may be getting a ducat to go to Receiving and Release for a photograph retake if the one on file cannot be digitized. He told me the institution purchased a scanner-digitizer and he will no longer be using blow-ups. Blow-ups? The puzzled look on my face encouraged the sergeant to elaborate. He stated, "I like to use your face during escape lectures and disguise training. The reason is that you look like the boy next door and would be easy to disguise.

Fancy that.

Sergeant Martinez continued, saying, "It's because you don't have any tattoos and don't look like a criminal."

"That's the point," I replied. "I'm not a criminal anymore."

Sergeant Martinez smiled and walked away. Why is it that only Christians can see beyond my blue inmate attire?

10:30 a.m.

```
STATE OF CALIFORNIA          DEPARTMENT OF CORRECTIONS
INMATE PASS                  CDC 129 (7/88)

INMATE'S NAME             CDC #          HOUSING #
WATSON                    D-67547        BG-167
ISSUED BY                 DATE:          PASS FROM:
            OCT
PASS TO:                  DATE:    1994  TIME:
Program Office                           1000
REASON:
UCC   PRIORITY
ARRIVAL TIME:             RECORDED BY:

DEPART TO:       TIME:    RECORDED BY:
```

I sat on the slatted wooden bench that is bolted to the wall in the Program Office hallway patiently waiting to be seen by the classification committee.

1:30 p.m.

Finally. The Program Administrator Alfred T. James and two counselors, in addition to my CCI Mr. May, were present as I was summoned into the classification room. After listening to the required, but unnecessary introductions and their commending me on remaining write-up free, I asked to be retained CCP (Continue Present Program). Mr. James told me that I still had to choose two other prisons as transfer options. "Okay, San Quentin and San Luis Obispo," I replied. "All right. That's it. Have a nice day," they said in unison.

As I exited the Program Office I thought about that "Have a nice day" dismissal. I'm sure they meant it, sort of, because in reality I am not supposed to have a nice day. This is prison and there is no escaping that despite my 'boy next door' appearance.

2:15 p.m.

Bamboozle me, huh? Come to find out by other inmates' experiences that I cannot be transferred from my sort-of level II gym setting unless I choose to be moved or I have become a disciplinary problem. Unfortunately, by telling the committee of the two other prisons as options, I have given the CSR the ability to transfer me. Hmm... Legally these inmates may be correct, but my experience is that those running the prison system can do whatever they want to suit their needs and desires.

Regardless, I have prayed and I must trust in God. I should not worry, though I do, having a queasy stomach and to constantly pee from overactive nerves. I go crazy with the back and forth between worry over the unknown and the proven confidence in God's protective hand that shelters me. Trust is a difficult thing as I am...I hate to say it...I am only human where my flesh and spirit are in constant battle against the principalities of darkness.

I am weak, Lord.

4:00 p.m.

Mail. A letter from Charlie. He paroled and has written from home. Praise God. Charlie has survived his ordeal and this gives me hope that I can too. Charlie's letter says, among other things, "Hang in there, Surf Dude."

I smile. I will with the support of family, friends, and God. It is another new year.

John 8:32, 36. *"Then you will know the truth, and the truth will set you free. So if the Son sets you free, you will be free indeed."*

✝ ✝ ✝

CONCLUSION

It is the end of another year in prison, and at a glance, not much has changed. I am still not any closer to freedom, my mental anguish and depravities still pound my spirit daily, and my need for hugs has not diminished.

So what has trusting in God gotten me? What have I gained? Christ has given me a restored soul. He has opened my eyes to the good that I can accomplish each day. I have become an example, not a perfect one, but one made perfect through Christ's shedding of blood and resurrection. I have become new.

In times of weakness and despair, I have prayed in earnest for God to take away my horrifying crimes, to change my past so that I don't make the choices that brought me to prison. I have begged Him to remove the pain I caused others and to wipe away my constant suffering behind these unforgiving walls. In those instances the Holy Spirit that is within me glows bright as God reveals the multitude of blessings He has bestowed on me and worked through me during my years of incarceration to the benefit of others.

I have been blessed beyond comprehension to have met and been enriched by a core of caring staff, who are supposed to be the enemy, and by wise men wearing blue, on whom society wants only to throw away the key.

I have also been bestowed with the privilege, while still residing in a cell, of saving my cellie's life after he had passed out from a blocked air passage by using the Heimlich maneuver. I have seen good where only evil is supposed to exist, and I know I can and will survive this self-imposed fire. I may have leapt into the fire, but God is the metallurgist who is turning my lead to gold.

Prison and Christ are the melding of a ten-thousand fold Samurai sword. The sufferings of prison life become a deep festering wound, but when Christ's teachings are applied, the wielder of the sword becomes a skilled surgeon methodically excising the malignancies to allow this suffering child to live a healthy spiritual life.

Maybe if an observer were fortunate, he would glimpse an out-of-place smile, or hear the echo of a laugh among the angry shouts. This is the continuing change in my life. This is the confident peace held permanently in my heart that I can run to when everyone and everything has lost all semblance of rationality. Jesus walks by my side during each day and watches over me while I sleep each night.

Prison will never be a place of enjoyment, but contained within these walls are lessons I could never have learned on the street. The most important lesson is; anyone can change through Jesus' love, and that whether or not society will ever pardon a wrong, God does. I can live with that.

The changes this past year have been in me as I become stronger in my faith and trust in Him. In the end, I have forfeited a societal life that was leading to a permanent death, and gained an eternal salvation with God.

To anyone going through trials, whether caused by your own actions, or by forces unknown to you, seek out Jesus for your refuge. He stands waiting at the door knocking. All you have to do is invite Him in. Your tribulations may not change, and your suffering may be great, but with Jesus you can endure to find the blessings hidden therein.

2 Corinthians 12:8-9. *Three times I pleaded with the Lord to take it away from me. But He said to me, "My grace is sufficient for you, for my power is made perfect in weakness."*

☦ ☦ ☦

EPILOGUE

On December 23, 1994, I was notified through the institutional mail that the CSR had decided that I would Continue Present Program. I will be retained here at California's Mule Creek State Prison for another year. My prayer was answered and I thank God for His Son and this Christmas gift.

FOLLOW-UP

Ed, the ex-professional volleyball player with the bull-buster's gait, remains a free man. He works in computer sales.

Charlie remains a free man. He completed college and is married.

December, 1994: As the Best Man, I attended Spencer and Lana's wedding. The ceremony was held on the patio of the visiting room. Lana was lovely in her best Sunday dress and Spencer was clean and pressed in state blues. One would have to toss a coin to decide which of the two beamed more with love. I was honored to participate.

February, 1995: Ron paroles. He moved to Arizona where he manages a muffler shop.

June, 1995: Ron's son, Joel, is transferred to Mule Creek State Prison, Facility B, where he joins our Bible fellowship.

October, 1995: O.J. Simpson is acquitted of murdering Nicole Simpson and Ron Goldman. Thirteen years later, O.J. is arrested in Las Vegas for robbing two sports memorabilia dealers. He is convicted of armed robbery and kidnapping and sentenced to up to 33 years in prison.

May, 1996: Spencer paroles. He and Lana create a loving home together.

April, 1996: *Swede* is transferred to Sweden. He is released from incarceration in 1998. *Swede* works for a software company.

May, 1996: Brain, the ex-police officer, paroles. He returned to the San Francisco Bay area where he works as a manager for a construction company.

November, 1996: Family (conjugal) visits are terminated by the California Legislature, affirmed by the courts, for most categories of inmates including lifers.

May, 1997: *Bull* paroles. He works building custom cabinetry.

June, 1997: Geronimo Pratt's (ex-Black Panther) conviction is overturned by the court and he is released. Geronimo works on behalf of men and women who are believed to be wrongfully incarcerated. Biography: *Last Man Standing: The Tragedy and Triumph of Geronimo Pratt.*

July, 1997: Aaron paroles to San Diego. The Department of Corrections would not allow him to parole to Oakdale, California, where his wife lives and where a job was waiting. He was required to return to the county of his commitment. Four months later, after accepting a ride from a friend, the friend fired shots at an enemy in another car. At trial, the friend testified that Aaron had no part in the shooting, but to no avail. Aaron was sentenced to 25 years to life under the Three Strikes law. Roni, Aaron's wife, remains faithful to him.

August, 2000: Doc Mahar paroles. He works as a physical therapist on cruise ships in the Caribbean.

July, 2003: While playing a 4th of July volleyball tournament, an opposing player, after attempting to spike the ball against my block, fell into the net and then onto my left knee, hyper-extending it and tearing ligaments. To save money, and because my injury is not life-threatening (new policy), medical staff would only provide me with one bag of ice. I have been unable to play volleyball since then.

July, 2003: (Date approximate) High school classmates, Linda and Jim, make contact with me to renew our friendship.

June, 2005: (Date approximate) Jennifer divorces her husband. Within a year she meets a man, falls in love and moves to Texas. I have not heard from her since.

January, 2006: Lana, Spencer's wife, passes away after a year-long battle with cancer. Despite his heart-breaking loss, Spencer does not stumble, but remains a valued asset to his community. Spencer works in promotional sales.

June, 2007: My mother, Kathleen, passes away in a hospice in Texas from complications brought about by a brain aneurysm. Her wish was for me to scatter her ashes in the ocean...someday. If it were not for my mother's love that Jesus allows me to feel every day, her passing would have crippled me.

July, 2007: I appear before the parole board. I am denied parole for four years. My next hearing is scheduled for 2011. It is all in God's hands and His divine time.

December, 2008: Vigilante Ellie Nesler dies at age 56 from breast cancer. After shooting her son's alleged molester five times in the head in a Toulumne County courtroom in 1993, Ms. Nesler pled guilty to manslaughter and served three years in prison. In 2002, Ms. Nesler was sentenced to six years for selling and possessing methamphetamine. Meanwhile, in 2005, at age 23, Ms. Nesler's son, William, was convicted of first-degree murder for stomping to death a man who was hired to clean the family's property in Sonora, California.

November, 2009: News Flash! The anchor of a Sacramento news station stated there are approximately 178,000 inmates incarcerated in California's prisons, costing taxpayers roughly $58,000 per inmate per year.

January, 2010: Due to the unconstitutionally substandard health care that has caused the needless deaths of hundreds of prison inmates, a three-judge federal panel ruled that overcrowding in California prisons prevents the state from providing the very basic of health care. The court ordered the state to reduce the inmate population from 200% to 137.5% of design capacity. The state of California appealed to the U.S. Supreme Court challenging the three judge panel's order.

June, 2010: The U.S. Supreme Court decides to review the appeal filed by the state.

July, 2010: During an appointment with the prison optometrist, he informs me that I have glaucoma. That sucks. I am going blind.

December, 2010: A historical novel I wrote about Market Hunters (waterfowl hunters and carvers) during the early 20th century, entitled: *A Thundering Wind* is published. I was right. There was a story about duck decoy carvers within the material my father mailed to me.

May, 2011: The United States Supreme Court rules in favor of inmates.

June, 2011: Elmer "Geronimo" Pratt dies. He spent 27 years in prison for a murder he did not commit. During his fourteen years of freedom, he held no anger, no bitterness, and no desire for revenge for the mistreatment by the justice system. What an example. Rest in peace.

June, 2011: I appear before the parole board. I have remained disciplinary free, obtained training in the Microsoft Office Suite, and received a glowing psychological evaluation. Denied. Three years.

July, 2011 Rick Stevens, the ex-Tower of Power lead singer, is granted parole.

July, 2011: I received a letter from the niece of my victim asking why I murdered her aunt. I prayed for guidance, and then responded with a detailed letter of the events surrounding the shooting, including apologies straight from my heart.

August, 2011: I received a second letter from the niece. The family understands, offering forgiveness along with wanting to come visit me, they believe I have been punished enough. They want to assist me in gaining parole.

THAT IS GOD'S HAND!!

To reconcile with this family, to be a part of bringing peace and understanding to their lives is worth every suffering moment I have experienced within prison.

Frank, the ex-professional football player, continues to be denied parole.

Coleman continues to be denied parole while remaining an exemplary inmate. In 2008 Coleman was transferred to the state prison located in Tehachapi, California.

Marty, the Freeway Killer's Assistant, continues to be denied parole.

Smitty continues to be denied parole. He devotes his time to working with E.O.P (emotionally challenged) inmates, and in his leisure time, he continues to write magazine articles as well as crime novels.

Wolf continues to be denied parole. He has grown his hair and beard long again.

The following dear friends and loving family members (real names) have remained, entered, or re-entered my life during times when I was at my lowest. They continue, despite the difficulties in their own lives, to send letters filled with love and encouragement: Mickie, Roxanne, Linda, Jim, Walt, Rod & Bonnie, Walt & Phyllis, Larry & Ann, Bruce & Eileen, Ed & Cathy, Ed & Joan, Gary & Suzy, Maneck, and Linda May. For each of them my heart bursts with love and gratitude for keeping me in their thoughts and prayers.

And for my father and JoAnne, together they have worked to fill the void left by the passing of my mother, while continuing to be an example of what loving parents should be. They never judge, but only love, helping and encouraging me in each endeavor and through every challenge, believing in me so that I have the strength to believe in myself. I am able to stand taller with squared shoulders because of them. I owe them everything and to be my very best at all times—to be as a straight arrow propelled down God's lighted path.

✝ ✝ ✝

AFTERWORD
by Jack "Murf the Surf" Murphy

In our society, from infancy to adulthood, we are taught that we are the masters of our destinies, that our choices determine our fate, that we are in control. It is against our human nature then to give up our free will to serve another. But, whether we realize it or not, our daily activities, our entire lives, are the result of decisions based on convictions that either work for or against the glory of God. A battle over the direction of our lives is constantly waged. *"For we do not wrestle against flesh and blood, but against principalities, against powers, against the rulers of darkness of this age, against spiritual wickedness in the heavenly places."* (Ephesians 6:12, KJV)

Many times the battle is lost to darkness. The result is spiritual and possibly physical incarceration. When a person ends up behind prison walls and razor-wire topped fences, the main concern that influences all decisions is how to survive and how to come out alive. There are two and only two choices in this battle for survival, for everyone, everywhere. It is either God's way (the light) or Satan's way (the darkness). Which "shot caller" do you follow? Do you continue to follow the one that led you to prison or the one who offers a new heart and a forgiven soul?

Not surprisingly, the ultimate shot caller in prison is not the convict gang leader who controls through fear, nor is it the insensitive guard, or the well-intentioned administrator. The authority above all authority, the ultimate "shot caller" is Jesus Christ. He who died on death row, and rose from the grave, so that none should perish, but rather, that everyone may be set free, both spiritually and physically, now and for eternity.

The life trials which Greg Watson is struggling through are not unlike those which I and millions of others have experienced. These times of great frustration, despair, loneliness, abuse, and threat of physical harm can be survived, because being a Christian, Greg's new heart is woven with a lifeline of salvation and eternal hope.

The apostle Paul wrote to the persecuted believers in Romans that *"The suffering of the present time is not worthy to be compared to the glory which shall be revealed in us."* (Romans 8:18, KJV) This hope continues to grow stronger with the power and the peace of the Holy Spirit. Like the blind man of Bethsaida who was given sight by Christ, our eyes will be opened to spiritual insights as we believe and surrender our will to Jesus.

Through challenges and trials, the Christian is strengthened to overcome spiritual forces of evil which would normally defeat a person. These trials eventually become a cherished fire that tests our metal, purifying the Christian into God's precious gold. *"My brethren, count it all joy when you fall into various trials, knowing that the testing of your faith produces patience. But let patience have its perfect work, that you may be perfect and complete, lacking nothing."* (James 1:2-4, KJV)

For myself, Greg, and other sinners like us for whom much has been forgiven, to be pardoned by Jesus is redemption that mere words cannot adequately describe. We can only pray that the fruits of our labor, in His Name, will loudly testify to the mercy, the grace, and the power of God to change even "a wretch like me".

Testimonies like Greg's are lights shining in the darkness, living evidence that cannot be denied as to the love of God. As a brother in Christ, I cheer and support Greg's honest testimony of successes and failures during his growth by fire. I pray that it will encourage others whose decisions have led them into bondage to seek the greatest freedom offered to mankind through the acceptance and joyful submission to the King of kings, Jesus Christ.

"...because of His great love for us, God, who is rich in mercy, made us alive with Christ even when we were dead in transgressions—it is by grace you have been saved. And God raised us up with Christ and seated us with Him in the heavenly realms in Christ Jesus." (Ephesians 2:4-6, NIV)

✝ ✝ ✝

BIOGRAPHY

Gregory Barnes Watson on
Mule Creek's Facility B Recreation Yard.

Gregory Barnes Watson

As a teenager in the 1970's, all indicators foretold a successful and productive life for Gregory, as he held AAU swimming records and excelled in big wave surfing in Hawaii. And during the United States bi-centennial, while living in Los Angeles, Gregory, skateboarding for Team Hobie, set a world record by skateboarding the 920 mile coastline from the Oregon border to Dana Point, California. Not only blessed with athleticism, Gregory received academic scholarships to college where he graduated and went on to law school.

It was during his legal training that Gregory became entangled with high level cocaine dealers as a shortcut to prosperity. In 1987, Gregory discovered that his shortcut had turned into a dead end when he was sentenced to 34 years to life for the shooting death of one of his suppliers. While in the cold, concrete box of Ventura County's jail cell, and realizing how far from the true path he had strayed, Gregory turned his life over to the will of God by accepting Jesus into his heart. After sentencing, Gregory was transferred to San Quentin where his infant spirituality was nurtured as he volunteered in the prison's Garden Chapel. While participating in the chapel's programs, Gregory was guided by the dynamic Chaplain Smith, guest speakers and fellow Christian convicts.

In 1990, Gregory was transferred to California's Mule Creek State Prison, where he continues to live his life for Jesus in the hope that he can be a positive example of God's infinite grace while facing daily tribulations.

☦ ☦ ☦

Jack "Murf The Surf" Murphy and Gregory Barnes Watson in San Quentin's Garden Chapel wearing San Quentin Surf Team tee shirts which were designed by Gregory.

Jack "Murf The Surf" Murphy

During the 1950's, Jack "Murf The Surf" Murphy was a flamboyant surfer and daring jewel thief who counted the fabulous Star of India sapphire as one of many acquisitions. A few years later, Murf's dubious luck ran out in Florida when he was sentenced to a double life sentence plus 20 years for a capital crime.

Society intended for Murf to die in the darkness of a prison cell but God had other plans. God sent Max Jones to take over the chaplaincy of the Florida State Prison where Murf was housed. During his rounds, Chaplain Jones stated to Murf with an undeniable radiance, "God loves you and His Son, Jesus Christ died for your sins." Skeptical, Murf watched for several months while his friends' hardened attitudes, hearts, and lives were being changed by God after they gave their lives to Jesus. Finally, seeking the same peace he witnessed in others, Murf asked Jesus into his own heart to begin a new life as a flamboyant evangelist for God. There was no longer darkness in Murf's cell, only Christ's light.

Because God did have other plans for Murf, his original parole date of 2006 was changed by the parole board to 1999, to 1991, to 1986, then finally, as Chaplain Jones had predicted: "In God's time the prison gates will open wide to allow a freight train to rumble through—sideways." On December 20, 1985, Murf was paroled to begin his ever-expanding ministry. In 1990 he began work with the Bill Glass Foundation, where Murf spread the simple but powerful message that "God loves you and His Son, Jesus Christ, died for your sins," bringing God's light to those still living in the darkness of sin. In 1996, Murf was inducted into the East Coast Surfing Hall of Fame. In August 2011, he became a Board member for International Network of Prison Ministries (prisonministry.net) He currently lives in Florida.

✝ ✝ ✝

9 780615 645544